EQUALITY AND
DISCRIMINATION UNDER
INTERNATIONAL LAW

EQUALITY AND DISCRIMINATION UNDER INTERNATIONAL LAW

WARWICK McKEAN

CLARENDON PRESS · OXFORD

1983

Oxford University Press, Walton Street, Oxford OX2 6DP
London Glasgow New York Toronto
Delhi Bombay Calcutta Madras Karachi
Kuala Lumpur Singapore Hong Kong Tokyo
Nairobi Dar es Salaam Cape Town
Melbourne Auckland
and associates in
Beirut Berlin Ibadan Mexico City Nicosia

Oxford is a trade mark of Oxford University Press

Published in the United States
by Oxford University Press, New York

British Library Cataloguing in Publication Data
McKean, Warwick A.
Equality and discrimination under international law
1. Civil rights (International law)
I. Title
341.4'81   K3240
ISBN 0–19–825311–7

Set by South End Typographics
Printed in Great Britain
at the University Press, Oxford
by Eric Buckley
Printer to the University

To Neville and Belle McKean

CONTENTS

viii   *Contents*

SELECTED ABBREVIATIONS

AD	Annual Digest of Public International Law Cases
AJIL	*American Journal of International Law*
All E.R.	All England Law Reports
ASIL	American Society of International Law
BYIL	*British Yearbook of International Law*
Can. YIL	*Canadian Yearbook of International Law*
CHR	United Nations Commission on Human Rights
CLJ	*Cambridge Law Journal*
Cmd., Cmnd.	United Kingdom Command Paper
CMLR	Common Market Law Reports
CR	International Court of Justice Court Record
ECHR	European Commission of Human Rights
ECOSOC OR	United Nations Economic and Social Council Official Records
GAOR	United Nations General Assembly Official Records
ICLQ	*International and Comparative Law Quarterly*
ICJ Rep.	Reports of judgments and advisory opinions of the International Court of Justice
I.L. Conf.	International Labour Conference
ILO	International Labour Organization
ILR	International Law Reports
JILI	*Journal of the Indian International Law Institute*
LNTS	League of Nations Treaty Series
L. of N. O.J	League of Nations Official Journal
LQR	*Law Quarterly Review*
MLR	*Modern Law Review*
PCIJ	Reports of judgments and advisory opinions of the Permanent Court of International Justice
PL	*Public Law*
O.J. Sp. Supp.	*League of Nations Official Journal Special Supplement*
RIAA	United Nations Reports of International Awards
UDHR	United Nations Universal Declaration of Human Rights
UNCIO	United Nations Conference on International Organization
UNRIAA	United Nations Reports of International Arbitral Awards
UNTS	United Nations Treaty Series

INTRODUCTION

ONE of the most constant themes underlying the great historical struggles for social justice has been the demand for equality. Maine pointed out that ancient law was largely a jurisprudence of personal inequalities in which every individual possessed a status imposed upon him independently of his own will and as a result of circumstances beyond his control, so that his legal position depended on whether he was a freeman or a slave, a noble or a commoner, a native or a foreigner, male or female. Most differences in status were 'natural inequalities' in that they depended upon birth or other unalterable circumstances.[1] A status was the condition of belonging to a class to which the law assigned certain legal capacities or incapacities.

Inequality exists in an extreme form in societies which are hierarchically structured on gradations of ranks and privileges, such as the feudal system, the Indian caste system, and the South African system of apartheid.[2] The widespread existence of slavery in many societies made possible the existence of a leisure class, and under Roman law a slave could not possess property or make contracts.[3] Marriage under most early legal systems was a relationship under which the husband possessed the property, so that a wife could not alienate it *inter vivos* or by will and nor could she make a contract on her own behalf.

Many laws prevented Jews from owning property, and illegitimate children suffered severe disabilities with respect to inheritance. Maine showed that most of the older types of personal inequality were being abolished in 'progressive societies', where they were felt to be no longer justified because of changes in economic conditions

[1] T. E. Holland, in his *Jurisprudence* (Clarendon Press, Oxford, 13th ed. 1924), 261, isolated sixteen varieties of status, i.e. sex; minority; *patria potestas* and *manus*; coverture; celibacy; mental defect; bodily defect; rank, caste, and official position; race and colour; slavery; profession; civil death; illegitimacy; heresy; foreign nationality; hostile nationality. C. K. Allen in his essay 'Status and Capacity', 46 *LQR* (1930), 277, 284 added criminality and bankruptcy. See also R. H. Graveson, *Status in the Common Law* (Athlone Press, London, 1953).

[2] See generally Bodenheimer, *Jurisprudence, the Philosophy and Method of the Law* (Harvard University Press, Cambridge, Mass., 1962), 179 ff. for a full treatment.

[3] 5 *Institutes* i.144.

and advances in scientific knowledge or in human understanding.
The Roman plebeians revolted against the exclusive rule of the
patricians on the ground that the existing political inequalities had
no basis in social reality and the French and Russian revolutions
largely resulted from discrimination by the nobles against the middle
and labouring classes, and the American revolution from unjust
treatment by Britain. Similarly, the Chartists sought the franchise
for the working classes, since by the 1830s it was regarded as
untenable to base voting rights on property qualifications alone.
Nothing aids the cause of a subject group more than demonstrating
that no reasonable basis for unequal treatment exists. Paine believed
that 'inequality of rights has been the cause of all the disturbances,
insurrections, and civil wars that ever happened.'[4]

Wollheim believes that equality can be regarded as the fundamental principle of liberalism[5] and it is a deep-rooted principle in
human thought that, unless there is a reason for it, recognized as
sufficient by some identifiable criterion, one man should not be
preferred to another.[6] Cahn believed that the sense of injustice
revolts against whatever is unequal by caprice[7] or, in Brecht's
words, 'it is unjust to discriminate arbitrarily among equal cases.'[8] It
has been shown that children will rebel against discrimination which
is entirely arbitrary and capricious,[9] and that in society co-operation
will be promoted by impartiality and impeded by discrimination.[10]

Though the importance of the principle of equality as an ideal is
obvious, the content of the principle is not nearly so apparent.
According to James Fitzjames Stephen, 'equality' is a word so wide
and vague as to be by itself almost unmeaning.[11] The essence of
'equality' as a component of 'justice' has been sought by many.
Aristotle believed in a form of distributive or proportional justice
where equal things should be given to equal persons and unequal

[4] Thomas Paine, *Works*, ed. J. P. Mendun (1878), i.454–5; Bodenheimer, op. cit.
[5] R. Wollheim, 'Equality and Equal Rights' in F. A. Olafson, ed., *Justice and
Social Policy* (Prentice-Hall, Englewood Cliffs N. J., 1961), 127.
[6] Sir Isaiah Berlin, 'Equality as an Ideal', 56 *Proceedings of Aristotelian Society*
(1955–6), 301, reprinted in Olafson, 128, 149.
[7] E. N. Cahn, *The Sense of Injustice, An Anthropocentric View of Law* (New York
University Press, 1949), and *The Predicament of Democratic Man* (Macmillan, New
York, 1961).   [8] 6 *Social Research* (1939), 58, 76.
[9] Jean Piaget, *The Moral Judgment of the Child*, trans. M. Gabin (1932).
[10] R. F. Bienenfeld, *Rediscovery of Justice*, (Allen and Unwin, London, 1947),
19–27.
[11] J. F. Stephen, *Liberty, Equality, Fraternity* (Cambridge University Press, 1873),
201.

things to unequal persons, or as Ulpian put it, *iustitia est constans et perpetua voluntas ius suum cuique tribuendi.*[12] This *suum cuique* formulation contained no explicit reference to the concept of equality but it implicitly recognized that persons in similar positions should not be treated unequally. Obviously, the weakness of this doctrine is that it makes no attempt to answer the question, 'what differences are relevant and what are not in determining whether individuals are equals or unequals?' The fact is that 'equality' is a term which is used in a great many different ways,[13] and this variety of usage has been a perpetual source of confusion. Does it mean simply 'sameness' or 'identity'? What is the relation to other principles of social justice? Is it a purely formal principle or does it have some content and if so, how is it to be discovered?

If the statement in the American Declaration of Independence that 'it is self-evident . . . that all men are created equal' is taken purely at face value, then it is clearly nonsense. Since Nature hands out its favours capriciously everyone differs in every single physical intellectual and moral characteristic that can be enumerated.[14] Nietzsche summed up his indictment of this maxim by saying 'Equality of all men is the biggest lie ever told.'[15] However, the statement was not meant to be taken in the sense that men are born with the same aptitudes and capabilities,[16] but rather in the sense of an 'artificial equality' to be pursued as the deliberate object of social policy;[17] i.e. in differentiating between men as members of society, distinctions such as sex, race, colour, religion, and language should not be taken into account where they are not strictly relevant to the purpose of a particular classification.

In his excellent essay, 'Equality as an Ideal', Berlin supports the principle that men should in every respect be treated in a *uniform* and *identical* manner unless there is a sufficient reason not to do

---

[12] *Digest*, 1, 1, 10. (And see Cicero's *De Finibus Bonorum et Malorum*, Book V.)

[13] R. H. Tawney, *Equality* (Allen and Unwin, London, 1952), 35.

[14] Frankel, 'The New Egalitarianism and the Old', *Commentary* (Sept. 1973), 58; J. Rawls, *A Theory of Justice* (Oxford University Press, 1971); G. Evans, 'Benign Discrimination and the Right to Equality', 6 *Fed. L. Rev.* (1974), 26.

[15] See *Gesammelte Schriften* (Musarion edition), XV, 488, XVI, 200.

[16] Though there is an element of truth in it. Hart includes in his minimum content of natural law necessary for a legal system the notion of 'approximate equality'. See H. L. A. Hart, *The Concept of Law* (Oxford University Press, 1961), 190–1. And see B. Williams, 'The Idea of Equality' in Laslett and Runciman, eds., *Philosophy, Politics and Society*, 2nd Ser. (Basil Blackwell, Oxford, 1962), 110–31.

[17] See e.g. Lester Ward, *Applied Sociology*, 22.

so.[18] The question then arises: 'What reasons are sufficient and why, and what attributes are relevant and why?' In order to answer these questions it is clear that values other than equality itself must be taken into account. The making of distinctions based on natural inequalities such as birth are usually condemned,[19] while others based on merit or efficiency usually are not. The question of what is a reasonable and relevant distinction must be decided by reference to other values in society which may alter from time to time.

Kelsen interprets the principle of equality to mean that only equals shall be treated equally. He states that the decisive question 'What is equal?' cannot be answered by the principle and accordingly a positive legal order may make any difference whatever between human beings the basis of a different treatment of its subjects without getting in conflict with the principle of equality, which is too empty to have practical consequences.[20] This purely formal view of equality is inadequate since the principle, as it is generally understood, does possess a 'minimum content' of 'fairness' or 'justice' which is derived from current community standards. It requires that any classification of individuals should be 'reasonable' and not 'arbitrary'. As Castberg commented, 'Everywhere, a law which for instance imposed special taxes on persons with long arms or short legs, red hair, or big ears would be regarded as unjust and unwarrantable, irrespective of whether the law was correctly applied in accordance with its content.'[21] Equality is not confined to the formal principle that persons placed in a particular classification however unreasonably or arbitrarily must be treated in the same fashion *inter se*.

There exists a wide measure of agreement among philosophers that there is a presumption in favour of 'mathematical' equality— that people should be treated in a substantially uniform way unless

---

[18] Berlin, 128 (italics added); cf. M. Ginsberg, *On Justice in Society*, (Penguin, Harmondsworth, Middlesex, 1965), 11, 42.

[19] See e.g. H. Spiegelberg, 'A Defense of Human Equality', 43 *The Philosophical Review* (1944), 101. (Aristotle was, however, prepared to accept certain natural inequalities. 'It is thus clear that there are by nature free men and slaves, and that servitude is agreeable and just for the latter. . . . Equally the relation of the male and female is by nature such that one is better and the other inferior, one dominates and the other is dominated.' (*Politics*, 1255a, 1254b, 1252b.) And see R. Dahrendorf, 'On the Origins of Social Inequality' in, Olafson, op. cit., 88.

[20] Hans Kelsen, *'What is Justice?'*, *Collected Essays* (University of California Press, Berkeley, Calif., 1957), 15.

[21] Frede Castberg, 'Natural Law and Human Rights' in 1 *Les droits de l'homme: Revue de droit international et comparé*, 15, 20.

there are 'intelligible' or 'relevant' reasons for treating them differently.[22] Aristotle was one of the first to imply that social inequalities, not equalities, are in need of some justification and that inequalities for which no adequate reason can be given are unjustified. It has been said 'men should never be treated unequally or differently in any respect except with justification, that is, until relevant grounds for discrimination have been shown.'[23] 'There should always be a sufficient reason for any difference in our treatment of our fellows;'[24] 'for every difference in the way men are treated, a reason should be given: When one requires further that the reasons should be relevant and that they should be socially operative, this really says something.'[25]

Often, the need to give acceptable reasons for differential treatment is conceded by those who practise colour discrimination. They might well agree that persons have a right to be treated in the same way unless there is a general and relevant principle of differentiation, but nevertheless maintain that such a principle exists, i.e. that some are black and others not. It would not be argued that the colour difference in itself constitutes a relevant reason but that it is correlated with other characteristics and attitudes which are relevant, such as insensitivity, stupidity, ineducability, irresponsibility, and so forth. The purported differentiating characteristics are often based on faulty generalizations, specious or unscientific arguments, or mere lack of data.[26]

Laski has pointed out that 'it is consistent with the principle of equality that men be treated differently so long as the differences are relevant to the common good'.[27] It is important to note that he does not say that it is consistent with the principle of equality that some men may be treated unequally. On the contrary, he is saying that the equality principle encompasses the possibility of differential

[22] For a hierarchy of standards, see Geoffrey Marshall, 'Notes on the Rule of Equal Law', in J. R. Pennock and J. W. Chapman, eds., *Nomos* IX (1967), 261.

[23] W. von Leyden, 'On Justifying Inequalities', 11 *Political Studies* (1963), 56, 67. (See also S. I. Benn and R. S. Peters, *Social Principles and the Democratic State* (Allen and Unwin, London, 1959).

[24] Leslie Stephen, 'Social Equality' in *Ethics* (1897), i.267.

[25] Williams, in Laslett and Runciman, 110, 123.

[26] Ibid. 113, and Richard Wasserstrom, 'Rights, Human Rights and Racial Discrimination', 61 *Journal of Philosophy* (1964), 628, 638–9.

[27] H. J. Laski, 'A Plea for Equality' in *The Dangers of Obedience* (1930), 232. Cf. W. K. Frankena, 'The Concept of Social Justice', in R. B. Brandt, ed., *Social Justice* (Prentice-Hall, Englewood Cliffs, N. J., 1962).

treatment; it does not necessitate treating people in an identical fashion. Some would go further and say that the more a society endeavours to secure equality of consideration for all its members, the greater will be the differentiation of treatment.[28]

If normative equality (social justice) permits and sometimes requires departures from numerical equality or identity of treatment, how is it to be decided which differences are permissible? The utilitarian 'greatest happiness of the greatest number' approach presents difficulties of quantification and could lead to disregard of minority interest. Rawls, on the other hand, argues in favour of a contractual model of normative equality in that just social arrangements are those which would result from a mutual acceptance of basic principle by a community of rational egoists seeking to organize a new society but ignorant of their status within it. The two principles which result are (1) each person will have an equal right to the most extensive liberty compatible with a like liberty for all and (2) the only differential treatment in the social and economic sphere that will be permitted will be that designed for the greatest benefit of the least advantaged or that attached to offices and positions equally open to all.[29] The criteria which suggest themselves as proper reasons for differential treatment include need, desert, or merit, and compensation, but how these are to be ranked depends on the nature and size of the particular claim.[30]

It is apparent that a prime difficulty with the term 'equality' is that it is used in both a narrow and a broad sense. First, it can be used in the sense of a 'mathematical', 'exact', 'strict', or 'numerical' equality which includes the ideas of 'identity' or 'sameness'. Alternatively, it is often used to mean 'true', 'effective', 'real', 'genuine', or 'normative' equality. This second formulation envisages a standard to be achieved and allows for 'special measures' or differences in treatment designed to bring persons up to a certain level. Thus, for example, to give old-age pensioners the same amount of money is an example of numerical or formal equality of treatment. To give them different amounts to bring their individual incomes up to a specified figure would be an application of the principle of real or genuine (normative) equality. Thus the latter notion involves the idea of

[28] See e.g. R. H. Tawney, op. cit., 39; J. Stone, *Human Law and Human Justice* (Stevens, London, 1965), 334.

[29] Rawls, 302. For criticism of Rawls's theory see R. Nozick, *Anarchy, State and Utopia* (Basil Blackwell, Oxford, 1974), and V. Haksar, *Equality, Liberty and Perfectionism* (1979).   [30] See Evans, op. cit.

compensatory treatment, or distributive justice. Certain under-
privileged persons or groups are given a 'boost' to bring them up to
the same basic level as others, on the analogy of the handicap
system employed in many sports.[31]
  Some philosophers have argued that to follow the maxim 'to each
according to his need' is to practise 'the most perfect form of equal
distribution.'[32] Raphael argues that to take special measures, to
give someone suffering from a disadvantage of some sort similar
opportunities to those enjoyed by others, is to accord him equal
treatment with those others. He says, 'There appears to be inequality
only because the means required in these circumstances to give me
equal treatment with other people is different from that employed
for other people'.[33] Similarly von Leyden argues that treating people
unequally is unjustifiable except when we must do so in order to
treat them equally in another more 'important' or 'fundamental'
respect.[34] He seems here to be using 'unequally' in the numerical
sense and 'equally' in the normative sense, and to be distinguishing
the two concepts.[35] This sort of analysis has been criticized by
others, especially Bedau who believes that 'Persons have [received]
an equal distribution, equal treatment, or equal rights etc., if and
only if they have received the *same* distribution, treatment, rights,
etc.'[36] This is a clear affirmation of the formal interpretation. In his
opinion, the other point of view was an attempt to justify inequalities
in the name of egalitarianism which would lead to the 'ironic consequence' that human justice has in many cases to be the justice of
mere equality simply because of the difficulties of assigning proportional equalities fairly.[37] Bedau is certainly correct in pointing out
that some writers have used equality in two different senses, but his
solution—scrapping the notion of distributive or real equality—is
hardly practicable, for it has become, as will be demonstrated, an
established usage in the interpretation of equality in legal instruments.

[31] See *Equality* (1965), a collection of essays by R. L. Carter, D. Kenyon, P.
Marcuse, L. Miller, 91–2; also, Stanley I. Benn, 'Egalitarianism and the Equal
Consideration of Interests', *Nomos* IX, 63, 75.
[32] e.g. G. Vlastos, 'Justice and Equality', in Brandt, 31; and D. D. Raphael,
'Equality and Equity', 21 *Philosophy* (1946), 118.   [33] Raphael, 126.
[34] Wolfgang von Leyden, 'On Justifying Inequality', 11 *Political Studies*, (1963)
56, 68.
[35] And cf. Frankena, op. cit., 23. 'Social justice is the equal (though not always
similar) treatment of all persons, at least in the long run.'
[36] H. A. Bedau, 'Egalitarianism and the Idea of Equality', *Nomos* IX, 3, 7.
[37] Ibid., 25.

Dworkin distinguishes the right to 'equal treatment' which he sees as requiring the numerical approach, from the right to 'treatment as equals' which is not a right to have some burden or benefit allocated equally (i.e. identically) but a right 'to be treated with the same respect and concern as everyone else.'[38]

If the word 'equality', when used unqualified, is taken to mean a normative equality in the sense outlined above, and 'difference' or 'differentiation' used to express the notion of exact or numerical inequality,[39] then much difficulty will be avoided. Honoré has attempted to solve the problem of usage by calling what is here referred to as normative equality 'social justice' and using 'equality' in the sense of numerical equality.[40] Although this solution is attractive, it is not ideal for the reason already given—that the normative-equality view involving the notion of 'special compensation' has gained acceptance in legal interpretations of the concept of equality. For instance, Freedman infers from a review of some cases decided by the United States Supreme Court interpreting the equality clause of the Fourteenth Amendment to the Constitution, that 'Consistent with the idea of equality, *if not essential to it*, is a recognition that inequality in treatment (compensatory treatment) may be necessary to provide an approximation of equality in status.'[41] Similarly, the concept of special measures of protection designed to promote real or genuine equality has become part of the notion of equal protection of the laws under other state constitutions, particularly that of India, and is well established in international law.

It will be seen that under international law the concept of equality of individuals includes two complementary notions: (1) *the principle of non-discrimination*, which is a negative aspect of equality designed to prohibit differentiation on irrelevant, arbitrary or unreasonable grounds; and (2) *the principle of protection or special measures*, designed to achieve 'positive' equality. This second principle is sometimes termed 'reverse' or 'benign' discrimination but these are misleading and unsatisfactory labels. The meaning and content of the term 'discrimination' has caused as much difficulty among

[38] R. Dworkin, *Taking Rights Seriously* (Duckworth, London, 1977), 227.
[39] e.g. Laski, n. 27 above.
[40] A. M. Honoré, 'Social Justice', 8 *McGill L. J.* (1962), 78; reprinted in a revised version in R. S. Summers, ed., *Essays in Legal Philosophy*, (Basil Blackwell, Oxford, 1968), 61. (And cf. n. 35 above.)
[41] Monroe H. Freedman, 'Equality in the Administration of Criminal Justice', *Nomos* IX, 250, 256.

lawyers as the term 'equality' has to philosophers. Does it just mean 'differentiation' *simpliciter*, or has it come to acquire a special meaning of 'unfavourable' or 'invidious' distinction in law? Other questions which arise are, *inter alia*, 'By what criteria is the quality of a classification of persons or a particular set to be tested in order to discover whether it offends the principle of equality, and by whom are these criteria to be established?'

'Discrimination' in ordinary usage has several meanings. It can be used neutrally to mean a mere distinction or differentiation or used in the complimentary sense of an accurate distinction.[42] On the other hand, 'to discriminate against' has always meant 'to make an adverse distinction'.

In 1949 two American commentators warned that there were two senses in which 'discrimination' was used which should not be confused. In one sense, to exercise discrimination was simply to be discerning, to be quick at recognizing differences, to be cognitively alert. In the second sense discriminatory action was action which was biased, prejudiced, unfair. Legislators should be discriminating in the first sense in that they must discern and recognize relevant distinctions and differences, i.e. classify reasonably. However, the type of discrimination forbidden by the equal protection clause was that suggested by the second sense of the term.[43] Although the confinement of the legal meaning of discrimination to the sense of unjustifiable differentiation has been attacked,[44] it is gaining acceptance in the United States.[45]

[42] See the definition of 'discrimination' in the Shorter Oxford English Dictionary (3rd ed.). However, the Random House Dictionary of the English Language (New York) defines the verb 'to discriminate' as 'to make a distinction in favor of or against a person or thing on the basis of the group, class or category to which the person or thing belongs, rather than according to actual merit'.

[43] See J. Tussman and J. tenBroek, 'The Equal Protection of the Laws', 37 *Calif. L. Rev.* (1949), 341, 358, n. 35. The requirement of motive or intent as an element of discrimination was overemphasized by these two writers.

[44] See e.g. J. S. Williams, '*Mulkey* v. *Reitman* and State Action', 14 (1) *UCLA Law Review*, (1966–7), 26, 31. 'Individuality consists in part of discrimination. We used to refer to a person of quality and sensible tastes as being a discriminating individual. This was a very apt description. He discriminated in favor of good literature, sensible political doctrine, quality friendships and the like. He showed good judgement. When the discretion to discriminate is taken away, individuality is gone.'

[45] e.g. *Gomillion* v. *Lightfoot* 364 US 339 (1960) and 22 *Ohio St. L. J.* (1961), 213; 21 *La. L. Rev.* (1961), 676. For an example of the traditional usage, see the 1949 Annotation of Discrimination in US Supreme Court Reports, 4 L. ed. 2d 1121, which states, 'Discrimination is here used in its broadest sense and includes *any* differential treatment whether of equal quality or not which may have been accorded to a member of a particular race by virtue of his membership of that race . . .'

Sørensen pointed out in 1956 that discrimination denoted only distinctions which are detrimental to the individual in question, and that favourable treatment was not discrimination unless it amounted to the granting of privileges to some groups to the detriment of others and thereby amounted to discrimination against those latter groups. Furthermore, discrimination comprised only such detrimental distinctions as were based upon the membership of individuals in social or other groups, and was not generally applicable to distinctions based on individual qualities. Although from a sociological point of view it might not be justifiable to classify women or men as specific social groups, detrimental differential treatment on such a ground is usually characterized as discrimination, since it means denying to an individual an equality which he ought to enjoy according to accepted social evaluations.[46] That the meaning of 'discrimination' is not just a verbal quibble is well illustrated by those who have argued that a blanket prohibition against discrimination had the adverse effect of precluding the state from taking ameliorative measures to remove the disabilities of the depressed classes in India.[47]

The word 'discriminate' taken alone is now commonly used in the pejorative sense of an unfair, unreasonable, unjustifiable or arbitrary distinction, not only in English but in other languages. Thus, in French, discrimination has been described as a *terme nouveau, toujours péjoratif*[48] and in German *Diskriminierung* means an adverse or unfavourable distinction.[49] The following unsatisfactory definition of '*discrimination*' appears in the 1960 Paris *Dictionnaire de la terminologie du droit international: 'Traitement différential. Distinction consistant à refuser à certains des droits ou avantages reconnues accordés à d'autres.'*[50] Nevertheless modern international usage now generally accepts that discrimination signifies any act or

[46] See M. Sørensen, 'The Quest for Equality', in *International Conciliation*, no. 507 (1956), 291.

[47] See e.g. S. M. Huang-Thio, 'Constitutional Discrimination under the Malaysian Constitution', 6 *Malaya L. R.* (1961), 1, 4; and *State of Madras* v. *Dorairajan* AIR 1951, SC 226.

[48] J. Pictet, *Les Principes du droit international humanitaire* (Comité internationale de la Croix-Rouge, Geneva, 1966), 41.

[49] See G. Jaenicke, *Der Begriff der Diskriminierung im modernen Völkerrecht* (1940), 12. But cf. the views of Austria, Report of Committee on the Elimination of Racial Discrimination 1978, GAOR 33rd sess., supp. no. 18, UN doc. A/33/18, para. 120. In Russian, the word 'discrimination' 'clearly referred to unfair, unequal treatment'. See UN doc. E/CN.4/S.R. 52, 11 (USSR delegate in Commission of Human Rights).

[50] At 217.

conduct which denies to individuals equality of treatment with other individuals because they belong to particular groups in society. As Jaenicke puts it '*Die Völkerrechtspraxis verwendet [den Begriff Diskriminierung] heute zur Bezeignung einer unzulässigen unterschiedlichen Behandlung.*'[51] International law, traditionally regarded as a law between states and inapplicable to individuals directly, did not take cognizance of personal status until quite recent times. One of the first important international achievements in alleviating personal inequalities was the large number of bilateral treaties concluded to ban the slave trade, and over the last fifty years it has been firmly established that human rights now fall within the purview of international law. The most significant development has been the strong affirmation of the principle of equality of persons in dignity and rights and the rejection of personal distinctions based on irrelevant criteria. International organizations have taken the initiative in procuring the outlawing of *de jure* and *de facto* distinctions between human beings on the grounds of race, colour, sex, religion, language, political or other opinion, national or social origin, birth, and other status. Discrimination against human beings on these grounds, which often gives rise to inferior status under municipal law, has been characterized by the international community as 'scientifically false, morally condemnable, socially unjust, and dangerous.'[52]

Just as certain types of discriminatory status have been rejected in municipal legal systems on the ground of public policy, so the international community has condemned discrimination as contrary to international policy. Under public international law, those kinds of status which predicate unreasonable and arbitrary inequalities are prohibited, while categories which give special protection to particular groups in order to enable them to attain real and genuine equality are permitted.[53]

[51] G. Jaenicke, 'Diskriminierung' in K. Strupp and H. J. Schlochauer, eds., *Wörterbuch des Völkerrechts* (W. de Gruyter, Berlin, 2nd ed. 1960–2), i.387–92. 'These days the practice of international law uses the term discrimination to signify inadmissible unequal treatment.'

[52] See the preambles to the United Nations Declaration on the Elimination of all Forms of Racial Discrimination, Nov. 1963, and to the convention on the same subject of Dec. 1965.

[53] Just as in municipal law those kinds of status which perpetuated inequality (such as coverture and illegitimacy) are disappearing, and those which provide protection (e.g. infancy and insanity) are surviving or even being introduced (e.g. the status of incompetency in California—cf. *Re Langley* [1962] Ch. 541) so, under international law, discriminatory types of status are being discouraged and special measures of

For example, the system of minority protection guaranteed by the League of Nations included certain obligations concerning the use of minority language and the creation and control by minorities of educational, charitable, religious, and social institutions. Such guarantees have been described as 'privileges', but as the Permanent Court stated, 'it is easy to imagine cases in which the equality of treatment of the minority whose situation and requirements are different would result in inequality in fact. Equality between members of the majority and minority must be an *effective and genuine equality*.'[54] As de Azcarate pointed out, for members of the minority to live on equal terms with the majority, it would be necessary for them to have the juridical, social, economic, and cultural institutions which would allow them to preserve their national consciousness and to cultivate and develop their own language and culture under the same conditions as the majority. For this purpose, protection against unfavourable discriminatory treatment is not enough; real equality—not merely formal but substantial—demands positive and special measures for the minorities.[55]

Although international conferences in the interwar period adopted resolutions condemning discrimination, it was not until the United Nations Charter that it was definitely laid down in an international instrument that human rights were to be available to all without distinction as to race, sex, language, or religion. The most important organ set up by the United Nations to deal with the question of equality was the Sub-Commission on the Prevention of Discrimination and Protection of Minorities, although minority protection fell into disfavour after the World War II since it was felt that it encouraged irredentism and that the Minorities Treaties had not provided adequate protection against Nazi intolerance and persecution. No minorities provision appeared in the Charter, nor did the United Nations guarantee the minority clauses in the peace treaties. The emphasis had changed.[56]

protection encouraged. As Frankena points out, 'the historical quest for social justice has consisted largely of attempts to eliminate certain dissimilarities as bases for difference of treatment and certain similarities as bases for sameness of treatment' (op. cit.).

[54] *Minority Schools in Albania* opinion. PCIJ (1935), ser. A/B, no. 64, 19.

[55] See P. de Azcarate, Y. Florez, *League of Nations and National Minorities: An Experiment* trans. E. O. Brooke (Carnegie Endowment, Washington, D. C., 1945), 24.

[56] Professor Kunz writing in 1954 (48 *AJIL* 282) wondered whether there might not be 'fashions in international law just as there are in neckties'. At the end of the first World War 'international protection of minorities was the great fashion: treaties in abundance, conferences, League of Nations activities, and enormous literature. Recently this fashion

The major work of the United Nations in this field has been concentrated on the negative aspects of the principle of equality. Conventions have been prepared dealing with, *inter alia*, genocide, political rights of women, equal pay for work of equal value, discrimination in employment and occupation, discrimination in education, racial discrimination, apartheid and discrimination against women; and non-discrimination provisions appear in many other instruments of which the most important are the 1966 Covenants on Human Rights and the European Convention of Human Rights, 1950.

An article on protection of minorities appears in the Covenant on Civil and Political Rights but in general the emphasis shifted from minorities to a more general concept of positive equality, i.e. special measures for the assistance of disadvantaged groups.[57]

In order to discover the extent to which there exist international norms, or standards of international law concerning the equality of individuals, the following will be examined:

(1) international treaties and declarations dealing with equality and discrimination;

(2) the practice and *opinio juris* of states and international organs, including the legal effect of United Nations recommendations;

(3) the decisions of international and municipal courts and the writings of jurists, not only as sources of law but also as 'law-determining agencies for ascertaining the contents of the actual rules of international law.'[58]

(4) whether or not the principle is a 'general principle of law' or part of the *jus cogens*.

has become almost obsolete. Today the well-dressed international lawyer wears human rights.' His wardrobe now includes 'special measures of protection' as well.

[57] See e.g. art. 1 (4) of the 1965 Convention on the Elimination of all Forms of Racial Discrimination.

[58] See E. Schwarzenberger and E. D. Brown, *A Manual of International Law* (Stevens, London, 6th ed. 1976), 18.

I

MINORITY PROTECTION AFTER
WORLD WAR I

1. *The Omission of Articles on Minorities and Religious and Racial
Equality from the League of Nations Covenant*

SEVERAL proposals were made for the inclusion of provisions on
minorities and on religious and racial equality in the League of
Nations Covenant, but all were finally discarded. In his Draft
Covenant of January 1919, President Wilson included a 'supplementary agreement', Paragraph VI of which provided, 'The League
of Nations shall require all new states to bind themselves as a
condition precedent to their recognition as independent or autonomous states, to accord to all racial or national minorities within
their jurisdiction exactly the same treatment and security, both in
law and in fact, that is accorded the racial or national majority of
their people.' D. H. Miller, the President's legal adviser, commented
that, while the purpose of the paragraph was beneficent, general
treatment was impossible because although equal religious and
cultural privileges should be accorded in all cases it would be
impracticable even locally for all racial minorities to have (for
example) their language used in official records.[1] The paragraph
was preserved in the third draft completed in January 1919, but this
'marked the zenith in the struggle at the Peace Conference for the
recognition and protection of minorities, and from that point the
decline began.'[2] The British suggested the omission of Paragraph
VI until after the special provisions to be contained in the territorial
treaties had been considered, and the Hurst–Miller draft[3] omitted
the paragraph altogether. Despite Wilson's efforts the Commission
failed to revive Paragraph VI because of the intransigence of the
British delegation caused in turn by the adamant stand of the

[1] D. H. Miller, *The Drafting of the Covenant* (Putnam, New York, London, 1928),
ii.91.
[2] J. Robinson and others, *Were the Minorities Treaties a Failure?* (Institute of
Jewish Affairs, New York, 1943), 9.
[3] Annex 1 of the English minutes of the 1st meeting of the Commission on the
League of Nations, in Miller, ii, doc. 19, 231–7.

Australian and New Zealand Prime Ministers who were concerned that the propriety of the treatment of their Aboriginal and Maori populations might come under the scrutiny of the League, despite the fact that the paragraph clearly applied only to new states not yet recognized as independent or autonomous.

It was surprising that no one suggested that *all* states should bind themselves in the League Covenant to accord equality of treatment to minorities within their jurisdiction, since in the proposed religious clause[4] it was provided that *all* states (whether existing or newly established) seeking admission to the League should undertake not to discriminate in law or fact on religious grounds. The omission of a general minorities clause in the Covenant in favour of specific provisions in the territorial treaties applying only to certain states was later to cause much bitterness and a sense of injustice in the states subject to minorities obligations, since many other states which also possessed minorities were not bound by similar provisions.

Paragraph VII of Wilson's third draft provided, 'Recognizing religious persecution and intolerance as fertile sources of war, the Powers signatories hereto agree, and the League of Nations shall exact from all new states and all states seeking admission to it the promise, that they will make no law prohibiting or interfering with the free exercise of religion, and that they will in no way discriminate, either in law or in fact, against those who practice any particular creed, religion, or belief whose practices are not inconsistent with public order or public morals.'[5]

When the Hurst–Miller draft was chosen as the working basis of the Commission, a committee chaired by Lord Robert Cecil concluded that, although it would be preferable to omit the religious article altogether, a milder formulation might suffice, i.e. 'The High Contracting Parties agree that they will not prohibit or interfere with the free exercise of any creed, religion or belief whose principles are not inconsistent with public order or public morals and that no person within their respective jurisdictions shall be molested in life, liberty, or pursuit of happiness by reason of his adherence to any creed, religion or belief.'[6] Had the Commission accepted this provision it would have appeared as Article XXI of the Covenant, but a majority opposed any religious clause and an excuse for abandoning

---

[4] Para. 7.   [5] Miller, ii, doc. 9, 105.
[6] Ibid., ii, doc. 19, 307. See E. M. House and C. Seymour, *What Really Happened at Paris* (Benn, London, 1921), 406–7, 209–22.

it was provided by a Japanese amendment which attempted to juxtapose the religious and racial questions. The effect was the defeat of both proposals.[7] According to Professor Zimmern, the reason for the amendment was that Japan was haunted by the problem of race relations. In her opinion the time was now ripe to set race relations once and for all on a basis of equality and this was to have been the Japanese contribution to the Covenant.[8]

House was eager to assist but soon noted that every solution was resisted by the Australian Prime Minister, and the British delegation, although generally unopposed, was unwilling to overrule him.[9] Because of this the Japanese decided to present the following resolution: 'The equality of nations being a basic principle of the League of Nations, the High Contracting Parties agree to accord as soon as possible to all alien nationals of states members of the League equal and just treatment in every respect making no distinction either in law or fact on account of their race or nationality.' A moderate speech in support of the resolution was made by the Japanese delegate who pointed out that the article as it stood attempted to eliminate religious causes of strife from international relationships and that, since the race question was also a standing difficulty which might become acute and dangerous at any moment in the future, it was desirable that there should be a provision in the Covenant dealing with it. The clause would enunciate the principle of equality between men as a basis of future intercourse and invite governments and peoples to devise the means of surmounting racial discrimination.[10] 'In spite of the nobility of the sentiments which inspired' the Japanese, Lord Robert Cecil suggested postponement of the discussion. The Commission pusillanimously agreed, believing that although questions of race and religion would 'certainly' be dealt with in the future by the League it 'would be better for the moment not to allude to them'[11] and the article was omitted. Miller observed that the proposal had served a good purpose at the meeting for it 'helped to make impossible any article on religious liberty in any form; any such article in the Covenant would have been most dangerous and perhaps fatal to the League; the subject was never

[7] Miller, ii, doc. 19, 323–5.

[8] A. E. Zimmern, *The League of Nations and the Rule of Law* (Macmillan, London, 1936), 262.

[9] E. M. House, *The Intimate Papers of Colonel House* (Benn, London, 1926) iv.320–1.

[10] Miller, ii.323–4.   [11] Ibid., ii.325.

again considered.'[12] Presumably it was felt that states would not brook any interference by the League in matters which traditionally had lain within their domestic jurisdiction, but it is arguable that racial and religious articles might have provided the League with a potent legal weapon to reinforce complaints about Germany's treatment of 'racial' and religious minorities in the 1930s.

It is important to note that while the 'religious' paragraph referred to persons generally within the states' jurisdiction and was cast in the negative, the 'racial equality' proposal applied only to *alien* nationals of states members of the League and imposed a positive duty to ensure equality of treatment. The 'religious' paragraph was a new excursion into the realms of state sovereignty since it imposed obligations with regard to a state's own nationals. The Japanese proposal, which had only sought equality of treatment of aliens with a state's own nationals, was not particularly radical since, in those countries where a state's treatment of its own nationals fell below the 'minimum standard' of international law, aliens would in any case be entitled to enjoy the international standard. Japan finally suggested the inclusion of a preparatory sentence in the Preamble, endorsing 'the principle of the equality of nations and just treatment of their nationals',[13] arguing that the wrongs of racial discrimination were the subject of deep resentment on the part of a large portion of the human race. It was only reasonable, therefore, that the principle of equality of nations and just treatment of their nationals should be laid down as a fundamental basis of future relations in the world organization, and the denial of this claim would, in the eyes of those peoples with reason to be keenly interested, reflect on their quality and status. Pride, the Japanese delegate ominously warned, was one of the most forceful and sometimes uncontrollable causes of human action.

Lord Robert Cecil replied that, while the British government realized the importance of the racial question, its solution could not be attempted without encroaching on the sovereignty of states members of the League. Either the points which the Japanese government proposed to add to the Preamble were vague and ineffective or they were of practical significance and, if the latter, they opened the door to serious controversy and to interference in the domestic affairs of states members of the League. Other important matters, such as religious liberty, the claims of the International Council of

[12] Ibid., i.269.　　　[13] Ibid., ii.387–94.

Women, and a great many other matters of this sort, had not been
included in the Covenant because they would have resulted in
infringements of the sovereignty of states.[14] Similarly, the United
States believed that, if the clause were substantial and not merely
formal, it would contravene that clause of the Covenant which
reserved to the members of the League matters solely within their
domestic jurisdiction.

This approach clearly begged the question since, if a matter is
regulated in the form of an international treaty, the matter regulated
ceases to fall exclusively within the domestic jurisdiction of the
parties to the agreement but is subject to an international regime to
the extent to which obligations are assumed under that agreement.
Merely to object that a treaty provision infringed the sovereignty of
states was no real objection, because most international agreements
affect the freedom of governments to act unilaterally to some extent.
The fact was that the matters which would now have been placed
under an international regime were matters that traditionally had
not been so subject, and certain states were afraid of taking a new
departure.

The importance Japan attached to the equality clause, and the
possibility that Japan might not join the League unless satisfied on
this point, were made perfectly clear and the form of the proposition
was such that it was not easy to object to it, since no delegate could
say that he objected to the principle of equality of nations or
favoured unjust treatment of nationals. However, the British Delegation feared that, despite the unobjectionable nature of the clause
in principle, its very vagueness might later enable investigation at a
later date of the White Australia policy and the general question of
the immigration of Eastern peoples into countries which found such
a possibility impossible to discuss.[15]

Most delegates did not see how the Commission could avoid
voting for the amendment. The Greek delegate noted that Japan
was not now taking a stand on the equality of races (which presumably

[14] Ibid., ii.389. The same objection was taken by the United States, i.465–6.

[15] Ibid., i.461–6, ii.389–90. It appears that Mr Hughes while endangering Japanese
membership of the League was simultaneously engaged in an attempt to ensure the
inclusion of Japan in the proposed ILO in order that her industrial competition might
be less dangerous for Australia. This led him to favour the complete separation of the
two organizations. (See J. T. Shotwell, ed., *The Origins of the ILO* (Carnegie
Endowment, New York, 1924), i.200.) At the same time Australia, Canada, and the
USA opposed the insertion into the Labour Charter of the principle of 'equality of
status and working conditions for foreign workers'.

he would have been unable to accept) but on the equality of nations themselves and the just treatment of their nationals. Moreover, the Japanese delegate had pointed out that his amendment did not involve any country in an obligation to pass any measures whatever in respect of immigration.[16]

Even President Wilson capitulated, stating that, although his own interest was 'to quiet discussion that raises national differences and racial prejudices', discussion of the matter had already 'set burning flames of prejudice'. 'How', he asked, 'can you treat on its merits in this quiet room a question which will not be treated on its merits when it gets out of this room?'[17] As Zimmern points out, this was a dangerous and short-sighted argument for it neglected the fact that, the issue having been raised, attention would inevitably attach to the vote and deductions would be drawn from it whichever way it went.[18]

When the amendment was pressed to a vote, eleven of the nineteen members present voted in favour, but to the astonishment of the delegates, President Wilson then ruled that in view of 'serious objections on the part of some of us' the amendment was not carried. In answer to M. Larnaude he explained that the practice of the Commission had been to require unanimity and that, since the objectors did not merely wish to make reservations but were insisting on their objections, he was obliged to declare the amendment defeated.[19] The Japanese delegate later described the President's ruling as 'somewhat sophistical, for the rule of unanimity was not then a *chose jugée*'.[20] Clearly the manœuvre was bitterly resented in Japan,[21] but, regardless of any question of procedure, the British objection was such that it was impossible for the Japanese proposal to become part of the Covenant.[22]

Despite President Wilson's insistence that the result was not a rejection of the principle of equality of nations and peoples, it was regrettable that no provision on the question, or on religious or racial equality, was included in the Covenant. Positive recognition

[16] Miller, ii.390.   [17] Ibid., i.462–3.   [18] Zimmern, 267.
[19] Miller, i.464. In favour of Japan, France, and Italy (2 votes each), Brazil, Chile, Guatemala, Yugoslavia, and Czechoslovakia (1 vote each). Only the affirmative votes were taken.
[20] Viscount Ishii, *The Foreign Policy of the Powers* (John Hopkins Press, Baltimore, 1935), 106–7.
[21] See the remarks of Baron Makino at the Peace Conference, 28 Apr. 1919, Miller, ii.704.
[22] Miller, ii.464.

of the legal right to equality of treatment of races and religious groups had to wait another thirty years for the United Nations Charter and subsequent instruments.

2. *The Protection of Minorities under the League*

Although clauses on minorities and racial and religious discrimination were finally excluded from the Covenant, a series of international instruments was drawn up in which stipulations for the protection of minorities in certain countries were guaranteed by the League[23] as conditions of the territorial settlements, and declarations were required from certain countries before they were permitted to join the League. Other instruments conferred on minority rights the character of positive international law. Clemenceau pointed out that the Treaty between the Allied and Associated Powers and Poland, which was intended as a model for the others,[24] did not constitute any new departure since it was the established procedure of European public law, when a new state was created or large accessions of territory were made to an existing state, that the formal recognition of the Great Powers should be accompanied by an undertaking by the state concerned, in the form of a binding international convention, to comply with 'certain principles of government'.[25] An early example was the Treaty of Sienna of 31 May 1815 between the Netherlands, Great Britain, Russia, Prussia, and Austria concerning the reunion of Belgium with Holland. The Treaty of Paris concluded on 30 March 1856, after the Crimean War, was the first to stipulate expressly that a class of citizens should not be deemed inferior to other classes for racial as well as for religious reasons. From then on, the question of racial and religious minorities received greater attention from governments, and in the

[23] *League of Nations Official Journal* (1929), 1134–9. Special minorities treaties were signed by Poland, Yugoslavia, Czechoslovakia, Romania, and Greece, and chapters on minorities were included in the peace treaties with Austria, Hungary, Bulgaria, and Turkey, while certain declarations were made by Albania, Estonia, Finland, Latvia, and Lithuania before the League Council.

[24] Analogous provisions were later included in the Treaties of St-Germaine-en-Laye, Neuilly-sur-Seine, Trianon and Lausanne. Twenty-two bilateral conventions were signed between various countries with regard to minorities—in particular between Austria and Czecholovakia, Poland and Czechoslovakia, Poland and Germany. The principle of minority protection was also recognized in Article 7 of the Treaty of Riga between Poland and the Soviet Union.

[25] H. W. V. Temperley, *History of the Peace Conference of Paris* (Hodder and Stoughton, London, 1920–4), v.437 ff.

Treaty of Berlin of 13 July 1878 religious toleration was made an indispensable condition of the recognition of Serbia, Montenegro, and Romania.

There were several important differences between the new treaties and these precedents.[26] First, it was decided not to include minority provisions in the treaties constituting the new states. This decision had far-reaching consequences, for, had the clauses for minority protection followed immediately after the territorial clauses, the fact that they were conditions for the transfers of territory would have been much clearer. Secondly, the guarantee of the provisions was vested in the League of Nations and not in the Great Powers. This was the most important innovation of the treaties in that it attempted to insulate the new states from intervention by other states purporting to protect a minority but actually seeking political advantage for themselves, a practice which had made the older systems unsuitable and ineffective. Instead, the responsibility for compelling compliance was given to the League Council which would not have private interests to serve. Thirdly, provision was made for the reference of dispute to the Permanent Court in order to facilitate impartial decisions and to avoid the dangers of political interference.

General provision was made in each treaty to assure the protection of life, liberty, and free exercise of religion to all the inhabitants of a state, without distinction as to birth, nationality, race, religion, or language.[27] Only nationals, however, were to enjoy civil and political rights and to possess equality before the law without distinction as to race, language, or religion.[28] Nationality was to belong as of right to all persons who could reasonably be considered as entitled to it by habitual residence, or birth, without any discrimination, and nationals were to be treated equally, regardless of race, language, or religion. Minorities whose distinguishing features were their

---

[26] See generally Sulkowski, *Problem of the International Protection of National Minorities* (1944); L. P. Mair, *The Protection of Minorities* (1928), 30–4; Tøre Modeen, *The International Protection of National Minorities in Europe* (Abo Akademi, Abo, 1969).

[27] e.g. art. 2 of the Polish Treaty. See L. of N. doc. C.L.110.1927, i.43.

[28] e.g. art. 7 of the Polish Treaty, L. of N. doc. C.L.110.927, i.43. The United Nations Secretary-General stated (UN doc. E/CN.4/sub.2/6) that the treaties and declarations recognized the equality of all persons before the law. It is clear, however, that under article 7 the principle applies only to nationals. It is difficult to see how non-nationals could be 'assured protection' under Article 2 if they were not entitled to equality before the law.

political views or which constituted a social or economic class were not given protection by the treaties.

As well as the non-discrimination provisions, 'racial, religious, and linguistic minorities' were accorded special rights which included:

(a) the right to use their own language in private intercourse, in commerce, in religion, in the press or in publications, or at public meetings;
(b) the right to have separate educational establishments;
(c) the right to possess their own religious and charitable institutions;
(d) the right to have an equitable share in the enjoyment of public funds;
(e) certain specific stipulations with regard to respect for the sabbath for Jews, family law, and rights for Muslims;
(f) certain traditional rights and, occasionally, a limited autonomy.

The right of appeal to the League Council or the Permanent Court was restricted to states members of the League Council, and it was stipulated that those provisions of the treaties *which concerned minorities of race, language, or religion* were to be placed under the guarantee of the League. These substantive provisions of the treaties and declarations upon which the edifice of the League minorities system was built, were strongly attacked. It was claimed that they were drafted in such circumstances and haste that they were, in the agreement of jurists, so loosely worded as to be sometimes unintelligible and frequently unworkable without the active co-operation and good will of the treaty-bound states.[29] Another delegate attacked the guarantee system as 'an ill-balanced structure erected haphazard and founded on political paradoxes.'[30]

An examination of the basic texts reveals a number of curious features which are inexplicable without reference to the limited purpose for which the treaties were intended. Thus, although the various instruments contained articles assuring protection of certain basic rights to *all* 'inhabitants' or 'nationals' of a state, the League guarantee only applied to the rights of 'members of racial, linguistic, or religious minorities'.[31] It can only be assumed that the general clauses were a half-hearted attempt to include in the treaties the

[29] 120 *O.J. Sp. Supp.*, 44.   [30] 125 *O.J. Sp. Supp.*, 42.
[31] L. of N. doc. C.L.110.1927, i.43.

humanitarian articles omitted from the Covenant. The fundamental
objection was that it was an assault on the doctrine of the sovereignty
of states, and interference in matters of domestic jurisdiction, to
attempt to regulate the way in which a state treated its own nationals,
but the framers of the minorities treaties considered that the protection of minorities had traditionally constituted an exception to
the domestic jurisdiction rule.

It was often emphasized that the minority system as it was constituted was limited and intended to deal with an exceptional *sui generis*
situation. Mr Anthony Eden remarked that 'the minorities treaties
were created to deal with a special problem existing in a given area
for a given time'.[32] Moreover, it was unequivocally pointed out in
the Madrid Report that it was not the purpose of the authors of the
treaties to set out principles of government which should be of
universal obligation. They did not consider the principle of religious
toleration to be applicable in all states, nor did they lay down
universal principles for the treatment of aliens.[33] Clearly the League
minority system was established for political rather than humanitarian
reasons and the notion that the international community should
concern itself with basic humanitarian questions such as racial or
religious equality had already been firmly rejected. It was only
where these matters might become a threat to international peace
or security that they were considered to be matters of international
concern.[34] There was no intention of declaring any humanitarian
norms applicable *erga omnes*; on the contrary any such intention
was specifically denied. The fact was that the humanitarian stipulations which President Wilson originally intended to be universal
and to apply to all members of the League were finally imposed on a
small number of states for political reasons.[35] Moreover, the system
did not protect rights inherent in the human person, but certain
categories of persons in certain categories of states. No major
power was subjected to minority obligations although several contained populations in a similar position to those guaranteed protection

[32] 130 *O.J. Sp. Supp.*, 60.
[33] L. of N. doc. C8.M5.1931, i.156, 161. (This section of the report was to be
quoted often in later years by those arguing against an extension of the minorities
system.)
[34] L. of N. doc. C8.M5.1931, i.94–7.
[35] 120 *O.J. Sp. Supp.*, 51. Mr Nintitch (Serbo-Croat-Slovene State) noted, 'As it
has so justly been remarked in this Assembly, the question of minorities is not merely
a humanitarian but also a political question . . . and in its present form much more
political.'

by the League in other states. Haiti alleged that, in the system as constituted, the principle of national cohesion and unity in each state was superseded by a system of discrimination in one and the same community (the League) and in one and the same state and these were the principal causes of most of the dissatisfaction caused by the minorities treaties.[36] Haiti also posed the vital question, 'What after all is this shifting, imprecise, and vague notion which we term a minority?' The treaties and declarations themselves made no attempt to define racial, linguistic, or religious minorities, nor did they establish any system of registration to enable the minority status of any person to be determined. It was decided by the Council that minority status could not be predicated on domicile, origin, or numerical strength.[37]

Two questions involving minority identity were referred to the Permanent Court for decision; the question of citizenship rights in the Polish Treaty and the *Upper Silesian (Minority School)* case.[38] Two basic principles for the protection of minorities were established in the treaties:

  (a) the principle of equality or non-discrimination;
  (b) the principle that persons belonging to minority groups should be guaranteed a number of special rights.

The essential difference between these two principles was that the first protected the members of minorities as individuals while the second conferred a number of special rights which could only be exercised by members of minorities acting in combination. The non-discrimination principle was negative. It did not require that individuals have to take positive action collectively to establish their rights but merely 'guaranteed' to persons 'belonging to racial, linguistic or religious minorities' the right not to be discriminated against in the exercise of civil and political rights which are enjoyed equally by other persons. The second principle, however, did not confer any rights on individuals *qua* individuals but instead allowed certain special guarantees which could only be exercised by members of minorities acting together, and which, it was hoped, would pacify the minorities by making them content with their new lot, reduce irredentist feeling and promote the conditions necessary for the establishment of complete national unity.[39]

---

[36] 130 *O.J. Sp. Supp.*, 40.   [37] 9 *L. of N. O.J.*, 888–93, 6 June 1928.
[38] PCIJ (1923), ser. B, no. 7, and PCIJ, ser. A, no. 15 (judgement no. 12).
[39] M. Ganji, *International Protection of Human Rights* (Droz; Minard, Geneva; Paris, 1962), 48–85.

The dangers inherent in giving minorities special group rights were realized at an early stage,[40] but the decision was taken not only to protect individuals considered separately but to attribute rights to minorities regarded as collective entities.[41] In the Assembly it was argued that the grant of special rights to minorities tended to crystallize group consciousness and prevent consolidation of the minorities into the political life of the state.[42] The opposing view was that a mere guarantee of basic rights to individuals would ignore the fundamental purpose of the system which was to enable certain groups to preserve their cultural identity. Considerable confusion existed concerning the extent to which 'cultural identity' or 'separate but equal' status was an aim of the system. Mr de Mello-Franco believed that those who conceived the system wished the elements of the population contained in such a group to enjoy a status of legal protection which might ensure the inviolability of the person under all its aspects and which might gradually prepare the way for conditions necessary for the establishment of a complete national unity.[43] Sir Austen Chamberlain commented that the object was to secure for the minorities that measure of protection and justice which would gradually prepare them to be merged in the national community to which they belonged, but this did not mean that the cultural characteristics of the minority population should be submerged or abolished.[44]

As it turned out the treaty provisions facilitated the dependence of minorities on neighbouring states rather than the new national states and the separate facilities set up provided ideal vehicles for interference by those other states. It eventually became apparent that Germany was using the ideology and instrumentality of the *Minderheitenschutz* to undermine neighbouring states and eventually the international status quo.[45] Moreover, the idea that the League guarantee would prevent the possibility of intervention by a state in favour of minorities in the territories of other states was over-

[40] By Mr de Mello-Franco (Brazil), L. of N. doc. C.8.M.5.1931, i.44–5; minutes of 37th sess. of Council, 9 Dec. 1925.
[41] P. Fauchille, *Traité de droit international public* (Rousseau, Paris, 1921–6) i.806. [42] 23 *O.J. Sp. Supp.*, 89. See generally: M. G. Jones, 'National Minorities, A Case Study in International Protection', 14 *Law & Contemporary Problems* (1949), 599–621.
[43] 39 *O.J. Sp. Supp.*, and see L. of N. doc. C8.M.5.1931, i.41–7.
[44] L. of N. doc. C.8.M.5.1931, i.87–92, 96, 101.
[45] 90 *O.J. Sp. Supp.*, 41; G. Kaeckenbeeck, *The International Experiment of Upper Silesia*, (Oxford University Press, 1942), 534.

optimistic and it has been suggested that the guarantee clause actually threw open the door to that intervention.[46] After Germany was admitted to the League in 1926, the minorities abandoned any pretence of loyalty towards the foreign government and, when 'minority cases' were brought by Germany before the Permanent Court, the illusion that minorities were protected by an international organization totally disappeared. Two states confronted each other before the Court.

[46] M. S. Korowicz, *Introduction to International Law* (Nijhoff, The Hague, 1959).

II

MINORITIES AND THE
LEAGUE OF NATIONS GUARANTEE

1. *The League Guarantee in Operation*

THE treaties and declarations generally stated that the 'treatment of minorities constituted obligations of international concern . . . placed under the guarantee of the League of Nations'.[1] The League Council was made the principal organ for the supervision of the provisions and had power to take 'proper and effective action' in the event of a breach of the treaty provisions 'so far as they concerned racial, linguistic or religious minorities'. The basic texts merely provided the skeleton to which the flesh and blood of the system were added[2] and the machinery for dealing with minority matters brought before the League was established by a series of reports and resolutions of the Council between 1920 and 1929 which were based on the Tittoni report adopted by the Council in October 1920.[3]

Differences of opinion on questions of law or fact could be referred to the Permanent Court by members of the Council but despite the fact that the Court, by the ease and simplicity of its procedure and its juridical reputation, could have played an important part in the minorities system, little use was in fact made of it. Most matters brought before the Court related to the *sui generis* Upper Silesian system. Three contentious matters were submitted to the court, all of which concerned the German minority in Poland. Two were eventually withdrawn[4] and the Court gave judgement in

[1] e.g. art. 12 of the Polish Treaty of 26 June 1919, L. of N. doc. C.L.110.1927.I.44.

[2] Mr de Azcarate, a former director of the League Minority Office, believed that had the League confined itself to allowing the mechanism established in the guarantee clause to function freely, the protection of minorities would never have been more than 'a brilliant conception expressed in solemn language but without the slightest degree of practical and positive value'. See P. de Azcarate, *League of Nations and National Minorities, An Experiment*, trans. E. O. Brooke (Carnegie Endowment, Washington D.C., 1945), 101.

[3] See L. of N. docs. C.24.M.18.1921, i and C.8.M.5.1931, i.

[4] (a) The case concerning the *Administration of Prince von Pless*, orders of 4 Feb. 1933–11 May 1933, PCIJ (1933), ser. A/B, nos. 52, 54, 59; (b) The case concerning *Polish Agrarian Reform and German Minorities*, order of 29 July 1933–2 Dec. 1933, PCIJ (1933), ser. A/B, nos. 58, 60.

one case only.[5] Five questions were submitted for advisory opinions, three concerning German minorities in Poland, one the Polish minority in Danzig, and one, the Greek minority in Albania.[6]

The latter judgment was of considerable importance. Article 5 of Albania's declaration stated, 'Albanian nationals who belong to racial, linguistic or religious minorities will enjoy the same treatment and security in law and in fact as other Albanian nationals. In particular, they shall have an equal right to maintain, manage and control at their own expense or to establish in the future, charitable, religious and social institutions, schools and other educational establishments, with the right to use their own language and teach their own religion freely therein.'[7] In its 1928 constitution Albania included articles in accord with the declaration, but in 1933 these were modified by the National Assembly to read, 'The instruction and education of Albanian subjects are reserved to the state and will be given in all state schools. Primary education is compulsory for all Albanian subjects and will be given free of charge. Private schools of all categories at present in operation will now be closed.' In the Court the Albanian representative stated that in Albania's opinion the law complied with Article 5 (1) of the Declaration. In January 1925 the Council asked the Permanent Court whether, 'regard being had to the above mentioned declaration of 2 October 1921 as a whole, the Albanian government is justified in its plea that as the abolition of private schools in Albania constituted a general measure applicable to the majority as well as to the minority, it is in conformity with the letter and spirit of the stipulations laid down in Article 5 (1) of that declaration.' The Court believed that the idea underlying the treaties for the protection of minorities was to secure for certain elements incorporated in a state, the population of which differed from them in race, language, or religion, the possibility of living peaceably alongside that population and co-operating amicably with it, while at the same time preserving the characteristics which distinguished them from the majority, and satisfying special

---

[5] *Rights of Minorities in Upper Silesia (Minority Schools)*, PCIJ, ser. A, no. 15, judgement no. 12 (26 Apr. 1928).

[6] *Settlers of German Origin in Territory Ceded by Germany to Poland*, PCIJ (1923), ser. B, no. 6; *Acquisition of Polish Nationality*, PCIJ (1933), ser. B. no. 7; *Access to German Minority Schools in Polish Upper Silesia*, PCIJ (1931), ser. A/B, no. 40; *Treatment of Polish Nationals and Other Persons of Polish Origin or Speech in Danzig*, PCIJ (1932), ser. A/B, no. 44; *Minority Schools in Albania*, PCIJ (1935), ser. A/B, no. 64.

[7] L. of N. doc. C.L.110.1927, i.3.

needs. Two things were necessary in order to attain this object: (1) to ensure that nationals belonging to racial, religious, or linguistic minorities should be placed in every respect on a footing of perfect equality with other nationals; (2) to ensure for minority elements suitable means for preserving their racial peculiarities, their traditions, and national characteristics.

These two requirements were clearly intertwined since there would be no 'true equality' between a majority and a minority if the latter were deprived of its own institutions and consequently compelled to renounce that which constituted the very essence of its being as a minority. 'Equality in law precludes discrimination of any kind; whereas equality in fact may involve the necessity of different treatment in order to attain a result which establishes an equilibrium between different situations.'[8] Far from creating a privilege in favour of the minority, as Albania alleged, Article 5 ensured that the majority should not be given a privileged situation compared with the minority. A similar view had been taken by the Court in the advisory opinion regarding *Settlers of German Origin* in the territory ceded by Germany to Poland. Interpreting Article 8 of the Polish treaty of 1919 (analogous to Article 5 of the Albanian declaration) the Court decided that a Polish statute of 14 July 1920 did not tend to create equality in fact. 'There must be equality in fact as well as ostensible legal equality in the sense of the absence of discrimination in the words of the law.'[9] As Lauterpacht remarked, the Court was in a position to make these important and progressive contributions to the minorities system because it proceeded from the assumption that its task was to give effect to what it called 'the value' of the minorities treaties.[10] The Court applied the principle of effectiveness.

A major reason why the Court was not used to a greater extent was that it was not open to the minorities themselves. Only a member of the Council could seise the Court of a dispute, and, as it turned out, only the German Government ever did so. Another

---

[8] Advisory opinion on *Minority Schools in Albania*, PCIJ (1935), ser. A/B, no. 64, 19. Cf. the view of the minority, Judges Hurst, Rostworowski, and Negulesco, at 26. In their view nothing in the wording of the Declaration permitted 'exact' equality to be disregarded in favour of 'a system of different treatment for the minority and majority, so as to establish an equilibrium between them'.

[9] PCIJ (1923), ser. B, no. 6, 24.

[10] H. Lauterpacht, *The Development of International Law by the International Court*, (Stevens, London, 1958), 261. See also M. G. Jones, 'National Minorities: A Case Study in International Protection', 14 *Law and Contemporary Problems* (1949), 599.

reason was the common belief that minority matters were political rather than legal. As the United Nations Secretary-General reported, the main object in a given case was not to state the law but to induce the state under obligations to give proof of goodwill and moderation.[11] States considered any international control over what they regarded as purely internal matters to be a serious infringement of their sovereignty. Therefore, it was believed that discreet advice and diplomatic action would be more likely to improve international relations and achieve the political objective of dampening tensions than legal proceedings which were strictly supervised and publicized thus providing a forum for condemnatory statements which could be used for irredentist propaganda.

Part III of the Geneva Convention relating to Upper Silesia, signed on 15 May 1922, contained provisions for the protection of minorities which differed in several important respects from the general minorities system. Division I, after recalling the decision of the Conference of Ambassadors in October 1921,[12] set out those articles of the Polish Minority Treaty which were applicable.[13] Division II contained specific stipulations regarding the rights of members of minorities in civil, political, and religious matters, in private education, public education, primary, technical and continuation schools, and in secondary and higher education; and it contained stipulations regarding the language to be used by the Administration and in the Courts. Division III set out a detailed procedure available for the protection of minorities.

The provisions for recourse to the Permanent Court were the same under the Upper Silesian system as those under the general League system but in practice the only *dispute* involving the Geneva Convention decided by the Court was *The Rights of Minorities in Upper Silesia* case[14] brought before the Court by Germany.

Large numbers of applications to admit children to minority schools were rejected on the grounds that 'the pupils did not belong

[11]   UN doc. E/CN.4/Sub.2/6, 41

[12]   *L. of N. O.J.* 1922, 117. This adopted the recommendation of the League Council that the protection of minorities in Upper Silesia should be ensured on the basis of 'an equitable reciprocity'. See the minutes of the extraordinary session of the League Council on the question of Upper Silesia, 11, and H. W. V. Temperley, *History of the Peace Conference of Paris*, (Hodder and Stoughton, London, 1920–4), ii.278, 391, 441.

[13]   Article 64 provided for the permanent application of the Polish Minority Treaty to the Polish area, whereas the German undertakings under Division I were to expire after fifteen years. (See L. of N. doc. C.L.110.1927, i.65 ff.)

[14]   See PCIJ (1928) ser. A. no. 15, 10.

to the German minority' and, following a petition from a German minority organ, the Minority Office transmitted the question to the Mixed Commission. In President Calonder's view, Article 74 imposed a subjective test for determining whether a person was exclusively a member of a minority or a majority, as did Article 131. 'Just as every citizen may freely decide whether he wants to belong to the minority or majority every person responsible for the education of a child has, according to Article 131, the right to choose freely between the majority and minority school.' He therefore directed the Polish authorities not to take action against the parents or guardians of children admitted into minority schools in accord with his opinion.[15] In January 1927 the Polish authority announced that it could not comply wholly with the President's opinion, whereupon the German minority organ applied to the League Council, which resolved that the Polish government should not insist on the measure taken by its local authorities to exclude children from minority schools because *inter alia* 'they did not belong to the German minority'. The Council considered that it would be 'inexpedient' to admit to the minority school children who spoke only Polish, and it decided to set up an inquiry as 'an exceptional measure designed to meet a *de facto* situation not covered by the Convention of 15 May 1922; it shall not be interpreted in any way as modifying the provisions of that Convention.'[16]

This was to be undertaken by the President of the Mixed Commission who would rely upon the opinion of an educational expert. If, following the expert's opinion as to a child's knowledge of German, the President declared that it would be useless for the child to attend a minority school, the child was to be excluded.

On 2 January 1928 the German government, in its capacity as a member of the League Council, referred the interpretation of the Convention to the Permanent Court, which at first sight appeared to take an objective view and held that Poland was justified in construing the minorities treaties to mean that the question whether a person did or did not belong to a racial, linguistic, or religious minority, and consequently was entitled to claim the advantages arising under the provisions with regard to the protection of

[15] PCIJ (1928), ser. A. no. 15; judgment no. 12.
[16] The exceptional circumstances were the fact that Polish parents wanted their children to enjoy the social status of a German school. The managerial and professional classes were largely composed of Germans. *L. of N. O.J.* (1927), 401; see also L. of N. doc. C.66.1927, i.

minorities, was a question of fact and not one of intention. Yet the court also held that a declaration as to minority status, 'freely declared according to his conscience', must set out what its author regarded as the true facts and that there was no unrestricted right to choose the language of instruction or the corresponding school. Moreover, the declaration contemplated by Article 131 and also the question whether a person did or did not belong to a racial, linguistic, or religious minority were subject to no verification, dispute, pressure, or hindrance whatsoever on the part of the authorities. As Judge Nyholm pointed out, *dissentiente*, to say that minority identity must be determined by objective criteria and then add that a declaration by the individual (however patently false) cannot be disputed is nothing more nor less than a confusion of legal and moral considerations and is in fact a contradiction in terms.[17] The eventual solution was based on an opinion delivered in 1934 by the President of the Mixed Commission under which a child's proficiency in German would be investigated by a committee consisting of two members, one appointed by each minority organization.[18]

In an advisory opinion delivered in March 1931 the Court decided that those children who had been excluded from German minority schools on the basis of language tests provided for in the Council's resolution could no longer be refused access to the schools for this reason.[19]

The most important innovation of the Upper Silesian system was the establishment of the right of individual petition. This was a notable landmark in the development of international law, in theory and practice, since for the first time individuals were given *locus standi* before international tribunals. Under the general procedure, individuals could not seise the Council of a matter by presenting a petition nor could they appear before the Council or the minority committees for oral hearings. Under the Geneva Convention, however, individuals or minority groups could petition the Mixed Commission and even the League Council directly and on the same footing as state representatives. Moreover, under the procedure developed by President Calonder, individuals could appear before the Mixed Commission and present oral statements as contending parties, though they could not appear in person before the League

---

[17] PCIJ, ser. A, no. 15; judgment no. 12, 32, 46–7, 64–5.
[18] G. Kaeckenbeeck, *The International Experiment of Upper Silesia*, (Oxford University Press, 1942) 333–5.   [19] PCIJ (1931) ser. A/B, no. 40, 20.

Council. This prepared the way for later developments such as the right of individual petition under the European Convention on Human Rights and under the Optional Protocol to the United Nations Covenant on Civil and Political Rights.

2. *Disillusionment with the League System and Proposals for the Future*

Within its general competence, the Assembly held many wide ranging discussions concerning the nature, purpose, and future of the minorities system. As early as 1922 Latvia proposed that the Assembly should consider 'Laying down the main lines for the general protection of minorities in the states members of the League of Nations' and in particular a system of legislation for minorities founded on the same basis in all countries. Instead, the Assembly accepted a resolution proposed by Professor Gilbert Murray of South Africa which expressed the hope that the states which were not bound by any legal obligations to the League with respect to . minorities would nevertheless observe in the treatment of their own racial, religious, and linguistic minorities at least as high a standard of justice and toleration as was required by any of the treaties and by the regular action of the Council.[20]

During discussion it was claimed that there were many minorities outside Europe which were treated in a 'fashion altogether peculiar and illegal', and called for consideration of the desirability of a general convention for the protection of minorities throughout the world.[21] Attention was drawn to the discontent of Indian minorities in South Africa, and Professor Murray was reminded that other things besides charity begin at home. Murray replied that Resolution IV was intended to cover situations 'where no legal obligations existed'. This was clearly the case, but it begged the primary question which was whether in fact legal obligations should be extended. The text was intended as a palliative to those advocating generalization to all League members of obligations to minorities.[22] The resolution reaffirmed in 1933[23] was to be constantly referred to in later discussions in the Assembly. The possible generalization of minority obligations was fully discussed in the Sixth Committee and a

[20] L. of N. doc. C.8.M.5.1931, i. 240, 243.
[21] L. of N. Records of 3rd Assembly, minutes of 6th comm., (16 Sept. 1922), 27.
[22] L. of N. 3rd Assembly, plenary meetings, 175, 177, 186.
[23] *L. of N. O.J.*, 120m *O.J. Sp. Supp.*, 72.

polarization of views became evident. Some delegates considered that the situation that existed where treaties and declarations for the protection of minorities imposed obligations only on certain states was contrary to the principle of equality of states while others believed that the special position of states bound by the treaties and declarations was the result of extraordinary conditions prevailing in those states, i.e. the creation of new minorities by territorial transfers after World War I.[24]

The same arguments were raised in the Assembly, and two parties formed; one wished to retain the status quo, while the other considered that the system applied unequally in its present form, a fault which could be remedied by extending it to all countries. This in turn raised the objection that many other countries did not possess minorities of race, language, or religion, which brought the wheel full circle to the most vexed question of all—how was a minority to be defined? These were the problems which were not easily soluble and they led inexorably to a gradual disenchantment with the notion of protection of minorities *qua* minorities, and assisted the change of direction towards the protection of the basic human rights of all individuals without discrimination, since the difficulties of defining a minority were thus avoided.

In 1925, Lithuania proposed that the Sixth Assembly should set up a special *ad hoc* committee to prepare a draft general convention to include all the states members of the League of Nations and to set forth their common rights and duties with regard to minorities.[25] Attention was drawn to the first resolution of the twenty-first conference of the Interparliamentary Union which met at Copenhagen in 1923 which stated: 'In view of the desirability of bringing about the adoption as principles recognized by international law, and by the constitutional law of States with a representative system of government, of the fundamental rights and duties of minorities of race or religion, the twenty-first Interparliamentary Conference asks the groups to lay before their respective governments the accompanying declaration on the rights and duties of minorities, and requests the International Parliamentary Bureau to transmit the said declaration to the League of Nations with a view to the drafting of a General Convention between the states on the basis of the principles set forth in the declaration.' France claimed to possess

---

[24] *L. of N. O.J.*, Records of 6th Assembly, minutes of 6th comm., 39 *O.J. Sp. Supp.*, (1925), 15 ff.   [25] Ibid., 41 (annex ii).

no minorities while Viscount Cecil said that to extend the suggested procedure to the whole world would impose a crushing burden upon the League. However, France's views revealed no reason prima facie why she should not sign a general convention while the British reply seemed tacitly to admit that minorities did exist in other countries but, since they provided no direct threat to European peace, they were not important enough to bother the Council. The Belgian delegate went further, arguing that an international regime for the protection of minorities, instead of safeguarding peace, might easily become a permanent cause of internal conflicts and lead to international conflicts. It is difficult to accept the logic of an argument that a system intended to safeguard peace in Europe would be likely to cause the opposite effect if generalized. The reply would probably have been that, while the minorities in Europe were a fact, generalization would create them where they did not exist, but his statement certainly revealed little faith in the League system set up to deal with the problem. Lithuania pointed out that states then entering the League were required to make declarations concerning their minorities, and inquired whether a mere denial by a state that it possessed any minorities would settle the matter; what was essential was a proper, objective definition of minorities.[26] Delegates to the Council pointed out the difficulties involved in defining minorities which were not just 'racial' groups incorporated in the body of a state forming a different 'racial' unit, but also possessed psychological, social, and historical attributes resulting from long periods of struggle and transfers of territory, which were their principal differentiating characteristics. A 'racially different' entity was not necessarily a minority which the League would protect. In the American continent there was national unity since the inhabitants had acquired rights, liberties, and prerogatives equally without distinction.[27] Mr de Mello-Franco referred to the dangers of creating a sense of group identity, and quoted with approval the view that 'The introduction into the laws of all countries of provisions protecting minorities would be enough to cause them to spring up where they were least expected, to provoke unrest among them, to cause them to pose as having been sacrificed and generally to create an artificial agitation of which no one up to that moment had dreamed'.[28]

---

[26] Ibid., 15–20. See also L. of N. doc. C.8.M.5.1931, i.64, and 39 *O.J. Sp. Supp.*, (meeting of 16 Sept. 1925), 17.   [27] L. of N. doc. C.8.M.5.1931, i.44–5.

[28] Baron Wittert van Hoogland speaking in Ottawa on 13 Oct. 1924, Ibid.

This statement considerably over-simplified the issues, in that it ignored the difference between subjective and objective minorities. A Jewish minority as such may not have existed in Germany, but one was created when discriminatory treatment was accorded to German Jews. This important distinction was illustrated by Mr Politis who agreed that it was difficult to understand at first sight why there were a large number of countries in Western Europe and America which looked upon themselves as possessing no minorities. The explanation was that in some countries there no longer existed any distinction in law and fact between minorities and the rest of the population since 'minorities' in those countries had become fused in a single population and had no desire to be regarded as minorities. Their sole reason for not wishing to be so regarded was that it was not in their interest, because they possessed, not only legally, but in fact, exactly the same status as other sections of the population. None the less, they were latent minorities, ready to awaken at any moment when their moral union with the rest of the population might be relaxed. This might be done in two ways: either the 'minority' might seek to secure a special position in the state, or the state itself might 'treat them differently from other sections of the population'.[29]

This sophisticated analysis of the nature of the minority problem was a milestone in the history of the developing law of human rights. The dangers of treating 'minority groups' as separate entities were understood and it was also realized that there might be an advantage in assuring certain basic rights to all the citizens of a state without discrimination. Discrimination in the way in which different persons enjoyed basic rights itself encouraged minorities groups to spring up to protect themselves. A view was to gain increasing support in later years that, although minorities should certainly be protected, it should not be as distinct groups, but as part of a general assurance of certain basic rights to all members of the population equally. The Permanent Court in its *Minority Schools in Albania* opinion, pointed out that true equality was not attained by forced assimilation or by imposing on all a strict regime acceptable to some but not to others.[30] It eventually came to be accepted that the best way of achieving the legal and political objectives of the minority system was by laying down a comprehensive list of basic rights and fundamental

[29] 120 *O.J. Sp. Supp.*, (1933), 49, 51.
[30] PCIJ (1935), ser. A/B, no. 64, 19.

freedom to be applied to *all* persons without distinction on the grounds of race, religion, sex, or language. The principal object to be achieved was equality of treatment by the proscription of discrimination, and this was the basis upon which an edifice of particular rights could be erected. These conclusions were not immediately inferred, however, and the proposal that minority protection should be generalized was frequently discussed during the Assembly debates in 1930. Poland would not agree to alterations in the present procedure unless it was proposed to establish a system of minority protection applying generally to all states members of the Council, which was the original plan of President Wilson, and would harmonize with the Third Assembly's fourth resolution of 21 September 1922.[31]

In 1932 Poland again declared that the system for the protection of minorities could only give 'complete satisfaction to the moral conscience of the world' if the essential condition was fulfilled that 'all minorities should be protected'. Polish public opinion could not understand how one minority east of a frontier enjoyed all the guarantees arising out of the treaties whereas a similar minority west of the same frontier was deprived of all protection. Justice should be the same for all, and the League would not possess moral authority while one group of minorities enjoyed legal guarantees under which they could appeal to the League while other minorities could only appeal to public opinion. Well-founded complaints could be met with the reply, 'The League cannot deal with this question because the state complained of is not subject to minority obligations.'[32]

In 1933 Sweden agreed with France that the famous 1922 resolution be reiterated but added that the Assembly must also consider the possibility of converting the moral principle contained in it into a *legal* undertaking. The Irish Free State went further and suggested that the defective provisions of the treaties should be reinforced by writing into a new draft convention, to be accepted and applied *generally*, the provisions which experience had shown to be necessary to safeguard certain fundamental human rights accorded as a matter of course in most countries of the world. Poland thereupon submitted a resolution:

[31] L. of N. Records of 11th Assembly, 6th comm., 90 *O.J. Sp. Supp.*, 25, 29.
[32] 104 *O.J. Sp. Supp.*, 142 (report of 6th comm., to the Assembly).

The Assembly of the League of Nations, considering that the minorities treaties at present in force and the declarations with regard to the international protection of minorities made before the Council by certain states are binding only on some of the Members of the League of Nations while other Members of the League still remain free of all legal obligations on the subject; Believing that such a state of affairs affords an international guarantee only to certain minorities, and leaves without international protection other minorities who are unable in any case to appeal to the League of Nations; Considering that such a distinction between protected and unprotected minorities conflicts with the sense of equity and justice; Taking into account the fact that those minorities of race, language or religion which are not covered by the present system of minorities protection, but have the same moral right as the protected minorities to the protection of the League of Nations, are to be found in practically all European and extra-European countries; Affirms that the present conditions of the international protection of minorities are not in accordance with the fundamental principles of international morality, and considers that this state of things should be remedied by the conclusion of a general Convention on the Protection of Minorities. Such Convention should involve identical obligations for all members of the League of Nations, and should ensure international protection to all minorities of race, language or religion; Requests the Council accordingly to appoint a Committee of Enquiry to study the problem and submit a draft general Convention on the Protection of Minorities to the next session of the Council.[33]

In Haiti's opinion it could not be maintained that international obligations freely assumed by states could affect the essential principles of their national and international sovereignty. The authors of the treaties had considered that the time had come when the rights of men as individuals should no longer be subject to arbitrary authority of the state, and the sovereignty of states which had not concluded minorities treaties would not be affected by assuming obligations with regard to minorities. It would be contrary to the fundamental principle of the equality of states to hold that what is obligatory for one category of states constitutes a violation of the sovereignty of another category of states in the same League. 'In view of the fact that there is not only one category of citizens of a State, described as a minority, which deserves attention, but that *all* the citizens of which human communities are made up are entitled to the same freedom and the same protection, the League of Nations must consider the problem as a whole from the aspects of the rights

---

[33] 120 *O.J. Sp. Supp.*, 28–59.

of man—that is to say, of the rights which men possess as such, whether they belong to a minority or a majority—and it must seek the solutions which are necessary, in accordance with the draft resolution.' This resolution provided,

The fourteenth Assembly of the League of Nations, Considering: That the minority treaties concluded in 1919 and 1920 by the principal Allied and Associated powers bind a certain number of states to respect the rights of men and of citizens; That the principle of the international protection of the rights of men and of citizens, solemnly affirmed in the Minorities Treaties is in harmony with the legal sentiments of the world today; That accordingly, the generalization of the protection of the rights of men and of citizens is highly desirable; That at the present time these rights might be so formulated as to ensure that every inhabitant of a State should be entitled to the full and entire protection of his life and liberty, and that *all* citizens of a state should be *equal before the law* and enjoy the same civil and political rights, *without distinction of race, language or religion*; Expresses the hope that a world convention ensuring the protection and respect of such rights may be drawn up under the auspices of the League of Nations.

In plenary session, the Haitian representative pointed out that this resolution had been adopted in November 1928 by the International Diplomatic Academy, attended by the most distinguished diplomats of seventy-three countries and that the same resolution, in essence, was adopted by the *Institut de Droit International* at its New York meeting in 1929. It had since been taken up by the Federation of League of Nations Unions, and represented 'the very essence of the juridical and moral conscience of the contemporary world.' Despite this formidable support the Haitian resolution was referred by the Plenary Session to the Agenda Committee, and shelved.[34]

The 1929 declaration of the *Institut*, its Declaration of the International Rights of Man, was of immense importance. Although the *Institut* was a private organization without any authority apart from the eminence of its members, its pronouncements were very influential and its declarations cannot be underestimated, particularly in view of the fact that the opinions of eminent jurists and publicists are a subsidiary source of international law. There was no doubt as to the distinction of its members, who had been elected from authorities in international law in Europe, America and Asia. The present declaration provided,

[34] L. of N. Records of 14th Assembly, plenary meetings, 115 *O.J. Sp. Supp.*, (30 Sept. 1933), 51, 57.

The Institute of International Law, Considering that the juridical conscience
of the civilized world demands the recognition for the individual rights
preserved from all infringement on the part of the state; That the declarations
of rights, written into a large number of constitutions and especially into the
American and French constitutions at the end of eighteenth century, are
ordained not only for the citizen, but for man; That the fourteenth Amendment of the Constitution of the United States prescribes as follows: . . . nor
shall any state deprive any person of life, liberty or property without due
process of law, nor deny to any person within its jurisdiction the equal
protection of the law; That the Supreme Court of the United States has
unanimously decided that by the terms of this amendment it is applicable
within the jurisdiction of the United States 'to every person without distinction
of race, colour, or nationality and that the equal protection of the laws is a
guarantee of the protection of equal laws'; That, moreover, a certain
number of treaties stipulate the recognition of the rights of man; That it is
important to extend to the entire world international recognition of the
rights of man;
Proclaims:

Article I
It is the duty of every state to recognize the equal right of every individual to
life, liberty and property and to accord to all within its territory the full and
entire protection of this right, without distinction as to nationality, sex,
race, language or religion.

Article II
It is the duty of every state to recognize the right of every individual to the
free practice, both public and private, of every faith, religion, or belief,
provided that the said practice shall not be incompatible with public order
and good morals.

Article III
It is the duty of every state to recognize the right of every individual both to
the free use of the language of his choice and to the teaching of such
language.

Article IV
No motive, based, directly or indirectly, on distinctions of sex, race, language
or religion empowers states to refuse to any of their nationals private and
public rights, especially admission to establishments of public instruction
and the exercise of the different economic activities and of professions and
industries.

Article V
The equality herein contemplated is not to be nominal but effective. It
excludes all discrimination, direct or indirect.

Article VI

Except for motives based upon its general legislation, no state shall have the right to withdraw its nationality from those whom, for reasons of sex, race, religion or language, it should not deprive of the guarantees contemplated in the preceding articles.[35]

Several points deserve comment. First, the declaration was clearly concerned with the legal equality of individuals generally. All persons were to possess certain basic rights without discrimination. It aimed to assure to individuals international rights and also imposes on nations a correlative duty towards all persons including their own nationals and thus repudiated the classical doctrine that only states are subjects of international law. P. W. Brown commented that it marked a new era which is more concerned with the interests and rights of sovereign individuals than with the rights of sovereign states.[36] Moreover, it was important evidence that questions of discrimination against persons in the enjoyment of basic rights were not considered to be questions solely or essentially within the juris-diction of states. Finally, the wording is very similar in some parts to that eventually included in the United Nations Charter, the Universal Declaration of Human Rights, and the Conventions later concluded on discrimination. The proposal of the Haitian delegate in the League Assembly, however, was the first occasion on which such a resolution was moved in the League.

Romania supported the Swedish and Polish suggestions but said that Haiti had put the subject on true ground. The question was not much wider and more serious than whether or not the Committees of Three should give reasons for their decisions or publish them; it was the question of a real charter of justice and humanity.[37] Mr Politis considered that the best solution of the problem which had absorbed the League so much was a combined system which would retain as a general regime applicable to all countries, recognition of the rights of man, whether a member of a majority or a minority, and whether liable to restrictions or a pure outsider, but which

[35] The Declaration of the International Rights of Man was adopted by the *Institut de Droit International* at its session of 12 Oct. 1929, in New York; 24 *AJIL* (1930), 126, 127.

[36] 24 *AJIL* (1930), 127. See for text, 35 *AJIL* (1941), 663–5. It is noteworthy that the Declaration was adopted on 12 Oct. 1929 (the 437th anniversary of the discovery of America by Columbus) by a very large majority, and Brown comments, it 'may be considered an expression of homage by the *Institut* to the New World for its contri-bution to the liberal development of International Law'.

[37] 120 *O.J. Sp. Supp.*, 47–51.

would replace political protection which was always artificial and arbitrary by objective and absolutely impartial protection based on law. This, he believed, was the direction in which international law was developing, and he referred to the 'general rules affirming the rights of man in the international sphere' laid down by the *Institut de Droit International* in 1929. Supporting the proposal to reiterate the 1922 resolution,[38] Politis undertook that Greece would collaborate in any reform to make the system of minority protection a rule of international law binding on all countries without distinction. He looked forward to major progress where all countries would be legally, and not just morally, obliged to grant minority privileges to all living in their territories, whether members of majorities or minorities, nationals or foreigners. Certain delegates agreed to a reference to the 1922 resolution reluctantly and only for the sake of securing uniformity since they considered that 'although it had not been possible, for the present, to proclaim it as an international obligation on all States to grant their racial, linguistic or religious treatment equal to that provided for in the special treaties, they were still convinced that such an obligation already existed in international law, and that consequently the resolution proposed to the Assembly could not call its existence into question'.[39] It would be difficult to find an argument more full of sophistry than this. If an obligation already exists in international law, then it is fatuous to claim that the time is not ripe for it to be proclaimed as such. Nevertheless the important point was that an *opinio juris* was agreed to exist and a further proposal endeavoured to make the matter more explicit, i.e. 'The Assembly considers that the principle expounded in Resolution I, which reaffirms the recommendation of 1922, must be applied without exception to all classes of nationals of a state that differ from the majority of the population in race, language or religion.'[40]

An almost identical proposal to that of 1933 was put forward by Poland in 1934, the difference lying in the final clause which called for an international conference to draw up a general convention on

[38] The Assembly reiterating the recommendation which it passed on 21 Sept. 1922, 'Expresses the hope that the states which are not bound by legal obligations to the League with respect to minorities will nevertheless observe in the treatment of their own racial, religious or linguistic minorities, at least as high a standard of justice and toleration as is required by any of the treaties and by the regular action of the Council'. 120 *O.J. Sp. Supp.*, annex 6, 72.

[39] See the summary of views by M. Holsti, rapporteur, ibid., 71.

[40] Ibid., 72, and see 115 *O.J. Sp. Supp.*, 88.

the protection of minorities and requested the Council to call such a conference within six months.[41] After again pleading the inequality of the system as it stood and advocating a permanent durable system, Poland declared that she was 'compelled to refuse from today all co-operation with international organs in the matter of the supervision of the application by Poland of the system of minority protection'.[42] This action, which was heavily criticized by other delegates, graphically illustrated the depth of Polish resentment at what she considered a complete denial of the doctrine of equality of states. This was the first act from which the collapse of the system followed. In the Sixth Committee the Haitian delegate made another far-sighted speech and drew some important conclusions.[43] Reference was made to President Wilson's intentions to protect rights inherent in the human person rather than minorities as such, and it was claimed that the principle of national cohesion of each state had been superseded by a system of discrimination in one and the same community, and in one and the same state. It was observed that, every time a human community had within its borders a specific category of citizens from a racial origin which differed from that of the population as a whole and which was treated differently, the outcome after a number of years had always been secession and war, sometimes leading to the dismemberment of the state itself. On the other hand whenever the precarious notion of a minority had been supplanted by the higher notion of the equality all citizens before the law without distinction of origin or race, the result had been assimilation and internal peace. Switzerland, and (somewhat prematurely) Canada, and the American republics were quoted as examples. The major weaknesses of the Polish proposals were pin-pointed by posing the question whether it was logical to attempt to generalize a system which most agreed had not given the results expected of it. There was first a desire to terminate an exceptional system and, secondly, a determination not to perpetuate the fostering of subversive forces capable of undermining national foundations. The answer was for the League to contemplate a guarantee under international jurisdiction of certain rights inherent in the human person to everybody irrespective of minority and majority allegiance, a solution which would also dispose of the objection, posed by the Belgian and French delegates, that generalization might create artificial minorities.

[41] L. of N. Records of 15th Assembly, 125 *O.J. Sp. Supp.*, 42 ff., 130.
[42] Ibid., 42–3.　　　　　　　[43] 130 *O.J. Sp. Supp.*, 40–5.

Logical and persuasive as the Haitian analysis of the existing system and the proposals *pro futuro* were, they did not evoke much immediate response from the other delegates, who generally preferred a more cautious approach.[44] Most ignored the Haitian suggestions completely because they were too radical, and reserved their comments mainly to exposing the weak links in the Polish proposal. Mr Anthony Eden, for the United Kingdom, saw the minorities system as an anomaly designed to deal with a *sui generis* problem which he believed would gradually wither away. He considered generalization dangerous and unnecessary. Similarly, the French delegation believed that to generalize the system would be to act like the sorcerer's apprentice. Both delegations ignored the arguments based on the inequality-of-states argument, apparently preferring to believe that, if the matter were quietly shelved, it would disappear, but they seized on Poland's inconsistency in wishing to generalize a system which she had criticized. The arguments were essentially negative, however, and made no reference to the Haitian proposal.

It was left to Mr de Valera of the Irish Free State to take a progressive view. He observed that the minorities problem reached its most acute form when a neighbouring minority became included in the ancestral home of another people, but at the same time, saw a definite point in the Polish proposal. A certain amount of protection was needed everywhere and this could be arrived at by an examination of the need for protection in several countries, to seek the greatest common measure. A suitable beginning would be to universalize 'those sacred rights of the individual which should not be taken away from him under any pretext'. He was convinced that agreement could be obtained on a universal measure of protection for minorities against unfair discrimination by majorities anywhere. This would remove the appearance that the protection of minorities required under the League system was *sui generis*, or the apprehension that a general convention might be an excuse for artificial agitation. In addition some minorities having special needs required extra protection over and above the universal minimum. Once this

---

[44] Iraq, Yugoslavia, the Netherlands, Sweden, Albania, and Bulgaria agreed that generalization should be examined but with reservations. Other states, eg. Switzerland, Argentine, Australia, the United Kingdom, France, Italy, and Uruguay, were either equivocal or opposed to the Polish proposal. Some states, notably Switzerland, condemned Poland's action in refusing to co-operate further with the League minority system. (See 130 *O.J. Sp. Supp.*, 38 ff.)

minimum protection was achieved any additional protection for minorities of the type referred to by the United Kingdom, i.e. those 'adjacent to a majority of their own race, language and religion recently transferred', could be added where necessary. Transference was the ideal solution of this type of problem but, where impossible, the best practical solution was to give a minority (if homogeneous and inhabiting a continuous area) the greatest amount of local autonomy consistent with the unity of the state. A conference should be held to prepare representations under two heads, (1) the rights of individuals which could be universally guaranteed; and (2) particular minorities problems which had arisen out of World War I. Though such a conference was never held, the common-sense suggestions made by Mr de Valera have been in fact the most fruitful in practice since then. Towards the conclusion of the Assembly debate, Poland, realizing that it could not hope for even a simple majority, asked that its proposal be not put to the vote, and the Haitian proposal was not voted upon either.

The history of the League debates shows a gradual disenchantment with the League minorities system, as it stood, and an inexorable movement towards the belief that there should be a universal protection of basic human rights in two steps: (1) the firm establishment of the principle of international legal equality of individuals by the proscription of discrimination on the grounds of race, religion, language, or sex; (2) the compilation of a list of those basic rights which were to be enjoyed by all without discrimination. The constructive suggestions made by the Haitian and Irish representatives eventually became the basis for later action for the international protection of individuals by the United Nations. The League of Nations assembly debates, although impotent so far as achieving any practical change in the existing minorities system, at least revealed its deficiencies and weaknesses, both in its theory and its machinery. Although the discussions appeared unproductive at the time, they sowed the seeds which were to flourish in the more favourable climate which existed after World War II.

III

THE POST-WORLD WAR II
PEACE TREATIES

THE present status of the post-World War I minorities treaties has given rise to considerable controversy. An unsatisfactory study prepared by the UN Secretariat was never considered by the UN Commission on Human Rights.[1] What the Secretariat's study attempted to do was to provide a viable legal explanation of a *fait accompli*—that the minorities treaties were generally considered to be a dead letter—since without exception legal writers who referred to the minorities treaties after World War II assumed that they were defunct and had been swept away with the dissolution of the League.[2] The general opinion was that the treaties had been replaced by the principle of universal respect for human rights and fundamental freedoms for all, but no legal explanation was offered to show why the treaties were defunct, only an analysis of the circumstances which brought about the disillusionment with the minority system.

It is a reasonable inference from the conduct of the parties both before and after the Secretariat's study was submitted that there was a general desire that the treaties should be terminated. The fact

---

[1] UN docs. E/CN.4/367, E/1371, E/1681. For an excellent treatment see N. Feinburg, 'The Legal Validity of the Undertakings concerning Minorities and the *clausula rebus sic stantibus*', in B. Akzin, ed., *Scripta Hierosolymitana* v *Studies in Law* (Magnes Press, Jerusalem, 1958), 95.

[2] M. Ganji, *International Protection of Human Rights* (Droz; Minard, Geneva; Paris, 1962), 81, concludes that only the minority provisions for the Aaland islands are still extant. See also, J. L. Kunz, 'The Future of International Law for the Protection of National Minorities', 39 *AJIL* (1945), 89, 94, and 'The Present Status of International Law for the Protection of Minorities', 48 *AJIL* (1954), 282; W. Rappard, 71 *Recueil des Cours* (1947), ii.87; G. Kaeckenbeeck, 70 *Recueil des Cours*, (1947), i.261; G. G. Fitzmaurice, 73 *Recueil des Cours*, (1948), ii.302; C. de Visscher, *Theory and Reality in Public International Law*, trans. P. E. Corbett, (Princeton University Press, 1957), 196; C. Rousseau, *Droit International Public*, (Sirey, Paris, 1953), 218–20; L. F. L. Oppenheim, *International Law*, ed. H. Lauterpacht (Longmans, Green, London, 8th ed. 1955) 654–5; J. B. Schechtman, 4 *Western Political Quarterly* (Mar. 1951), i–ii: R. de Nova, 11 *Howard L. J.* (1965) 275, 282–4; I. L. Claude, *National Minorities: An International Problem* (Random House, New York, 1955), 152–3; Comments of World Jewish Congress, UN doc. E/C2/136, and the authorities collected in L. B. Sohn and, T. Buergenthal, *International Protection of Human Rights* (Bobbs-Merrill, Indianapolis, 1973), 305–6.

that no state disputed the findings of the study nor made any real attempt to have the issue debated, though it appeared for several years on the Commission's agenda, is evidence of a general, tacit agreement that the minorities treaties were no longer in force. Factors that influenced this *opinio juris* were no doubt the activities of the Sub-Commission on Prevention of Discrimination and Protection of Minorities and the proposal to include an article dealing with minorities in the Draft Covenant on Civil and Political Rights.[3]

The only way in which the matter would be finally settled now, in view of the unfortunate failure of the Economic and Social Council to request an advisory opinion from the International Court of Justice, would be for a state to bring contentious proceedings against another party alleging infringement of the provisions. In this unlikely event the Court might possibly accept a *clausula rebus sic stantibus* argument,[4] but a more likely course would be to accept the simplest solution and declare that the conduct of the parties since the war evidenced a tacit agreement that the obligations were no longer binding, and that a state could not now be allowed to resurrect them.

A number of miscellaneous equality provisions appear in treaties following World War II. Most emphasize the negative aspect of equality by concentrating on non-discrimination provisions, but special measures for positive minorities protection were included in later instruments. Thus the peace treaties signed with the Allied and Associated Powers in 1947 provided that each state concerned should take all measures necessary to secure to all persons within their jurisdiction, without distinction as to race, sex, language, or religion, the enjoyment of human rights and of the fundamental freedoms including freedom of expression, of press and publication, of religious worship, of political opinion, and of public meeting.[5] The protection afforded by this provision extends to all persons under the jurisdiction of the states concerned and not just to nationals as in the post-World War I treaties.

---

[3] *Yearbook of the International Law Commission* 1963, ii.70–1.

[4] See A. Renouf, 'The Present Force of the Minorities Treaties', 28 *Can. B. R.* (1950), 804.

[5] See art. 15 of the Treaty with Italy (49 United Nations Treaty Series, 3); art. 3 (1) of the Treaty with Romania (42 UNTS, 3); art. 2 of the treaty with Bulgaria (41 UNTS, 21); art. 2 (1) of the Treaty with Hungary (41 UNTS, 135); art. 6 of the treaty with Finland (49 UNTS, 203). The same provision appeared in article 6 (1) of the State Treaty with Austria of 1955 (217 UNTS, 223). (See E. Schwelb, 'The Austrian State Treaty and Human Rights', 5 *ICLQ* (1956), 265.)

Three states were, in addition, required to undertake that the laws in force in their countries should not, either in their content or their application, discriminate or entail any discrimination between persons of the nationality of that state, on the ground of race, sex, language, or religion, whether in reference to their persons, business, professional or financial interest, status, political or civil rights, or any other matter.[6] The clause gives rise to difficulties. The first concerns its relationship to the initial provision since that refers to all citizens, but the additional clause covers nationals alone; one uses the term 'distinction' while the other employs 'discrimination'.

The basic provision does not forbid the prohibition of aliens from exercising those human rights which adhere to one in one's capacity as a national of a state, e.g. the right to vote or work in that state, whereas the additional provision prohibits 'invidious or unreasonable distinctions' being drawn between *nationals* with respect to rights and freedoms that are not necessarily basic or fundamental of all persons in all places, but which only belong to persons as nationals, e.g. the right to vote.[7] It would not be improper to draw a 'reasonable distinction' between persons on the basis of race, sex, language, or religion, by, for example, providing separate lavatories for men and women.

Though the 1947 treaties do not provide special measures of protection for minorities, the Austrian State Treaty contains clauses for the protection of Slovene and Croat minorities in Carinthia, Burgenland, and Styria. Article 7 (1) provides that Austrian nationals belonging to these minorities shall enjoy the same rights on equal terms with all other Austrian nationals, including the right to their own organizations, and meetings and press in their own language. The paragraph does not add much to the earlier non-discrimination provisions, although the right to a press in their own language is a positive measure of protection. Article 7 (2) entitles minorities to elementary instruction in the Slovene or Croat language and to a

[6] Art. 3 (2) of the Treaty with Romania (42 UNTS, 3); art. 2 (2) of the Treaty with Hungary (41 UNTS, 135); and art. 6 (2) of the Austrian State Treaty (217 UNTS, 223). It was not included in the other treaties. See also *The Paris Peace Conference*, 1946, *Selected Documents*, 200–2, US State Department 1946; and S. D. Kertesz, 'Human Rights in the Peace Treaties', 14 *Law and Contemporary Problems* (1949), 627, 635.

[7] See e.g. art. 8 of the Austrian State Treaty which makes this explicit: 'Austria shall have a democratic government based on elections by secret ballot and shall guarantee to all citizens free, equal and universal suffrage as well as the right to be elected to public office without discrimination as to race, sex, language, religion or political opinion.'

proportionate number of their own secondary schools, while Article 7 (3) accepts this language as an official language in the said districts, in addition to German. The 1955 Treaty therefore is much fuller than the Treaty of St-Germain-en-Laye of 1919.[8] Article 7 (4) provides that Austrian nationals of the said minorities shall participate in the cultural, administrative, and judicial systems of the said territories on equal terms with other Austrian nationals. It is not altogether clear what 'on equal terms' means in this paragraph. Schwelb considered it to be a provision 'to prevent discrimination and to safeguard equality' rather than a provision 'granting special protection and privileges'.[9] Nevertheless, if the 'real or genuine equality' interpretaton is adopted, then it should be interpreted to mean that minority participation in the cultural, administrative, and judicial systems in the particular territories may be more than that of other nationals, if this is necessary for them to enjoy *de facto* equality.[10]

Before signing the 1947 peace treaty, Italy executed an agreement with Austria providing for the fair treatment of the German-speaking minority in South Tyrol, which has been termed 'notorious' by one commentator.[11] It provided for elementary and secondary teaching for the German-speaking minority, and for the exercise of autonomous legislative and executive regional power. In addition, the Italian Constitutional Law of 29 February 1948 containing the special statute for Trentino-Alto Adige contained elaborate provisions on representation and the use of languages.[12]

In the Trieste Settlement between Italy and Yugoslavia,[13] the Special Statute does not use the term 'minority', but refers to the 'Yugoslav ethnic group in the Italian administered area'. There are

---

[8] It is noteworthy that, whatever force this treaty may still have in international law, Section V of Part III forms part of Austrian constitutional law by virtue of Article 149 of the Federal Austrian Constitution, and thus exists side by side with the 1955 Treaty. (See E. Schwelb, 'The Austrian State Treaty and Human Rights', 5 *ICLQ* (1956), 265.)   [9] Schwelb, op. cit.

[10] See *Minority Schools in Albania* opinion, PCIJ, ser. A/B, no. 64.

[11] The De Gasperi–Gruber agreement of 5 Sept. 1946 has given rise to considerable controversy. See the debate in the General Assembly's Special Political Committee, UN doc. A/SPC/S.R.177–84, and R. de Nova, 'The International Protection of National Minorities and Human Rights', 11 *Howard L. J.* (1965), 275–86.

[12] See Struye Report, Council of Europe, *Documents of the Assembly* (1959), doc. 1002, app.

[13] Agreement of 5 Oct. 1951 by Great Britain, The United States, Italy, and Yugoslavia. See E. Schwelb, 'The Trieste Settlement and Human Rights', 49 *AJIL* (1955), 240–8.

several non-discrimination provisions and special economic safeguards, and provision is made for the use of the minority language in public documents, court sentences, official announcements, and correspondence with administrative and judicial authorities.[14] Another important agreement, between the Federal Republic of Germany and Denmark, dealt with the minorities in Schleswig.[15] This was based on the twin principles of non-discrimination and the special protection of language and cultures, and provided for minority schools.

These developments were examined in a Council of Europe Report prepared by Mr Paul Struye who believed that the special arrangements concluded for the benefit of minorities can be grouped into five categories: culture, language, religion, education, and political rights.[16] A proposal to include a provision for minority protection in the Fourth Protocol to the European Convention for the protection of Human Rights and Fundamental Freedoms signed in 1963 was not proceeded with, on the somewhat specious excuse that the matter was *subjudice*, because of the *Belgian Linguistics* case.[17]

Other bilateral treaties containing provisions for minority protection have been concluded, in particular the Treaty of Friendship and Mutual Aid between Poland and Czechoslovakia in 1947, and the treaty between India and Pakistan in 1950.[18] The former guaranteed the possibility of national, political, cultural, and economic development to Czechs in Poland and Poles in Czechoslovakia 'within the limits of the law, and on the basis of reciprocity'. The latter granted political representation to the respective minorities at both the central and provincial level, and provided for control systems by both local and international committees.[19]

[14] See H. Lannung, 'The Rights of Minorities', in *Mélanges offerts à Polys Modinos* (Paris, Éditons A. Pedone, 1968), 181, 189–90.
[15] Declaration of 29 Mar. 1955 (see G. Heraud, 'Les accords germano-danois de minorités', in *Mélanges en l'honneur de Gilbert Gidel* (Sirey, Paris, 1961), 313.
[16] Council of Europe, *Documents of the Assembly* (1959), doc. 1002. (30 Apr.). See also docs. 508, 731, 770 (para 53), 999, and 1299, and Res. 136.
[17] See below, ch. 12.
[18] Cf. also the Constitution of Cyprus 1960, HMSO, Cmnd. 1093; and the debate in the General Assembly's 1st comm., 20th sess., (1965), UN doc. A/C1/P.V.1409–13. See also Moses Moskowitz, *The Politics and Dynamics of Human Rights* (Oceana, Dobbs Ferry, N.Y., 1968), chs. 9 and 10.
[19] Treaty of 8 Apr. 1980. See A. Demichel, 'L'évolution de la protection des minorités depuis 1945', 64 *Revue Générale de Droit International Public* (1960), 22, 39 48 and generally; also R. de Nova, 'The International Protection of National Minorities and Human Rights', 11 *Howard L. J.* (1965), 275–88, and the authorities collected in Sohn and Buergenthal, 334–5.

Some commentators have taken too narrow a view of the meaning of equality in that they seem to believe that equality means merely the prevention of discrimination, and that positive protection therefore gives more than equal rights to minorities.[20] But, as the *Minorities Schools* case pointed out, such treaties required equality in fact, not merely formal equality or 'ostensible legal equality in the sense of the absence of discrimination in the words of the law'.[21] This being so, the denial of special protection to minorities may deny equality of treatment. As de Azcarate pointed out in 1945, equality has both a negative aspect (non-discrimination) and a positive aspect (special measures of protection).[22] 'Equality in law' no longer means purely formal or absolute equality, but relative equality, which often requires differential treatment.

[20] Thus J. L. Kunz states that the provisions of the Special Statute of Trieste are arranged 'on the basis of the distinction between the safeguarding of equality (prevention of discrimination) and the positive protection of minorities'. ('The Trieste Settlement and Human Rights', 49 *AJIL* 240, 244.)

[21] *Minority Schools in Albania*, PCIJ, ser. A/B, no. 64, 12–20 (quoting *German Settlers in Poland* PCIJ, ser. B. no. 6, 24). Lannung, 182–3, interprets the *Minority Schools in Albania* case as stating that 'though the first step necessary to protect minorities is to place them in every respect on a footing of perfect equality with the other nationals of the state, the second necessary step is to ensure for them "suitable means for the preservation of their racial peculiarities, their traditions and their national characteristics" '.

[22] P. de Azcarate, *League of Nations and National Minorities: An Experiment*, trans. E. O. Brooke (Carnegie Endowment, Washington D.C., 1945), 24.

IV

DEVELOPMENTS UNDER THE UNITED NATIONS

1. *The Equality of Individuals under the United Nations Charter*

DURING the period preceding World War II, the basic defects and inadequacies of the League minorities system had become gradually more evident. It was considered by many to be based purely on political expediency rather than on any real concern for the protection of human rights, and to be discriminatory in two senses. First, it was thought to offend the principle of equality of states since the obligations devolved on some states only. Secondly, only 'minorities' were to have their basic rights guaranteed. That most states found this unsatisfactory was demonstrated in the League Assembly debates, but apart from these, the activities of several other international organizations and the opinions of writers showed a growing preference for the notion that certain basic rights should be enjoyed by all persons everywhere, without distinction. Most important was the 1929 Declaration of the International Rights of Man,[1] but in 1936 a Declaration on the Foundation and Leading Principles of Modern International Law, approved by the International Law Association, the *Union Juridique Internationale*, and the *Académie Diplomatique Internationale*, included a section on the international rights of the individual.[2] Article 28 provided that every state ought to assure to every individual within its territory complete protection of the right to life, liberty, and property without distinction as to nationality, sex, race, language, or religion.[3] The Inter-American Conference on Problems of War and Peace held in Chapultepec in 1945 considerably influenced American states. Article XLI of the Final Act read:

The Inter-American Conference on War and Peace Problems, Considering that World Peace cannot be maintained unless men are able to exercise their

---

[1] See ch. 2 above, p. 39.

[2] The declaration was drawn up at the suggestion of the 1930 Hague Conference on the Codification of International Law. See A. Alvarez, *Exposé motifs et déclaration des grands principes du droit international moderne* (Éditions internationals. Paris, 1936), 10–11.

[3] See *Yearbook of the International Law Commission* (1956), ii.230.

basic rights without distinction of race or religion, resolves: (1) to reaffirm the principle recognized by all American nations of equality of rights and opportunity for all without distinction as to race or religion; (2) to recommend to the Governments of the American republics that, while maintaining freedom of speech and publication, all effort should be made to prevent in their respective countries anything that could provoke discrimination among individuals on grounds of race or religion.[4]

In the Dumbarton Oaks proposals for a new form of international organization after the war, the major powers included only one reference to human rights or fundamental freedoms. Under Chapter IX, Section A, the organization was 'to promote respect for human rights and fundamental freedom'.[5] A quite different emphasis was to prevail at San Francisco where the promotion of human rights was elevated to a major purpose of the organization and many states and international organizations suggested amendments incorporating the principles of equality and non-discrimination. The most striking omission was the lack of any amendments advocating the protection of minorities as such, demonstrating a clear determination to abandon what was regarded as an outmoded and unsuccessful system and to replace it with two principles: first, that individuals should enjoy certain basic rights, and, secondly, that those rights should be enjoyed by persons without distinction as to race, sex, language, or religion. Throughout the discussions on human rights at the United Nations Conference on International Organization, the minorities treaties were not referred to, but a considerable amount of influence was brought to bear in favour of 'a new covenant' and a fresh approach.[6] The atmosphere prevailing can be gauged from two extracts. P. B. Potter said that the new Charter had accepted in place of the old system of minorities protection, 'a more radical method of the bill of rights in terms of the individual'.[7] Similarly as Mr. Fr. Collin put it, '*Désormais, les droits que possèdent les hommes en tant que tels, sans distinction de race, de religion, de langue, et même de sexe, seront garantis sur le plan international, qu'il s'agisse de minorités ou de majorités.*'[8]

---

[4] Acta Final de la Conferencia Interamericana sobre Problemas de la Guerra y de la Paz, Ciudad de Mexico.   [5] UNCIO Doc., iv.13.
[6] See e.g. C. A. Baylis 'Toward an International Bill of Rights', *P. O. Quarterly* (1944); P. Edson 'The Story Behind the Human Rights Plan', *San Francisco News*, 16 May 1945; V. Riesel, *New York Post*, 30 Apr. 1945; J. Robinson, *Human Rights and Fundamental Freedoms in the Charter of the United Nations* (Institute of Jewish Affairs, New York, 1946); 'Free World Recommends a Charter for the U.N.', '*Free World*' ix (1945), no. 5.
[7] 39 *AJIL*, 548.   [8] *Tribune de Genève*, 2 July 1945.

Numerous amendments to Chapter I (Purposes) of the Dumbarton Oaks proposal were submitted and the most detailed proposal included a declaration of fundamental human rights.[9] That individual equality and the repudiation of the doctrine of racial division and discrimination should be included in the aims of the organization had been stressed by a number of speakers in the opening addresses at the Conference,[10] and the four-power amendment was finally incorporated in the Charter with only minor changes. Thus Article 1 (3) includes among the purposes of the United Nations the following aims: 'To achieve international co-operation in solving international problems of an economic, social, cultural, or humanitarian character, and in promoting and encouraging respect for human rights and for fundamental freedom for all without distinction as to race, sex, language, or religion'. Proposals were also made for the inclusion of references to human rights among the principles of the organization,[11] but ultimately no specific references were included. A Haitian proposal that Chapter II of the Dumbarton Oaks proposals should contain, as a corollary, the principle of racial and religious non-discrimination, was opposed by the United Kingdom which argued that membership qualifications should not be defined too precisely, and this view was accepted by the Committee.[12]

A formula emphasizing the principle of non-discrimination was included in Article 13 of the Charter. Under Article 13 (b) the General Assembly was to initiate studies and make recommendations for the purpose of 'assisting in the realization of human rights and fundamental freedoms for all without distinction as to race, sex, language or religion'. Under Article 55 (4) the United Nations was to promote 'universal respect for, and observance of, human rights and fundamental freedom for all without distinction as to race, sex, language or religion', and members were to have an obligation under Article 56 'to take joint and separate action in co-operation with the Organization for the achievement of the purposes set forth in Article 55'. The Economic and Social Council was to have responsibility in this field for discharging the United Nations function (Article 60) and could make recommendations for the purpose of promoting respect for and observance of human rights and fundamental

[9] Doc. 215 I/1/10 (11 May 1945), UNCIO Docs., vi.536–51.
[10] See e.g. Sir Ramaswami Mudaliar of India, UNCIO Docs., i.245.
[11] See J. Robinson, op. cit., 50–54.
[12] See docs. 215 I/1/10 and G/7 (b) (1) UNCIO Docs., vi.563; doc. 242 I/2/11, UNCIO Docs., vii.24; and doc. 423 I/1/20, UNCIO Docs., vi.310-12.

freedoms for all (Article 62 (2)). This latter article anomalously did not include the proviso 'without distinction as to race, sex, language or religion', but it did include the phrase 'for all'. It has been objected that it may have been unwise to limit possible types of distinction to race, sex, language, or religion,[13] since other types of distinction may occur, either open or disguised, based on opinion, country of origin, nationality, social status, or whatever. However, the phrase did not attempt to limit definitively the types of distinction forbidden, but merely enumerated the most common forms; the affirmative 'equality' formulation 'for all' is the important part.[14] Later formulations such as that in Article 14 of the European Convention on Human Rights not only give a longer list of types of invidious distinctions but usually add a phrase such as 'or other status' to show that these are not exhaustive.

Article 68 provides that 'The Economic and Social Council shall set up commissions in economic and social fields and for the promotion of human rights, and such other commissions as may be required for the performance of its functions'. The express reference to human rights, originally suggested by Belgium, was opposed by the Soviet delegate but insisted upon by the United States delegation since 'there would be profound disappointment' if it were not included. Finally the Committee unanimously accepted the above wording in Article 68, and made the appropriate recommendation to the Commission.[15]

Among the basic objectives of the trusteeship system was included the encouragement of 'respect for human rights and for fundamental freedoms for all without distinction as to race, sex, language or religion' Article 76(c)) and reference is also made in the Preamble. 'We, the peoples of the United Nations, determined . . . to reaffirm faith in fundamental human rights, in the dignity and worth of the human person, in the equal rights of men and women . . . have resolved to combine our efforts to accomplish these aims.'[16]

The Charter provision which has caused the greatest difficulty and has been a fertile source of controversy particularly with respect

[13] J. Robinson, 54.

[14] N. Robinson, *The Universal Declaration of Human Rights* (Institute of Jewish Affairs, New York, 1958), 104.

[15] UNCIO Docs. 725 11/3/42 (1 June 1945) and 924 11/12 (12 June 1945).

[16] Composed by Field-Marshal Smuts. See J. P. Humphrey, 'The U.N. Charter and the Universal Declaration of Human Rights', in D. E. Luard, ed., *The International Protection of Human Rights*, (Thames and Hudson, London, 1967), 39, 41.

to questions of discrimination and human rights has been Article 2 (7): 'Nothing contained in the present Charter shall authorize the United Nations to intervene in matters which are essentially within the domestic jurisdiction of any state or shall require the Members to submit such matters to settlement under the present Charter; but this principle shall not prejudice the application of enforcement measures under Chapter VII.' The article was based on the four-power amendment to the Dumbarton Oaks proposals to be included in Chapter II.[17] Originally the domestic jurisdiction provision was only to apply to peaceful settlements of disputes.[18]

Dr Evatt of Australia opposed the proviso, arguing that it would be much more efficacious to affirm the protection of minorities to be a matter of international concern (and hence outside the ambit of the clause) or to include an international agreement for their proper treatment. This would have made it plain that nothing in the amendment would limit the power of the Security Council to intervene. Similarly, France had proposed that the proviso be replaced by the words, 'unless a clear violation of essential liberties and human rights consitutes in itself a threat capable of compromising peace', since recent experience had shown that it was desirable for the Organization to intervene to protect unfortunate minorities.[19] This proposal was not accepted, on the grounds that it only dealt with one of the cases envisaged as falling under the exception clause. The rejection of the proposal was a grave error which was to cause incalculable difficulty later, particularly with regard to the South African and Rhodesian questions.[20]

Suggestions that where conflicts arose as to whether a matter was one of international or domestic jurisdiction, they should be referred to the International Court, and that the word 'solely' should be used instead of 'essentially' were not accepted,[21] mainly due to the intransigence of the United States representative, Mr Dulles.[22] The resulting article provoked a bitter comment from Professor Rappard: 'As almost all, if not all, measures violating the fundamental rights of the individual, however defined, are held to be matters of domestic

[17] Doc. 2 (French) G/29 (5 May 1945), UNCIO Docs., iv.889.

[18] Ch. 8, s. a, art. 7, Dumbarton Oaks Proposals, UNCIO Docs., iv.13.

[19] Ibid. See also J. Huston, 'Human Rights Enforcement Issues of the United Nations Conference on International Organisations', 53 *Iowa L. R.* (1967), 272–90.

[20] Myres S. McDougal and W. M. Reisman, 'Rhodesia and the United Nations: The Lawfulness of International Concern', 62 *AJIL* (1968), 1, 13–14.

[21] Doc. 1070, I/1/34 (i) d, (18 June 1945).

[22] See the *New York Times*, 16 June 1945.

jurisdiction one cannot escape the conclusion that the United Nations have denied themselves the possibility of protecting such rights by international legal action.'[23] This was too pessimistic a prediction, however, and it now seems to be generally agreed that human rights and freedoms, having become the subject of a solemn international obligation, and one of the fundamental purposes of the Charter, are no longer matters essentially within the domestic jurisdiction of the members of the United Nations. This view gained acceptance from the beginning despite the objections of South Africa.[24] When the United States Senate Foreign Relations Committee was holding its hearings on the Charter, a senior draftsman replied affirmatively to the question whether the United Nations could investigate matters of racial discrimination or racial situations (for instance on the southern shores of the Mediterranean) which, though originally domestic, might have explosive effects.[25]

Similarly, the eminent French jurist, René Cassin, was of the opinion that the International Court, if seised of a dispute concerning a serious violation of human rights, would regard it as a question of positive international law. He thought it clear that recommendations regarding human rights were different from other recommendations since Articles 55 and 56 of the Charter created a general obligation for states to cooperate with the United Nations in promoting respect for human rights and a general obligation obviously carried more weight when given practical form by a recommendation. While no one could affirm that, in the matter of human rights, competence was withdrawn from states and conferred exclusively on the United Nations, neither could one maintain that Article 2(7) applied to human rights in the same way as it applied to political questions

[23] 243 *Annals*, 119. Quoted by J. Robinson, op.cit. in n. 11 above, 46.

[24] H. Lauterpacht, *International Law and Human Rights* (Stevens, London, 1950), 178. As Dugard points out, few states today accept South Africa's claim to the absolute protection of Article 2 (7) in respect of apartheid. 'Instead, the majority appear to have accepted the view that International Law, prompted by the human rights provisions in the Charter, has evolved sufficiently to include discriminatory legislation within a state as a matter fit for action by the international community.' C. J. R. Dugard, 'The Legal Effect of United Nations Resolutions on Apartheid', 83 *South African L.J.* (1966) 44, 53. (See also GAOR, 7th sess., 1st comm., 226–7.)

[25] U.S. Senate hearings before the Committee on Foreign Relations, 979th Congress, 1st sess., July 9–13, 1945, 309–12. Senator Alben Barkley added: 'Almost every problem that concerns international relations must originate somewhere and that somewhere usually is within the domestic boundaries of one nation and may leap over into another nation and create an international situation.' See L. B. Sohn, in *18th Report of Commission to Study the Organization of Peace* (1968), Supplementary Paper.

essentially within the domestic jurisdiction of a state.[26] In support, Mr Cassin referred to Article 62 (2) to show that the right of the international community to intervene in matters of human rights, though less extensive than its right to intervene in some other international questions, was more extensive than its right to intervene in purely political issues.[27] Professor Manley O. Hudson has said that the Charter supplies a clear recognition of limits on the old concept of domestic jurisdiction. 'Certain subjects covered by the Charter were not previously covered by international legislation, but one can no longer contend that they fall within the range of merely domestic jurisdiction. The principal of those subjects is that of human rights.'[28] Similarly Professor Higgins believes that, if a state is in breach of an obligation concerning human rights, there is no reason why a resolution to this effect should be considered to contravene the state's domestic jurisdiction.[29]

Clearly the reservation is inoperative when a treaty obligation

[26] See UN doc. E/CN.4/S.R.405, (29 July 1953), 4–16. Mr Cassin earlier made the same point in the Third Committee during the drafting of the Universal Declaration of Human Rights, where he said that Article 2 (7) could not be involved when, 'By the adoption of the declaration, the question of human rights was a matter no longer of domestic but of international concern', (GAOR, 3rd sess., 3rd comm., (1948), 61). Similarly, Mr de Leon (Panama) wished to object to the 'oft-repeated sophistry' that the United Nations was helpless to prevent the violation of human rights because under Article 2 (7) it could not interfere in matters which were within the domestic jurisdiction of states. 'If the Charter had any significance at all, human rights were international, they were the common property of all mankind.' (Ibid., 43.)

[27] See M. Ganji, op. cit., *118 International Protection of Human Rights* (1962), for a similar view, and R. Brunet, *La Garantie Internationale des Droits de l'Homme d'après la Charte de San Francisco* (Grasset, Geneva, 1947), 167–8.

[28] M. O. Hudson, 'Report on the Development of International Law', *Proceedings of the American Society of International Law* (1948), 11. (See also Myres S. McDougal and G. C. K. Leighton, 'The Rights of Man in the World Community', 14 *Law and Contemporary Problems* (1949), 490 ff.; J. L. Kunz, 'The United Nations Declaration on Human Rights', 43 *AJIL* (1949), 316, 318.

[29] R. Higgins, *The Development of International Law through the Political Organs of the United Nations* (Oxford University Press, London, 1963), 118–30. See also: M. S. Rajan, *United Nations and Domestic Jurisdiction*, (Asia Publishing House, London, 2nd ed. 1961), 73 and generally; H. Lauterpacht, *International Law and Human Rights* (Stevens, London, 1950), ch. 10; Sir C. H. M. Waldock, 'General Course on International Law', 106 *Recueil des Cours* (1962), ii.173–91, and 31 *BYIL* (1954), 96–142; Sir G. Fitzmaurice, 'General Course on International Law' 92 *Recueil des Cours* (1957), ii.59–67; McDougal and Reisman, op. cit., 1; N. de M. Bentwich, 'The Limits of the Domestic Jurisdicion of a State', 31 *Grotius* (1955), 59; E. Lauterpacht, 'Some Concepts of Human Rights', 11 *Howard Law Journal* (1965), 264, 266.

is involved[30] since, if states agree to regulate a matter of treaty, they cannot afterwards claim that the matter is not of international concern. Nevertheless it is important not to take too facile an approach towards the question of domestic jurisdiction, because it may still restrict international competence, for example, by express limitations set out in international instruments such as the domestic remedies rule, and reservations as to recognition of the competence of international bodies to investigate complaints,[31] or by indirect influence.[32]

Unlike the League Covenant, which specifically excluded mention of racial and religious equality, and the Dumbarton Oaks proposals for the Charter, which contain one brief reference to human rights and fundamental freedoms, the United Nations Charter drawn up at San Francisco has as one of its basic provisions the promotion of human rights, in particular equality and non-discrimination. One delegate to the Third Committee went so far as to say that the 'United Nations Organization had been founded principally to combat discrimination in the world'.[33] As in the Covenant, no specific reference was made to protection of minorities, for reasons already given. There was a sharp reaction against the protection of minorities *per se* and a desire to make a fresh start. The trend at San Francisco was not favourable to special measures of protection since the interests of minority groups were generally believed to be adequately safeguarded by the faithful observance of the principle of non-discrimination.[34] It will be suggested below that this principle, though highly beneficial, was not sufficient in itself and that the notion of special measures of protection has been reintroduced in a form which does not refer specifically to minorities.

The neglect of minorities *qua* minorities at San Francisco did not

[30] See *Peace Treaties* case, ICJ Rep. 1950, 65, 70–1; *Nationality Decrees in Tunis and Morocco*, PCIJ, (1923), ser. B, no. 4, 24; I. Brownlie, *Principles of Public International Law*, (Oxford University Press, 2nd ed. 1973), 535; J. E. S. Fawcett, 14 *Law and Contemporary Problems* (1949), 438, 449–50.

[31] e.g. arts. 8 (2), 9 (2) and 15 of the European Convention on Human Rights, which allow a certain margin of appreciation to the states parties in matters such as national emergency, public order, etc.

[32] J. E. S. Fawcett, 'Human Rights and Domestic Jurisdiction', in Luard, op. cit., 286–302, concludes, 'even where international standards of human rights have been accepted by agreement and machinery established to enforce them, the old Adam of sovereignty can still fight a delaying action at many points.'

[33] UN doc. A/C3/S.R.100, 7.

[34] M. Sørensen, 'The Quest of Equality', in *International Conciliation*, no. 507 (Mar. 1956), 291, 302–7.

mean that minority protection was to be ignored by the United Nations altogether. On the contrary, a sub-commission was set up to deal with the problem under the Commission on Human Rights.[35] Under the interim arrangements concluded at San Francisco, a preparatory commission was established to make provisional arrangements for establishing United Nations organs. The executive Committee recommended six commissions, first place among which was given to the Commission on Human Rights (the only commission specifically required by Article 68 of the Charter). Its functions were to be to assist the Council to carry out its responsibility under the Charter to promote human rights, on the basis that its studies and recommendations would encourage the acceptance of higher standards in this field and help to check and eliminate discrimination and other abuses.

In particular the work of the Commission was to be directed towards the following subjects:

(a) formulation of an international bill of rights;
(b) formulation of recommendations for an international de-claration or convention on such matters as civil liberties, status of women, freedom of information;
(c) protection of minorities;
(d) prevention of discrimination on grounds of race, sex, language, or religion;
(e) any matters within the field of human rights considered likely to impair the general welfare or friendly relations between nations.

Studies, recommendations, and the provision of information and other services were to be undertaken at the request of the General Assembly, or the Economic and Social Council, either on its own initiative or at the request of the Security Council or of the Trustee-ship Council.[36]

Prevention of discrimination was thus to be an important part of the Commission's work and it is noteworthy that protection of

[35] Mr Dehousse of Belgium said of the Economic and Social Council, 'Even minority questions fall properly within its province, but under another name and, though on a wider territorial basis, without the special guarantees which in this connection would result from the system of the League of Nations.' ECOSOC Official Records, 1st sess., 9.
[36] Report by the Executive Committee to the Preparatory Commission of the United Nations, UN doc. PC/EX/113/rev.1 (12 Nov. 1945), 52–3, and report of the Preparatory Commission, doc. PC/20, 36.

minorities, which found no mention in the Charter, was included among the Commission's major purposes. At its first session, the Economic and Social Council established the Commission on Human Rights and a sub-commission on the status of women,[37] but at its second session, the status of the latter was raised to that of a full commission[38] and the Commission on Human Rights was empowered to establish a sub-commission on the protection of minorities and a sub-commission on the prevention of discrimination. Since their subject matter was likely to overlap, the Commission eventually decided to combine the proposed sub-commissions into one which would: (1) examine what provisions should be adopted in the definition of the principles which should be applied in the field of the prevention of discrimination on the grounds of race, sex, language, or religion, and in the field of the protection of minorities, and make recommendations to the Commission on urgent problems in these fields; (2) perform any other functions which might be entrusted to it by the Council or the Commission on Human Rights.[39]

The elevation of the Sub-Commission on the Status of Women to the status of a full commission brought about the curious result that while matters involving discrimination generally and the protection of minorities were to be dealt with by just one sub-commission of the Commission on Human Rights, the status of women was thought to warrant a full commission. This demonstrates that great importance was attached to the principle of equality of the sexes even in the early stages. The Commission on the Status of Women immediately adopted guiding principles. 'Whereas a woman is as much human as a man, she should share freedom and equality in the interests of the well being of society and to achieve a democratic peace by eliminating fascist ideology.' Its purpose was to raise the status of women, irrespective of nationality, race, language, or religion, to equality with men in all fields of human enterprise, and to eliminate all discriminations against women in statutory law and in the maxims, rules, and interpretations of customary law. The Council reaffirmed that the fundamental purpose of the Commission was to develop proposals for promoting equal rights for women and eliminating discrimination on the grounds of sex in legal, political, economic, social, and educational fields.[40] It can thus be seen that

[37] ECOSOC Res. E/20 (15 Feb. 1946). See ECOSOC OR, 1st sess., 163–4.

[38] See United Nations Yearbook 1946, 529, ECOSOC OR, 2nd sess., 402, and UN docs. E/56/Rev.1 and E/84.

[39] United Nations Yearbook 1946, 528.   [40] Ibid., 530.

the foundation stone of the machinery set up under the Economic and Social Council to protect human rights was the principle of equality; the alpha and omega of human rights programmes was to be that rights were to be enjoyed by all people everywhere without discrimination.

2. *The Inclusion of References to the Prevention of Discrimination and the Protection of Minorities in the Universal Declaration of Human Rights*

A major task for the Commission on Human Rights after establishing its sub-commissions was to submit suggestions concerning the proposed International Bill of Rights. Before it had been decided whether the Bill should comprise a declaration or a convention or both,[41] it had been agreed that the Bill should contain an unequivocal statement of the principle of equality of rights of individuals. The General Assembly had referred to questions of discrimination and equality in several resolutions,[42] in particular in Resolution 103 (1)[43] which declared that it was in the higher interests of humanity to put an end to religious and so-called racial persecution and discrimination, and called on governments and responsible authorities to conform both to the letter and to the spirit of the United Nations Charter and to take the most prompt and energetic steps to that end. Several references to equality appeared in the documentation prepared for the Commission's first session[44] and at an early meeting it discussed the 'status of equality without distinction as to race, sex, language or religion', following a communication from a non-governmental organization in consultative status.[45]

[41] See UN doc. E/CN.4/S.R.25.

[42] e.g. Res. 44 (1) concerning the treatment of persons of Indian origin in South Africa; Res. 56 (1) concerning the political rights of women; Res. 96 (1) concerning the crime of genocide.

[43] 48th plenary meeting of the General Assembly (29 Nov. 1946), UN doc. A/64/add.1, 200.

[44] In the second document prepared (E/CN.4/2), a quotation appeared from the Draft Declaration on the Rights and Duties of Man of the Inter-American Juridical Committee, Article XVIII, which stressed the right of all persons to equality before the law and stressed that there should be no privileged classes. Similarly Document E/CN.4/11 contained an Indian draft resolution for the General Assembly which, *inter alia*, requested freedom and equality before the Law and recognition of the right of every human being to equality without distinction of race, sex, language, religion, nationality, or political belief.

[45] The Catholic Welfare Association. See UN doc. E/CN.4/W.18, also the statements from the Preparatory Committee for the International Refugee Organization, UN doc. E/CN.4/41.

Although one representative described the principle of equality of rights as 'a very ambiguous one',[46] others claimed that it was a very clear principle which had been defined for centuries. Every person was a citizen of the United Nations and this should be recognized and incorporated in the Bill of Rights. Mr Cassin agreed, quoting the famous phrase from Article 1 of the 1789 French Declaration of Rights: 'Men are born and remain free and equal before the law.' This was a broad definition but it was not in his view necessary to specify the principle in too much detail. Chile favoured a text recognizing the principle of equality of man before the law since equality before the law implied enjoyment of the other rights, but Belgium opposed the immediate acceptance of the principle of equality since it was necessary to define the concrete rights attached to the concept. Mr Cassin thought it essential that the Commission should at least assert the fundamental principle of the unity of the human race and define the principle of equality in the fundamental articles of the Declaration, pointing out that Hitler had begun by asserting the inequality of men before attacking men's liberties. The Chinese representative reminded members that, as they were speaking on the morrow of a war waged in the name of racial inequality, it was necessary to examine the principle of equality. In the initial draft outline of the International Bill of Human Rights prepared by the Secretariat, it was proposed that 'no one should suffer any discrimination whatsoever because of race, sex, language, or religion or political creed. There should be full equality before the law in the enjoyment of rights enunciated in the bill of rights.' Moreover, states possessing 'substantial numbers of persons differing in race, language, or religion from the majority of the population, should give such persons the right to establish and maintain out of an equitable proportion of public funds, schools, cultural and religious institutions, and they should be entitled to use their own language before the courts and other authorities and organs of state and in the press and in public assembly'.[47]

The drafting committee went further and suggested articles stipulating that all men are brothers entitled to freedom and personal equality and dignity of rights, that all persons are equal before the law, and that everyone is entitled to the rights and freedoms set forth in the declaration without distinction as to race, sex, language,

[46] Mr Malik (Lebanon). See UN doc. E/CN.4/S.R.13, 2.
[47] See UN doc. E/CN.4/AC1/3 annex a and add.1.

or religion.[48] The latter article gave rise to a long debate interspersed with a good deal of procedural wrangling, but it was eventually decided that since 'race' included 'colour' it was unnecessary to include the latter term.[49] The Soviet delegate considered the article 'decidedly inadequate' since, in his view, it was not enough to state that men were equal. Rather the concept had to be given a concrete content and a juridical character by affirming that men had equality before the law and the same rights in economic, political, cultural, and social life irrespective of race, sex, religion, or social status. Secondly, it should be stated that any advocacy of hatred or racial conflicts and any action establishing privileges or discrimination of any kind were crimes punishable by the law of a state. Although a text to this effect was rejected by the Sub-Commission, it did adopt a recommendation to include clauses condemning incitement to violence against religious groups, nations, races, or minorities.[50]

When the question of including a minorities clause arose, problems of definition at once arose and the Indian delegate suggested that a section of the International Court be requested to define minorities from the legal point of view.[51]

The Sub-Commission approved the proposed Article 36 concerning minorities by a small majority and also articles providing *inter alia* that individuals should be free to leave their own country and to change their nationality to that of any country willing to accept them, that everyone should have equal opportunity to engage in public employment and to hold public office in the state of which he is a citizen, and that access to examination for the public service should not be a matter of privilege and favour.[52] The Sub-Commission rejected a Soviet proposal that advocacy of national, racial, or religious hostility, or of national exclusiveness, or hatred, or contempt, as well as any action establishing a privilege or discrimination based on distinctions of race, nationality, or religion, should constitute a crime and should be punished by the law of the state. Mr Cassin properly pointed out that implementation clauses should not be included in the Declaration, and others found it odd for the Soviet Union to oppose implementation of human rights

[48] UN doc. E/CN.4/21.
[49] UN doc. E/CN.4/Sub.2/S.R.4, 6 ff. It was reintroduced later; see n. 55 below.
[50] UN docs. E/CN.4/Sub.2/21 and E/CN.4/Sub.2/S.R.8, 10.
[51] UN docs. E/CN.4/Sub.2/S.R.11; E/CN.4/Sub.2/S.R.12, 7, 9; S.R.11; S.R.24; S.R.27; S.R.33.
[52] See generally the report of the Sub-Commission, 1st sess., UN doc. E/CN.4/52.

provisions generally and yet propose the insertion of provisions of implementation in an article of the Declaration.[53] The United States view was that 'unlawful' should not be included in the Declaration on the grounds that it would be difficult to distinguish the purpose and meaning of the declaration from that of the covenant.[54]

The Commission's first draft declaration[55] was to be considerably revised later. In January 1948 the Commission on the Status of Women suggested that 'men' in draft Article 1 should be replaced by 'people' and 'like brothers' by 'in the spirit of brotherhood' and that Draft Article 13 should be amended to provide that men and women have equal rights to dissolve as well as to contract marriage.[56]

At the third session of the Commission on Human Rights the chairman, Mrs Roosevelt, pointed out that equality did not mean identical treatment for men and women in all matters, for there were certain cases, as, for example, the case of maternity benefits, where differential treatment was essential.[57] This was a clear affirmation that 'equality' was here being used in its normative and not its formal sense. As finally adopted[58] Article 1 read: 'All human beings are born free and equal in dignity and rights. They are endowed with reason and conscience and should act towards one another in a spirit of brotherhood.'

In the draft declaration submitted by the drafting committee to the Commission's third session, Article 3 provided:

(1) Everyone is entitled to all the rights and freedom set forth in this Declaration, without distinction of any kind, such as race (which includes colour), sex, language, religion, political or other opinion, property status, or national or social origin.

(2) All are equal before the law regardless of office or status and are

[53] UN docs. E/CN.4/Sub.2/21 and E/CN.4/S.R.34 and 35.

[54] UN docs. E/CN.4/82 and E/CN.4/77.

[55] This included, *inter alia*, Article 1: 'All men are born free and equal in dignity and rights. They are endowed by nature with reason and conscience and should act towards one another like brothers'; and Article 3: 'Everyone is entitled to all the rights and freedoms set forth in this declaration without distinction of any kind such as race, which includes colour, sex, language, religion, political or other opinion, property status or national or social origin.' The report included two variants of Article 36 (the minority clause), one suggested by the Sub-Commission, and the other by the drafting committee. UN doc. E/600.

[56] UN doc. E/615, 12; ECOSOCOR 6th sess., supp. no. 5; see Res. 120 VI (3 Mar. 1948), and UN docs. E/737 and E/CN.4/99.

[57] UN doc. E/CN.4/S.R.50, 9.

[58] GAOR, 3rd sess., 3rd comm., 125. And see UN doc. A/C3/228.

entitled to equal protection of the law against any arbitrary discrimination or against any incitement to such discrimination in violation of this Declaration.[59]

Chile considered that the wording of Paragraph 1 would imply that discrimination was permitted with respect to rights not listed in the Declaration; so, on the suggestion of the Chinese representative, the words 'or other' were inserted between 'property' and 'status'.[60] An important and instructive debate ensued over a proposal to delete the word 'arbitrary' before 'discrimination'.[61] Most delegations supported this change since, although there was no desire to suppress useful and necessary distinctions, there was general agreement that 'discrimination' already meant 'invidious distinction'. It was felt that the word discrimination used alone had a derogatory connotation, and discrimination which harmed men was quite different from any distinctions established to assist certain groups which required special aid.[62] Others demurred, being of the opinion that 'arbitrary' should be maintained because all discrimination was not necessarily invidious; for instance protection for reasons of old age was a useful and commendable type. Discrimination required an adjective on this view since alone it meant merely 'distinction'.

Although the proposal to delete 'arbitrary' before 'discrimination' was adopted, Mr Cassin then committed a volte-face, and made a suggestion which would have considerably weakened the article had it been adopted. In order to allay the doubts of those who were of the opinion that 'discrimination' did not mean an 'invidious' distinction in law he proposed the inclusion of the words 'in violation of the principles of this Declaration' after 'discrimination'.

The difficulty with the Cassin amendment is that, while the original version of Article 3 (2) purported to prohibit *any* discrimination, the new proposal would have restricted its operation to the rights recognized in the Declaration, but as was pointed out, there were certain 'rights', such as the right to travel on railroads, not specifically mentioned in the Declaration, which should be covered by the non-discrimination clause. Moreover, the enjoyment of the

[59] UN doc. E/CN.4/95, annex A, 5; and cf. the Panamanian proposal in UN doc. E/CN.4/AC2/S.R.3, 2. [60] UN docs. E/600 and E/CN.4/S.R.52, 3, 5.

[61] UN docs. E/CN.4/99, E/CN.4/82/add. 8, and E/CN.4/S.R.52, 6, 8. See also the comments by Parvez Hassan, 'The Word "Arbitrary" as used in the Universal Declaration of Human Rights: "Illegal" or "Unjust" ', 10 *Harvard International L.R.* (1969), 225, 255 ff.

[62] See the views of Mr Cassin (France), Dr Chang (China), and Mr Santa Cruz (Chile), UN doc. E/CN.4/S.R.52, 8–17.

rights set forth in the Declaration without any distinction based on status had already been covered in Draft Article 3 (1). Nevertheless, by voting to eliminate the word 'arbitrary', the Commission clearly accepted the view that 'discrimination' in the context of human rights, meant 'invidious distinction'. Article 6 of the Commission's final draft read: 'All are equal before the law and are entitled without any discrimination to equal protection of the law against any discrimination in violation of this Declaration and against any incitement to such discrimination.'[63]

This was a curious formulation because the notion of 'equal protection against discrimination' is ambiguous, and the phrase 'without any discrimination' quite necessary.[64] The draft article is circular in that it entitles one to be equally protected (which must include the notion of non-discrimination) against discrimination in violation of the convention, without any discrimination; which is hardly illuminating. Matters were improved in the Third Committee by an undebated Australian amendment which added 'and equal protection' after 'equal protection of the law' and before 'against', thus clearly separating the clause into two distinct halves, and altering the sense.[65]

When the equality and non-discrimination articles were discussed in the Third Committee, it was explained that after mature consideration the Commission on Human Rights had decided to employ two separate articles. The fundamental difference was that, while Draft Article 2 established that everyone was entitled to the rights and freedom set forth in the Declaration and followed logically from Article 1, Draft Article 6 had a more limited field and defined the legal status of all human beings within the national limits of sovereign powers and states. The former set forth the principle of non-discrimination while the latter ensured the individual protection of the law against discrimination within his own country; the two ideas, though similar, were not absolutely identical. Despite this explanation, the drafting of the articles was not entirely felicitous and there was no compelling reason for not amalgamating them.

[63] Dr Chang (China) said that the drafting committee had decided that the phrase 'in violation of this Declaration' should qualify the phrase 'against any discrimination' and *not* 'without any discrimination'. UN doc. E/CN.4/ S.R.53, 7.

[64] Mr Wilson (United Kingdom), UN doc. E/CN.4/S.R.54, 3.

[65] GAOR, v, 3rd sess., 3rd comm., (1948), summary records, 237. See also the Venezuelan view at 235. Draft Article 6 was approved by the Third Committee in parts (ibid., 240–1).

Draft Article 6 embodies several concepts:

(1) equality of all before the law;
(2) equal protection of the law without discrimination;
(3) equal protection of the law against discrimination in violation of the Declaration;
(4) equal protection of the law against incitement to such discrimination.

It is unclear what the relationship is between the ideas expressed in (1) and (2). Does formulation (2) mean that there should be laws which should be applied equally, or that all are equally entitled to the protection of whatever laws existed?[66] No conclusive answer to this question was ever given although, according to the Australian representative, it meant that all individuals are entitled to equal treatment under whatever laws existed.[67] The better view appears to be that it is formulation (1) and not (2) which embodies this principle. 'Equally before the law' means that everyone is entitled to the impartial application of the law, whatever that law may be.[68] A statement that certain rights are to be equally enjoyed by everyone, irrespective of race, sex, religion, or other status merely means that only those rights are to be enjoyed equally by all. The 'equal protection' formulation, on the other hand, has a much broader application and means that the substantive provisions of the law should apply to everyone equally. This does not mean that everyone should be treated in exactly the same way but that they should not be discriminated against, i.e. treated differently on irrational, arbitrary, or capricious grounds,[69] and this is the idea contained in the 'equal protection' clause in the Fourteenth Amendment to the United States Constitution.

Nor is it easy to discover what concept (3) adds to Draft Article 2 for, under this provision, 'any distinction' based on a non-exhaustive list of types of status with regard to entitlement to the rights and freedoms proclaimed in the Declaration is improper. An amendment providing that 'everyone should have the right to an effective remedy

[66] See e.g. United Kingdom representative in the Commission, UN doc. E/CN.4/S.R.52, 15; Philippine representative in 3rd comm., op. cit., 234.

[67] UN doc. E/CN.4/S.R.52, 15.

[68] cf. A.V. Dicey's formulation of the Rule of Law, in *Introduction to the Study of the Law of the Constitution* (Macmillan, London, 10th ed. 1959), 193.

[69] cf. G. Evans, 'Benign Discrimination and the Right to Equality', 6 *Fed. L. Rev.* (1974), 26.

by the competent national tribunals for acts violating the fundamental rights granted him by the constitution or by law' was also
adopted and became Article 8 of the Declaration.

A subcommittee set up to examine the totality of the Declaration
'solely from the standpoint of arrangement, consistency, uniformity
and style' also improved the substance of the text by separating the
unwieldy Draft Article 6 (now Article 7) into two sentences:[70] 'All
are equal before the law and are entitled without any discrimination
to equal protection of the law. All are entitled to equal protection
against any discrimination in violation of this Declaration and against
any incitement to such discrimination.[71] This text makes it much
more obvious that the first sentence applies generally to any 'right'
which might be the subject of a legal claim, while the second
sentence refers to human rights and freedoms included in the
Declaration itself. It would thus be incompatible with the first
sentence of Article 7 for a state to introduce by law any kind of
discrimination in the sense of an invidious or unreasonable distinction, regardless of whether the 'right' with regard to which the
discrimination is made is one protected by the Declaration or not.
However, it only provides for equal protection of the *law*, and if a
discrimination is not made or sustained by law, it will not be
construed as violating the Declaration, unless it concerns a right
included in the Declaration, in which case the second sentences of
Article 7 and Article 2 are relevant. Article 7 first spells out Article
2 in a more positive manner. The *law* must protect every person
against any invidious distinction being drawn with respect to his
entitlement to the rights enumerated in the Declaration.

Article 2 (1) in its final form provides, 'Everyone is entitled to all
rights and freedoms set forth in this Declaration, without distinction
of any kind, such as race, colour, sex, language, religion, political or
other opinion, national or social origin, property birth or other
status.'

Article 2 (2) was added at a very late stage, after the United
Kingdom moved the deletion of Article 3 and the substitution of the
following proviso: 'Furthermore, no distinction shall be made on
the basis of the political, jurisdictional, or international status of
the country or territory to which a person belongs, whether it be

[70] UN doc. A/C3/400/rev.1, annex a.
[71] Art. 3 having been deleted, (3rd comm., op. cit., 863); see GAOR, 3rd sess., pt. 1
(1948), ii.535 (UN doc. A/777); GAOR, 3rd sess., pt. 1 (plenary), vol. ii,183rd meeting.

independent, trust, non-self-governing or under any other limitation
of sovereignty.' This paragraph, though strictly unnecessary in view
of the first paragraph, which refers to *any* distinction, was added for
emphasis. It does not prevent reasonable distinctions being made
on the basis of nationality—e.g. the denial of the right to vote—but
would prohibit differentiation between foreigners *inter se* with regard
to entitlement to rights set forth in the Declaration. Other articles
also involve the equality principle. Slavery, which is prohibited by
Article 4, clearly involves a denial of the equal rights of all persons
of liberty, while Article 5 provides that 'Everyone has the right to
recognition everywhere as a person before the law'.[72]

Procedural equality before the tribunals is dealt with in Article 10
which provides that everyone is entitled to a fair and public hearing
by an independent and impartial tribunal, in the determination of
his rights and obligations and of any criminal charge against him.
Men and women are entitled to equal rights as to marriage and
everyone, 'without any discrimination' has the right to equal pay for
equal work.[73]

One major omission from the Declaration is any specific mention
of minorities *per se*. Article 31 of the drafting Committee's version
contained minority provisions but these were opposed by some
delegations which argued that the problems of minorities would be
automatically solved by the complete implementation of the
Declaration and that, since human rights were to be enjoyed equally
by all, there was no need to grant special rights to minority groups.
It was claimed that to confer rights on groups as such would go
beyond the scope of the Declaration. The Commission decided to
delete the proposed article, and it also rejected Soviet proposals (1)
to provide that cultural groups should not be denied the right to free
self-development (as ambiguous) and (2) to grant national minorities
the right to have schools in their mother tongue.[74] In the Third
Committee several delegations argued that the problem of minorities
was complicated by the differing structure of the various states and
that some countries might not be able to agree to the inclusion of
minorities provisions in a universal declaration, because national
unity might be disrupted by any attempt to apply them. Others
believed that it was impossible in a single article to include both the

[72] UN doc. E/CN.4/95, annex a.
[73] Art. 23 (2). The proviso is clearly superfluous in view of Article 2 and the second
part of Article 7.
[74] UN docs. E/CN.4/S.R.73, 5–6, 10 and E/CN.4/S.R.74, 4–6.

views of the new world, which in general wished to assimilate immigrants, and the old world in which entrenched racial and national minorities existed. It was also contended that the rights of minorities were already fully protected in Article 2 and in the articles on: freedom of thought, conscience, and religion; freedom of the press and opinion; freedom of assembly; the choice of education; and the right to participate in the cultural life of the community.[75] The problem was referred back to the Sub-Commission for further study and a separate resolution on minorities was finally adopted by the General Assembly as Resolution 217 III (C).[76] It has been pertinently observed that the omission from the Universal Declaration of Human Rights of any reference to minorities only served 'to encourage a comfortable illusion and to nurture a solemn complacency. . . . The essence of equality is the refusal to recognize irrelevant distinctions, not the erasure of all distinctions.'[77] The Universal Declaration of Human Rights was finally adopted *nem. con.* and proclaimed on 12 December 1948 as Resolution 217 III (A). it was not intended to be a legally binding instrument at the time it was drafted, but there are grounds for believing that it has since achieved the status of customary law.[78]

Article 6 of the Draft Declaration on the Rights and Duties of States, 1949, provided that 'Every State has the duty to treat all persons under its jurisdiction with respect for human rights and fundamental freedoms *without distinction as to race, sex, language, or religion.*' Although it was argued that the italicized words should be omitted because the Charter merely laid down an aim to be achieved and not a duty, their inclusion was approved by a narrow majority,[79] and the provision was described by the United States delegate to the Sixth Committee as 'an extremely important pioneering effort'.[80]

[75] GAOR, 3rd sess., 3rd comm., 716, 731. See arts. 18, 19, 20, 26, 27 respectively of the Declaration.
[76] GAOR, 3rd sess., (1948), Resolutions, 77–8. UN doc. E/1371.
[77] M. Moskowitz, *The Politics and Dynamics of Human Rights* (Oceana, Dobbs Ferry, N.Y., 1968), 169; see also J. W. Bruegel, 'A Neglected Field: The Protection of Minorities', 4 *Human Rights Jo.* (1971), 413; J. Claydon, 'The Transitional Protection of Ethnic Minorities: A Tentative Framework for Enquiry', 13 *Can. YIL* (1975), 25, and E. I. Daës, in E. von Caemmerer and others, eds., *Festschrift für Pan J. Zepos* (Katsikalis, Athens, 1973), ii.41. See generally T. Buergenthal and L. B. Sohn, *International Protection of Human Rights* (Bobbs-Merrill, Indianapolis, 1973), 213–336, for a collection of materials and bibliography.
[78] H. Lauterpacht, *International Law and Human Rights*, 397.
[79] See G. Whiteman, *Digest of International Law*, v.244–6.
[80] GAOR, 4th sess., 6th comm., 168th meeting, 167.

V

THE UNITED NATIONS ORGANS

1. *The Sub-Commission on the Prevention of Discrimination and the Protection of Minorities*

THREE organs were created by the United Nations *specifically* to deal with questions of discrimination. The Sub-Commission on the Prevention of Discrimination and the Protection of Minorities and the Commission on the Status of Women were established as subsidiary organs of the Economic and Social Council in 1946, while in 1952 the General Assembly set up an *ad hoc* commission to study the racial situation in South Africa. Only the Sub-Commission, which was set up by the Commission on Human Rights as a subsidiary organ with no power to make independent decisions, was empowered to deal with both discrimination and minority issues generally.[1] It was to consist of a committee of experts to carry out functions on behalf of its parent body. Under its terms of reference, the Sub-Commission was (1) to examine what provisions should be adopted in the definition of principles which were to be applied in the field of prevention of discrimination on the grounds of race, sex, language, or religion and in the field of protection of minorities and to make recommendations to the Council on urgent problems in these fields; and (2) to perform any other functions which might be entrusted to it by the Council or the Commission on Human Rights. Thus, the Sub-Commission was of a *sui generis* nature, in that it was designed to function as an advisory, not a political organ. Although its members were to be chosen with regard to the geographical distribution of their states, they were not to sit as the representatives of those states but as experts in their own right. This was a distinction not always fully appreciated by members of the Sub-Commission or governments, but on the whole members were aware that they were experts, not delegates, and according to a former member this gave 'zest, flexibility, and effectivensss' to proceedings.[2] While most

---

[1] See UN doc. E/CN.4/S.R.6.

[2] R. Hiscocks, 'The Work of the United Nations for the Prevention of Discrimination', in *Die moderne Demokratie und ihr Recht*, (*Festschrift für Gerhard Leibholz*) (Mohr, Tubingen, 1966), 713, 728.

members genuinely appeared free to decide questions as they thought fit, others, though they tended to be 'officials', at least went through the motions of not following instructions. This eager and independent attitude resulted in a number of initial difficulties concerning the nature of its tasks which took some time to resolve and led to a great deal of frustration. The Sub-Commission's activities can be classified into three main periods. From 1946 to 1951 there was a preliminary period of ground clearing in which only a small amount of constructive work was accomplished. In the second phase from 1952 to 1961 some valuable progress was made, and since 1962 earlier work has borne fruit and the role and the emphasis of the Sub-Commission have changed.

Important matters considered by the Sub-Commission at its early sessions included the Draft Declaration on Human Rights, and it was responsible for the introduction and wording of several articles relating to discrimination, including Article 2 of the Universal Declaration. It also agreed upon a trail-blazing definition of the terms 'prevention of discrimination' and 'protection of minorities', and initiated enquiries into the validity of existing minority treaties and carried out important studies on various forms of discrimination and minority problems. In general, however, the period up to 1951 was one of frustration and dissatisfaction.

A major complaint was that the meetings of the various United Nations bodies responsible for discrimination were not co-ordinated, which resulted in much time being wasted.[3] Since committees often sat simultaneously, the reports and recommendations of subsidiary bodies were sometimes not discussed for up to eleven months; at its sixth session, for example, the Commission on Human Rights had to consider the reports of both the second and third sessions of the Sub-Commission. Eventually, a system was established whereby the Sub-Commission met in January, the Commission in March, the Council in the Summer and the General Assembly in the Autumn, and this expedited matters considerably. Not all the problems associated with a hierarchical pyramid of organizations were obviated. Often, suggestions which had been rejected by the Sub-Commission reappeared when the same subject was discussed in the Commission or the Council or in the General Assembly, rather in the manner of an appeal proceeding to higher courts. Occasionally

[3] See generally M. Moskowitz, *Human Rights and World Order* (Oceana, Dobbs Ferry, N.Y., 1958), 54 ff.

this meant that the same points were wearily reargued *ab initio* in up to four different organs.

Another difficulty was the enormous amount of time wasted by the Sub-Commission on procedural wrangling. In the early sessions more time seemed to be spent in the 'interstices of procedure' than on substantive issues. Undoubtedly the major bone of contention with the Commission concerned the way in which the Sub-Commission had conceived its functions under its terms of reference since it believed a principal part of its task to be the recommendation of practical measures of implementation. Once certain general principles were laid down, the next stop in the Sub-Commission's view was to make them effective and operational. In its first report the Sub-Commission requested leave to convene at the earliest possible date in order to formulate proposals for machinery to implement the provisions of the proposed Universal Declaration of Human Rights dealing with discrimination and minorities.[4] Similarly, it considered that 'in order satisfactorily to fulfil its task and effectively to protect minorities, it must have at its disposal for the purposes of its future work, all information that it may require in order to distinguish between genuine and spurious minorities which might be created for propaganda purposes.' It recommended that UNESCO be invited to consider creating a committee of world educational leaders to study and select basic principles of democracy and universal education in order 'to combat any spirit of intolerance and hostility as between nations and groups'. To allow itself more latitude in organizing its programme the Sub-Commission requested a revision of its terms of reference, and, in May 1949, the Commission resolved that it should 'undertake studies, particularly in the light of the Universal Declaration of Human Rights, and to make recommendations to the Commission concerning the prevention of discrimination of any kind relating to human rights and fundamental freedom and the protection of racial, national, religious and linguistic minorities'.[5]

At its second session in June 1949, the Sub-Commission recommended the establishment of national co-ordinating committees to assist with the speedy implementation of the principles and rights enunciated in the Universal Declaration. Another resolution

---

[4] ECOSOC OR, 6th sess., supp. no. 11, UN doc. E/CN.4/52, 9–16.
[5] Report of the 5th sess., of the Commision on Human Rights, ECOSOC OR, 9th sess., supp. no. 10, UN doc. E/1371, 6.

recommended that non-governmental organizations (in consultative status under Article 71 of the Charter) be invited to furnish such information as might assist it to determine whether, to what extent, and why, any particular group was being discriminated against on the basis of the categories referred to in Article 2 of the Universal Declaration.[6]

The most far-reaching recommendation was one which proposed a basic revision of the procedure for handling complaints received by the United Nations which alleged violations of human rights. Instead of the mere note-taking procedure laid down by the Council in 1947, the Sub-Commission suggested accepting a right of petition by individuals and groups on much the same lines as in the Upper Silesian system under the League. Until machinery of implementation was established under the proposed Covenant on Human Rights, the Sub-Commission proposed that it be given authority to examine communications alleging the existence of urgent problems in the field of discrimination brought to its attention by governments, United Nations members, special agencies, and non-governmental organizations, as well as communications and petitions originating from private individuals which, in the Secretary-General's opinion, indicated the existence of urgent problems. Moreover, the Sub-Commission proposed that it be given authority to request further information from states and individuals or groups concerned, in order to make any necessary recommendations. Until this could be achieved it recommended the adoption of several interim measures for minority protection.[7]

Alas for enthusiasm; the Commission did not share the sub-Commission's 'activist' view of its role and rejected all those recommendations calling for practial action.[8] The implementation proposals were rejected on the grounds that the Commission had not yet completed consideration of the measures to be included in the proposed Covenant on Human Rights and the interim procedures suggested by the Sub-Commission were therefore 'premature'.

This rebuff was hardly surprising in the light of the Commission's conception of its own programme which was that the proclamation

[6] UN doc. E/CN.4/351, Res. II.
[7] UN docs. E/CN.4/351, Res. 6, and E/CN.4/352, Res. 5.
[8] UN docs. E/CN.4/358. See ECOSOC OR, 11th sess., supp. no. 5, also UN doc. E/1371 and E/CN.4/181.

and legal enactment of human rights should precede any attempt to implement them. The Universal Declaration of Human Rights of 1948 was not intended to have any legally binding effect and only after the proposed covenants were signed and ratified would it be possible to deal with specific problems and complaints. It was feared that any positive action might be interpreted as violating the domestic jurisdiction clause (Article 2 (7) of the Charter), about which states were particularly sensitive, and jeopardize the covenants. The Sub-Commission therefore maintained a conception of its role quite different from that of the Commission and the Council. It saw little point in pursuing studies and making reports as ends in themselves but, on the contrary, perceived as its task proposing concrete measures for the prevention of discrimination and the protection of minorities. From this viewpoint, nothing could have been more negative than the Commission's treatment of the two reports. As a former director of the human rights division of the United Nations Secretariat pointed out, it was as if governments, having led the Sub-Commission down the perilous road of minorities, had also conspired to lie in wait for it and finally to liquidate it.[9] Since the Council would not approve recommendations calling for practical action and was not convinced of the value of studies *in vacuo*, it decided that the role into which the Sub-Commission found itself forced did not justify its existence any longer. After a report from the *Ad Hoc* Committee on the Organization and Operation of the Council and its Commissions, which pointed out that the Sub-Commission had been unable to establish a satisfactory work programme, the Council determined in September 1951 that it be discontinued until the end of 1954.[10]

Nevertheless, this action did not herald its demise. Out of the ashes of frustration and ineffectiveness which marked the end of the first period of its existence was to arise a phoenix of central importance in United Nations activity in the field of human rights over the next decade. The programme of studies which had been discredited and rejected, eventually became the cornerstone of its activities simply

[9] J. P. Humphrey, 'The United Nations Sub-Commission on the Prevention of Discrimination and the Protection of Minorities', 62 *AJIL* (1968), 869, 874. 'Obviously, the crime of the Sub-Commission was that it had taken its job too seriously. It was actually interested in legislation, and worse, in enforcement of legislation.' (Ibid., 875).

[10] First report, *Ad Hoc* Committee, ECOSOC OR, UN doc. E/1991; ECOSOC OR, 13th sess., supp. no. 1, Res. 414 BI (XIII).

because there were no other alternatives acceptable to the majority of states. About this time it became clear that, even if the covenants on human rights were ever completed at all, they would take a long time. There were several reasons for this. An atmosphere of political uncertainty and suspicion currently existed in which states were not eager to enter into any new international obligations, especially ones as broad and far reaching as those set forth in the draft covenants. Concern over becoming parties to any measure which might qualify states' domestic jurisdiction and a corresponding unreadiness to accept the idea of implementation led to disenchantment with the view that broad general omnibus treaties were the best method of protecting human rights. An educational approach and a study programme were the obvious solutions to fill the vacuum created by the retreat from the legal approach towards human rights, and the Sub-Commission was in an ideal position to assist.

When the Council resolved to discontinue the Sub-Commission it took over responsibility for dealing with matters for which the latter was responsible and accordingly requested the Secretary-General to report on how member states and the Secretariat itself considered the Council should deal with questions relating to discrimination and minorities. The Secretariat thereupon proposed the study of forms and types of discrimination.[11] Meanwhile, in 1952, following strong pressure from states, the General Assembly asked the Council to reconsider its decision temporarily to discontinue the Sub-Commission, and the Council accordingly rescinded its decision and extended the Sub-Commission's life, requesting it to pay particular attention to the prevention of discrimination. Since, under its terms of reference, the Sub-Commission's task was to undertake studies, it embarked on a series of enquiries relating to discrimination in education, occupation and employment, political rights, religious rights and principles, residence and movement, immigration and travel, and certain family rights.[12] This second and extremely fruitful phase, concentrated on education rather than legislative activities. An important reason for the move towards an educational approach was the change in United States policy in April 1953 when John Foster Dulles, US Secretary of State, during hearings on the Bricker constitutional amendment, announced that the United States was

[11] ECOSOC OR, 13th sess., special supp. no. 1, Res. 414 (XIII) (UN doc. E/2229).

[12] GA Res. 532 (VI) B, GAOR, 6th sess., vol. ix; Resolutions, 29–30; Res. 443 (XIV), ECOSOC OR, 14th sess., supp. no. 1; UN doc. E/CN.4/669, Res. A.

opposed to international efforts to promote human rights and fundamental freedom by compulsion, including treaties or covenants on human rights, and that education was a more appropriate means for the United Nations to carry out its charter obligations.

In 1952, the International Labour Organization was asked to study discrimination in Employment and Occupation, while the Sub-Commission itself undertook a study of discrimination in Education, in conjunction with UNESCO and these provided the models for later studies.[13] A special rapporteur was chosen to undertake a study with the aid of the Secretariat, in three stages: (1) the collection and analysis of materials; (2) the preparation of the report; (3) recommendations. Recourse for information was had to governments, the Secretariat and experts, special departments, non-governmental organizations, and the Commission, as well as to the best available literature. Each report was prepared on a global basis and in a 'tactful' manner, specialist attention being given to matters typical of general tendencies and to areas in which discrimination had been successfully overcome by positive government action. A positive rather than a negative approach was chosen so that *de jure* and *de facto* human rights situations could be exposed to the searchlight of world public opinion. Government action would thus be stimulated and other member states would learn by example. Reports were prepared on conditions in each state and returned to that state's government for comment, before they received publicity in the Sub-Commission, the Commission, the Council, the General Assembly, and non-governmental organizations. On the basis of the reports, recommendations were made usually calling for declarations and conventions to be drawn up to deal with the subject matter of the study. Thus the ILO drew up a convention on discrimination in employment and occupation, while UNESCO prepared a convention on discrimination in education. In later years, following the successful completion of these pioneer studies, special rapporteurs were appointed to undertake studies of discrimination in other fields, including religious rights and practices, political rights, the right of everyone to leave any country including his own and to return to his own country, persons born out of wedlock, equality in the administration of justice, and racial discrimination in political, economic, social, and cultural spheres.[14]

It would be facile to maintain that the Sub-Commission's first

[13] UN doc. E/CN.4/Sub.2/rev.1.   [14] See ch. 6, n. 32, below.

phase showed the futility of a legal approach towards questions of discrimination while the second phase showed the advantages of a purely educational approach. The true explanation would seem to be that international conventions can be concluded successfully only when they deal with a circumscribed topic which has been thoroughly explored so that states can have little doubt as to the exact nature of the legal obligations into which they are entering.

After 1952, the minorities protection side of the Sub-Commission's activities fell into abeyance since the Commission would not adopt its recommendations. It could not even agree on a definition of 'protection of minorities' and the matter was returned to the Sub-Commission 'for further study'.[15] One reason for this was that several members were sensitive over minorities problems of their own, but a second and more important reason was the legacy of the bitterness resulting from the League minorities system which was seen as a cause of dissension. Many also believed that the general protection of human rights obviated the need for special minorities protection. As a result the Sub-Commission became exasperated at its carefully prepared recommendations being returned and, after another attempt in 1954 in which three resolutions were all passed back, it decided to shelve the problem until a more positive attitude prevailed.[16]

The third period of the Sub-Commission's activities can be traced back to the arrival of a number of new nations, all of which were extremely sensitive to racial issues which in turn made the United Nations more receptive to action designed to prevent discrimination. Consequently the Sub-Commission was requested to assist in the preparation of recommendations and conventions for adoption by the General Assembly, and between 1963 and 1965 it prepared the early drafts of the Declaration and Convention on the Elimination of All Forms of Racial Discrimination and the proposed Declaration and Convention on the Elimination of All Forms of Religious Intolerance. These developments, marking the return to a more specifically legal approach, were of immense importance. They meant that the Sub-Commission and to some extent the Commission on Human Rights itself had become drafting committees of the General Assembly. In 1965, it was proposed that the name of the

---

[15] See generally: Felix Ermacora, *Der Minderheitenschutz in der Arbeit der Vereinten Nationen* (Braumueller, Vienna, 1965).
[16] See UN docs. E/CN.4/Sub. 2/S.R.513–15.

Sub-Commission be changed to the 'Permanent Committee of Experts of the Commission on Human Rights' but no action was taken.[17] A proposal that the Commission on Human Rights should be promoted to the rank of Council, since the General Assembly rather than the Economic and Social Council was not its true parent, did not succeed either.[18]

The Council then resolved to submit to the Sub-Commission for 'initial study' all the material transmitted by governments to the Secretary-General in their Periodic Reports on Human Rights.[19] The plan was that the Sub-Commission should not just study the reports in so far as they related to discrimination or minorities, but should study them thoroughly, in all their aspects, and report thereon, through the Commission, to the Council.

This programme was approved and, at the second meeting of the Sub-Commission in 1967, the United States expert proposed that the Sub-Commission's rapporteur be appointed special rapporteur (1) to prepare, with the assistance of the Secretariat for consideration by the Sub-Commission at the present session, a short study covering, in so far as possible, salient developments and trends in civil and political and in economic, social, and cultural rights during the period under review; (2) to submit draft comments in so far as possible for the consideration of the Sub-Commission.[20] Consequently an Israeli special rapporteur was appointed who prepared a study which included an annex summarizing information submitted by non-governmental organizations, some of which was critical of certain governments. A débâcle followed in the course of which the Soviet expert moved that the annex be destroyed and this was agreed to by the Sub-Commission. It is not surprising, therefore, that at its next session the Commission called upon the Council to decide that new arrangements rendered unnecessary the initial study of periodic reports.[21]

At its twenty-third session, the Commission authorized the Sub-

[17] ECOSOC OR, 41st sess., supp. no. 8, and UN doc. E/4184, 119. See also UN docs. E/CN.4/L.768 and CHR Res. 4 (XXI). [18] See Humphrey, 883.
[19] ECOSOC Res. 1074 C (XXXIX), para. 15 (28 July 1965). ECOSOC OR, 39th sess., supp. no. 1, UN doc. E/4117, 24–5. See Committee on Periodic Reports, UN doc. E/CN.4/A.C.18/S.R. 8, 3–6.
[20] UN docs. E/CN.4/Sub.2/S.R.483, 3; E/CN.4/Sub.2/1.429; E/CN.4/915; E/CN.4/Sub.2/S.R.484, 3.
[21] UN docs. E/CN.4/Sub.2/458; E/CN.4/Sub.2/R.1 (annex iv); E/CN.4/Sub.2/S.R.504, 17; E/CN.4/Sub.2/S.R.505, 4; ECOSOC Res. 1230 (XLII) (6 June 1967), ECOSOC OR 42nd sess., supp. no. 1, UN doc. E/4393, 12–13.

Commission to undertake the consideration of two other important matters, both closely related to its prime functions. First, it was requested to consider the question of slavery, 'including the slavery-like practices of apartheid and colonialism'.[22] This was the culmination of a campaign waged by the Anti-Slavery Society to establish an expert body which could study information submitted by governments under the Supplementary Convention on Slavery, 1956. Second, it was authorized to examine information relating to gross violation of human rights and fundamental freedom as exemplified by the policy of apartheid as practised in the Republic of South Africa and in the territory of South West Africa, under the direct responsibility of the United Nations and now illegally occupied by the government of the Republic of South Africa, and to examine information relating to racial discrimination as practised notably in Southern Rhodesia.[23] All these developments gave the Sub-Commission an important supervisory role over a wide range of issues intimately concerned with the principle of individual equality.

The early history of the Sub-Commission can be summed up as one of qualified success. It did not manage to deal adequately with the question of minorities, but it was very active in the field of discrimination, although 'Apart from the great issues of war and peace, and economic development, there has been no issue with which the United Nations has been more concerned than that of discrimination, and no organ of the United Nations had played a more imaginative or constructive role in this matter than has the Sub-Commission'.[24] Since 1970 the Sub-Commission has been relatively inactive in respect of its prime functions and instead has carried out tasks on behalf of the Commission of Human Rights. For example, in respect of its procedures for handling complaints of violations of human rights.[25] The extent of this development is demonstrated by the fact that in 1979 the Sub-Commission recommended that its name be changed to the Sub-Commission on Human Rights.[26]

[22] ECOSOC OR, 42nd sess., supp. no. 6; UN doc. E/4322, Res. 13 (XXIII), 209.
[23] ECOSOC OR 42nd sess., supp. no. 1; UN doc. E/4393, Res. 1235 (XLII), 17–18.
[24] Humphrey, 871–2.
[25] ECOSOC Res. 1503 (XLVIII) (1970).
[26] See I. Brownlie, *Basic Documents on Human Rights* (Oxford University Press, 2nd ed. 1981), 15–20, and Th. C. Van Boven, 'The United Nations Commission on Human Rights and Violations of Human Rights and Fundamental Freedoms', 15 *Neth. Int. L. Rev.* (1968), 374–93.

2. *The Meaning of 'Prevention of Discrimination' and 'Protection of Minorities'*

Early in its first session, the Sub-Commission agreed on a description of its two tasks, the prevention of discrimination and the protection of minorities. It did not attempt a *legal* definition but merely indicated the considerations which should be taken into account in framing the proposed Universal Declaration of Human Rights.[27]

'Prevention of discrimination' was described as the prevention of any action which denies to individuals or groups of people equality of treatment which they may wish; and 'protection of minorities' as the protection of non-dominant groups which, while wishing in general for equality of treatment with the majority, wish for a measure of differential treatment in order to preserve the basic characteristics which they possess and which distinguish them from the majority of the population. This protection applied equally to individuals belonging to such groups and wishing the same protection. It followed that differential treatment of such groups or of individuals was justified when it was exercised in the interests of their contentment and the welfare of the community as a whole. The characteristics meriting such protection were race, religion, and language but in order to qualify for protection, a minority must owe undivided allegiance to the government of the state in which it lived and its members must be nationals. If a minority wished for assimilation and was debarred, the question was one of discrimination and should be treated as such.

These useful and important descriptions were the major contributions of the Sub-Commission's first period. One illuminating conceptual breakthrough contained in the definitions was the clear distinction made between 'differentiation' which may be justified in the interests of true equality, and 'discrimination', which meant in this context 'unwanted', 'unreasonable', or 'invidious' distinction and was never justifiable. During the discussion of Miss Monroe's working paper by the Sub-Commission it was suggested that the words 'equality of treatment' should replace 'treatment which they may wish' in the first definition since 'the opposite of discrimination is equality'.[28]

In the Commission on Human Rights some delegates considered

---

[27] UN docs. E/CN.4/Sub.2/36 and E/CN.4/Sub.2/S.R. 14 and 15. See ECOSOC OR, 6th sess., supp. no. 11, UN doc. E/CN.4/52, 10–11.

[28] See UN doc. E/CN.4/Sub.2/S.R.15, 1 ff.

that the description of 'prevention of discrimination' was 'loose and unscientific' for two reasons. First, the mention of equality of treatment without qualification was unacceptable since absolute equality of treatment was obviously impossible to achieve.[29] The insertion of the word 'justified' before 'equality' was suggested, but this was opposed on the ground that the word 'equality' used here in its legal sense did not mean 'absolute' equality but 'fair' or 'justified' equality and there was therefore no need for a qualifying adjective. The replacement of the phrase 'which they may wish' by 'granted to them in accordance with international law concerning the protection of the rights of individuals or groups' was proposed, but it was objected that such rights were not yet affirmed by international law and that it would be begging the question to demand the application of a law which did not exist.[30] It is instructive to recall here Abraham Lincoln's comments on the assertion of human equality in the US Declaration of Independence:

They did not mean to assert the obvious untruth that all men were then actually enjoying that equality yet or that they were about to confer it immediately upon them. In fact they had no power to confer such a boon. They meant simply to declare the right so that the enforcement of it might follow as fast as circumstances permit. They meant to set up a standard maxim for a free society which should be familiar to all, constantly looked to, constantly labored for, and even though never perfectly attained, constantly approximated to, and thereby constantly spreading and deepening its influence and augmenting the happiness and value of life of all people of all colours everywhere.[31]

Finally the Commission approved the Sub-Commission's text on the prevention of discrimination, but no decision was reached on

[29] See UN doc. E/CN.4/S.R.32–41.

[30] The record reads: Prof. Dehouse (Belgium) 'confirmed the fact that there was no provision in International Law for the protection of human rights'. This is in marked contrast to a statement made by Lord Dukeston (UK) in the Commission regarding Article 2 of the proposed Covenant. He said that if it was implied in the Convention that those rights and freedoms in the Bill were not part of general international law the Commission would be giving substance to the argument that no action could be legally taken against states which had not acceded to the Convention. He had no qualms about the suggestion that to say in the Covenant that human rights and fundamental freedoms were part of interntional law would be to admit that those rights and freedoms could be enforced by states which were not parties against states which are parties to it. Such rights and freedoms were part of the law of nature which was the foundation of all law and of international law. See UN doc. E/CN.4/S.R.41.

[31] Address of 26 June 1857. See J. G. Nicolay and J. Hays, eds., *Complete Works of Abraham Lincoln* (New York, 1894), 330–1.

the protection of minorities.[32] In an excellent memorandum the Secretary-General pointed out that the Sub-Commission's definitions indicated a fundamental difference between the prevention of discrimination and the protection of minorities.[33] Discrimination implied any act or conduct which denied to certain individuals equality of treatment with other individuals because they belonged to particular social groups. To prevent discrimination some means had to be found to suppress or eliminate inequality of treatment which may have harmful results, aiming at the prevention of acts which implied that an unfavourable distinction was made between individuals solely because they belonged to certain categories or groups of society. The prevention of discrimination meant the suppression or prevention of any conduct which denied or restricted a person's right to equality.

The protection of minorities, on the other hand, although similarly inspired by the principle of equality of treatment of all peoples, required positive action. Concrete service was rendered to the minority group such as the establishment of schools in which education is given in the native tongue of the group's members. The principle of equality inspired such measures, for if a child received its education in a language not its mother tongue, this might imply that the child was not treated on an equal basis with those children who did receive their education in their mother tongue. The protection of minorities therefore required positive action to safeguard the rights of minority groups provided that the people concerned wished to maintain their difference of language and culture. Applying the principle of prevention of discrimination in this example, no child could be excluded from any school because its mother tongue or cultural background differed from that of the majority of children attending school.

Since the ultimate goal of protection of minorities thus differed from that of discrimination, the two questions had to be dealt with differently. No contradiction existed in aiming simultaneously at the protection of minorities and the prevention of discrimination, because in each case it was desired to obtain and effectively maintain equality of treatment of all peoples. The difference arose from the wishes of the people concerned, for those affected by any plan

[32] ECOSOC OR, 6th sess., supp. no. 1; UN doc. E/600, para. 39, 11; see UN doc. E/600, para. 40, 11.

[33] UN doc. E/CN.4/Sub.2/40. See ECOSOC Res. 116 (VI) B, ECOSOC OR, 6th sess., Resolutions, 17.

designed to protect minorities were free to choose whether they wished to maintain the culture of their national, linguistic, or religious group. Prevention of discrimination and the protection of minorities represented different developments of the same idea of equality of treatment for all peoples. One required the elimination of any distinction imposed, whereas the other required safeguards to pre-serve certain distinctions voluntarily maintained.

Any plan aimed at the prevention of discrimination should be based on guiding principles such as the United Nations Charter and the Universal Declaration which were in turn based on other grounds of a natural law quality, in particular the ethical concept of the dignity of the human person which implied that human beings must be treated as ends in themselves and not as mere means to ends. The two principles which flowed from this ethical *Grundnorm* were the principle of individual freedom and the principle of the equality of all human beings before the law.

To eliminate the ambiguity of the word equality, it should be considered to refer only to moral and juridical equality as proclaimed in the Universal Declaration of Human Rights. Such equality did not exclude admissible differentiation based on conduct imputable to the individual, e.g. industriousness, idleness, carefulness, decency, merit, lawfulness etc., and it did not exclude differentiation based on physical and mental capacities and abilities which though not imputable to the individual had a social value. Rather, juridical equality excluded any difference based on grounds not imputable to the individual which should not be considered as having any social or legal meaning such as colour, race, and sex, and social generic categories such as language, political or other opinions, nationality or social origin, property, birth, or other status. This meant that the term 'discrimination' should be delimited to 'any conduct based on a distinction made on grounds of natural or social categories which have no relation either to individual capacities or merits or to the concrete behaviour of the individual person'.

The report, which went on to discuss both legal and educational measures for preventing discrimination, was welcomed by the Sub-Commission which decided to use it as a working paper, and the subject was fully discussed during the early stages of its third session.[34] The Soviet expert criticized the Secretary-General's memorandum for tending to minimize the importance of legislative measures in

[34] UN docs. E/CN.4/Sub.2/S.R.43 and 44.

the prevention of discrimination and argued that the proviso that legislation should be enacted 'subject to social conditions' was dangerous, since experience showed that legislation if strictly applied could prevent discrimination and even eliminate it altogether 'thus ensuring the protection of minority rights'. This view failed to recognize that one of the purposes of the report was to point out that the protection of minorities was not achieved merely by the prevention of discrimination. Other Soviet objections to the memorandum were that it dealt with questions outside its competence which would divert the Sub-Commission's attention from its basic tasks, and was generally 'unsatisfactory and ineffective'. The questions considered to be outside the Sub-Commission's competence somewhat surprisingly included the rights of women and illegitimate children, matters with which the Sub-Commission quite properly concerned itself in later years.

Other members thought more highly of the document. The French member considered that the Sub-Commission's efforts should not be directed against differentiation *per se* but against differentiation which tended to produce inequality and prejudice the rights of a given group. The Sub-Commission should be guided by the 'fundamental principle' that non-discrimination was a matter of natural law and therefore 'the duty and responsibility' of all nations whether or not signatories to the proposed Covenant. Presumably he did not accept that there already existed a duty of non-discrimination under positive international law for he went on to add that, though the Declaration was 'valid and *morally binding*', a violation of a duly signed Covenant would be far more serious since it would be an offence against international law.

The UNESCO representative pointed out that educational and legal measures were in fact two aspects of the same line of effort. The history of United Nations activity in the field of individual equality showed that while education was a necessary prerequisite for legislative activity, law itself can have a profound educative influence. In retrospect, the Secretary-General's memorandum can be seen as a milestone in the progress of understanding the juridical meaning of equality and its related concepts, prevention of discrimination and protection of minorities. It reaffirmed that these two concepts are not unrelated or contradictory, but are complementary methods of attaining equality of treatment for all persons. Although the study profoundly influenced later thinking, there have been many occasions when it has not been referred to when it would have been relevant and pertinent to do so, and some delegates have appeared to be completely ignorant of its valuable insights and conclusions.

VI

INTERNATIONAL STUDIES
OF DISCRIMINATION

1. *Racial Discrimination in Non-Self-Governing and Trust Territories*

RACIAL discrimination has been of prime concern to the United Nations Committee on Information from Non-Self-Governing Territories since its inception, but unfortunately little notice has been taken of its work, particularly its excellent analysis of the nature of discrimination, produced as early as 1952.[1] It was pointed out that there was a fundamental distinction between discriminatory laws and protective measures designed to safeguard the rights of indigenous inhabitants.[2] The Committee classified existing laws as differential or concessionary, and protective or discriminatory. By differential or concessionary legislation it meant those laws which reflect the different religious, traditional, and cultural aspirations of the different communities and which originate with and are maintained by the will of the particular communities concerned.[3] It was emphasized that such laws are necessary and beneficial so long as they represent the will of the inhabitants. Protective legislation might also be necessary and beneficial but required frequent reconsideration since, with the evolution of society, its purposes might become unnecessary and it might degenerate into discrimination. Discriminatory laws imposed disabilities on persons by reason of race and were contrary to the principles of the Charter and the Universal Declaration. The Committee also emphasized that every citizen should have the legal right to challenge executive actions or legislative measures which impair his equal status and opportunity, and stressed the role of legislation in moulding public

[1] See report of the Committee on Information from Non-Self-Governing Territories, UN doc. A/2219, pt. iii, and pt. i, annex ii b.

[2] UN doc. A/AC.35/S.R.70 (20 Oct. 1952).

[3] UN doc. A/2219, pt. iii (Race Relations), 53–6, paras. 26–30. Paragraph 5 of the draft resolution recommended that where existing laws provided particular measures of protection for sections of the population, they should frequently be examined in order to ascertain whether their protective aspect was still predominant. See also UN doc. A/AC.35/S.R.70, 7–10.

opinion. No principle in the field of education was more important than that of equality of opportunity. for all racial, religious, and cultural groups and, although respect should be paid to the wishes of a group desiring to establish particular educational facilities, the general welfare of the whole community must not be prejudiced thereby and a differential system must not lead to discrimination against any group.

In the Fourth Committee the opinion was expressed that racial discrimination only existed where a person or ethnic group was deprived of certain political or civil rights or placed at a disadvantage because of race or colour. There was no discrimination where limitations were imposed because of a person's lack of qualifications or a group's backwardness, so long as the limitations were merely temporary.[4] This was a clear acceptance of the principle that although some differentiations may be legitimate and therefore not discriminatory, any protective measures must not be continued longer than is strictly necessary or they will become restrictions or privileges not based on the particular disabilities (which have disappeared) but on the irrelevant grounds of race or ethnic group. Because the draft resolution touched on the distinction between discrimination and protective measures it was drawn to the attention of the Commission on human rights.[5] The resolution adopted by the General Assembly recommended to the members responsible for the administration of non-self-governing territories the abolition in those territories of discriminatory laws and practices contrary to the principles of the Charter and of the Universal Declaration.[6] It also recommended that the administering members should examine all laws, statutes, and ordinances in force in the non-self-governing territories under their administration and their application with a view to abolishing any discriminatory provisions or practices;[7] that, in any non-self-

[4] See report of 4th committee, 7th sess., UN doc. A/2296. Also UN docs. A/C4/S.R.260–2; GAOR., 7th Sess., 4th Comm., (1 Nov. 1952), 84.
[5] UN doc. A/C4/S.R.262, GAOR., 7th sess., 4th comm., 94–6. The Yugoslav representative doubted whether there was any fundamental difference between discriminatory laws and practices and protective measures.
[6] GA Res. 644 (VII), especially para. 7. The resolution was adopted at the Assembly's 402nd plenary meeting on 10 Dec. 1952, the fourth anniversary of the adoption of the Universal Declaration, by 51–0, 1 abstention, and reaffirmed in 1958. UN docs. A/4090, 35; A/3873, 34–6; A/4068.
[7] Arts. 1, 2, 3, 5. In the Fourth Committee the United Kingdom introduced an amendment to add the words 'of a racial or religious character' at the end of

governing territory where laws were in existence which distinguish between citizens and non-citizens primarily on racial or religious grounds, these laws should similarly be examined; that all public facilities should be open to all inhabitants of the non-self-governing territories without distinction of race; and that, where laws were in existence providing particular measures of protection for sections of the population, they should frequently be re-examined in order to ascertain whether their protective aspect was still predominant, and whether provision should be made for exemptions in particular circumstances.

In 1957, the International Labour Organization had adopted Convention 107[8] which required special measures to be adopted for the protection of institutions, persons, property, and labour of indigenous and tribal populations when their social, economic, and cultural conditions prevented them from enjoying the benefits of the general laws of the country to which they belonged. Such special measures were not to be used as a means of creating or prolonging segregation or prejudicing the enjoyment of general citizenship rights without discrimination. Due account must also be taken of cultural and religious values and customary laws existing among such populations; education programmes should be adapted to their special needs and, so far as practicable, teaching should be provided in the mother tongue.

In 1960, the Committee on Information from Non-Self-Governing Territories recognized and welcomed the progress achieved since 1947 in abolishing a number of forms of racial discrimination and improving race relations in many territories. It nevertheless recognized that discrimination on the grounds of race and colour continued to exist, particularly in some African territories where European minorities frequently exercised political, social, and economic privileges denied to the indigenous population. The quickest way to abolish discrimination would be the establishment of political equality among all members of

Paragraph 2 (UN doc. A/C4/L.215), and this was adopted. However, in plenary session the United Kingdom introduced another amendment to delete these words and insert 'such' between 'any' and 'discriminatory' (UN doc. A/L.127), and this was adopted at the 402nd meeting. The United Kingdom representative explained this volte-face by saying that some representatives had pointed out that the first amendment was unduly restrictive. (See UN doc. A/P.V.402, 343.)

[8] 328 UNTS, 249. The Convention came into force on 2 June 1959.

plural communities.[9] The General Assembly, endorsing the Committee's view that racial discrimination was a violation of human rights and a deterrent to progress in the territories, called for the extension to all inhabitants of the full exercise of political rights, particularly the right to vote and the establishment of equality among the members of all races inhabiting the territories.[10] The administering powers' reports often noted that not all differential treatment was undesirable and that, during the transition of a people from a primitive society to a new nation, it was necessary to provide certain legislation as a means of protection.[11]

United Nations practice thus endorses the view that the equality principle permits and sometimes requires differences of treatment so long as four conditions are satisfied: (1) The differential treatment must consist of protective measures designed to promote the welfare of a particular indigenous group; (2) It must be wanted by such groups; (3) It must be based on the needs of a particular group and not its race or colour classification;[12] (4) It must not be continued for longer than is strictly necessary. Should any of these conditions not be satisfied then the differential treatment will be invidious and therefore discriminatory.

Under Article 76 (c) of the Charter, a basic objective of the trusteeship system is 'to encourage respect for human rights and for fundamental freedoms for all without distinction as to race, sex, language or religion'. At an early session the Trusteeship Council adopted resolutions on discrimination[13] and in 1949 the General Assembly, recalling the provisions of Article 76 (c), recommended 'the abolition of discriminatory laws and practices contrary to the principles of the Charter and the Trusteeship Agreements in all Trust Territories in which such laws and practices exist'.[14] The Trusteeship Council 'should examine all laws, statutes and ordinances as well as their application in the Trust Territories and make positive

---

[9] Survey and report by the Secretary-General (6 Mar. 1961) UN doc. A/AC.35/L.334.
[10] GA Res. 1536 (XV), GAOR, 15th sess., supp., no. 15, UN docs. A/4371 and A/4785; and supp. no. 16, UN docs. A/4684, 27. See also the information submitted by the United Kingdom Government (1958–9) in UN doc. A/4760. See also GAOR, 10th sess., (1955), supp. no. 16, 29. [11] UN doc. A/4785, 64.
[12] This is not to say that particular ethnic groups may not be classified according to race or colour for convenience, but the *reason* for the classification must be the degree of backwardness or need, and not race or colour *per se*. [13] Res. 49 (IV) and 50 (IV).
[14] GA Res. 323 (IV), GAOR, 4th sess., Resolutions, 39.

recommendations to the Administering Authorities concerned with a view to the abolition of all discriminatory provisions or practices'.[15] It was pointed out that discrimination and differential treatment were not the same thing and, as explained in the Trusteeship Council,[16] the differential treatment employed in the trust territories had been adopted to safeguard the interests of the indigenous inhabitant, was not aimed against any one racial group but applied to all foreigners, and was justified by Article 74 (d) of the Charter.[17] Although differential treatment might work against the interests of foreigners, it was nevertheless justified for the well-being and advancement of the inhabitants of the territories, and measures which at first sight appeared discriminatory were in fact in the best interests of the indigenous inhabitants.[18] After 1960 most of the activities of the United Nations organs with regard to discrimination in non-self-governing and trust territories centred on the implementation of the Declaration on the Granting of Independence to Colonial Countries and Peoples, 1960,[19] and the condemnation of apartheid.

Paragraph 5 declared *inter alia* that 'Immediate steps shall be taken, in Trust and Non-Self-Governing Territories or all other territories which have not yet attained independence, to transfer all powers to the peoples of those territories, without any conditions or reservations, in accordance with their freely expressed will and desire, without any distinction as to race, creed or colour in order to enable them to enjoy complete independence and freedom'.

Equality and non-discrimination were stressed by several speakers[20]

[15]	This paragraph was described by the USSR in the Fourth Committee as 'vague and obscure'. UN docs. A/C4/S.R.98, 34; and A/C4/L.13, and revs. 1–2.

[16]	UN docs. A/C4/S.R.97 and 98 (12 Oct. 1949), and report of Trusteeship Council, UN doc. A/933.

[17]	4th comm., 97th and 98th meetings. See the remarks of the Australian representative, UN doc. A/C4/S.R.97, 39. Article 74 (d) of the Charter provides that one of the objectives of the trusteeship system is 'to ensure equal treatment in social, economic, and commercial matters for all Members of the United Nations and their nationals and also equal treatment for the latter in the administration of justice without prejudice to the attainment of the foregoing objectives', i.e. the UN members and their nationals were to be equal *inter se*. This did not prevent special measures for the advancement of the indigenous peoples.

[18]	UN doc. A/C4/S.R.98, 43. For later discussions see GAOR, 10th sess., (1955), supp. no. 4, 63–70.

[19]	GA Res. 1514 (XV), adopted at the 947th plenary meeting on 14 Dec. 1960. See also UN docs. A/PV.925–39 and 944–7.

[20]	See UN docs. A/PV.927, 933, 937 and 939; GAOR, 15th sess., plenary meetings 927, 1099, 1161–2, 1199–200.

in debates on the declaration, which has been extremely influential, and the dynamic 'Committee of Twenty-Four' established to assist in implementing it has taken over many of the functions previously exercised by the Committee on Information from Non-Self-Governing Territories and the Trusteeship Council. Other important developments were the United Nations efforts to eradicate apartheid, and many resolutions progressively stronger in tone have been adopted on the question.[21] While in 1952 fifteen United Nations members either voted for or abstained on a South African motion to declare the General Assembly incompetent to deal with apartheid,[22] and seventeen states opposed establishing a three-member Commission to study the racial situation in South Africa,[23] in 1963 only South Africa and Portugal opposed a peremptory resolution addressed to the former.[24]

In 1962 the General Assembly appealed to members to break off diplomatic and trade relations with South Africa[25] and the following year it called upon members and upon the specialized agencies to take appropriate measures and to intensify their efforts to dissuade the South African government from pursuing its apartheid policies, requesting them to implement fully the Security Council resolution of 4 December 1963[26] which requested South Africa to 'cease forthwith its continued imposition of discriminatory and repressive measures which are contrary to the principles and purposes of the Charter and which are in violation of its obligations as a member of the United Nations and of the provisions of the Universal Declaration of Human Rights'. It also called upon states to cease selling or shipping arms to South Africa which itself was asked to liberate all persons imprisoned, interned or subject to other restrictions for having opposed apartheid.[27] This was done largely at the instigation of the Special Committee on Apartheid which produced a great deal

[21] The texts of all the resolutions on racial discrimination in South Africa up till 30 Aug. 1964 can be found in UN doc. S/AC14/L.3/add.1.

[22] See UN doc. A/PV.401, 38–41.

[23] GA Res. 616 (VII), and 721 (VIII).

[24] GA Res. 1978 (XVIII). See further, ch. 7 below.

[25] GA Res. 1761 (XVII). See UN doc. S/AC14/L.3/add.1, 28. At the same time the Assembly decided to establish a special committee of representatives nominated by the Assembly's President to keep South African racial policies under review and report to the General Assembly as appropriate. This became known as the Special Committee on the Policies of Apartheid of the Republic of South Africa.

[26] GA Res. 1978 (XVIII).

[27] Security Council res. of 7 Aug. 1963. See UN doc. S/AC14/L.3/add.1, 33.

of documentation.[28] In 1965, at the suggestion of the Committee, the General Assembly established a United Nations trust fund to provide legal assistance to South Africans and relief to refugees.[29] At the same time it began to prepare the ground for action under Chapter VII of the Charter which had already established an expert committee in 1964 to undertake a technical study of the possibility, effectiveness, and implications of measures which could be taken by the Council.[30] In 1961, the International Labour Conference requested South Africa to withdraw from membership of the ILO until she had abandoned her apartheid policy, and she finally withdrew in 1964.[31]

2. The Studies Undertaken by the Sub-Commission on the Prevention of Discrimination and the Protection of Minorities. The Work of Non-Governmental Organizations, and United Nations Seminars

The studies carried out since 1952 by special rapporteurs appointed by the Sub-Commission have been immensely valuable, in elucidating the meaning and content of the principles of equality and non-discrimination, and have established several general principles.[32]

[28] See for instance the study on apartheid prepared by the special rapporteur appointed on the question. UN doc. E/CN.4/949 and add.1–5. See also the study of the group of experts under Mrs. Myrdal (Sweden), UN doc. S/5658, and the report of the UN seminar on apartheid, UN doc. ST/TAO/HR.27, and the report of the UN seminar on racial discrimination, UN doc, ST/TAO/HR.34.

[29] GA Res. 2054 (XX). See UN doc. E/4226.

[30] See UN doc. S/AC14/L.3/add.1, 40. See ch. 7 below.

[31] See UN doc. A/5454; also ILO policy statements and reports concerning apartheid in labour matters, International Labour Conference (Geneva), 1966; M. Moskowitz, *The Politics and Dynamics of Human Rights* (Oceana, Dobbs Ferry, N.Y., 1968), 190.

[32] See the study of discrimination in education (C. D. Ammoun), E/CN.4/Sub.2/181/rev.1 (1956); the study of discrimination in respect of religious rights and practices (A. Krishnaswami), E/CN.4/Sub.2/200/rev.1 (1959); the study of discrimination in respect of political rights. (H. Santa Cruz), E/CN.4/Sub.2/213/rev.1 (1961); and an updated study E/CN.4/Sub.2/370 (1976); the study of discrimination in respect of the right of everyone to leave any country, including his own and to return to his own country (J. D. Ingles), E/CN.4/Sub.2/220, (1962); the study of discrimination against persons born out of wedlock, (V. V. Saario), E/CN.4/Sub.2/265, (1966); the study of racial discrimination in the political, economic, social and cultural spheres (H. Santa Cruz), E/CN.4/Sub.2/288 (1968); the study of equality in the administration of justice (Abu Rannet), E/CN.4/Sub.2/296 (1969); the question of slavery and the slave trade in all their practices and manifestations, including the slavery-like practices of apartheid and colonialism (M. Awad), E/CN.4/Sub.2/322 (1971); the study of the rights of persons belonging to ethnic, religious, and linguistic minorities (F. Capotorti), E/CN.4/Sub.2/384; the problem of the applicability of

(1) It was generally agreed that the term 'discrimination' is not synonymous with 'differential treatment' or 'distinction'. Rather, 'discrimination' in the sense used in the studies meant some sort of distinction made with respect to a person according to his classification into a particular group or category rather than by taking account of his individual merits or capacities.[33]

(2) In order to constitute discrimination, the distinctions, exclusions, or limitations made on the basis of such classifications must be adverse to the interests of the particular individual and unwanted by him.

(3) No undue preferences should be given to individuals because of such classifications.[34]

(4) Distinctions, exclusions, or limitations are not discriminatory if they are reasonable or justified.[35]

(5) Certain distinctions are legitimate if they are special measures designed to achieve rather than to prevent equality in the enjoyment of rights.[36]

existing international provisions for the protection of human rights to individuals who are not citizens of the state in which they live (Baroness Elles), E/CN.4/Sub.2/ 392; the study of the individual's duties to the community and the limitations on human rights and freedoms under article 29 of the Universal Declaration of Human Rights (E. I. Daës), E/CN.4/Sub.2/413; the study of discrimination against indigenous peoples (J. M. Cobo) E/CN.4/Sub.2/415; the study of the prevention and punishment of the crime of genocide (N. Ruhashyaniko) E/CN.4/Sub.2/416.

[33] In his study of racial discrimination in the political, economic, social and cultural spheres, Mr Santa Cruz adopts the definition of the verb 'to discriminate' which appears in the Random House Dictionary of the English Language, i.e. 'to make a distinction in favor or against a person or thing on the basis of the group, class or category to which the person or thing belongs, rather than according to actual merit'. UN docs. E/CN.4/Sub.2/288, 44, and E/CN.4/Sub.2/370, para. 66. In the study of discrimination in religious rights and practices, Mr Krishnaswami stated that 'in this field more than any other, differential treatment meted out to individuals and groups is not always synonymous with discrimination'. UN doc. E/CN.4/Sub.2/200, 5. See also the draft study of equality in the administration of justice, UN doc. E/CN.4/Sub.2/289, 94.

[34] UN doc. E/CN.4/Sub.2/213, 28; the study of discrimination against persons born out of wedlock, UN doc. E/CN.4/Sub.2/265, 25, refers to 'discriminating distinctions'.

[35] Thus the disqualification from the exercise of political rights of aliens, of nationals who have not yet reached the age specified by law, or of insane persons is not normally considered to be discriminatory. See UN doc. E/CN.4/Sub.2/213, para. 117, 44. If unjustified distinctions of any kind prevent the full enjoyment of a right, such distinctions are discriminatory (UN doc. E/CN.4/Sub.2/220, 23). In the view of Mr Saario, most differences between the status of persons born in and out of wedlock are discriminatory in nature; (UN doc. E/CN.4/Sub.2/265, 29).

[36] Thus it is legitimate to provide special education for a separate population group in its own language or in accordance with its own cultural traditions, and to provide special measures for blind, deaf, disabled, or otherwise physically or mentally handicapped persons, and for specially gifted persons. See UN doc. E/CN.4/Sub.2/181, para. 51, 24.

(6). However, such special measures are only legitimate if they are temporary, i.e. not applied for a longer period than is necessary to redress the *de facto* inequality between groups due to the economic, social, and cultural conditions prevailing before the adoption of the measures.[37]

(7) It is not necessary for a discriminatory motive to exist if discrimination exists in fact, although *mala fides* obviously aggravates a discriminatory practice and is much more to be condemned.[38]

(8) Some limitations, distinctions, or restrictions, although prima facie legitimate and non-discriminatory, may in fact affect only a particular group or affect it to a greater degree than others and this should be taken into account in determining whether they are legitimate.[39]

(9) The grounds of distinction in Article 7 of the Universal Declaration of Human Rights are illustrative not exhaustive.[40]

(10) Neither the Universal Declaration nor any United Nations pronouncement establishes the priority of one right over another so that the principles of equality and non-discrimination are not to be denied in order to express other rights.[41]

(11) The principle of equality does not exclude the possibility of differentiations based on merit, physical or mental capacity, talent or innate ability, but is primarily concerned with differentiations based on race, colour, descent, and national or ethnic origin.[42]

[37] UN doc. E/CN.4/Sub.2/181, 24.

[38] Ibid., para. 63–6, 27–8. Although the use of the adjectives 'static' and 'active' to qualify 'discrimination' had been discarded by the special rapporteur, the terms did indicate 'tendencies' in his view. Discriminatory practices due to economic, social, political, and historical factors were much more widespread than practices resulting from a deliberate policy of discrimination. Nevertheless a deliberate policy was never conducted in a vaccum but always as a result of such factors. Moreover it was difficult to determine the existence of such deliberate intention. Did it for instance lie solely in positive measures or could it also be discerned in negligence, inaction, or delay in taking positive steps to combat discriminatory practices? Article 1 of the Convention on the Elimination of All Forms of Racial Discrimination, and Article 1 of the Draft Convention on the Elimination of All Forms of Religious Intolerance (UN doc. A/7177, annex iii) define discrimination as acts having a certain 'purpose or effect'.

[39] UN doc. E/CN.4/Sub.2/200, para. 45, 32. 'Only when public authorities refrain from making any adverse distinctions against, or giving undue preferences to individuals or groups, will they comply with their duty as concerns non-discrimination.'

[40] UN docs. E/CN.4/Sub.2/213, paras. 26–7, 15 and E/CN.4/Sub.2/265, 25.

[41] UN doc. E/CN.4/Sub.2/265, 27. See also art. 30 of the Universal Declaration of Human Rights. Article 29 of the Declaration provides that only reasonable limitations may be imposed on the exercise of the rights and freedoms enumerated therein.

[42] UN doc. E/CN.4/Sub.2/288, paras. 46–8. 'Racial Discrimination is the very negation of the principle of equality, and therefore an affront to human dignity.' UN doc. E/CN.4/Sub.2/370, paras. 68, 69.

The importance of these studies in contributing to the understanding of the meaning of the principles of non-discrimination and equality cannot be underestimated, and they have had a profound influence on the thinking of the Sub-Commission.[43]

Another indication of the importance attached to the eradication of discrimination by international bodies can be discerned in the activities of non-governmental organizations, which have held two conferences devoted to the subject. In 1954, the Economic and Social Council authorized the Secretary-General to convene a conference at which non-governmental organizations might exchange views concerning the most effective means of combating discrimination, and consider the possibility of establishing common objectives and programmes.[44] The conference which met at Geneva from 31 March to 4 April 1955 recommended the adoption either of a comprehensive charter such as the Covenants on Human Rights or conventions relating to particular and clearly defined subjects as well as the establishment of recourse, individual and collective, to international bodies. The importance of the role of legal measures on both the international and the national planes was emphasized by many speakers who believed that action to eradicate discrimination could only be effective in the field of law, which has besides a profound educative influence. The need for some kind of tribunal where outstanding cases of prejudice and discrimination could be heard by eminent jurists was also stressed.[45]

Subsequently, the hope was expressed that competent organs would be established, where they did not already exist, to receive, to examine and, if necessary, to report publicly on complaints and petitions with regard to violations of human rights and thus with regard to discrimination contrary to the Charter of the United Nations, the Universal Declaration of Human Rights, and to international conventions.[46]

[43] See the reports of the 16th–20th sessions of the Sub-Commission, UN docs. E/CN.4/873; E/CN.4/882; E/CN.4/903; E/CN.4/930; E/CN.4/947; A/6660; A/6404; A/6934; A/7177.

[44] Resolution 546 (XVIII). See UN doc. E/N.G.O./Conf.1/8 (Final Act of the United Nations Conference on Non-Governmental Organizations interested in the Eradication of Prejudice and Discrimination).

[45] UN docs. E/N.G.O./Conf.1/S.R.2, 6, 19, and E/N.G.O./Conf.1/S.R.5,7. It was suggested that had there existed between 1933 and 1939 an independent tribunal for the examination of complaints where the voice of the people might have made itself heard, the history of the past few years might have been very different. See also UN doc. E/N.G.O./Conf.1/S.R.7, 4.

[46] Res. D, para. 3, UN doc. E/N.G.O./Conf.1/8, 15.

An early draft had employed the term 'illegal discrimination' but its use was criticized as injudicious, and likely to give rise to misunderstandings and difficulties of interpretation. According to the rapporteur the phrase was used to avoid getting involved with 'legal discrimination' such as the Swiss law which deprived women of their political rights, since such discrimination 'could not be dealt with by an international tribunal for human rights'. This curious explanation was disapproved on the grounds that it could be interpreted to mean that certain types of discrimination were acceptable, and the adjective 'illegal' was deleted.[47] It was also recognized that discrimination imposed inferior status on certain groups and individuals on the grounds of race, nationality, religion, language, sex, etc., and should not be confused with positive action to ameliorate the political, social, and economic welfare of under-privileged groups.[48]

The Second Conference of Non-Governmental Organizations Interested in the Eradication of Prejudice and Discrimination, convened in 1959, had as its prime concern 'such discriminatory behaviour as deprives individuals of equal rights or makes distinctions based on race, colour, sex, language or religion'.[49] The importance of conventions and competent organs to deal with complaints was re-emphasized and it was agreed that non-governmental organizations should urge governments to ratify the ILO Convention on Discrimination of the previous year and similar international instruments.[50] Resolution 8 (II) stated that it is essential nowadays to enact laws everywhere actually guaranteeing equality to women.

It is not discriminatory to permit religious groups to maintain their own schools or to allow the children of minority groups to be taught in the faith or language of that group, and nor is it necessarily discriminatory to emphasize different kinds of vocational education for men and women.[51] In judging whether or not a particular act is discriminatory, the sensibilities of the individuals or groups affected by the action as well as the reason or intention prompting it must be considered, and it is essential that care should be taken to respect individual differences and not to confuse equality with sameness.[52]

[47] UN doc. E/N.G.O./Conf.1/S.R.7, 3–5.
[48] UN doc. E/N.G.O./Conf.1/S.R.3, 7. One delegate said that too much attention should not be given to discrimination at the expense of equality. If rights and freedoms were recognized for all, there was no room for discrimination. E/N.G.O./Conf.1/S.R.2, 8.   [49] UN doc. N.G.O./Conf. 2/7, para. 41, 16.
[50] E/N.G.O./Conf.2/S.R.2, 8; and see Res. 7 (II), UN docs. E/N.G.O/Conf.2/7; E/N.G.O./Conf.2/S.R.2, 7.   [51] UN doc. E/N.G.O./Conf. 2/7, 26.
[52] UN docs. E/N.G.O./Conf. 2/7, para. 42, 17; E/N.G.O./Conf. 2/S.R.1, 8.

Special measures for certain social groups such as women and children or the sick and indigent are also an essential part of the equality principle. This does not mean that they should have privileges but only that individual situations should be taken into account; 'Rights are equal but special understanding for individuals is essential.'[53]

Useful seminars have been organized under United Nations auspices for the study of particular issues in the field of human rights. Most important have been the seminar on the multi-national society[54] held in 1965, and the seminars on apartheid,[55] and the elimination of all forms of racial discrimination,[56] held in 1968.

At the first seminar it was the general opinion that the essential aim to be achieved was equality of treatment in every sphere and that the state's preventive function in the matter of discrimination calls in turn for protective action to safeguard minority rights.[57] However, it was stressed that separate rights for groups *qua* groups should only be envisaged in the linguistic, cultural, or religious fields, and the primary consideration was the wish of the particular group to maintain its ethnic characteristics.[58] It was agreed that all governments should promote and protect the rights of ethnic, religious, linguistic, or other national groups not only through the adoption of constitutional and legislative provisions but also through the promotion of activities consistent with the political, economic, and social conditions of the state or country concerned. An immigrant group could be treated differently in some respects from an indigenous group, e.g. the majority should be under no obligation to subsidize the teaching of the language of an immigrant group. Presumably the reason for this view was that by their free choice the immigrants had undertaken to join a new community with its different linguistic traditions, and so by the operation of a kind of estoppel, they could not thereafter expect that community to subsidize an alien language, although it should be allowed to be taught privately. Moreover, when a minority group sought special privileges beyond those fundamental freedoms recognized *erga omnes* these privileges

---

[53] UN doc. E/N.G.O./Conf.2/S.R.2, 12.
[54] See UN doc. ST/TAO/HR.23.
[55] UN doc. ST/TAO/HR.27.   [56] UN doc. ST/TAO/HR.34.
[57] UN doc. ST/TAO/HR.23, paras. 30, 35, 47, 144.
[58] Discrimination against a group which wishes to use its own language was considered to be reprehensible and a type of 'cultural genocide'. By the same token, if a group preferred to integrate with the rest of the community then the compulsory continuation of its own language would be discriminatory.

should satisfy the test of reasonableness.[59] The seminar on apartheid agreed that the greatest single indictment of apartheid was its total disregard for the dignity of the individual personality and the sacredness of family life.[60] Free choice was emphasized and it was pointed out that the policy of separate development was not one agreed to by the different population groups but was imposed upon them.[61]

The seminar on racial discrimination recognized that special and concrete measures should be taken, when the circumstances so warranted, to ensure the adequate development and protection of certain racial groups or individuals belonging to them for the purpose of guaranteeing the full and equal enjoyment of human rights and fundamental freedoms. An important discussion took place on the legitimacy of reservations and quotas. According to one view, reservations and quotas were a fundamental means of promoting equality in law and in fact for persons who had been victims of discrimination, but others believed that it would be preferable to make special facilities available to backward groups in order to enable them to meet the general standards of merit.[62] Though the second view is attractive, systems of reservations and quotas are not necessarily inconsistent with the principle of equality, as long as they are of a strictly temporary nature and are maintained no longer than is necessary to achieve the objectives for which they are imposed, i.e. the rescue of backward groups from their economic and cultural disabilities. The crucial point was made that although under certain circumstances reservations and quotas may be appropriate, they must always be of limited duration.

The seminars generally approved the suggestion that further

[59] Ibid., paras. 37, 63.

[60] UN doc. ST/TAO/HR.27, 12. GA Res. 2105 (XX), which referred to apartheid as a 'crime against humanity', was also approved, as were the reports of the United Nations Commission on the Racial Situation in South Africa; GAOR, 8th sess., supp. no. 16, UN doc. A/2505 and add.1; 9th sess., supp., no. 16, UN doc. A/2719; 10th sess., supp. no. 14, UN doc. A/2953) and those of the Committee on South West Africa (GAOR 15th sess., supp., no.12, U.N. doc. A/4464; 16th sess. UN doc. A/4926.

[61] UN doc. ST/TAO/HR.27, 12. It was also agreed that apartheid was a policy based on 'the general principles of differentiation corresponding to differences of race and/or colour and/or level of civilisation; as opposed to assimilations'; and 'of the maintenance and perpetuation of the individuality (identity) of the different colour groups of which the population is composed, and of the separate development of those groups in accordance with their individual nature, traditions and capabilities; as opposed to integration'. See report of the special rapporteur, Dr Ganji, UN doc. E/CN.4/949.   [62] UN doc. ST/TAO/HR.34, paras. 147-55.

measures of implementation should be introduced, and favoured the appointment of a United Nations high commissioner or ombudsman for human rights. A large measure of agreement on the nature of the principles of equality and non-discrimination was demonstrated, and the views expressed on the importance of special measures of protection, the difference between discrimination and legitimate distinctions, the relevance of motive on the part of authorities, and the wishes of individuals and groups, were to exert a seminal influence in the future.

VII

THE CONVENTIONS AND
DECLARATIONS (1)

1. *Conventions or Recommendations*

SINCE the United Nations was founded, a substantial number of instruments aimed at the practical realization of the principle of individual equality have been prepared under its auspices. The treaty approach to human rights was not begun without considerable hesitation on the part of member states. It was objected that it would be impracticable to bind nations by international legal norms because these would be subject to many interpretations, and that abstract concepts could not be transformed into binding obligations without enormous difficulties. Moreover, it would mean that subjects traditionally regarded as part of a state's domestic jurisdiction would become subject to international scrutiny and derogate from state sovereignty.[1]

Nevertheless, the desire to lay down certain international legal norms to govern the relationship between states and their subjects and states *inter se* was particularly strong in the aftermath of World War II. Since it was realized that human rights questions would be under the scrutiny of the international community, it was thought preferable that they should be dealt with on a legal rather than a political plane. Although a Convention for the Prevention and Punishment of Genocide,[2] the 'crime of crimes',[3] was concluded as early as 1946, states were still very cautious about the notion that human rights instruments could lay binding obligations on states. This was demonstrated during the drafting of the Universal Declaration of Human Rights which, it was carefully pointed out, did not purport to be a treaty, or a statement of law or legal obligations.[4]

---

[1] See generally M. Moskowitz, *Human Rights and World Order* (Oceana, Dobbs Ferry, N.Y., 1958), ch. 7.

[2] Some representatives in the Sixth Committee thought that a declaration on genocide would be a more suitable instrument. See e.g. G. Kaeckenbeeck (Belgium), GAOR, 3rd sess., 6th comm., 65th meeting, 22.

[3] See P. N. Drost, *The Crime of State II, Genocide* (Sythoff, Leyden, 1959), Introduction.

[4] Mrs Roosevelt, GAOR, 3rd sess., Pt. 1, UN doc. A/PV.180; see also UN doc. A/PV.181, and H. Lauterpacht, *International Law and Human Rights*, (Stevens, London, 1950), ch. 17.

One major achievement of the Universal Declaration was to resolve doubts concerning the possibility of obtaining a consensus among disparate states on the statement and definition of fundamental human rights. Thereafter, the idea that conventions could be suitable instruments for realizing the protection of human rights became more acceptable, although there was still a large number of states which would have preferred recommendations alone. The arguments for and against conventions in this field were summarized in the debates on the ILO's 1951 Equal Remuneration Convention[5] in the International Labour Conference.[6] A majority of delegates believed that sufficient recommendations existed already[7] and that what was now required was an obligatory pact; a convention would deal only with the principle of discrimination in pay while the recommendation would cover methods of application. C. W. Jenks took the view that civil liberties were proper subjects for treaty regulation, and that conventions might be more effective instruments than recommendations in this field. This was the better approach since even covenants which are not universally accepted may fulfil a useful function with regard to states where rights and freedoms need the 'stimulus and consecration of such international recognition'.

A 'happy compromise'[8] was eventually reached in each case. Both types of instrument were adopted simultaneously, the conventions laying down the basic objectives to be attained, while the recommendations suggested measures for achieving them. These were examples of 'promotional' conventions which did not impose on the ratifying states strict obligations of immediate application but sought to promote defined objectives and policies and to set out standards to be achieved.[9] Most of the 'equality' conventions can be classified under this head although some are of immediate application and others are mixed with some obligations taking effect immediately, but with others to be introduced gradually to avoid the difficulties and dislocations which an immediate obligation might cause.[10] The

[5] See ch. 10 below.

[6] For an argument against conventions, see Sir Guildhaume Myrddin-Evans, I.L. Conf., 34th sess., rec. of procs., 351–3.

[7] I.L. Conf., 34th sess. of procs.; see particularly Bose (Indian Workers), 354; de Alba (Mexican Government), 356; Bar-Yaakov (Israeli Workers), 357.

[8] In the words of C. W. Jenks, *Human Rights and International Labour Standards* (Stevens; Praeger, London; New York, 1960), 131–2, and 139–41.

[9] See C. W. Jenks in 19 *Zeitschrift für Ausländiches Öffentliches Recht und Völkerrecht* (1958), 197.

[10] See for instance, I.L. Conf., 34th sess., Rec. of procs., 336, 348.

Genocide Convention is a treaty requiring immediate application by member states, while the Supplementary Convention on Slavery of 1956[11] is an example of a treaty whose aims are to be achieved progressively. Other examples of primarily promotional conventions are the Convention on the Political Rights of Women, 1953,[12] the ILO Discrimination (Employment and Occupation) Convention, 1958,[13] the UNESCO Convention on Discrimination in Education, 1960,[14] the Consent to Marriage, Minimum Age for Marriage, and Registration of Marriage Convention, 1962,[15] and the Covenant on Economic, Social, and Cultural Rights, 1966. Examples of 'mixed' conventions are the Convention on the Elimination of All Forms of Racial Discrimination, 1965, and the Covenant on Civil and Political Rights, 1966. The arguments for and against conventions were canvassed *ab initio* during the drafting of most of these instruments. During discussion on the Convention on the Political Rights of Women, the Economic and Social Council and some members of the Commission on the Status of Women considered that the principles could better be achieved by a continuing process of education and periodic reports, than by an international convention,[16] but the arguments against a convention were rejected because it was pointed out that the Inter-American Convention on the Granting of Political Rights to Women, 1948, had hastened the evolution of electoral legislation in several member states.[17]

The common pattern which emerged was for a declaration to be drafted followed by a convention. The Universal Declaration preceded the Human Rights Covenants by eighteen years,[18] and the Declaration on the Elimination of All Forms of Racial Discrimination, 1963, preceded the Convention on the same subject by two years. Though a Declaration on the Elimination of Discrimination against Women was adopted by the General Assembly in 1967, a convention was not drafted until 1980. It has been well said that

[11] 266 UNTS, 3.   [12] 193 UNTS, 135.   [13] 362 UNTS, 31.
[14] 429 UNTS, 93.   [15] 521 UNTS, 231.
[16] See e.g. UN docs. E/CN.6/184, 4, 8, and E/CN.6/S.R.71, 83.
[17] The Convention signed at Bogotá in 1948 provided, 'The High Contracting Parties agree that the right to vote and to be elected to national office shall not be denied or abridged by reason of sex'.
[18] By the time the Covenants were drafted, the Universal Declaration had probably achieved the status of customary international law, and the Covenants must to some extent be considered codificatory; thus the Universal Declaration contains binding principles of law even among states which have not ratified the Covenants and between states which have signed and states which have not, in their relations *inter se*.

human rights instruments stand for equality, progress, and civilization. They answer a deep-seated longing for universal recognition in law, as well as in fact, of the equality of all men not only as members of an organic species with common biological needs, but as moral and social beings with common psychological wants and common requirements inherent in the nature of any human society.[19]

2. Genocide

Although it has been argued that the Genocide Convention should not be classified as a convention for the protection of human rights but as one for the preservation of international peace,[20] it is intimately connected with the principle of individual equality in its negative aspect, the prevention of discrimination. It seeks to prevent the most severe form of discrimination—the physical destruction of persons on the ground that they belong to certain national, ethnic, racial, or religious groups. As the International Court of Justice stated in its advisory opinion on *Reservations to the Genocide Convention*, 'The Convention was manifestly adopted for a purely humanitarian and civilizing purpose. It is indeed difficult to imagine a convention which might have this dual character to a greater degree, since its object on the one hand is to safeguard the very existence of certain human groups and on the other to confirm and endorse the most elementary principles of morality.'[21]

Its purpose was, however, limited to preventing the destruction of groups—it did not seek to guarantee their equality in any positive

---

[19] Moskowitz, 83. The measures of implementation adopted in the various conventions will not be discussed here. See particularly E. Schwelb, 'The International Convention on the Elimination of All Forms of Racial Discrimination', 15 *ICLQ* (1966), 996, 1031–57; *Mélanges offerts à Polys Modinos* (Éditions Pedone, Paris, 1968), 270; 62 *AJIL* (1968), 827: also M. E. Tardu, *Human Rights: The International Petition System* (1979–80); A. R. Wilkoc, 1–2 *N. Y. Univ. Jo. of Int. Law and Politics* (1968–9), 277; K. Das and others, 4 *Human Rights Jo.* (1971), 207 ff.; P. Schaffer and D. Weissbrodt, 2 *Human Rights Jo.* (1969), 632; F. Capotorti, *Proceedings of the Nobel Symposium on the International Protection of Human Rights* (Oslo, 1967); L. B. Sohn, The United Nations and Human Rights, 18th report of the Commission to Study the Organization of Peace (1968), 120 ff.; A. Cassesse, 5 *Human Rights Jo.* (1972), 375; L. B. Sohn and T. Buergenthal, *International Protection of Human Rights* (Bobbs-Merrill, Indianapolis, 1973).

[20] A. K. Kuhn, 'The Genocide Convention and State Rights', 43 *AJIL* (1949), 498–9.

[21] ICJ. Rep. 1951, 23. (See also comments of Myres S. McDougal and R. Arens, 'Genocide Convention and the Constitution', 3 *Vanderbilt* L. R. (1950), 683; and E. I. Daës in *Festschrift für Pan J. Zepos*, ii.82.)

sense.[22] It is not proposed to examine the Genocide Convention in detail,[23] but merely to examine its relevance to the prevention of discrimination and protection of minorities. What is clear is that the Convention does not itself create the international crime of genocide—it merely spells out in detail the particular acts which parties to the convention undertake to prevent and punish. The International Court has said that the principles underlying the Convention are principles which are recognized by civilized nations as binding on states, even without any conventional obligation.[24] The interest taken by the United Nations in the problem of genocide originated from the influence of Professor Lemkin, who coined the expression 'genocide'.[25] At its first session in 1946 the General Assembly unanimously adopted Resolution 96 (I): The General Assembly,

Affirms that genocide is a crime under international law which the civilized world condemns and for the commission of which principals and accomplices, whether private individuals, public officials or statesmen, and whether the crime is committed on religious, racial, political or any other grounds, are punishable;

Invites the member states to enact the necessary legislation for the prevention and punishment of this crime;

Recommends that international co-operation be organized between states with a view to facilitating the speedy prevention and punishment of the crime of genocide, and to this end,

[22] GAOR, 3rd sess., 6th comm., 75th meeting (15 Oct. 1948), 110, 111, 114. The Polish representative said: 'The Convention on Genocide must seek to protect human beings whatever the colour of their skin, the god they worshipped and the national groups to which they belonged. Those who needed protection most were those who could not alter their status. For them the idea of equality was of the very greatest importance.'

[23] See Drost, op. cit.; Robinson, *The Genocide Convention* R. Lemkin, 'Genocide as a Crime under International Law', 41 *AJIL* (1947), 145, and 'Genocide' in 15 *The American Scholar*, no. 2, (1946); Anonymous Contribution, 'Genocide: A Commentary on the Convention', 58 *Yale L. J.* (1948–9), 1142; Oppenheim, i.745 ff., 914; P. B. Perelman, 'Genocide Convention', 30 *Nebraska* L. R. (1950), 1; J. L. Kunz, 'The United Nations Convention on Genocide', 43 *AJIL* (1949), 738; Myres S. McDougal and R. Arens, 'The Genocide Convention and the Constitution', 3 *Vanderbilt* L. R. (1950), 683; UN publication, *The Crime of Genocide: A United Nations Convention aimed at preventing destruction of groups and punishing those responsible*, 4th ed. (1956), UN doc. UN ST DPI (O2) G.32; US Department of State publication no. 341 6 (1949); also the extensive bibliography in Robinson, 153–8; and UN doc. E/CN.4/Sub.2/416.

[24] *Reservations to Genocide Convention*, ICJ Rep. 1951, 23. See also Rosenne, *Yearbook of the ILC* (1963), 74.

[25] From the Greek 'genos' and the Latin 'cide'. See R. Lemkin, 'Genocide' in 90 *The American Scholar* (1946), no. 2, and 'Genocide as a Crime under International Law', 41 *AJIL* (1947), 145.

Requests the Economic and Social Council to undertake the necessary studies with a view to drawing up a draft convention on the crime of genocide to be submitted to the next regular session of the General Assembly.

Consequently, the Economic and Social Council instructed the Secretary-General to prepare, with the assistance of experts, a draft convention which was transmitted to governments for comment[26] and submitted to the General Assembly which reaffirmed that genocide was an international crime entailing national and international responsibility on the part of individuals and states.[27] The Council thereupon established an *ad hoc* committee to draw up a draft convention and this was transmitted to the General Assembly's third session.[28]

The Assembly's Legal Committee did not refer the draft to the International Law Commission but proceeded with it itself.[29] Article I provided 'The Contracting Parties confirm that genocide is a crime under international law whether committed in time of peace or of war which they undertake to prevent and punish.'

Some representatives, believed that, if genocide was already a crime, Article I would not add anything substantive and should either be deleted or transferred to the Preamble, but Soviet motions to this effect were defeated.[30] It was generally agreed that, although General Assembly resolutions were not mandatory and could not proclaim new rules of law, its resolutions could affirm already existing law and as such were binding on members, particularly if adopted unanimously, and this view appears to have been accepted by the International Court of Justice.[31]

Article II defines genocide for the purposes of the Convention as 'any of the following acts committed with intent to destroy in whole or in part, a national, ethnical, racial or religious group as such: (a) Killing members of the group; (b) Causing serious bodily or mental

[26] Res. 47 (IV) adopted on 28 Mar. 1947; see UN doc. E/447, and Res. 77 (V) (6 Aug. 1947).

[27] GA Res. 180 (II) (21 Nov. 1947), and GA Res. 174 (II).

[28] See ECOSOC Res. 117 (VI) (3 Mar. 1948), UN doc. E/794, ECOSOC OR 7th sess., 3rd year, supp. no. 6; also ECOSOC Res. 153 (VII), (28 Aug. 1948).

[29] UN doc. A/PV.142; GAOR, 3rd sess., 6th comm., 63rd meeting ff. (For a full account of the drafting history of the Convention, see Drost, op. cit., 1–7.) See UN docs. E/CN.4/136 and E/CN.4/S.R.76.

[30] GAOR., 3rd sess., 6th comm., 4–5, 51; also UN doc. A/C6/256.

[31] See in particular the views of the Polish and Czech representatives, 6th comm., op. cit., 45–6; also those of M. Kaeckenbeeck (Belgium), ibid., 22.

harm to members of the group; (c) Deliberately inflicting on the group conditions of life calculated to bring about its physical destruction in whole or in part; (d) Imposing measures intended to prevent births within the group; (e) Forcibly transferring children of the group to another group.' The question of definition caused substantial controversy.

First, it was disputed whether or not political groups should be protected under the first paragraph. Although political groups had been included in General Assembly Resolution 96 (I) this did not require them to be protected under the Convention, which left the General Assembly free to decide what groups were to be brought within its scope. One argument against the inclusion of political groups distinguished natural status acquired by accident of birth from types of status which could be discarded at will—the Convention should protect the former but not the latter.[32] No substantial reasons were adduced for this view except that political groups were said to be difficult to identify. That the distinction is unsound is illustrated by the fact that religious groups were included, whereas linguistic groups which are 'natural' rather than a matter of choice were excluded.[33] Nevertheless, political groups were not included in the first paragraph, an omission which left a serious gap in the Convention.

The groups referred to in Article II are 'national, ethnical, racial, or religious'.[34] The exact meaning of 'national group' was never clarified, and it has been objected that 'ethnical' adds little to 'racial'. The former term is preferable to the latter, the correct application of which is highly controversial.[35]

Secondly, a major question which faced the Sixth Committee was whether or not to include 'cultural' genocide. The Secretariat had included a Draft Article III:[36]

[32] 6th comm., op. cit., 60, 99, 101, 111, 115.

[33] Drost, 23, submits that difference of language as the distinctive and offensive characteristic of a persecuted minority does not seem likely to occur apart from disparity of religious tenets and principles, diversity of national character, and inspirations or dissimilarities of racial features and colour of skin. It would seem that the *Belgian Linguistics* case belies this view. See below, ch. 12.

[34] Mr. Kaeckenbeeck (Belgium) pointed out that the wording used was derived from the minorities treaties. (6th comm., op. cit., 116.) An American amendment to add economic and similar groups (UN doc. A/C6/214) was not accepted.

[35] Drost, 62. Are Jews for instance a racial group? Cf. *Mills* v. *Cooper* [1967] 2 QB, 459; *King-Ansell* v. *Police* [1979] 2 NZLR, 531 (NZ Court of Appeal); See in particular the judgment of Richardson J. at 540.

[36] UN doc. E/447.

In this Convention, genocide also means any deliberate act committed with intent to destroy the language, religion or culture of a national, racial or religious group on the grounds of the national or racial origin or religious belief of its members such as: (1) Prohibiting the use of the language of the group in daily intercourse or in schools, or the printing and circulation of publications in the language of the group; (2) Destroying or preventing the use of libraries, museums, schools, historical institutions and objects of the group.

Cultural genocide was included by a large majority in the *Ad Hoc* Committee but rejected by the General Assembly. Some delegations supported the draft article on the grounds that 'cultural genocide' aimed at the destruction of a group of human beings as such. It did not destroy the group physically but it insidiously abolished all its differentiating cultural characteristics and was therefore just as effective in the long term.[37] On the other side it was argued for several reasons that genocide should be defined strictly to mean the physical destruction of human groups. First, there was an essential difference between cultural genocide and genocide as defined in Article II,[38] and it showed a lack of logic and sense of proportion to include in the same convention, both mass murders in gas chambers and the closing of libraries;[39] second, 'cultural genocide' fell within the sphere of human rights or rights of minorities.[40] Cultural genocide might encompass acts which should be earnestly condemned and an international treaty or declaration could be drawn up to deal with the matter specifically, but the Genocide Convention was not the proper instrument for this purpose. There was sympathy for the aims of Draft Article III but not for the method;[41] thirdly, it was felt that the notion of cultural genocide was too vague and indefinite for a convention defining criminal acts, and might give rise to abuses. It would be difficult, for example, to estimate the scope of education policy.[42]

Eventually it was decided to draw the Third Committee's attention to the need for the protection of language, religion, and culture within the framework of an international declaration on human

[37] The principal holders of this view were the Soviet bloc countries, plus China, Pakistan, and Venezuela, (6th comm., op. cit., 193–5, 202, 205; also GAOR, 3rd sess., vol. i.)

[38] 6th comm., op. cit., 200, 203 (USA); also GAOR, 3rd sess., (plenary) i.821 (USA).

[39] As the Danish representative succinctly put it, 6th comm., op. cit., 199.

[40] Ibid., 197, 201, 203, 205–6, plenary sess., op. cit., 837.

[41] 6th comm., op. cit., 197–204.　　　　　　　　　　　　　　　　[42] Ibid.

rights, and the draft article was deleted.[43] This was the correct decision, not because the object of the proposed article was at fault, but because the Genocide Convention was not the ideal instrument in which to include specific measures to protect minorities.[44]

The requirement for a subjective element in Article II has been bitterly criticized in that it would enable those accused of genocide to escape punishment by claiming that there was no *mens rea*. Proposals to replace 'committed with intent to destroy' by objective words such as 'resulting in the destruction of' were criticized on the grounds that this would make it impossible to distinguish between genocide, ordinary murder, and war crimes.[45] One writer has claimed that the failure to condemn attempts against the lives of human groups in objective terms meant that the convention had failed in its purpose and would never achieve the slightest impact or effectiveness.[46]

Article III of the Convention, as finally adopted, lists the acts which shall be punishable: (a) genocide; (b) conspiracy to commit genocide; (c) direct and public incitement to commit genocide; (d) attempt to commit genocide (e) complicity in genocide. A Soviet amendment in the Sixth Committee to add a paragraph penalizing all forms of public propaganda aimed at provoking genocide was rejected.[47] Under Article IV persons committing genocide or any of the other acts enumerated in Article III shall be punished, whether they are constitutionally responsible rulers, public officials, or private individuals. Persons charged with genocide are to be tried by competent tribunals of the state in the territory of which the act was committed, or 'by such international penal tribunal as may have jurisdiction with respect to those Contracting Parties which shall have accepted its jurisdiction'.[48]

---

[43] 6th comm., op. cit., 206; UN doc. A/C6/216.

[44] Amendments to reintroduce protection against cultural genocide were rejected in plenary session. UN docs. A/770, A/766; plenary sess., op. cit., 847–8. A defeated Venezuelan amendment would have narrowed the concept of cultural genocide to the protection of three matters: religious edifices, schools, and libraries. Drost, 43, describes 'cultural genocide' as a 'far-fetched expression for a far removed subject'.

[45] See GAOR, 3rd sess., pt. 1, 6th comm., 73rd meeting. Also Drost, op. cit., 82; E/CN.4/Sub.2/416, 26.

[46] N. Jacobs, 'A propos de la définition juridique du génocide', *Études internationales de psycho-sociologie criminelle* (1969), nos. 16–17, 56.

[47] The amendment was in two parts: the first was more an anti-discrimination than an anti-genocide measure. It provided that all forms of public propaganda (press, radio, cinema, etc.) aimed at inciting racial, national, or religious hatred should be penalized. The second provided that all acts of public propaganda aimed at provoking acts of genocide should be penalized. Both were rejected. (6th comm., op. cit., 254.)

[48] Arts. 5 and 6; plenary sess., op. cit., 848; UN doc A/766.

The Convention was unanimously adopted by the General Assembly on 9 December 1948, the day before the adoption of the Universal Declaration of Human Rights.[49] A second resolution invited the International Law Commission to study the desirability and possibility of establishing an international judicial organ for the trial of persons charged with genocide[50] but, in 1957, the General Assembly deferred consideration of the question until it took up again the question of defining aggression and the question of a draft code of offences against the peace and security of mankind.[51] Nevertheless, measures have been taken to encourage states to implement the Genocide Convention and furnish information on implementation.[52]

An up-to-date study of the whole question was submitted to the Sub-Commission in 1978 by a special rapporteur.[53] Among his recommendations was a proposal that an *ad hoc* committee should be set up to investigate allegations of genocide brought to the knowledge of the Commission by member states or international organizations if supported by sufficient prima-facie evidence. Appropriate new instruments could be adopted to improve the effectiveness of the existing convention which was only a point of departure. The 1973 Convention on apartheid had already entered into force and the Declaration and Convention on Religious Intolerance, 'one of the decisive causes of genocide' should be accelerated. Articles VI and IX were seen to be largely ineffective and, in the absence of an International Criminal Court, the adoption of the principle of universal jurisdiction was argued. This would offer the choice between extradition to the country where the crime was alleged to have been committed and jurisdiction by the state on whose territory the indicted person was found. A protocol providing for this solution was favoured by some states as an interim measure until an international penal tribunal could be established but it was also pointed that the goal could be achieved merely by national

---

[49] GA Res. 260 (III) A. See 78 UNTS, 277. The Convention entered into force on 12 Jan. 1951.

[50] Ga Res. 260 (III) B.   [51] GA Res. 1187 (XII).

[52] e.g. The International Association for the Prevention of Crime, at its Second International Conference in Paris, 10–13 July 1967, recommended more education measures relating to the equality of rights of all races and the irrational nature of discrimination. See G. Lavasseur, 'The Prevention of Genocide', 8 *Journal of the International Commission of Jurists* (1967), 76, 80. See also UN docs. E/CN.4/Sub.2/ rev.1; E/CN.4/Sub.2/S.R.516–19; E/CN.4/Sub.2/L.479; E/CN.4/Sub.2/S.R.516 and 519.   [53] Mr. Nicodème Ruhashyaniko. UN doc. E/CN.4/Sub.2/416.

legislation. Recent conventions on apartheid, hijacking, and internationally protected persons have all provided for universal jurisdiction.[54] Universal jurisdiction is not an ideal solution since it could lead to differences of interpretation by state courts but it is the best that can be achieved until a universally recognized international criminal court can be established.

The interest of the Sub-Commission in the question emphasizes the organic connection of genocide with the principle of individual equality. In the words of the famous French jurist René Cassin, racial discrimination not only denies freedom and equality to members of another group but on what appear to be the most plausible grounds it develops into genocide under all its forms.[55] As the President of the General Assembly pointed out on the adoption of the Convention in 1948, fundamental rights had formerly been protected by international conventions against piracy, the slave trade, and traffic in women and children. The Convention on Genocide protected the fundamental right of a human group to exist as a group; by approving it, the General Assembly had in accordance with Article 13 of the Charter, promoted 'the progressive development of international law and its codification'.[56]

3. *Apartheid*

The desirability of an international penal tribunal and of extending the scope of universal jurisdiction was also canvassed in the discussion on punishing apartheid. This matter, which greatly concerned the United Nations political organs from their inception, was referred to an *ad hoc* group of experts to be studied from the point of view of international penal law. In its 1972 report[57] it was accepted that penal international law, though still a customary unwritten law in the process of formation, was an essential part of public international law.[58] It is the discipline which, with a view to the defence of

[54] Ibid., 47–56. See UN Resolutions 3068 (XXVIII) and 3166 (XXVIII), and the ICAO Conventions on the Suppression of Unlawful Seizure of Aircraft, 1970, and Suppression of Unlawful Acts against the Safety of Civil Aviation, 1971.

[55] R. Cassin, 'Twenty Years after the Universal Declaration: Freedom and Equality', in 8 *Journal of the International Law Commission* (1967), 1.

[56] Plenary sess., op. cit., 852 (Dr. Evatt).

[57] UN doc. E/CN.4/1075 (15 Feb. 1972). The report was prepared by Mr Ermacora (Austria).

[58] J. Graven, 'Les Crimes Contre l'Humanité' 76 *Receuil des Cours* (1950), i.433. Similarly, P. Guggenheim, *Lehrbuch des Völkerrechts* (Verlag für Recht und Gesellschaft, Basel, 1951), ii.541, and A. Verdross, *Völkerrecht*, (Springer, Vienna, 5th ed. 1964), 220.

international order, defines crimes against the peace and security of mankind, provides for their punishment, and lays down the rules governing the responsibility of individuals, states, and other legal entities.[59] It was accepted that these crimes need not be enumerated in conventions in order to be punishable, so long as they were already deemed criminal under general international law. Some crimes had been enumerated since the Nuremberg and Tokyo Trials and in General Assembly Resolution 95 (I), and were set out in the Genocide Convention and the 1949 Geneva Conventions. Failure to ratify these conventions, however, would not mean that a state was free from obligations under international penal law, for these exist independently of the conventions in question, as was pointed out in the *Genocide* case. The report noted that the Convention on the Non-Applicability of Statutory Limitations to War Crimes and Crimes Against Humanity described 'inhuman acts resulting from the policies of apartheid' as a form of crime against humanity and as crimes under international law.

The question then was to determine what acts are inhuman acts which may be considered crimes under international law. Although many General Assembly resolutions had condemned apartheid policies as crimes against humanity these were not strictly legal texts and did not usually particularize the acts condemned. Constant repetition and reiteration of the resolutions would, however, give rise to a nascent customary law. The group of experts suggested how the crimes could be defined *rationae personae* and *rationae materiae* but recommended that the terms should be clearly defined by the General Assembly in a revised genocide convention[60] and should include acts of cultural genocide. Since an international penal court did not yet exist, prosecution and punishment had to be left to national bodies, which made jurisdiction over states virtually impossible and raised strong doubts as to the effectiveness of international penal law in general.

Instead of revising the Genocide Convention, however, the General Assembly decided to draft a separate Convention and Protocol on Suppressing and Punishing the Crime of Apartheid,[61] a course which gave rise to considerable opposition. The United States

[59] S. Glaser, *Droit international pénal conventionnel* (Bruylant, Brussels, 1970), 165.   [60] See UN doc. E/CN.4/984/add.18.
[61] UN docs. E/CN.4/1111, A/9003, and A/9095 and add.1; ECOSOC OR, 54th sess., supp. no. 6 (XX). See also GA Res. 2786 (XXVI) and 2922 (XXVII), and ECOSOC Res. 1784 (LIV).

expressed misgivings about the use of international conventions to achieve political ends, however desirable, but also claimed that the matter was adequately covered by the racial discrimination and genocide conventions. Also, while deploring apartheid as a travesty of human rights, the United States did not accept the assumption of the draft convention that apartheid was already generally regarded as a crime against humanity.[62] Such crimes were so grave that at the current stage their legal definition must be strictly construed. Other states whose populations included racial minorities expressed reservation about the extension of the meaning of apartheid in the draft.

The term 'crime of apartheid' is generally defined in Article II as including similar policies and principles of racial segregation and discrimination to those practised in Southern Africa and in particular a list of 'inhuman acts' committed for the purpose of establishing and maintaining the dominance by one racial group of persons over any other racial group of persons.

This definition was attacked as ambiguous, as lacking clarity and judicial precision, and for covering forms of racial discrimination other than apartheid. Other legal arguments were directed to Article IV, which required state parties to adopt legislative and other measures to bring to trial and punish those guilty of the crime of apartheid. Several states claimed that they could only legislate extraterritorially in rare cases, e.g. piracy, and that they were unable to accept the legitimacy of provisions which purported to authorize states to exercise penal jurisdiction in respect of acts committed outside their jurisdiction by persons not their nationals. As one delegate pointed out, to extend criminal jurisdiction in this manner, or to agree that others were entitled to do so in the absence of an established international criminal jurisdiction, would be to allow of the possibility that, by simply drawing up a treaty to which they were all parties, a small group of states could assume power to declare an act an international crime and enforce the treaty regardless of the attitude of the rest of the international community.[63] Nevertheless, as the Permanent Court stated in the *Lotus* case,[64] far from laying down a general prohibition to the effect that states may not extend the application of their laws and the jurisdiction of their

[62] GAOR, 23rd sess., 3rd comm., 2002–8th meetings.
[63] Miss Williams (New Zealand); UN doc. E/AC7/S.R.719.
[64] PCIJ ser. A, no. 10. And see *Israel* v. *Eichmann* (1961), 36 ILR, 5; 56 *AJIL*, 805, 808.

courts to persons, property, and acts outside their territory, international law leaves them in this respect a wide measure of discretion which is only limited in certain cases by prohibitive rules. The principle of universal jurisdiction has recently been accepted without much protest for hijacking, war crimes,[65] and crimes against diplomats in addition to piracy. If it is correct that the right to punish war crimes 'is not confined to the state whose nationals have suffered or on whose territory the offence took place but is possessed by any independent state whatsoever, just as is the right to punish the offence of piracy'[66] then it is not a large step to accept that other acts repeatedly declared to be international crimes or crimes against humanity are not so confined. However, the combined weight of the objections, particularly from states possessing common law systems and the Nordic states, indicates that the principle of universality is not yet generally regarded as extending so far.

Another stumbling-block was Article IX which purported to confer duties on the Commission on Human Rights, since it was doubted whether the parties were competent to direct or increase the work load of existing United Nations bodies. Moreover, the Commission might find itself in the difficult position of supervising the implementation of an instrument which most of its members had not acceded to and did not support.

It is difficult to escape the conclusion that the convention was drafted too hastily and without adequate legal assistance. Proposals to refer the draft to the International Law Commission or to the Sixth (Legal) Committee were not proceeded with, the former showing little concern in the matter. Although the ILC President[67] noted 'with deep interest' the recommendation of the *ad hoc* working group that inhuman acts resulting from apartheid should be made subject to sanctions by means of an international convention and 'warmly supported' United Nations efforts to bring about wider participation in humanitarian conventions and observance of their provisions, there was no suggestion that the ILC should examine the convention although it was being drafted at the time.[68] It is

[65] See the *Amelo* trial, UN War Crimes Commission, 1 *Law Reports of Trials of War Criminals*, 35; *Zyklon B* case, ibid., 93; *Hadamar* trial, ibid., 46; Geneva Conventions 1949, 75 UNTS, 62, 116, 236, 386. Also W. B. Cowles, 'Universality of Jurisdiction over War Crimes', 33 *Calif. L. R.* (1945), 177 ff.; and A. R. Carnegie, 'Jurisdiction over Violations of the Laws and Customs of War', 39 *BYIL*, 402.

[66] As the UN War Crimes Commission states, 15 *Law Reports of Trial of War Criminals* (1949), 26.   [67] Prof. Castaneda.

[68] See report of the ILC, 25th sess., 1973, A/9010/rev.1.

curious that the ILC 'would not have time' to consider the study in depth and this abdication of responsibility may be blamed for many of the defects in the Convention, which entered into force on 18 July 1976.[69]

In 1977 the General Assembly considered a report of an *ad hoc* committee on an international convention against apartheid in sport[70] and proclaimed a declaration on the subject and requested the Committee to draft a convention. This would *inter alia* forbid sporting contact with countries practising apartheid, require the refusal of finance or assistance to teams, individuals, or sporting bodies and set up an international commission against apartheid in sport.

4. *Slavery*

Slavery was one of the first subjects involving the denial of fundamental human rights to be dealt with by treaty. A large number of bilateral treaties were concluded during the nineteenth century,[71] and in 1926 a general convention on slavery was prepared under the auspices of the League of Nations.[72] In addition, an *ad hoc* committee on Slavery was set up by the Economic and Social Council in 1949 to take note of 'information received from many sources which indicated that other forms of servitude, in addition to slavery and the slave trade, existed to a considerable extent in many parts of the world'.[73] In its 1951 report the *ad hoc* committee, though accepting the definitions of slavery and the slave trade contained in Article 1 of the 1926 Convention,[74] questioned whether these definitions

---

[69] The Convention had 35 signatures followed by 25 ratifications and 20 accessions at 1 Sept. 1978. This was less than one third of UN membership.

[70] See GAOR, 33rd sess., supp. no. 36 (A/33/36); GA Res. 31/6/F and 32/105m.

[71] See Lord Halsbury, *Statutes of England*, 2nd ed. (1951), xxv.1015.

[72] 60 LNTS, 253. See also UN publication E.68 XIV.6, 41. The Convention came into force on 9 Mar. 1927. (Article 22 of the League of Nations Covenant stated *inter alia* that the mandatories were to be responsible for the prohibition of abuses such as the slave trade.)   [73] UN doc. E/1454. ECOSOC Res. 238 (IX).

[74] Slavery is defined in Article 1 of the 1926 Convention as 'the condition of a person over whom any or all of the powers attaching to the right of ownership are exercised'. The slave trade included 'all acts involved in the capture, acquisition or disposal of a person with intent to reduce him to slavery: all acts involved in the acquisition of a slave with a view to selling him or exchanging him: all acts of disposal by sale or exchange of a slave acquired with a view to being sold or exchanged, and, in general, every act of trade or transport in slaves'. See Secretariat memorandum, *The Suppression of Slavery* (1951).

embraced all the types of servile status the abolition of which should be promoted by the United Nations.[75]

In 1953 the General Assembly approved a protocol prepared by the Secretary-General under which states would agree to transfer the functions of the League under the 1926 Convention to the United Nations.[76] The Economic and Social Council noted a report from the Secretariat concerning the desirability of a supplementary convention on slavery,[77] and in 1955 appointed an *ad hoc* committee to draft a supplementary convention on slavery and servitude.[78] A conference of plenipotentiaries subsequently adopted the Supplementary Convention on the Abolition of Slavery, the Slave Trade, and Institutions and Practices Similar to Slavery, and opened it for signature and ratification.[79] The Supplementary Convention is particularly relevant to the equality principle because it spells out in detail certain types of status which are invidious and illegal under international law. An attempt had been made to enumerate types of conditions resembling slavery in the 1926 Convention but these were omitted on the grounds that the conditions listed came within the definition of slavery in Article 1 and no further enumeration was necessary.[80]

The types of status to be completely abolished or abandoned 'progressively and as soon as possible' are enumerated in Article 1: (a) debt bondage, or the status or condition arising from a pledge by a debtor of his personal services or those of a person under his control as security for a debt; (b) serfdom, which is the status of a tenant who is by law, custom or agreement, bound to live and labour on land belonging to another person and to render some determinate service to such other person whether for reward or not, and is not free to change his status; (c) any institution or principle

[75] UN doc. E/1988 (4 Apr. 1951).
[76] GA Res. 794 (VIII). (In accordance with ECOSOC Res. 475 (XV)).
[77] UN doc. E/2540; ECOSOC Res. 525 A (XVII). The report of Mr Engen (the special rapporteur) is contained in UN doc. E/2673/add.1–5); UN docs. E/2540/add.4 and E/AC.43/L.1; and ECOSOC Res. 525 B (XVII).
[78] ECOSOC Res. 564 (XIX) (7 Apr. 1955); UN doc. E/2824 (15 Feb. 1956).
[79] ECOSOC Res. 608 (XXI); UN doc. E/Conf.24/S.R.24; 266 UNTS, 3; also UN publication E.68 XIV, 6, 44. The Convention came into force on 30 April 1957. For the Final Act of the Conference, see UN doc. E/Conf./24/23. Also UN doc. E/Conf.24/S.R.1–24. See generally J. A. C. Gutteridge, 'Supplementary Slavery Convention 1956', 6 *ICLQ* (1957), 449.
[80] Debt slavery, sham adoption, childhood marriage, traffic in women, etc. See Secretariat memorandum, *The Suppression of Slavery* (1956), 16; and *L. of N. O.J.*, 7th sess., of the Assembly, 44 *O.J. Sp. Supp.*, 416.

whereby (i) a woman, without the right to refuse, is promised or is given in marriage on payment or consideration, (ii) the husband of a woman, his family or his clan has the right to transfer her to another person for value received, or (iii) a widow on the death of her husband is liable to be inherited by another person; (d) any institution or procedure whereby a child or young person under the age of eighteen is delivered to another person whether for reward or not with a view to the exploitation of the child or young person or of his labour.

Article 2 provides that, with a view to bringing to an end the institutions and practices mentioned in 1 (c), the states parties undertake to prescribe, where appropriate, suitable minimum ages of marriage, and to encourage facilities whereby the consent of both parties to the marriage is freely expressed in the presence of competent civil or religious authorities, and to encourage registration of marriages.[81]

This matter was taken up by the Commission on the Status of Women which prepared a draft convention on consent to marriage, minimum age for marriage, and registration of marriage[82] which was adopted by the General Assembly in 1962.[83] A further recommendation on the subject, adopted by the General Assembly in 1965, requested member states to take legislative action to specify the minimum age for marriage, which in any case should not be less than fifteen.[84]

There was a division of opinion over whether the institutions and practices dealt with in the Supplementary Convention should be

---

[81] Other important articles of the Supplementary Convention include Article 3 under which the parties undertake that the slave trade is to be a criminal offence under their laws; Article 4 under which any slave taking refuge on a vessel of a state party is to be considered *ipso facto* free; Article 5 which provides that mutilating, branding, or otherwise marking a slave or a person of servile status shall be a criminal offence liable to punishment, under the laws of the states parties; Article 6 which makes criminal under the laws of the states parties the act of enslaving, inducing slavery, or conspiracy to enslave; Article 9 which does not permit reservations; Article 10 which provides for disputes to be submitted to the ICJ; Article 12 under which the Convention is to apply to all non-self-governing, trust, colonial, and other non-metropolitan territories. (Cf. also art. 22 (b) of the Convention on the High Seas, 1958.)

[82] See UN doc. E/3360, report of 14th sess., of the Commission on the Status of Women, ch. 4.

[83] See the 1140–8th meetings of the 3rd comm., GAOR, 17th sess., 3rd comm.; UN doc. A/5273, para. 66; 521 UNTS, 231. The Convention came into force on 9 Dec. 1964.

[84] GA Res. 2018 (XX) (6 Oct. 1955); see UN doc. A/Conf.32/4, P.88 (Principle II).

abolished at once or progressively. Some representatives felt that the words 'progressively and' would weaken the article but the view which prevailed was that the immediate abolition of such practices would cause 'considerable disorganization'.[85] As it turned out the decision to make the Convention merely promotional was extremely unfortunate and provided excuses for dilatoriness.[86] Moreover, it hardly seems that the possibility that 'disorganization may ensure' is relevant when basic human rights to equality and liberty are in issue.[87]

Despite its imperfections, the Convention was an important step forward in the progressive realization of the principle of equality of individuals by providing for the removal of degrading types of status by which a person is subject to the control and will of another. Had the Supplementary Convention been prepared more recently it is likely that other examples of practices similar to slavery would have also been included. Recent resolutions adopted by United Nations organs on the question of slavery and the slave trade have added the phrase 'including the slavery-like practices of apartheid and colonialism'.[88] In 1968 the Council authorized the Sub-Commission to study measures which might be taken to implement the 1926 and 1956 Conventions and the recommendations included in other United Nations resolutions concerning the slavery-like practices of apartheid and colonialism. It also called for the total eradication of these latter practices as practised particularly in Rhodesia, South West Africa, and South Africa, and affirmed that the master and servant laws currently enforced in these countries constituted clear manifestations of slavery.[89]

[85] UN doc. E/2824, 17–18. The words 'progressively and as soon as possible' were inserted in the 1926 Convention because 'it was recognized that in certain cases in the past the attempt to do away with slavery and similar conditions in an abrupt manner, although noble in its inspiration, had resulted in unforeseen hardships for the individuals whose condition it was sought to alleviate, and even in grave social upheavals'. See 44 O.J. Sp.Supp. (1926), 416.

[86] Cf. the result of the 'with all deliberate speed' decision in *Brown* v. *Board of Education*, below, ch. 15.

[87] The Geneva Conference adopted Article 1 of the Convention as 'Each of the States Parties to the Convention shall take all practicable and necessary legislative and other measures to bring about progressively and as soon as possible the complete abolition of the following institutions and practices.'

[88] See e.g. CHR Res. 13 (XXIII); ECOSOC OR, 42nd sess., supp. no. 6 (UN doc. E/4322), 209; CHR Res. 14 (XXIV); ECOSOC OR, 44th sess., supp. no. 4 (UN doc. E/4475) ch. 18; ECOSOC Res. 1330 (XLIV) (31 May 1968); ECOSOC OR, 44th sess., supp. no. 1 (Resolutions), UN doc. E/4548.

[89] Res. 1330 (XLIV), 31 May 1968. ECOSOC OR 44th sess., supp. no. 1, (Resolutions), UN doc. E/4548.

Thus United Nations organs gradually came to the view that certain types of racial discrimination were manifestly akin to slavery. Other conventions on practices similar to slavery include the Forced Labour Convention, 1930,[90] and the Abolition of Forced Labour Convention, 1957, in which compulsory labour is forbidden *inter alia* for the purpose of racial, social, national, or religious discrimination.[91] In addition, Article 4 of the European Convention on Human Rights prohibits slavery or servitude and forced or compulsory labour[92] as does Article 8 of the Covenant on Civil and Political Rights, 1966.[93]

Although these instruments demonstrate substantial progress in the progressive realization of the principle of equality of individuals, since they prohibit *pro futuro* those degrading types of status by which a person is subjected to the control and will of another, the problem of enforcement remained. The 1971 study[94] suggested somewhat tentatively that 'at the proper time' the United Nations might find it convenient to consider a consolidated convention aimed at eradicating all forms of servile status and establishing an international supervisory body with functions similar to those of the International Narcotics Control Board. In the meantime, better co-operation with Interpol and the adoption by states of measures ensuring strict and severe punishment for serious offences were advocated. As a consequence the Sub-Commission was directed to

[90] Article 2 (1) of the Convention defines 'forced or compulsory labour' as 'all work or service which is extracted from any person under the menace of a penalty and for which the said person has not offered himself voluntarily'. However, work or service carried out as part of normal civic obligations, in execution of a penal sentence or in national emergency is not prohibited. See also the report of the UN/ILO *Ad Hoc* Committee on Forced Labour (1953), UN doc. E/2431, and reports of the ILO Committee on Forced Labour (1956), vi, no. 2, and (1957), iv, no. 2.

[91] I.L.O. Convention no. 105. Adopted by I.L.O. General Conference, 25 June 1957. See UN doc. A/Conf.32/4, 46–8. See also the Convention for the Suppression of the Traffic in Persons and the Exploitation of the Prostitution of Others, 1949. This convention was approved by the General Assembly in Resolution 317 (IV) on 2 Dec. 1949. (See Ibid., 48–51.) For the other conventions on traffic in persons and white slavery see UN docs. ST/LEG/SER.D/2, 137–154.

[92] See generally J. E. S. Fawcett, *The Application of the European Convention of Human Rights* (1969), 41–57; the *Iversen* case No. 1468/62, 6 *Yearbook of the European Convention on Human Rights, 278-332*. Article 4(3) provides that the term 'forced or compulsory labour' shall not include work done in the ordinary course of detention permitted under Article 5, nor military service, emergency services, or normal civic obligations.

[93] Article 8 (3) contains provisions obviously based on Article 4 (3) of the European Convention. See also the comments of the Secretary-General in UN doc. A/2929, 33–4. [94] UN doc. E/CN.4/Sub.2/322 (16 July 1971), para. 83.

examine the possibility of permanent machinery to advise on the elimination of slavery, and the suppression of traffic in persons and exploitation of prostitution, and the Secretary-General prepared a survey of national legislation on the issue.[95] It is regrettable that, despite this progress, no international body yet exists to receive and consider complaints from individuals claiming to be the victims of violations of the slavery conventions.

5. *Religious Belief: the Neglected Discrimination*

One of the first studies requested by the Sub-Commission was that on religious rights and practices[96] published in 1959, and religious intolerance was described in the Genocide Study as 'one of the decisive causes of genocide'.[97] Nevertheless, no other subject has been so shunned and neglected and the story of the drafting of instruments on the topic has been 'a tale punctuated by hypocrisy, procedural jockeying, and false starts'.[98] A declaration and convention on religious intolerance was requested by the General Assembly in 1962 at the same time as it called for similar instruments on racial discrimination, but although the latter were completed by 1965, the religious intolerance drafts were not acceptable to the Assembly.[99] One reason for the lack of progress was the curious 1967 decision of the General Assembly to call for the preparation of a convention before a declaration. This was a wholly illogical move since declarations, which are not binding and possess no enforcement procedures, are stated at a higher level of generality than conventions. A declaration would have assisted the resolution of controversial

---

[95] UN doc. E/CN.4/Sub.2/370 paras. 99, 114, 163; ECOSOC Res. 1695 (LII), paras. 6, 12, 13; UN docs. E/CN.4/Sub.2/327, E/CN.4/Sub.2/350, and E/CN.4/Sub.2/410.   [96] UN doc. E/CN.4/Sub.2/200/rev.1 (A. Krishnaswami)
[97] UN doc. E/CN.4/Sub.2/416 (N. Ruhashyankiko).
[98] R. S. Clark, 'The United Nations and Religious Freedom', *New York University Journal of International Law and Politics* (1978), 197–220; H. Jack, '58 words, Two Commas: Snail-like Motion Toward a UN Declaration for Religious Freedom' and 'The Human Rights Commission at Geneva' (1975), both reprinted in R. Woito, ed., *World Without War Council, International Human Rights Kit*, 154, 162; S. Neff, 'An Evolving International Norm of Religious Freedom: Problems and Prospects', 7 *Calif. Western Int. L.J.* (1977), 543; McDougal, Lasswell and Chen, 'The Right to Religious Freedom and World Public Order: The Emerging Norm of Non-discrimination'. 74 *Mich. L.R.* (1976), 865; J. Claydon, 'The Treaty Protection of Religious Rights: UN Draft Convention on the Elimination of All Forms of Intolerance and of Discrimination Based on Religion or Belief', 12 *Santa Clara Lawyer* (1972), 403.
[99] UN docs. A/6347; A/7777; A/7930; A/8330; A/9322; A/9134; E/CN.4/1145.

issues and the formation of a consensus among states and could have been followed by a convention in due course.[100] By the time the decision was reversed in 1973 much time had been wasted.

A working group was set up at each session of the Commission on Human Rights from 1974 in order to speed up the work, but in 1979 it was 'noted with regret'[101] that the Commission had so far adopted only the title and preamble of a draft declaration. It was pointed out in the Third Committee by the representative of the Holy See that although the question had been discussed for a third of a century and a consensus regarding the necessity for a convention existed, almost no progress had been achieved, and 'it was evident that certain forces were trying to prevent the declaration from becoming reality'.[102] In contrast to progress in other fields the working group had not even reached agreement on basic guidelines, and sixteen years after drafting commenced it could not even be agreed that Article 18 of the Civil and Political Rights Covenant should be the basis for Article 1 of the Declaration. Action by the United Nations had been neither prompt nor energetic and discrimination based on religion or belief was the 'neglected discrimination'.[103]

This failure reflects the complexity and confusion of the issues and the critical problem was that of defining the limits of the freedom. Although, since 1967, the drafts have included the words 'Intolerance and Discrimination based on Religion and Belief' in their titles to make it clear that they deal with non-theistic and atheistic as well as theistic beliefs, many matters remained highly controversial. States feared that religious divisions would be exacerbated if United Nations instruments gave substance to the vaguely worded provisions of the Universal Declaration and Covenant. A principal stumbling-block has been the controversial provisions concerning the way in which religious beliefs may be manifested.[104] Some states objected to a right to maintain places of worship which they claimed would encourage divisive proselytizing and threaten security.[105] Further differences arose over the right to withdraw children from state schools to obtain religious education

---

[100] Clark, 208.

[101] UN doc. A/C3/33/S.R.67. See GA Resolutions 1781 (XVII) (1962), 3027 (XXVII) (1972), 3069 (XXVIII) (1973), 3267 (XXIX) (1974), 31/138 (1976), 32/143 (1977), and 33/106 (1979).

[102] Cardinal Chelli, UN doc. A/C3/33/S.R.60, para. 115.

[103] UN docs. A/C3/33/S.R.60-7, and A/8330.

[104] Art. 3 (2) of the Draft Convention; UN docs. A/7930; A/8330.

[105] UN docs. A/C3/S.R.148, 6-8.

even though such provisions are already found in other instruments.[106]

It is regrettable that, at the end of the twentieth century, religious intolerance and bigotry should remain, as they have over the centuries, a prime cause of division between states. No topic has divided mankind more and it is unlikely that the United Nations will find acceptable solutions quickly.

[106] Art. 13 (3) and (4) of the Convenant on Economic, Social, and Cultural Rights; art. 5 of the Convention Against Discrimination in Education. Cf. the *Minority Schools in Albania* case, PCIJ (1935), ser. A/B no. 64.

VIII

THE CONVENTIONS AND DECLARATIONS (2)

1. *The Discrimination (Employment and Occupation) Convention, 1958*

SINCE it was generally considered that studies falling within the scope of the specialized agencies should normally be carried out by the agencies concerned, the study of discrimination in employment and occupation was placed on the International Labour Organization's agenda.[1] The guiding principle on discrimination is to be found in the Declaration of Philadelphia, 1944, at which the International Labour Conference confirmed that 'all human beings irrespective of race, creed or sex, have the right to pursue both their material well-being and their spiritual development in conditions of freedom and dignity, of economic security and equal opportunity'. In its preliminary report the ILO reviewed the progress to date and referred to the conclusions of the Sub-Commission and to the Secretary-General's memorandum on *The Main Types and Causes of Discrimination*,[2] noting that it was by no means easy to determine the extent in certain cases to which observable differences in treatment were caused by natural factors as opposed to artificial and discriminatory factors.[3] A trend since 1944 towards fuller implementation of the principle of equal opportunity for all and an evolution in public opinion was observed, and the report recommended specific and positive measures directed towards eradicating discrimination where it existed and promoting equality of treatment in the field of employment generally. Because national situations varied widely, any international instrument had to be conceived in the most flexible terms but at the same time administrative machinery was necessary. The grounds of discrimination enumerated in Article 2 (1) of the Universal Declaration were accepted as the basis for discussion.

[1] UN docs. E/CN.4/669 Res. A; E/CN.4/Sub.2/120; E/CN.4/Sub.2/156; and E/CN.4/703, Res. C; ECOSOC Res. 545 C (XVIII), 820th plenary meeting; I. L. Conf., 40th sess., report VII (1).

[2] UN doc. E/CN.4/Sub.2/40/rev. 1., ch. 10.

[3] I.L. Conf., 40th sess., 1947, report VII (1), 8.

A second report analysed the substance of the replies to a questionnaire and set out some draft conclusions. Discrimination was tentatively defined to include (a) any adverse distinction which deprives a person of equality of opportunity or treatment in employment and occupation and which is made on the basis of race, colour, sex, religion, political opinion, national extraction, or social origin; and (b) as appropriate in national circumstances, such other adverse distinctions affecting a person's employment or occupation as may be specified by the member concerned after consultation of representatives of employers' and workers' organizations.[4]

Although the report acknowledged that beneficial disctinctions such as special legislation for women workers and temporary privileges to assist integration should not come within the definition of discrimination, this view was not reflected in the draft conclusions.[5]

The Committee of Experts on Discrimination, which was set up to prepare a draft, realized that this definition of discrimination was not entirely satisfactory since it was not made clear that the term did not apply to objective differentiation based on the genuine needs of different types of employment[6] and the draft convention introduced the proviso that distinctions in respect of access to a particular employment based on the inherent requirements thereof should not be deemed to be discrimination.[7] A further draft article provided that the following should not be deemed to be discrimination; (1) special measures of protection or assistance provided for in other conventions or recommendations adopted by the International Labour Conference; (2) other special measures designed to meet the particular requirements; of persons who for reasons such as sex, age, disablement, family responsibilities, or social or cultural status are generally recognized to require special protection or assistance.[8] It is surprising that this article did not follow Article 1 which defined discrimination, since it obviously qualifies that definition.

---

[5] The question of what distinctions were reasonable was referred to in the Sub-Commission where it was pointed out that the grounds of discrimination in Article 2 of the Universal Declaration did not apply simply in the case of employment, since there might be linguistic, sex, or other qualifications which were legitimate in a particular type of job. See UN doc. E/CN.4/740, 57.

[6] I.L. Conf., 40th sess., 1957, rec. of procs., app. 10, 741.

[7] I.L. Conf., 42nd sess., 1958, report IV (1), 29.

[8] According to the Secretary-General's report, 'cultural status' referred to the position of tribal populations and 'social status' (added by the Committee) to depressed classes or castes which might need special training opportunities. See I.L. Conf., sess., 1958, rec. of procs., app. 6, 713.

Several members of the Sub-Commission doubted whether the definition was sufficiently comprehensive and precise and criticized the term 'adverse distinction' since there was no indication as to who should determine whether or not a distinction had an adverse effect and the government concerned might well not admit the existence of discrimination. The omission from the list of prohibited grounds of discrimination, of language, age, citizenship, and trade union affiliation was criticized and the term 'national extraction' queried.[9] The ILO Committee on Discrimination agreed after lengthy discussion that distinctions, exclusions, or preference made on the basis of national extraction meant distinctions between the nationals of a ratifying state made on the ground of foreign ancestry or foreign birth, and the Committee accepted a French government amendment which sought to make clear that discrimination included both adverse and preferential treatment.[10]

Article 1 as finally accepted provided that:

(1) For the purpose of this convention the term 'discrimination' includes:
  (a) Any distinction, exclusion or preference made on the basis of race, colour, sex, religion, political opinion, national extraction or social origin, which has the effect of nullifying or impairing equality of opportunity or treatment in employment or occupation;
  (b) Any other distinction, exclusion or preference which has the effect of nullifying or impairing equality of opportunity or treatment in employment or occupation as may be determined by the Member concerned after consultation with representative employers' and workers' organizations, where such exist, and with other appropriate bodies.

(2) Any distinction, exclusion or preference in respect of a particular job based on the inherent requirements thereof shall not be deemed to be discrimination.

It is disappointing in view of this latter provision that the list of prohibited discriminations in Article 1 (1) (a) did not include language, age, or citizenship. Irish amendments to omit the word 'sex' from Article 1 (1) and to permit the reservation of certain occupations to men, widows, or unmarried women were overwhelmingly defeated, as was an attempt by the employers' members to include trade union affiliation. Although this omission was described by the United Kingdom employers' adviser as hypocritical, unjustifiable,

[9] UN doc. E/CN.4/764, paras. 42–6.
[10] This definition appears deficient in that it does not necessarily prohibit discrimination against foreigners or stateless persons. See Mr Krishnaswami, UN doc. E/CN.4/778, 15; I.L. Conf., 42nd sess. 1958, app. 6, 710, 713 and report IV (1), 30.

and unrealistic,[11] the closed shop was defended by the workers' representatives on the grounds that trade union history showed the need for union security arrangements and that nothing in the convention prevented a non-union member from working. Article 4 provided that measures affecting an individual suspected of or engaged in activities prejudicial to the security of the state should not be deemed to be discrimination, but provided for a right of appeal to a competent body, while Article 6 resolved a controversy over Article 35 of the ILO Constitution by providing that every member should apply the Convention to its non-metropolitan territories.

Under Article 3, parties were required to undertake certain duties 'by methods appropriate to national conditions and practice'[12] and Paragraph (b) was particularly important, since members undertook 'to enact such legislation and to promote such educational programmes as may be calculated to secure the acceptance and observance of the policy'. It is noteworthy that a country had no obligation to enact legislation if it 'calculated' that it would be ineffective and the United Kingdom and Canadian Government members ensured that this interpretation was recorded in the *travaux préparatoires*. The omission of any direct obligation to legislate was heavily criticized by the USSR representatives who claimed that the convention was seriously deficient in failing to lay down a clear and binding obligation on governments to prohibit discrimination by law and to eradicate it in practice, and to prohibit propaganda in favour of racial discrimination.[13] It is clear that although such obligations did not appeal to the majority of delegates at that time, with the presence of many new nations in the United Nations, a movement towards the Soviet view has since taken place. Most delegates cherished no illusions as to the limited nature of the convention but it was, nevertheless, a useful beginning because it formulated norms and principles and gave 'a habitation and a name to the noble idea of equality of opportunity or treatment in employment or occupation'.[14] No special measures of implementation were included to the disappointment of some delegates[15] but there

---

[11] 26th sitting of I.L. Conf., 42nd sess., 1958, rec. of procs., 415.

[12] 42nd sess., 1958, app. VI, 711-12.

[13] 42nd sess., 1958, rec. of procs., 405; UN doc. E/CN.4/778, 14.

[14] See e.g. Mr Bocabo (Philippine Government Adviser) 42nd sess., 1958, rec. of procs., 406.

[15] See C. W. Jenks, *Human Rights and International Labour Standards*, (Stevens; Praeger, London; New York, 1960), 85.

were obligations to report to the Director-General and to reply to questionnaires from the Governing Body of the ILO.[16]

The prime achievement of the Convention was the definition of discrimination (resulting from the combined operation of Articles 1 and 5) which made an important contribution to the understanding of the juridical meaning of discrimination and influenced the drafting of later texts. It acknowledged unequivocally that special measures of protection are not discriminatory distinctions if they are designed to promote real equality of opportunity and treatment. Moreover, distinctions, exclusions, or preferences required by the peculiar nature of a particular job were not invidious but necessary and reasonable and should not be described as discriminatory.

2. *The Convention on Discrimination in Education, 1960*

Discrimination in Education was not dealt with in the same way as discrimination in employment and occupation but was the first subject to be studied by the Sub-Commission itself.[17] A three-stage procedure was adopted: (1) collection, analysis, and verification of material, (2) the production of a report, (3) recommendations for action. The report was to be undertaken on a global basis with respect to all the grounds of discrimination condemned by the Universal Declaration, with special attention given to instances where discrimination had been successfully overcome. It was emphasized that the report should be factual and objective and should deal with the *de facto* as well as the *de jure* situation as well as demonstrate the general trend of legislation and the development of principles concerning discrimination in education. It should evaluate their effect on the elimination or reduction of discrimination, and determine whether the discrimination was static or retrogressive. Questions to be investigated were whether the causes of discriminatory principles were economic, social, political, or historical and whether or not they resulted from a policy designed to originate, maintain, or aggravate such principles. In particular, collaboration with other United Nations bodies, especially the ILO and the Commission on the Status of Women, was urged, and it was stressed that the report should serve to educate world public opinion. More generally, it was urged that the various studies on discrimination

---

[16] See the report of the ILO representative to the Sub-Commission, UN doc. E/CN.4/778, 17.   [17] UN doc. E/CN.4/703, paras. 35-9.

should serve not only the purpose of bringing to the fore discriminatory principles that might still exist, but should also serve the purpose of formulating the general principles of international law recognized by civilized nations with respect to non-discrimination in each particular field so that principles and recommendations could be formulated.[18] This approach was disapproved of by several members who believed that the Sub-Commission had not been called upon to make any contribution to the codification of international law. A better view was taken by the special rapporteur[19] who believed that the existence or significance of such principles should not be overlooked and saw no reason why the Sub-Commission should refrain from defining certain general principles of law recognized by civilized nations which fell within the terms of its competence. It was hoped that the education study would be a pilot study and prove to be a model for all special studies of human rights, which would become the greatest project of the United Nations in the non-political field.[20]

In his progress report for the seventh session of the Sub-Commission, in 1954, the special rapporteur reviewed the attempts made by the United Nations to define discrimination precisely and scientifically.[21] A long discussion took place on the question of definition since it was agreed that neither the Sub-Commission nor the Commission on Human Rights had ever considered its early text to be a legal definition of discrimination. Should an effort first be made to prepare a more precise definition? The view which prevailed was that the Sub-Commission should not tie the hands of the special rapporteur and the wisdom of this approach was soon demonstrated.[22] In his progress report, the special rapporteur distinguished static discrimination, which results from social climate, economic situation, and geography, and deliberate discrimination, the result of human will, actual, active, and premeditated.[23] The concept of 'international

[18] UN doc. E/CN.4/Sub.2/165, para. 18.

[19] Mr Ammoun who replaced Mr Masani as special rapporteur of the study of Discrimination in Education on the expiration of his term on the Sub-Commission (See UN docs. E/CN.4/703 S.99 and E/CN.4/Sub.2/155).

[20] UN doc. E/CN.4/Sub.2/S.R.117, 8.

[21] In particular the Sub-Commission text in UN doc. E/CN.4/52, s. 5; i.e. 'The prevention of discrimination is the prevention of any action which denies to individuals or groups of people equality of treatment which they may wish.' See UN doc. E/CN.4/Sub.2/163.

[22] The 7th sess., of the Sub-Commission, UN doc. E/CN.4/711.

[23] UN doc. E/CN.4/Sub.2/163, para. 134.

discrimination' was also introduced, i.e. the situation in which though a person may be treated in the same fashion as his other fellow citizens, he may nevertheless suffer inequality in comparison with the people of another country.[24] Several members of the Sub-Commission criticized the term 'international discrimination' on the grounds that the special rapporteur had confused discrimination with *de facto* inequality between nations which resulted from the uneven distribution of the world's natural wealth and resources. At the same time they recognized that the existence of these inequalities tended to encourage discrimination and should not be overlooked.[25] It was considered that the Sub-Commission should not concern itself with the innumerable inequalities existing between countries in the economic, social, and political fields since these required other remedies.

Members were divided on the distinction between 'active' discrimination, the result of deliberate action and 'static' discrimination, the result of social, political and historical circumstances. In the final report, the notion of international discrimination was practically eliminated in deference to the views of the Sub-Commission and Unesco, though the need for action against the economic causes of discrimination was recognized and the epithets, 'static' and 'active' were also avoided on the ground that they might have enabled some states to evade their responsibilities by alleging that certain discrimination was 'static' and therefore beyond their control.[26]

Although the special rapporteur's distinctions were intended to elucidate the nature of discrimination, in fact they tended to confuse the issues. Natural or *de facto* inequalities resulting from physical, intellectual, economic, and other similar differences between persons or peoples do not in themselves involve the concept of discrimination. Rather, discriminatory activity involves either positive action, or a policy of inaction and inertia on the part of those in authority over others, and discrimination occurs where distinctions are made or allowed to continue for irrelevant and unjustifiable reasons. Although the Sub-Commission acknowledged that protective and compensatory measures intended to help backward groups achieve equality of opportunity do not constitute

[24] UN doc. E/CN.4/Sub.2/L.92, paras. 39–48.
[25] 8th sess., of the Sub-Commission, UN doc. E/CN.4/721, 174th-88th meetings.
[26] UN doc. E/CN.4/Sub.2/181/rev.1, 27.

discrimination,[27] it nevertheless condemned any form of *numerus clausus* or quota system on the grounds that this ignored the principle of equal treatment for all, while failing to take into account the merits of each individual case.[28] Differentiation based on population ratio was said to constitute a form of discrimination, since it ignored the particular individual claim in favour of a blanket classification. As early as 1955, therefore, many of the affirmative action and so-called benign discrimination issues, which were to trouble the United States Supreme Court nearly a quarter of a century later, were canvassed by the Sub-Commission. In his report, the special rapporteur recommended the preparation of an international convention for the prevention of discrimination in education, which would include appropriate provisions of the Draft Covenant on Economic, Social, and Political Rights plus a number of fundamental principles formulated as the result of his study,[29] and the establishment of machinery to examine and dispose of complaints arising under the Convention.[30] Unesco declared itself willing to undertake the task, emphasizing the need for a detailed definition of statutory obligations and perhaps the imposition of sanctions,[31] but the Sub-Commission itself was equally divided, the special rapporteur and the Soviet bloc being generally in favour of a convention, the Western countries considering the proposal premature and likely to weaken the Universal Declaration and distract attention from the draft Covenants.[32] Finally the Commission on Human Rights decided that Unesco should be invited to prepare an 'appropriate international instrument',[33] and in December, 1960,[34] the General Conference of Unesco unanimously adopted a Convention and Recommendation on Discrimination in Education.[35] The Sub-Commission's study of discrimination in education was found to be

1960

[27] See UN doc. E/CN.4/721, s. 5.   [28] UN doc. E/CN.4/740.

[29] UN doc. E/CN.4/Sub.2/181, 238.   [30] UN doc. E/CN.4/Sub.2/198.

[31] UN doc. E/CN.4/Sub.2/L.103, paras. 22, 23.

[32] UN doc. E/CN.4/740.

[33] UN docs. E/CN.4/740, Res. B, 47, and E/29270. (Resolution C contained nine fundamental principles to elaborate further the principles enunciated in the Universal Declaration.) See UN docs. E/CN.4/740, Res. C, 49; E/CN.4/Sub.2/S.R.198–213.

[34] Report of 11th sess., of Sub-Commission, UN doc. E/CN.4/778, Res. E. See also E/CN.4/Sub.2/197 and note by the Secretary-General, E/CN.4/Sub.2/201.

[35] At its 11th session. See UN doc. E/CN.4/Sub.2/210 and annex iii; Unesco doc. 11 C/15. The Committee met in Paris 13–29 June 1960. Draft instruments prepared by a special committee of government experts and a number of amendments were examined by an *ad hoc* working party and eventually accepted by the General Conference.

'a basic and permanent source of inspiration',[36] as were the Universal Declaration, the draft Covenants on Human Rights, the Convention and Recommendation Concerning Discrimination in Respect of Employment and Occupation, 1958, and the work of the Commission on Human Rights, the Commission on the Status of Women, and the Sub-Commission. It had been suggested that the Convention might lay down general principles and specific rules of immediate application while the Recommendation might deal with technical measures, intended gradually to eliminate *de facto* inequalities ascribable to geographic, economic, and social circumstances, but it was decided that a choice between two instruments identical in content but different in legal effect was preferable.

Article 3 imposed on states a number of specific undertakings to be carried out at once 'to eliminate and prevent discrimination within the meaning of this convention', i.e. the repeal or modification of statutory provisions, the adoption of remedial measures, and the prohibition of differences of treatment and of preferences and restrictions in certain fields. Article 4 dealt with equality of opportunity and treatment in education and set goals to be achieved progressively, i.e. universal education, equivalent educational standards in all institutions of the same level, and the eradication of illiteracy. In addition, it contained a specific obligation to formulate, develop, and apply a national policy which would tend to promote such equality of opportunity and treatment and was thus a 'framework text' defining the aims and stages of national policy with regard to the objectives included in Article 26 of the Universal Declaration. Article 5 set forth a number of principles in application of which the parties were to adopt 'necessary measures', while under Article 6, state parties undertook to pay 'the greatest attention' to any further recommendations adopted by Unesco defining the measures to be taken against discrimination and promoting equality of opportunity and treatment. Article 7 obliged states to include information on action taken and difficulties encountered in applying the Convention, in their periodic reports to the Unesco General Conference.

'Discrimination' was defined in Article 1 as 'any distinction, exclusion, limitation or preference, which being based on race, colour, sex, language, religion, political or other opinion, nationality

---

[36] Unesco doc. 11 C/15, paras. 14 and 18–20.

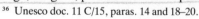

or social origin, economic condition, or birth, has the purpose or effect of nullifying or impairing equality of treatment in education and in particular: (a) Of depriving any person or group of persons of access to education of any type or any level; (b) Of limiting any person or group of persons to education of an inferior standard; (c) Subject to the provisions of Article 2 of this Convention, of establishing or maintaining separate educational systems or institutions for persons or groups of persons; or (d) Of inflicting on any person or group of persons conditions which are incompatible with the dignity of man.' Three things were required: (1) some sort of distinction, exclusion, limitation, or preference which (2) must be based on one of the grounds therein mentioned and (3) must have the purpose or effect of nullifying or impairing equality of treatment.

This definition does not include discrimination based on 'other status' because some committee members considered that the expression was too imprecise for a convention, covered *de facto* inequalities which could only be eliminated gradually,[37] and did not have a 'discriminating character'. This was a surprising objection since the Convention obliged parties first to remove all barriers preventing equality of access to education, and second to formulate, develop, and apply policies tending to promote equality of opportunity and treatment in education. If a distinction, exclusion, limitation, or preference has the 'purpose or effect of nullifying or impairing equality of treatment', then *a priori* it should not be permitted to continue. The issue was approached from the wrong point of view. It should have been examined not from the point of view of the factors on which distinctions, etc. are forbidden, but should have asked the question 'What grounds are there which can justify differential treatment?' It is surprising to note that 'capacity or intellectual aptitude'[38] was proposed as a forbidden differentiating status, because this prohibition would directly contradict the nature of most educational systems, in which individuals are classified and progress according to ability. What is necessary is that all should have *equal opportunity* to develop their capacities to the full under the system without distinctions being made on criteria irrelevant to an education system. Nationality was not included among the factors of discrimination but under Article 3 (c) foreign nationals resident in a territory were given the same access to education as the citizens

---

[37] Unesco doc. 11 C/15, para. 27.   [38] Unesco, doc. 11 C/15 para. 36.

of that territory. This did not imply the grant of free education or other advantages which may be granted to nationals.[39]

Article 2 allowed for situations which 'when permitted in a state'[40] should not be deemed to constitute discrimination. Thus the establishment and maintenance of 'separate but equal' educational systems for the two sexes was permitted provided that there really was 'equivalent access, an equally well qualified staff, and the same or equivalent courses of study'. The conditions reflect the views of the Commission on the Status of Women. During the drafting of the Declaration on Discrimination against Women several women's organizations criticized the use of the word 'equivalent' in this article and proposed that it be replaced where it is used the first time by 'equal' and where it is used the second time by 'identical' since it was felt that the term 'equivalence' might in fact permit the introduction of types of discrimination under its cover.[41] Similarly, separate educational systems 'for religious or linguistic reasons' were permitted.[42] General permission for separate systems was suggested but rejected on the ground that the door would be open for a whole series of exceptions, as were amendments to include 'pedagogical reasons' or 'for other justifiable or precise reasons'.

At first sight it may appear that the combined effect of Article 1 (1) (c) and Article 2 would not permit the estalishment of separate educational systems or institutions for special cases, e.g. of handicapped children. However, under Article 1, a distinction, exclusion, limitation, or preference is only discriminatory when it has the purpose or effect of nullifying or impairing equality of treatment in education. Such special institutions would not have this purpose or effect but, on the contrary, constitute special measures to raise deprived persons to a condition of genuine equality.[43] It is nevertheless regrettable that the Convention did not contain a specific acknowledgement of the legality of such special institutions. The committee considered that the rejection of the amendments did not mean that separate schools might not exist since such a possibility

[39] See report of working party, UN doc. E/CN.4/210, annex iii, para. 14.
[40] See UN doc. E/CN.4/210, annex iii, para. 9.
[41] See Unesco doc. 11 C/15, annex iii, para. 38; UN doc. E/CN.6/426, 39–42.
[42] Art. 2 (2). The education had to be in accord with the wishes of the parents or guardians and participation optional. A distinction willingly assented to is not discrimination. In addition the education had to conform to standards laid down or approved by competent authorities, in particular for education of the same level. See working party report, UN doc. E/CN.4/210, annex iii, para. 11.
[43] Cf. *Minority Schools in Albania* case PCIJ, (1935) Ser. A/B, no. 64.

was provided for in Article 2 (3) but this does not seem to be correct. Article 2 (3) allows for the maintenance and establishment of private educational institutions if their object is not to secure the exclusion of any group but to provide educational facilities in addition to those provided by public authorities, provided they conform to certain standards, but it does not mention special *public* educational institutions. Even Article 5 does not authorize special public schools; all that paragraphs (b) and (c) recognized was the right of parents to choose educational institutions other than those maintained by the public authorities, so long as they conform to certain minimum standards, to ensure the religious and moral education of children in accord with their own convictions. National minorities could maintain schools and teach their own language so long as members of minorities were not prevented from understanding the culture and language of the community as a whole, and participating in its activities; national sovereignty was not prejudiced, general standards were maintained, and attendance at such schools was optional.

In the Sub-Commission it was objected that Article 1 did not appear to distinguish between discrimination of a permanent nature and temporary provisions designed solely to repair damage already done, and might even be interpreted as prohibiting such measures.[44] However, *travaux préparatoires* indicate that special measures to meet special requirements of persons in particular circumstances, such as backward children, the blind, immigrants, and illiterate populations were not 'unjustified' preferences.[45] It is unfortunate that this was not made clear in the Convention itself.

The General Conference decided to modify Article 8 of the Draft Convention in order to provide that disputes concerning the interpretation or application of the Convention should be referred to the International Court of Justice at the request of the states parties to the dispute and not, as originally proposed, by only one of those states. It also adopted a resolution requesting the preparation of a draft protocol by an *ad hoc* committee of government experts instituting a conciliation and good offices committee competent to seek a settlement of disputes which may arise between states parties concerning the application or interpretation of the Convention.[46]

[44] UN docs. E/CN.4/815, para. 131, and E/CN.4/Sub.2/S.R. 316–9.
[45] See Unesco doc. 11 C/15, annex iii para. 36 (report of Special Committee), and E/CN.4/Sub.2/210 annex iii, para. 13 (report of working party).
[46] See Records of the General Conference of Unesco, 11th sess. (1960), Proceedings (14 Dec. 1960), 476–81; also Unesco doc. 11 C/36 and annex 1.

IX

THE CONVENTIONS AND DECLARATIONS (3)

1. *The Covenants on Human Rights, 1966*

On 16 December 1966 the General Assembly approved resolutions adopting the International Covenant on Economic, Social, and Cultural Rights, and the International Covenant and Optional Protocol on Civil and Political Rights.[1] The two draft covenants had been under consideration by the General Assembly since 1954, and the drafting of the general articles was completed in the Third Committee in 1963. This to some extent accounts for the fact that the treatment of the concepts of discrimination and equality of individuals was less sophisticated and informed than in the 1965 Convention on the Elimination of All Forms of Racial Discrimination.[2] Unfortunately, no attempt was made to define 'discrimination' for the purposes of the Covenants and this failure was responsible for much of the confusion and uncertainty about the nature of the concept which was revealed in the course of the debates. The Commission on Human Rights had completed its preparation of the draft articles by 1954, and in many respects the drafting was superior to that finally adopted by the Third Committee.[3]

The work of the Third Committee will be considered in the same order as the articles were adopted, since earlier debates influenced later drafting. Articles 23, 25, 26, and 27 of the Covenant on Civil and Political Rights were prepared during the Sixteenth Session, in October and November, 1961.[4] Special provision was made for the

---

[1] GA Res. 2200 A (XXI). The General Assembly unanimously adopted the Covenant on Economic, Social, and Cultural Rights, 105–0; and that on Civil and Political Rights by 106–0. The Optional Protocol to the latter was adopted by 66–2 with 38 abstentions. See *UN Yearbook* 1966, 418. These instruments came into force on 3 Jan. 1976, 23 Mar. 1976, and 28 Mar. 1979 respectively.

[2] See p. 152 below and Annex I.

[3] The early drafting history of the Covenants is outlined in the annotation prepared by the UN Secretary-General in 1955; UN doc. A/2929, 5–20. The work of the Commission on Human Rights is contained in ECOSOC OR, ESC (XIV), supp. no. 4, paras. 92–289 and annexes i, ii and iii; ESC (XVI), supp. no. 8, paras. 24–214 and annexes i and ii; ESC (XVIII), supp. no. 7, paras. 24–231 and annexes i, ii and iii.

[4] Report of the 3rd comm., UN doc. A/5000. Article 23 (equality of spouses in marriage) is considered in ch. 10 below.

equality of individuals in respect of the suffrage and the conduct of public affairs. Article 25 provided that 'every citizen should have the right and the opportunity, without any of the restrictions mentioned in Article 2, and without unreasonable restrictions: (a) to take part in the conduct of public affairs, directly or through freely chosen representatives; (b) to vote and to be elected at genuine periodic elections which shall be by universal and equal suffrage and shall be held by secret ballot, guaranteeing the free expression of the will of the electors; (c) to have access, on general terms of equality, to public service in his country'.[5]

The phrase, 'without any of the distinctions mentioned in Article 2' is superfluous, since Article 2 (1) applies to 'the rights recognised in the present convention' and *a fortiori* to Article 25[6] and its only effect is to raise doubts concerning the strength of the application of Article 2 (1) with respect to other articles.

The inclusion of the phrase 'on general terms of equality' in subparagraph (c) was pointless, since the non-discrimination provision in Article 2 is included by special reference in the first sentence of the article, but it was unconvincingly argued that the proviso had been carefully drafted to prevent certain groups from monopolizing the public service, while guaranteeing to the state the opportunity to appoint to such service persons of the right age and competence.[7] Another view was that the proviso would permit the establishment of the necessary distinctions relating to qualifications for public service which were different from the distinctions forbidden by Article 2 (1). These explanations defer to the 'absolute' or 'identity' notion of equality, i.e. that without the proviso, any person could claim access to public service whether or not he possessed proper qualifications. Correctly interpreted, however, Article 2 (1) does not prevent the drawing of distinctions on the grounds of merit or capacity, nor does the equality principle require identical treatment for all, or forbid relevant and reasonable distinctions. Moreover, the principle 'without unreasonable restrictions'—a phrase at the very heart of the concept of equality—was specifically included in the first sentence of Article 25.[8]

Article 26 of the Covenant deals specifically with equality and discrimination and is undoubtedly one of the major articles of the

[5] Art. 23 of the Commission's draft. UN docs. A/5000, 28; E/2573, annex i b.
[6] UN docs. A/2929, 173; E/CN.4/S.R.364–6.
[7] UN doc. A/C3/S.R.1096, 180–3.
[8] UN docs. A/5000, 29; A/C3/S.R.1096.

Covenant although it possesses formidable defects. The basic difficulty was that the term 'discrimination' was not itself defined and
was consequently used in different senses in the debates. Article 26
was originally intended to deal also with discrimination in respect of
the rights and freedoms protected by the Covenant, but it was felt
more appropriate to include this clause in Article 2 (1) with other
general provisions.[9]

The Commission's draft read: 'All persons are equal before the
law. The law shall prohibit any discrimination and guarantee to all
persons equal and effective protection against discrimination on
any ground such as race, colour, sex, language, religion, political or
other opinion, national or social origin, property, birth, or other
status.'[10] Certain misgivings were expressed concerning the inclusion
of the phrase 'All persons are equal before the law' on the ground
that it might be interpreted to mean that the law should be the same
for everyone, or to preclude the imposition of reasonable legal
disabilities upon certain categories of individuals such as minors or
persons of unsound mind. In reply it was correctly explained that the
expression was not substantive but procedural and intended to ensure
equality, not identity, of treatment which did not preclude reasonable
differentiations between individuals or groups of individuals.[11]

The Third Committee amendment brought the article into line
with Article 7 of the Universal Declaration, i.e. 'All persons are
equal before the law, and are entitled without any discrimination to
equal protection of the law.'[12] The Indian view was that, while
procedural equality before courts and tribunals had already been
incorporated in Article 14 of the Draft Convention, Article 7 of the
Universal Declaration incorporated two further ideas, (a) the
equality of all persons before the law and (b) the equal protection of
the law, but the latter had been omitted from the first sentence of
Draft Article 24.[13] It is difficult to see why two formulations were
necessary since the statement 'All persons are equal before the law'
can be subsumed in the clause 'All persons are entitled to equal

[9] UN doc. A/2929, 177 ff. Article 2 (1) corresponds to Article 14 of the European
Convention on Human Rights. No general equality clause was included in the
European Convention. Article 26 of the Covenant (Article 24 of the Commission
draft), was adopted by the Third Committee before it considered Article 2 (1).

[10] Draft art. 24. See UN docs. A/5000, 30; E/2573, annex i b; A/C3/S.R.1097.

[11] UN doc. A/2929, 177–9.

[12] The Indian amendment was adopted by 68–1, 8 abstentions. See UN doc.
A/C3/L.945/rev.1, and rev.1/corr.1. Cf. art. 14 of the Indian Constitution.

[13] UN doc. A/C3/S.R.1097, 187.

protection of the law' which also incorporates the principle of non-discrimination.[14]

The 'equal before the law' formulation is much weaker than the 'equal protection of the law' principle since it merely provides that people should be treated alike except where the *law* provides otherwise. The essence of the latter principle is that the law should treat people in the same way except where there is reasonable justification for not doing so.

An important amendment[15] which sought to insert 'In this respect' at the beginning of the second sentence was widely supported for a number of reasons, most of which can be traced back to the failure adequately to define 'discrimination' or 'equality' in the Covenant.[16] It was generally agreed by both sides that the amendment would confine the scope of the article by limiting the prohibition of discrimination to the principle of equality before the law but what this meant was never made clear in the confused debate which followed. Those favouring the amendment believed that the original text applied to discrimination in private and social relationships not subject to legal regulation and argued that such discrimination by private individuals would be difficult to prove and prevent; serious problems of practical limitation would arise and the article would be vague and unworkable. Since all states practised certain *distinctions*, the amendment was 'logical' and would 'clarify' the text.[17]

An important exchange of views took place on the meaning of the terms 'discrimination' and 'distinction'.[18] Two delegates pointed out that a question of substance was involved and that there were cases in which the law was justified in making *distinctions* between individuals or groups;[19] e.g. the imposition of reasonable legal

[14] See UN docs. A/C3/S.R.1099, 193–5; A/C3/S.R.1100, 202. The Iraqi delegate thought that equality before the law and non-discrimination were two entirely different principles. UN doc. A/C3/S.R.1098, 191. And see G. Evans, 'Benign Discrimination and the Right to Equality', 6 *Fed. L. Rev.* (1974), 26.

[15] Proposed by Greece and the UK; UN docs. A/C3/L.946; A/2910/add.1; A/C3/S.R.1102. For the text of art. 26 see n. 26 below.

[16] UN docs. A/C3/S.R.1097, 187; A/C3/S.R.1098, 191; A/2929; E/CN.4/Sub.2/335.

[17] UN docs. A/C3/S.R.1097, 188; A/C3/S.R.1098, 191; A/C3/S.R.1101, 202; A/C3/S.R.1100, 198; A/C3/S.R.1102, 209; A/C3/S.R.1099, 194.

[18] UN docs. A/C3/S.R.1098, 189, 192; A/C3/S.R.1099, 193 and 195; A/C3/S.R.1100, 197; A/C3/S.R.1101, 204.

[19] A/C3/S.R.1099, 193. (Some representatives opposed to the amendment took the view that the South African apartheid laws were 'in conformity with the principle of equality before the law' for they were expressly directed at the entire population of South Africa, but were none the less 'discriminatory'. (UN docs. A/C3/S.R.1101, 202, 204 (Polish and USSR reps.) For a similar view see UN doc. A/C3/S.R.1098, 190.)

disabilities upon certain categories of individuals such as minors or persons of unsound mind, restrictions on military forces, differential treatment as between aliens and nationals in matters of extradition, and similar *reasonable differentiations* were not precluded, since such distinctions were not discriminatory in the sense of being unfavourable and odious distinctions which lacked any objective or reasonable basis.

This sensible and informed approach was supported by other representatives who pointed out that differential treatment such as the granting of certain social benefits contingently on citizenship should not be regarded as discrimination since it was not unjust or unreasonable and, moreover, not the kind of distinction with which Draft Article 24 was concerned. 'Discrimination' had a well-defined legal meaning and neither the nationalization of foreign property nor the refusal to grant civic rights to aliens should be regarded as discriminatory;[20] the principle of equality before the law incorporated the principle of non-discrimination, and neither meant that all persons should receive identical treatment.[21]

A more primitive approach considered (1) that discrimination in its legal sense included legislation protecting certain groups as well as income tax differentials, and (2) that the second sentence 'conflicted with three-quarters of the legislation in force in democratic societies'.[22] This approach was criticized on the ground that differentiations in such matters as taxation, treatment of aliens, or special protective measures in social legislation were not discriminatory. The word discrimination 'as everyone knew' was used here in 'a negative sense' only, to mean a distinction of an unfavourable and not a favourable kind; discrimination in the present context possessed its 'classical judicial meaning' and did not cover private individual preferences.[23] Legitimate distinctions established by states between adults and minors, men and women, or nationals and aliens should never be considered discriminatory measures.[24]

It has been pointed out that the argument that the obligations of the second sentence should serve to implement the principle set out

[20] UN doc. A/C3/S.R.1100, 197. (The nationalization of foreign property is not necessarily discriminatory but it may be so if alien property is nationalized and national property exempted. See *Anglo-Iranian Oil Company* case, ICJ, pleadings 93–4, and Gillian White, *Nationalization of Foreign Property* (Stevens, London, 1961), ch. 6.)   [21] See the Malayan view, UN doc. A/C3/S.R.1100, 199.
[22] UN doc. A/C3/S.R.1101, 201. Cf. *Gudmundsson* v. *Iceland*, European Commission on Human Rights, Application no. 511/59.
[23] UN doc. A/C3/S.R.1102, 209–10.   [24] UN doc. A/C3/S.R.1101, 204.

in the first was similar to a mathematical proposition of multiplying a nought by a nought—the same result would be obtained, namely nought,[25] and the article approved by the Third Committee was thus 'an accumulation of tautologies'.[26] It provided that the law should prohibit any discrimination in respect of the entitlement not to be discriminated against, and that the law should guarantee to all persons equal and effective protection against discrimination in respect of their entitlement to equal protection of the law. Thus the second sentence adds no normative content to the article and the prohibition of 'any discrimination' in the original draft was removed.

A minorities clause, adopted after brief discussion as Article 27 of the Civil and Political Rights Covenant,[27] reads: 'In those states in which ethnic, religious or linguistic minorities exist, persons belonging to such minorities shall not be denied the right in community with other members of their group, to enjoy their own culture, to profess and practise their own religion or to use their own language.' It was pointed out that the concept of a minority, 'which was closely linked to the principle of non-discrimination' was difficult to define, for some groups demanded autonomy while others wished only to retain their own characteristics without being subjected to discrimination by the state in which they lived.[28] While Article 2 (1) and Article 26 contained a general prohibition of discrimination, differential treatment might be granted to minorities in order to ensure them real equality of status with the other elements of the population[29] and this was a welcome acknowledgement that differential treatment was not necessarily discriminatory and that *de jure* and *de facto* equality were not the same thing.

Later minorities studies have stressed that the principle of non-discrimination is an absolute pre-condition to the effective

---

[25] UN doc. A/C3/S.R.1101, 202 (by the Polish representative).

[26] In the words of E. Schwelb, 'The International Convention on the Elimination of all Forms of Racial Discrimination', 15 *ICLQ*, 996, 1019. Article 26 as approved by the General Assembly reads: 'All persons are equal before the law and are entitled without any discrimination to equal protection of the law. *In this respect*, the law shall prohibit any discrimination and guarantee to all persons equal and effective protection against discrimination on any ground such as race, colour, sex, language, religion, political or other opinion, national or social origin, property, birth, or other status.'

[27] The text is almost identical to that suggested by the Sub-Commission in 1950. (UN doc. E/CN.4/358, 22). i.e. 'Persons belonging to ethnic, religious, or linguistic minorities shall not be denied the right . . .' The wording was changed as a concession to those who claimed no 'minorities' existed within their territories.

[28] UN doc. A/C3/S.R.1103, 214.

[29] UN doc. A/2929, 181. (For a discussion of art. 2 (1), see p. 148 below).

implementation of special rights in respect of culture, language, and religion. At the 1965 seminar in Yugoslavia on the multinational society, the essential aim was said to be the attainment of equality in every sphere. The two mandatory principles were: (1) the majority must not practise against the minority any form of discrimination whatever but must extend to it every cultural freedom and an absolute equality of opportunity; (2) the minority must have the right and facilities to play an active role in the social life of its country of residence. The State's preventive function in the matter of discrimination in turn called for protective action to safeguard the rights of minority groupings.[30] Capotorti has emphasized that, while the two concepts are distinct in the sense that equality and non-discrimination imply a formal guarantee of uniform treatment for all individuals, whereas protection of minorities implies special measures in favour of members of a minority group, the purpose of these measures none the less is to institute factual equality between the members of such groups and other individuals. More succinctly, 'this shows that prevention of discrimination of the one hand, and the implementation of special measures to protect minorities, on the other, are merely two aspects of the same problem: that of fully ensuring equal rights to all persons'.[31]

On the question of definition the Commission agreed that the word 'minorities' in this context should cover 'only separate or distinct groups, well-defined, and long established on the territory of a state'.[32] Minorities provisions should not be applied so as to obstruct the process of assimilation, since such tendencies might endanger the unity and security of the state, but any assimilation that might take place must be clearly voluntary and members of minority groups should not be deprived of the rights enjoyed by other citizens of the state so as to enable them to integrate should they so desire.[33] A proposal that these extra rights be stated more specifically (i.e. to possess their national schools, libraries, museums, and other cultural and educational institutions) was rejected by the

[30] UN doc. ST/HAO/HR/23, para. 26. See also J. W. Bruegel, 'A Neglected Field: The Protection of Minorities', 4 *Human Rights Jo.* (1971), 413; J. Claydon, 'The Transnational Protection of Ethnic Minorities: A Tentative Framework for Enquiry', 13 *Can. YIL* (1975), 25.

[31] UN doc. E/CN.4/Sub.2/384/add.5, 14.

[32] UN docs. A/2929, 181 (para. 184); E/CN.4/S.R.369, 370. Several representatives in the Third Committee stated that Article 25 should not be used to encourage the emergence of new minorities and this was not disputed. UN doc. A/C3/S.R.1103, 1104.   [33] UN docs. E/CN.4/S.R.257, 368, 369, 370.

Commission.[34] A strange confusion appeared to exist over whether minorities included only alien groups which had settled within a territory, or whether they could be autochthonous. It was objected that the indigenous population of Latin America should not be recognized as a minority, but treated as a vital part of the nation and assisted in attaining the same levels of development as the rest of the community, and similarly that Australian Aborigines could not be considered a 'minority' within the meaning given to the term by the Commission.[35] On the contrary, however, the Commission's text, and its explanation of it, does not support this interpretation nor does there seem to be any desirable reason why it should. There is no important distinction between the goal of the minorities provisions, i.e. giving extra rights to non-dominant groups in a community over and above those enjoyed by the population as a whole in order to achieve a *de facto* equality, and granting special protection to indigenous, 'backward' groups. The real fear behind the attitude taken by some representatives was that the attaching of the label 'minority' to an autochthonous group might support 'minority consciousness' and possible seccessionist tendencies based on the principle of self-determination of peoples.[36]

Thus the search for a comprehensive formal definition of 'minority' did not meet with more success on this than on previous occasions. In his excellent *Study on the Rights of Persons Belonging to Ethnic, Religious and Linguistic Minorities* presented to the Sub-Commission in 1977, Mr Capotorti stated that it would be illusory to suppose that a definition likely to command general approval could be achieved, however valuable it might be on the doctrinal plane. He nevertheless posited two core propositions: (1) there exists within a state's population distinct groups possessing stable ethnic, religious, or linguistic characteristics which differ sharply from those of the rest of the population (as the Permanent Court pointed out, the existence of such groups is a question of fact); (2) in principle they must be numerically inferior to the rest of the population. Where groups of roughly equal numerical size coexist, however Article 27 applies to them all, and in the case of very small groups, states should not be required to adopt special measures of protection beyond a reasonable proportionality between the effort involved and the benefit to be derived from it. It is a question of fact whether it would be a

---

[34] UN doc. A/2929, 182.   [35] UN doc. A/C3/S.R.1103.
[36] Cf. UN docs. E/CN.4/L.222; E/CN.4/S.R.256, 257, 369.

disproportionate burden on the resources of a state to grant a group special status. Apart from these objective criteria there is also a subjective requirement that the members of a group should desire to preserve their own characteristics. This common will can usually be derived from the group's behaviour. Capotorti thus proposes that for the purposes of Article 27 the term 'minority' may be taken to refer to 'a group numerically inferior to the rest of the population of a state, in a non-dominant position whose members—being nationals of the State—possess ethnic, religious or linguistic characteristics differing from those of the rest of the population and show if only implicitly, a sense of solidarity, directed towards preserving their culture, traditions, religion or language'.

Although in the Universal Declaration of Human Rights and other instruments prior to 1950 the term 'racial minorities' was generally used, this term gradually fell out of favour as being unscientific. 'Ethnic group' was preferred since this was a wider term including groups which saw themselves or were seen by others as possessing different characteristics or culture regardless of whether they differed in inherited, racial, or national characteristics. It is also clear from Article 27 that rights are conferred on persons and not upon groups, although naturally such rights will be exercised by individuals 'in community with the other members of the group'. An individual is free to choose between voluntary assimilation with the majority and preservation of his distinctive characteristics in co-operation with other members of the group. Although the wording of Article 27, 'persons . . . shall not be denied the right . . . to enjoy their own culture' does not prima facie place any positive obligation on states to adopt legislative measures or to undertake expenditure, Articles 13–15 of the Covenant on Economic, Social, and Cultural Rights clearly place positive obligations on states concerning the provision of education and cultural life and these apply to minorities as well as majorities.[37] At the United Nations seminar on the promotion and protection of the rights of national, ethnic, and other minorities in 1974, several participants considered it to be the responsibility of governments to guarantee in law and

[37] See E/CN.4/Sub.2/286, paras. 155–7. As E. I. Däes points out, 'minority protection' is needed only where special conditions require 'positive measures' over and above the 'universal minimum' to assure real equality of rights. 'Minority protection' is thus a complementary factor or corollary to the principle of human rights and its 'positive' nature should be emphasized. (E. Von Caemmerer and others, eds., *Festschrift für Pan J. Zepos*, (Katsikalis, Athens, 1973) ii.41).

practice the maintenance and preservation of group traditions and customs and to provide for their autonomous development where necessary by public financing.[38] It is surely correct to argue that Article 27 taken in its proper context requires states to adopt legislative and administrative measures to enable its objectives to be achieved since conservation of a group's culture and language can only be guaranteed by establishing institutions. 'Only the effective exercise of the rights set forth in Article 27 can guarantee observance of the principle of the real, and not only formal, equality of persons belonging to minority groups. The implementation of these rights calls for active and sustained intervention by states. A passive attitude on the part of the latter would render such rights inoperative.'[39]

Such a teleological approach is in line with the views expressed in the Secretary-General's memorandum *The Main Types and Causes of Discrimination* where it is stated that, while the prevention of discrimination means the suppression or prevention of any conduct which denies or restricts a person's right to equality, the protection of minorities, although similarly inspired by the principle of equality of treatment of all peoples, requires positive action. Concrete service includes the establishment of schools in which education is given in the native tongue of members of the group, provided, of course, that the people concerned wish to maintain their difference of language and culture.[40]

If Article 27 does not require positive measures it is not easy to see how it adds anything to the general equality and non-discrimination provision of Article 2 (1). Article 27 must be interpreted as an additional provision to ensure for members of minorities, independently of the other rights set out in the Covenant, the right to special assistance to practise their own culture, language, and religion. This is a natural corollary of the clear principle which has emerged in United Nations practice that a general prohibition of discrimination does not constitute an obstacle to differential treatment for minorities in order to ensure them real equality of status with the rest of the population.[41] The need for the adoption of special measures to aid disadvantaged minority groups in appropriate circumstances was also recognized by the World Conference to

---

[38] UN docs. ST/TAO/HR/49, para. 79.
[39] UN doc. E/CN.4/Sub.2/384/add.2, 78.
[40] UN publication sales no. 49 XIV 3, paras. 6 and 7.
[41] UN doc. A/2929, para. 183.

Combat Racism and Racial Discrimination held in Geneva in 1978.[42]

A proposal to include a non-discrimination clause in the article was rejected in the Commission on the grounds that Article 2 (1) was adequate in this respect[43] and it was agreed that the limitations clause in Article 18[44] applied to minorities and majorities alike.

Articles corresponding to Article 2 (1) of the Universal Declaration were included in both Covenants. Article 2 (2) of the Covenant on Economic, Social and Cultural Rights provided, 'The State Parties to the present Covenant undertake to guarantee that the rights enunciated in the present Covenant will be exercised without discrimination of any kind as to race, colour, sex, language, religious, political or other opinion, national or social origin, property, birth, or other status.'[45] This is similar to the clause approved by the Commission with the significant difference that the word 'distinction' in the original text was replaced by 'discrimination' and the debates reveal an illuminating discussion.[46] 'Distinction' was not defined in the Commission's text and a valiant effort to remedy the situation was made by the Indian representative who, believing it essential to make clear that protective measures would not be construed as 'distinctions' within the meaning of the paragraph, proposed an explanatory proviso: 'Special measures for the advancement of any socially and educationally backward sections of society shall not be construed as "distinction" under this article.' Alternatively, he suggested the insertion of an explanatory statement in the report.[47] There were fears that the guarantee of rights without *distinction* as to, *inter alia*, national origin or other status might be interpreted as

---

[42] UN doc. A/33/262, para. 20 and item 7 of Programme of Action, para. 21.

[43] UN doc. A/2929, 182 (para. 187).

[44] Article 18 (3) reads: 'Freedom to manifest one's religion or beliefs may be subject only to such limitations as are prescribed by law and are necessary to protect public safety, order, health or morals or the fundamental rights and freedoms of others.' Cf. arts. 8 (2), 9 (2), 10 (2) and 11 (2) of the European Convention on Human Rights, 1950.

[45] UN docs. A/5365, 13–23; A/C3/L.487; A/3307, 34. (Consideration of Article 2 was postponed in 1955 until after the substantive articles had been drafted.)

[46] UN doc. A/C3/L.1028/rev.1 and rev.2. (The Commission's text of Article 2 (2) read: 'The State Parties hereto undertake to guarantee that the rights enunciated in this Covenant will be exercised without *distinction* of any kind such as race, colour, sex, language, religion, political or other opinion, national or social origin, property, birth, or other status.' See UN docs. E/2573, annex 1 a; A/5000, 56–61; E/CN.4/Sub.2/335, para. 14; A/C3/S.R.1181–5, 1202–7.)

[47] UN doc. A/C3/S.R.1182, 241. See also Belgian contribution, UN doc. A/C3/S.R.1202, 337.

forbidding states to place any restrictions on the rights of aliens such as, for example, their freedom to take up employment in a country. These fears led most representatives to favour the substitution of 'discrimination' for 'distinction', to eliminate ambiguity.[48] This would indicate that what was to be avoided at all costs was 'arbitrary distinction giving rise to privilege'. Distinctions, the purpose of which was to protect the weak, such as labour legislation favouring women and children, or underdeveloped regions, and made 'in fact to restore equality', were in no way prohibited.[49] The amendment was questioned on legal grounds since the United Nations Charter and Universal Declaration of Human Rights both employed 'distinction', and the juridical meaning of 'without distinction' in Paragraph 2 was not that states should practise non-discrimination but that they should act independently of such distinctions listed in the paragraph. If the term 'discrimination' was used, a state might apply unequal treatment to different groups of people and claim that this did not constitute 'discrimination' but distinct treatment of distinct groups, and this danger was the greater since there was 'no generally accepted legal definition of discrimination'.[50] As one representative put it, 'discrimination' differed from 'distinction' in United Nations terminology—differentiation was not the same thing as discrimination which meant 'unjustified differential treatment'. Those who attempt to differentiate must then *justify* their differential treatment as reasonable in all the circumstances.

Other representatives supported this approach[51] and said that it was evident that 'discrimination' was a broader and clearer term than 'distinction' from the Unesco and ILO Conventions on Discrimination. Discrimination evoked the idea of injustice, prejudice, and anything that offended human dignity, and was practised by dominant groups against defenceless minorities. Drawing distinctions did not necessarily involve discrimination—there could be valid distinctions made between children and adults or men and women. 'Discrimination' had come to mean 'unfair distinction' both in legal terminology and in everyday speech; arbitrary actions were precluded but legitimate distinctions allowed. These extracts demonstrate that 'discriminations' had acquired a separate technical

[48] UN docs. A/C3/S.R.1182, 241; A/C3/S.R.1202, 338; A/C3/S.R.1203, 341.
[49] This refreshing approach was taken by the Italian representative, Mr Capotorti, a distinguished former member of the Sub-Commission.
[50] UN doc. A/C3/S.R.1203, 343.
[51] UN docs. A/C3/S.R.1203–5; E/CN.4/Sub.2/335, paras. 14, 15.

legal meaning from 'distinction' and was the more suitable term. The change was adopted by an overwhelming majority.[52]

Article 2 (3) of the Social and Economic Covenant provides, 'Developing countries with due regard to human rights and their national economy, may determine to what extent they would guarantee the economic rights recognized in the present Covenant to non-nationals.' This was the most contentious clause in the Covenant, and the voting showed a clear division between the 'developing countries' and the Soviet bloc on the one hand, and the 'Western powers' on the other.[53] The argument ran that since very few developing countries could afford to guarantee to everyone the rights to work and to form trade unions, to social security or to an adequate standard of living, it was necessary to distinguish between nationals and non-nationals. The amendment was not 'discriminatory' but aimed at eliminating economic inequality to which the nationals of developing countries were subjected.[54] Not surprisingly, other representatives disagreed, taking the view that Article 2 (3) had destroyed the 'basic principle of the Covenant—namely non-discrimination' or was an unjustified discrimination against some individuals contrary to the whole concept of human rights.[55] Despite these strictures, Article 2 (3) can be justified as reasonable and not therefore discriminatory, if the premises (i.e. economic necessity in view of the exceptional conditions prevailing in the developing nations) can be accepted. It is nevertheless unfortunate that the term 'developing country' was not fully defined as it does not have a settled meaning.[56]

Article 2 of the Covenant on Civil and Political Rights, adopted in 1963, has been described as the key provision of that Covenant.[57] Article 2 (1) provides: 'Each State Party to the present Covenant undertakes to respect and to ensure to all individuals within its territory and subject to its jurisdiction, the rights recognized in the present Covenant without *distinction* of any kind such as race, colour, sex, language, religion, political or other opinion, national or social origin, property, birth or other status.' This is substantially

[52] 76–2, 13 abstentions. See UN doc. A/5365, 22.

[53] The article was narrowly adopted 41–38, 12 abstentions. Article 2 as a whole was adopted by 51–4, 33 abstentions. UN docs. A/5365, 22–3; A/C3/L.1027/revs.1–4; A/5365, 15–16.

[54] e.g. the Indonesian representative. UN doc. A/C3/S.R.1202, 336.

[55] UN doc. A/C3/S.R.1207, 362.

[56] Cf. UN docs. A/C3/S.R.1204, 349; A/C3/S.R.1205, 352; E/CN.4/Sub.2/335, paras. 14, 15.   [57] UN doc. A/C3/S.R.1257, 237.

the same as the text adopted by the Commission.[58] Surprisingly, the word 'distinction' was not replaced by 'discrimination' as it had been in the corresponding Article 2 (2) of the Covenant on Economic, Social, and Cultural Rights in the previous year although it was pointed out that 'discrimination' rather than 'distinction' was used in the ILO and Unesco conventions,[59] and in the United Nations instruments. Delegates preferred 'distinction' because the Charter and the Universal Declaration both employed it, and 'discrimination' would introduce a different shade of meaning implying action; 'distinction' would permit no differentiation of any kind whereas 'discrimination' had acquired a separate shade of meaning. Alternatively the change was considered unnecessary because 'distinction' was followed by qualifying words leaving no room for doubt as to its meaning.[60] One representative incorrectly alleged that the word 'distinction' had been preferred to 'discrimination' in Article 2 (2) of the Covenant on Economic, Social, and Cultural Rights. On the other hand, the Italian and Peruvian representatives considered that 'discrimination' should replace 'distinction' for the sake of logic and terminological consistency with the corresponding clause in the sister covenant.

The arguments in favour of retaining 'distinction' were far less cogent than those adduced by the Committee the previous year in favour of 'discrimination'. A major reason for the change of attitude was that the composition of the Committee had largely changed since 1962. The arguments in favour of 'discrimination' have already been stated—it has acquired a much richer legal meaning—and the retention of 'distinction' required reservations to be made to accommodate special measures of protection. Further confusion resulted from the employment of the phrase 'protective discrimination'. Provision had to be made for legitimate special measures designed to safeguard and protect the rights of certain socially and educationally backward groups of the population, and it was proposed that Article 2 should be followed by an explanatory paragraph, i.e. 'Special measures for the advancement of any socially and educationally backward sections of society shall not be construed as "distinction" under this article.'[61]

To describe such measures as 'protective discrimination' is only

---

[58] UN docs. A/2929, 47–9. And A/C3/S.R.100–3, 176–7.
[59] UN doc. A/C3/S.R.1257, 238, 239, 240.
[60] UN doc. A/C3/S.R.1258, 241–5.
[61] UN doc. A/C3/S.R. 1257, 239.

confusing if 'discrimination' is to have the legal meaning ascribed to it in the Third Committee the year before, i.e. 'arbitrary and unreasonable distinction'. Mr Capotorti pointed out that use of 'discrimination' in the article would meet the point, since although a measure taken on behalf of a backward group might be called a distinction, it could in no sense be called discrimination. Unfortunately, the Italian representative did not insist on this point since he understood that a Committee would be established to harmonize the language of the Draft Covenants after their adoption, and the matter could be straightened out there. This did not in fact occur. Nevertheless, the crucial point—that measures adopted to accelerate the progress of retarded population groups should not be deemed to constitute 'distinctions' in the sense of Article 2—was accepted by the Third Committee, and specifically stressed in its report.[62] This disposed of the claim that 'distinction' would permit 'no differentiation of any kind' albeit in a clumsy fashion. The more sophisticated provisions of the Convention on the Elimination of all Forms of Racial Discrimination, 1965, which contains a definition of discrimination and a provision excepting special circumstances from its ambit, are much to be preferred to the badly drafted discrimination provisions of the Covenants.

The failure to include the word 'discrimination' in Article 2 (1) of the Convention on Civil and Political Rights is particularly astonishing since the derogation clause, Article 4 (1) does employ the term: 'In time of public emergency which threatens the life of the nation and the existence of which is officially proclaimed, the States Parties hereto may take measures derogating from their obligations under this Covenant to the extent strictly required by the exigencies of the situation provided that such measures are not inconsistent with their other obligations under International Law, and *do not involve discrimination solely on the ground of race, colour, sex, language, religion, or social origin.*'

This clause was adopted by the Third Committee without any discussion of the meaning of 'discrimination'.[63] The Commission had agreed that reference to the various grounds for non-discrimination set forth in Article 2 (2) of the Universal Declaration would not be appropriate since legitimate restrictions might in some cases be imposed on certain categories mentioned therein. The principal

[62] UN docs. A/C3/S.R.1258, 244-5; A/C3/S.R.1259, 249.
[63] UN docs. E/2573, annex 1 b; A/2929, 65-70.

value of Article 4 in this context is that it recognizes that derogations in time of emergency are still subject to the overriding peremptory proviso that they must not be applied in a discriminatory fashion or used as a cloak for discrimination.[64]

Article 14 of the Covenant on Civil and Political Rights deals with the procedural equality of all persons before courts and tribunals,[65] and sets out in detail the minimum guarantees in respect of a criminal charge to which everyone is entitled 'in full equality'. It also provides for special measures of protection to which everyone is entitled, such as legal assistance without payment if a person is indigent, and the free assistance of an interpreter if necessary. Thus the article does not require mere identity of treatment. On the contrary, in order to achieve a genuine equality of opportunity in putting a case before a court or tribunal, it insists on certain positive measures of protection in appropriate cases. The article was opposed by some representatives on the grounds that Article 26 already included the principle of equality before the law but it was generally agreed that arbitrary distinctions in the administration of justice should be specifically prohibited.[66]

Article 24 of the Covenant on Civil and Political Rights is designed to protect the rights of children: 'Every child shall have, without any *discrimination* as to race, colour, sex, language, religion, national or social origin, property or birth, the right to such measures of protection as are required by his status as a minor, on the part of his family, society, and the state.'[67] Several representatives would have welcomed a general non-discrimination clause, but others were unable to support it because, while no child should be subjected to discrimination on the ground of sex, race, colour, religion etc., many legislatures did distinguish in matters of inheritance between children born in and out of wedlock, a distinction regarded by many countries as necessary to safeguard the family and the interests of legitimate children. Consequently, the phrase 'without any discrimination' was discarded in favour of an enumeration of the

[64] Cf. art. 15 of the European Convention on Human Rights, 1950, which does not include the non-discrimination proviso.

[65] The first sentence of Article 14 (1) provides, 'All persons shall be equal before the courts and tribunals.' And see UN doc. A/2929, 118–25.

[66] See e.g. UN docs. E/CN.4/S.R.107, 109, 110, 318 and 323. Also, UN docs. E/CN.4/L.124; E/CN.4/253 and GAOR 9th sess., 3rd comm., 580th meeting, para. 13.

[67] UN docs. A/C3/L.1014 and L.1174; A/5365, 3–10; A/5655, 14–20. The article was adopted 60–1, 14 abstentions.

grounds of discrimination.[68] The Polish sponsors explained that 'national origin' referred not to aliens but to different ethnic groups living in a country and that had they wished to refer to the distinction between children born in and out of wedlock, they would have chosen the word 'filiation' rather than 'birth'. The importance of Article 24 lies in the fact that, apart from Articles 14 and 27, it is the only provision in the Covenant on Civil and Political Rights which refers to special measures of protection. It is clear from the text that discrimination cannot be interpreted to forbid necessary differential treatment.

Article 10 of the Covenant on Economic, Social, and Cultural Rights also provides for special protection for children and for mothers 'during a reasonable period before and after childbirth'. This would appear to recognize that measures of protection in order not to be discriminatory must be temporary. The principle of equality required positive measures to assist those who are subject to natural disabilities, but these are not to be continued longer than necessary to remedy a particular situation.

This review of the Covenants demonstrates that, although they are largely concerned with the principles of equality and non-discrimination, much confusion and uncertainty still existed at the time of drafting as to their nature and content. It is unfortunate that a greater attempt was not made to compare the work of other United Nations organs in the field and to investigate the experience of domestic courts in interpreting equality clauses under municipal constitutions. One major reason for the lack of proper analysis was the speed with which the drafting committees changed their composition. There was often little continuity between sessions and it was regrettable that an effort was not made to ensure that representatives who had begun the drafting of particular instruments were permitted to make use of their experience and complete the tasks assigned to them.

2. *The Racial Discrimination Convention*

In 1962 the General Assembly requested the Economic and Social Council to prepare a draft declaration and convention on the elimination of all forms of racial discrimination, and on 20 November 1963 the General Assembly, on the Recommendation of its Third

---

[68] UN doc. A/C3/L.1174/rev.1.

Committee, proclaimed the United Nations Declaration on the Elimination of all Forms of Racial Discrimination.[69] No attempt was made to define 'discrimination' explicitly in the Declaration, but references in the Preamble to the Charter and in the Universal Declaration show that it was to mean the denial of equality of dignity and rights before the law. Discrimination between human beings on the grounds of race, colour, or ethnic origin by a 'state, institution, group or individual' in matters of human rights and fundamental freedoms is condemned, as is the encouragement, advocacy, and support of such action by the state (Articles 1 and 2). The second paragraph of Article 2 is particularly important since it specifically provides that special measures may be taken in order to secure adequate development or protection of individuals belonging to certain racial groups, with the object of ensuring the full enjoyment by such individuals of human rights and fundamental freedoms. Such measures were not to be maintained after the need for them had disappeared, nor were they to have as a consequence the maintenance of unequal or separate rights for different racial groups. The Canadian co-sponsor said that until quite recently the need had been felt for a categorical proclamation of the right to non-discrimination and there had been a widespread suspicion of any special measures that might be regarded as relics of a discriminatory system, whereas the most urgent need now was to provide the facilities necessary to enable minorities to attain equality as rapidly as possible. The purpose of the clause, as Mr René Cassin put it, was to provide temporary 'compensatory inequalities' in order to achieve true equality in fact for racial groups in inferior positions.[70]

Article 3 dealt with the special efforts to be made to prevent discrimination in the fields of civil rights, access to citizenship, religion, employment, occupation, and housing, and for equal access to public places and facilities. Article 4 provided for the revision of laws and policies tending to create or perpetuate racial discrimination, and for positive legislation to prohibit discrimination and measures to combat prejudice, while Article 5 specifically condemned segregation and apartheid policies 'which shall be ended

[69] 13th sess. (1961), UN doc. E/CN.4/815, paras. 176, 185. Draft texts were prepared by the Sub-Commission and the Commission (UN docs. E/CN.4/846 and annex; E/3743; A/5603). See comments by Matthew J. Whitehead II, 'The Elimination of Racial Discrimination: The United Nations' Proposed Solution', 11 *Howard L.J.* (1965), 583–93.

[70] UN docs. E/CN.4/L.655 and corr.1–2; E/CN.4/L.658; E/CN.4/S.R.759–60.

without delay'. Discrimination in access to political and citizenship rights, especially the suffrage and public service is prohibited by Article 6, and Article 7 called for 'equality before the law and equal justice under the law' and for an effective remedy and protection against discrimination before independent national tribunals. Article 8 covered education and information with a view to eliminating discrimination and to promoting understanding and tolerance, referring specifically to the purposes and principles of the Charter, the Universal Declaration, and the Declaration on the Granting of Independence to Colonial Countries and Peoples. Article 9 provided for legislation and other measures to prosecute and/or outlaw organizations which promote or incite to racial discrimination or violence for discriminatory purposes. This was the most controversial article in the Declaration and the final compromise text did not satisfy all delegates, some of whom felt that certain amendments would violate the principles of freedom of speech and association.[71] Article 10 enjoined the United Nations and its agencies to do all in their power to promote measures and studies with a view to abolishing racial discrimination, while Article 11 reaffirmed the obligation of states to promote respect for and observance of human rights and fundamental freedoms in accordance with the United Nations Charter, and added that the provisions of the present Declaration, the Universal Declaration, and the Declaration on Colonialism should be 'fully and faithfully observed'.

The Declaration was a preliminary reconnaissance of the content of the principle of non-discrimination. Following its unanimous adoption, the General Assembly requested the Sub-Commission and the Commission to give absolute priority to the preparation of a draft convention.[72] It was agreed that the wording and contents of the Convention should necessarily differ from that of the Declaration since the Convention would set out strict legal obligations to be undertaken by the parties, whereas the Declaration stated general principles applicable to groups and individuals as well as to states and governments.

[71] Report of 3rd comm. of GA, UN docs. A/5603, paras. 114–48, and A/C3/S.R.1227–32; A/C3/L.1090 and add.1.
[72] GA Res. 1906 (XVIII) (20 Nov. 1963); Sub-Commission, 16th sess., UN docs. E/CN.4/873; A/C3/L.1010; E/CN.4/873; E/CN.4/Sub.2/S.R.406–18; 420, 422–5, 427–9; E/CN.4/Sub.2/L.308, and add.1, rev.1, corr.1. Other drafts were submitted: UN docs. E/CN.4/Sub.2/L.309; E/CN.4/Sub.2/L.314; see also Commission on Human Rights, report on 20th sess., 1964. ECOSOC OR 37th sess., supp. no. 8; UN doc. E/3873.

The preamble takes as self-evident the principle that all are equal before the law[73] and are entitled to the equal protection of the law against any discrimination or incitement to discrimination, and *inter alia* rejects doctrines of superiority based on racial differentiation, specifically mentioning apartheid. The first paragraph assumed that the Charter was based on the principle of the dignity and equality inherent in all human beings and that it imposed on all members of the United Nations the obligation to ensure, promote, and encourage universal respect for and observance of human rights and fundamental freedoms for all, without distinction as to race, sex, language, or religion. Objection was made to this at the Commission's first discussion of the draft by the United Kingdom on the ground that the Charter did not impose an obligation of that kind on member states, so that the paragraph was 'an erroneous interpretation of the Charter'.[74] Dr Schwelb has pertinently inquired what national interest of the United Kingdom, *i.e.* of the country where, for centuries, civil liberties have been better protected than anywhere else, was supposed to be served by the British Government coming out strongly against the principle of effectiveness in the interpretation of the basic instrument of the international community, contrary to the teachings of the most respected British scholars of our time, contrary to the views of the majority of the International Law Commission, and contrary also to the opinion on the same problem expressed by the British Government in the Third Committee in 1965.[75]

Although the obligation of states under general international law and Article 56 of the Charter to ensure respect for human rights in their own territories was reaffirmed by other states, the immediate result of the United Kingdom intervention was the adoption of a joint text which omitted any reference to 'obligation' or 'ensuring' respect for human rights.[76]

'Racial discrimination' is defined for the purposes of the Convention in Article 1 (1) as 'any distinction, exclusion, restriction, or preference, based on race, colour, descent or national or ethnic

[73] Inserted in the 3rd comm., on the motion of Romania (UN doc. A/C3/L.1219) as amended by the UK (UN doc. A/C3/L.1230). [74] UN doc. E/CN.4/S.R.775, 779.
[75] E. Schwelb, 'The International Convention on the Elimination of All Forms of Racial Discrimination', 15 *LC LQ*, 996, 1029; (1949) *Yearbook of ILC* 179, 287–8; UN doc. A/C3/S.R.1344
[76] See statements by the representatives of The USSR, The Ukraine, and Poland. UN docs. E/CN.4/S.R.776, 777, 779; E/CN.4/L.686/rev.1. Text proposed by Lebanon, Philippines, and India. Also ECOSOC OR, 37th sess., supp. no. 8, UN doc. E/3873, paras. 29–31.

origin which has the purpose or effect of nullifying or impairing the recognition, enjoyment or exercise, on an equal footing, of human rights and fundamental freedoms in the political, economic, social, cultural or any other field of public life'.

This definition is similar to those in the 1960 Convention against Discrimination in Education, and the 1958 Discrimination (Employment and Occupation) Convention. Thus there is reference to certain acts or omissions based on a number of specified grounds which have a certain purpose or effect, i.e. nullifying or impairing equality of treatment in particular fields, and all three conventions include the phrase 'distinction, exclusion or preference' while the 1960 Convention adds 'limitation' and the 1965 Convention 'restriction', but there does not appear to be any normative distinction between these terms. The principal differences are due to the fact that, whereas the 1958 and 1960 Conventions deal with acts or omissions on a large number of prohibited grounds but have a circumscribed area of effect (i.e. education or employment and occupation), in the 1965 Convention the proscribed acts or omissions are based on restricted grounds but cover a far wider range of effects. The earlier conventions dealt with discrimination on many grounds but in restricted fields, the latter with few grounds but with unrestricted scope. The 1965 Convention thus marked the beginning of a new trend under which the grounds of discrimination mentioned in the Universal Declaration were treated seriatim.

This is not to suggest that the 1965 Convention confines itself to race *strictu sensu* since it also includes the allied grounds of 'colour, descent, or national or ethnic origin'. 'Descent' was included for the first time in a discrimination instrument by a late amendment but its normative meaning is unclear though it may well include the notion of 'caste', which is not easily subsumed under the concepts of national or ethnic origin.

The discrimination prohibited in the Convention is not restricted to rights contained in the Universal Declaration but includes rights in the 'political, economic, social, cultural or any other field of public life'. Were this not so, Section 5 (f) would have been inconsistent with Article 1 (1).

The Third Committee, in order to make clear that the Convention did not prohibit or condemn distinctions based on alien status introduced Article 1 (2) which read 'This Convention shall not apply to distinctions, exclusions, restrictions or preferences made by a State Party to this Convention between citizens and non-citizens.' [77] Differential treatment is thus permitted only on the ground of citizenship or lack of it; other articles of the Convention make it clear that distinctions etc. made with regard to aliens on the basis of race, colour, descent, or national or ethnic origins are prohibited and condemned.

Article 1 (3), also inserted by the Third Committee, provides, 'Nothing in this Convention may be interpreted as affecting in any way the legal provisions of States Parties concerning nationality, citizenship or naturalization, provided that such provisions do not discriminate against any particular nationality.' This clause, intended to allow certain disabilities of naturalized persons [78] to be maintained, prima facie permits certain distinctions which would otherwise constitute discrimination as defined in Article 1 (1). Although the proviso does not permit discrimination against any particular nationality (presumably used here in its politico-legal sense) the use of the word 'discriminate' at first sight suggests that states parties may refuse their nationality on purely racial grounds. A refusal to grant naturalization on one of the grounds mentioned in Article 1 (1) is permitted by Article 1 (3) which takes precedence over other articles in the Convention by virtue of its opening phrase. Thus immigration policies which deny citizenship to individuals on racial grounds such as the White Australia policy, are apparently not made illegal by the Convention. Nevertheless, in order to give some effective meaning to Article 5 (d) (iii), which prohibits discrimination with regard to the right to nationality, it appears that a person may not be deprived of his nationality on racial grounds. [79] The exception

[77] UN docs. A/C3/L.1238; A/6181, particularly paras. 30–7; E/CN.4/Sub.2/335, paras. 38–9.

[78] Notable among such disabilities are: (i) Articles I and II of the US Constitution (under which nationality by birth or for terms of years are conditions precedent for eligibility for the Presidency and Congress respectively); (ii) Sections 14 and 20 of the British Nationality Act, 1948; (iii) Article 55 of the Mexican Constitution 1948, and Article 94 of the Columbian Constitution. See *United Nations Yearbook of Human Rights* 1948, 355 and UN docs. E/CN.4/S.R.809, 786, and A/C3/S.R.1307.

[79] This is also the view of Schwelb, op. cit., 1008–9 who also refers to the agreement between three Scandinavian countries of 21 Dec. 1950 (s. 10 of each of the Citizenship Acts of Denmark, Norway, and Sweden) under which, in certain circumstances, a national of one 'contracting country' has the right to acquire that of any of the others. Probably this agreement would not be construed as discriminating against any particular nationality, but as a contractual provision for the mutual benefit of three homogeneous countries with geographic, cultural, and economic ties. It does not have 'the purpose or effect of nullifying or impairing' the human rights of others under general international law.

of aliens *qua* aliens from the enjoyment on an equal footing of the human rights and fundamental freedoms protected by the Convention is a clear restriction on the universality of the principle of equality, but it is made inevitable by the existence of sovereign states. It is unfortunate that the restrictions upon aliens were not made more selective. While it may be reasonable to prevent aliens from exercising certain rights (e.g. the franchise, or ownership of certain natural resources) there seems no reason why a non-citizen should be liable to be prevented from exercising e.g. freedoms of thought, conscience, and religion (Article 5 (d) (vii)), freedoms of opinion and expression (Article 5 (d) (ix)), the right to equal participation in cultural activities (Articles 5 (e) (vi)), or the right of equal access to public places (Article 5 (f)). Yet, unless it can be demonstrated that he is being discriminated against on racial grounds rather than lack of citizenship, there is no redress under the Convention. The 1965 Convention thus provides less protection than the Unesco Convention of 1960 in which states undertake to give foreign nationals resident within their territory the same access to education as that given to their own nationals.[80]

Two of the most important provisions of the Convention are Articles 1 (4) and 2 (2). Article 1 (4) provides, 'Special measures taken for the sole purpose of securing adequate advancement of certain racial or ethnic groups or individuals requiring such protection as may be necessary in order to ensure such groups or individuals equal enjoyment or exercise of human rights and fundamental freedoms shall not be deemed racial discrimination, provided, however, that such measures do not, as a consequence, lead to the maintenance of separate rights for different racial groups and that they shall not be continued after the objectives for which they were taken have been achieved.' Under Article 2 (2) states parties are required to take certain special and concrete measures 'when the circumstances so warrant' to 'ensure the adequate development and protection of certain racial groups or individuals belonging to them, for the purpose of guaranteeing them the full and equal enjoyment[81]

[80] UNESCO Convention against Discrimination in Education 1960, art. 3 (e). Cf. in this connection art. 5 (e) (iv) of the 1965 Convention.
[81] The phrase 'full enjoyment' in the Sub-Commission's draft was objected to in the Commission by a number of undeveloped countries on the grounds that it was physically impossible for them to guarantee to all their nationals the enjoyment of all the economic, social and cultural rights set forth in the UDHR and Article 5 of the Draft Convention. Moreover if full enjoyment was granted only to underdeveloped

of human rights and fundamental freedoms. These measures shall in no case entail as a consequence the maintenance of unequal or separate rights for different racial groups after the objectives for which they were taken have been achieved.'

Articles 1 (4) and 2 (2) are both based on the second paragraph of Article 2 of the 1963 Declaration. In Article 1 (4) the principle of 'special measures' qualifies the definition of discrimination, but in Article 2 (2) it is made one of the fundamental obligations of the Convention. The Sub-Commission's text was expanded in the Commission after a number of amendments had been sought to make it clear that measures adopted solely for the adequate development or protection of racial groups or individuals should not be deemed to be preference or discrimination.[82] The provisos in both clauses emphasize in similar wording that special measures are for a temporary and limited purpose and are not to result in the maintenance of unequal or separate rights for certain groups after the objectives sought are achieved. Thus crash programmes which allow special privileges or 'preferences' to underdeveloped groups do not conflict with the principle of non-discrimination so long as they cease when the members of such groups achieve a real *de facto* equality with the rest of the community.

A definition of discrimination which incorporates the notion of special temporary measures, not as an exception to the principle but as a necessary corollary to it, demonstrates the fruition of the work of the Sub-Commission and the method by which the twin concepts of discrimination and minority protection can be fused into the principle of equality.

The other fundamental obligations of the Conventions are generally set out in Article 2 (1) under which the parties undertake to 'condemn racial discrimination' and 'to pursue by all appropriate means and without delay a policy of eliminating racial discrimination in all its forms and promoting understanding among all races'. To achieve this end the parties are required (1) to take certain immediate action and (2) to support and promote policies of non-discrimination. Some provisions of Article 2 (1) require the parties

racial groups this would be tantamount to discriminating against the rest of the population. On a Lebanese amendment, the Commission replaced 'full' by 'equal' (UN docs. E/CN.4/L.691 and L.696; E/CN.4/S.R.786–7). However, the Third Committee adopted a seventeen power amendment including the phrase 'full and equal enjoyment'. (UN doc. A/C3/L.1226 and corr.1.)

[82] See UN doc. E/3873, paras. 76–82.

to take or refrain from practical action. They must not themselves engage in any act or practice of racial discrimination against any person, group, or institutions and must ensure that all national and local public authorities and institutions conform with this obligation (Article 2 (1) (a)). They must not sponsor, defend or support racial discrimination by any person or organization (Article 2 (1) (b)), and must take effective measures to review governmental, national, and local policies, amending, rescinding, or nullifying any laws or regulations which have the effect of creating or perpetuating discrimination wherever it exists (Article 2 (1) (c)). Article 2 (1) (d), undoubtedly the most important substantive provision in the Convention, provides, 'Each State Party shall prohibit and bring to an end by all appropriate means including legislation as required by the circumstances, racial discrimination by any persons, group or organization.'

In a simple straightforward manner a comprehensive obligation is placed on the parties to ensure that racial discrimination is terminated within their jurisdiction. One promotional clause was added as Article 2 (1) (e),[83] i.e. 'Each State Party undertakes to encourage, where appropriate, integrationist multiracial organizations and movements and other means of eliminating barriers between races, and to discourage anything which tends to strengthen racial discrimination.' There is obviously no comparison between the normative strengths of subparagraphs (d) and (e).

Under Article 3, racial segregation and apartheid are condemned and state parties undertake to prevent, prohibit and eradicate all practices of this nature in territories under their jurisdiction. The special reference to apartheid was made despite the fact that it had been agreed not to include any reference to specific forms of racial discrimination,[84] and that Articles 1, 2, and 5 made it perfectly clear that separate facilities on racial grounds were not permissible.

Article 4 controversially required states parties to condemn all propaganda and all organizations which are based on ideas or theories of superiority of one race or group of persons of one colour or ethnic origin, or which attempt to justify or promote racial hatred and discrimination in any form, and to undertake to adopt immediate and positive measures designed to eradicate all incitement to or acts

---

[83] UN docs. E/3873 paras. 108–9, 132; A/6181, paras. 48-9; A/C3/L.1217.
[84] UN docs. E/CN.4/873, paras. 69–72; E/CN.4/Sub.2/C.308; UN docs. A/C3/L.1244; A/6181, para. 9; A/C3/S.R.1313; A/C5/S.R.1313.

of such discrimination. This clause posed the dilemma of how conflicts of human rights were to be resolved. Where is the line to be drawn between the principle of non-discrimination and the principle of freedom of expression?[85] The first paragraph was introduced to subparagraphs (a), (b), and (c), which spelt out the obligations of the parties in detail. *Inter alia*, they must declare to be offences punishable by law all dissemination of ideas based on racial superiority or hatred, incitement to racial discrimination, as well as all acts of violence or incitement to such acts against any race or group of persons of another colour or ethnic origin, and also the provision of any assistance, including finance, to racist activities. They must declare illegal and prohibit organizations and propaganda activities which promote and incite racial discrimination, and must recognize participation in such organizations or activities as an offence punishable by law. Finally, public authorities or institutions whether national or local, were not to be permitted to promote or incite racial discrimination.

A compromise was reached in the Third Committee, whereby the subparagraphs of Article 4 were made subject to a clause requiring the specific obligations of the parties to be exercised with 'due regard to the principles embodied in the Universal Declaration of Human Rights and the rights expressly set forth in Article 5 of this Convention'. Despite its casual inclusion this was an important amendment since for the first time an international convention had incorporated a reference to the Universal Declaration in a substantive article.[86] (A reference to the Declaration had been included in the Preamble to the Convention on the Political Rights of Women, 1953.) The juridical value of inserting a reference to the Declaration was questioned inasmuch as 'a declaration was not a binding instrument'.[87] This obviously begs many questions but, in any case, if something originally 'non-binding' is incorporated by reference into a 'binding' instrument, it becomes binding in that context.

[85] UN docs. E/CN.4/837, paras. 73–83; E/3873, paras. 144–188; A/6181, paras. 60–74.

[86] UN docs. A/C3/L.1243; A/C3/L.1245; A/C3/S.R.1315; E/C3/S.R.1315, A/6181, paras. 64, 72, and 74.

[87] By India, UN doc. A/C3/S.R.1313. Articles 19 and 20 of the UDHR are subject to limitations under Article 29 (2) for the purpose of securing due recognition and respect for the rights and freedoms of others and of meeting the just requirements of morality, public order, and general welfare in a democratic society, so that the reference to the UDHR could be described as circular. (See Schwelb, op. cit., 1024, n. 138.)

Article 5 spells out in detail the basic obligations laid down in Article 2. States parties 'undertake to prohibit and to eliminate racial discrimination in all its forms and to guarantee the right of every one, without distinction as to race, colour or national or ethnic origin, to equality before the law notably in the enjoyment of the following rights'. This is followed by a list of rights, culled primarily from the Universal Declaration. The opening paragraph contains the clearest affirmation so far of the principle of equality of individuals before the law. It is stated both negatively and positively: (1) Discrimination is to be prohibited and eliminated; (2) Equality before the law is to be guaranteed. The Sub-Commission's draft had contained a reference to equality before the law in a subparagraph followed by a detailed list of certain rights in respect of which the states parties were to prohibit racial discrimination.[88] Surprisingly the words 'descent' and 'national origin' were omitted (cf. Article 1 (1)).

The list of rights 'notably' to be protected is divided into six sections.

(1) 'The right to equal treatment before the tribunals and all other organs administering justice' (Article 5 (a)).

The Sub-Commission's text employed the words 'equal justice under the law' which the Commission considered too vague. 'The right to equal treatment before the courts' had been proposed, but the above text was substituted to ensure that administrative and other tribunals should clearly be seen to be included.[89] The transfer of 'equality before the law' from subparagraph (a) to the introductory paragraph highlights the sometimes forgotten distinction that the right to equal treatment before organs administering justice is only one of many facets of equality before the law.

(2) 'The right to security of person and protection by the State against violence or bodily harm, whether inflicted by government officials or by any individual group or institution' (Article 5 (b)).

(3) 'Political rights, in particular the rights to participate in elections—to vote and to stand for election—on the basis of

[88] UN docs. E/CN.4/L.699 and rev.1; E/3873, paras. 201–5; E/CN.4/S.R.796–800; E/CN.4/S.R.796, 6–7, 133.
[89] UN docs. E/CN.4/L.708; E/3873, paras. 198, 206, 207.

universal and equal suffrage, to take part in the Government as well as in the conduct of public affairs at any level and to have equal access to public service' (Article 5 (c)).

The somewhat clumsy parenthetic explanation of the right to participate in elections was added in the Third Committee.[90] Despite the use of 'everyone' rather than 'citizen' in the opening paragraph the rights enumerated in Article 5 may of course be withheld from aliens *qua* aliens under Article 1 (2).

(4) 'Other civil rights, in particular: (i) the right to freedom of movement and residence within the border of the State; (ii) the right to leave any country, including one's own, and to return to one's country; (iii) the right to nationality; (iv) the right to marriage and choice of spouse; (v) the right to own property alone as well as in association with others; (vi) the right to inherit; (vii) the right to freedom of thought, conscience and religion; (viii) the right to freedom of opinions and expression; (ix) the right to freedom of peaceful assembly and association' (Article 5 (d)).

It is curious that, while Article 2 refers to rights and freedoms in the political, economic, social, cultural, or any other field of public life, Article 5 speaks only of 'civil rights' and some rights, such as the 'right to inherit' (whatever content this may have), which are hardly in the field of public life. Nor does this right appear in the Universal Declaration.[91] The addition of 'and choice of spouse' after 'marriage' in Article 5 (d) (iv) was aimed at the repeal of 'anti-miscegenation' statutes.[92]

(5) 'Economic, social and cultural rights, in particular: (i) the rights to work, to free choice of employment, to just and favourable conditions of work, to protection against unemployment, to equal pay for equal work, to just and favourable remuneration; (ii) the right to form and join trade unions; (iii) the right to housing; (iv) the right to public health, medical care, social security and social services; (v) the right to education and

---

[90] UN docs. A/C3/L.1218; A/6181, para. 80.

[91] Somewhat surprisingly the inclusion of the 'right to inherit' was proposed by a Communist state. (See Polish amendment, UN doc. E/CN.4/L.699.)

[92] UN docs. A/C3/L.1225; A/6181, paras. 62, 64; A/C3/S.R.1306. See also E. Schwelb, 'Marriage and Human Rights', 12 *American Journal of Comparative Law*, (1963), 337, 371–6.

training; (vi) the right to equal participation in cultural activities' (Article 5 (e)).

Despite the wording of Article 5 (d) and (e) it would seem that no further obligations, apart from those which may exist independently, are imposed upon states parties actually to ensure the enjoyment of the rights listed. The only obligation is to ensure the right of all to equality before the law in the enjoyment of these rights where they are vouchsafed to anyone at all. For this reason, the inclusion of 'equal' in Article 5 (e) (vi) would appear superfluous.

Under Article 5 (e) (ii) states parties are obliged to prohibit and bring to an end (Article 2 (d)) racial discrimination with regard to the right to join trade unions. This goes further than the 1958 Discrimination (Employment and Occupation) Convention, under which parties undertook to seek the co-operation of employers and workers associations in promoting the acceptance and observance of a non-discrimination policy.

(6) 'The right of access to any place or service intended for the general public such as transport, hotels, restaurants, cafés, theatres and parks' (Article 5 (f)).

This right does not appear in the Universal Declaration.

Under Article 6, states parties undertake 'to assure to everyone within their jurisdiction, effective protection and remedies through the competent national tribunals and/or state institutions against any acts of racial discrimination which violate his human rights and fundamental freedoms contrary to this Convention, as well as the right to seek from such tribunals just and adequate reparation or satisfaction for any damage suffered as a result of such discrimination'. Unlike the same phrase in the European Convention of Human Rights, the words 'everyone within their jurisdiction' should be treated with caution since they must be read subject to Article 1 (2) of the Convention. The word 'national' before 'tribunal' was inserted in the Commission and means 'municipal' as opposed to 'inter-national'.[93] Although there is a necessary implication that national tribunals must be enabled by municipal law to afford protection and grant remedies, a proposal to include a clause specifically stressing this point was rejected.[94]

[93] UN doc. E/3873, paras. 220, 222.
[94] UN docs. A/C3/L.1223; A/C3/S.R.1316, 1318; A/6181, paras. 96–7.

Article 7 obliges states parties to adopt immediate and effective measures particularly in the fields of teaching, education, culture, and information with a view to combating prejudice which leads to racial discrimination and to promote understanding, tolerance, and friendship among nations and racial or ethnical groups as well as to propagating the purposes and principles of the United Nations Charter, the Universal Declaration, the United Nations Declaration on the Elimination of All Forms of Racial Discrimination, and the present Convention. This is merely a hortatory portmanteau clause of little normative importance.

The 1965 Convention was the most radical instrument so far adopted in this field. Despite its title it is not only a Convention on the Elimination of Racial Discrimination but one which also enshrines the positive aspect of the principle of equality. It was the first general international instrument in which the taking of the special practical measures to ensure the 'full and equal' enjoyment of human rights and fundamental freedoms was made mandatory on the parties. In addition it provided for measures of implementation which though much weaker than those provided for under the European Convention on Human Rights, are considerably stronger than those included in the International Covenants on Human Rights of 1966.[95]

[95] For a United States view of the scope of the rights established, see W. J. Dehner jun., 'Multinational Enterprise and Racial Non-Discrimination: United States Enforcement of an International Human Right', 13 *Harv. Int. L.J.* (1974), 71.

X

THE CONVENTIONS AND
DECLARATIONS (4)
EQUALITY OF THE SEXES

1. *Equal Treatment and Remuneration for Women*

(a) *ILO Convention no. 100.* Article 41 of the International Labour Organization Constitution, 1919, proclaimed the 'special and urgent importance' of the principle that men and women should receive equal remuneration for work of equal value.[1] This principle was recognized in a great many subsequent instruments,[2] implicitly included in the preamble to the United Nations Charter which referred to 'equal rights of men and women', and explicitly in Article 23 (2) of the Universal Declaration of Human Rights which stipulates that 'everyone without any discrimination has the right to equal pay for equal work'.

Both a convention and a supplementary recommendation were adopted.[3] The former provided that where rates of remuneration are governed by law or subject to administrative control, the obligation was to ensure that the principle of equal remuneration was applied, and where rates were determined by the parties or by independent wage-fixing bodies, the obligation was to promote its application.[4]

[1] A similar clause appears in the preamble to the amended constitution of 1948.

[2] Sec. 37 (1) of the Employment (Transition from War to Peace) Recommendation, 1944, provided that 'in order to place women on a basis of equality with men in the employment market, steps should be taken to encourage the establishment of wage rates on the basis of job content without regard to sex'. The 1947 Convention on Social Policy in Non-Metropolitan Territories, Article 18 (1), declares that 'it shall be an aim of policy to abolish all discriminations among workers on grounds of race, colour, sex' with regard to wage rates which shall be fixed according to the principle of equal pay for work of equal value to the extent that the principle is recognized in the metropolitan territory. In various resolutions the International Labour Conference has asked the governing body to draw the attention of governments to this principle with a view to establishing it in law and custom by legislation and administrative action.

[3] See reports V (1) and (2), 33rd sess. of I.L. Conf., Geneva, 1950, and reports VII (1) and (2), 34th sess., of the I.L. Conf., Geneva, 1951. Also 33rd sess., rec. of procs. 334–57, report of Committee on Equal Remuneration; and app. viii, 506–8.

[4] Article 2 provides, '1. Each Member shall, by means appropriate to the methods in operation for determining rates of remuneration, promote and, in so far as is consistent with such methods ensure the application to all workers of the principle of equal remuneration for men and women workers for work of equal value. 2. This

Disappointingly, there was a failure adequately to define the phrase 'equal remuneration for men and women workers for work of equal value'. Under Article 1 (b) this phrase is to refer to 'rates of remuneration established without discrimination based on sex', but this circular definition does not add anything to the original. 'Discrimination based on sex' itself is not defined but if it had been would it not have included notions of inequality between the sexes? What was required was guidance as to the meaning of equality in this context. One delegate maintained that 'equal' clearly meant 'identical' in both cases,[5] and another denied that the language was unclear or vague, arguing that the fact that Article 1 defined remuneration in terms of rates was in a sense an answer to those who said 'equal value' was not defined. Where a time rate applied, if no quantity or output considerations applied to men, neither should they apply to women. Where incentive schemes operated, if women produced less, they should receive less.[6] This is a sensible interpretation but the article does not make it absolutely clear that this is what was intended. Three amendments sought to clarify the term 'work of equal value' to emphasize that the work should be performed under exactly the same conditions as regards technique and process, and that quality, quantity, and output should be 'equal'. Others took the view that remuneration as defined in Article 1 (a) included elements not related to the quality or quantity of work, and that the definition in 1 (b) should be restricted to the fundamental principle.[7]

principle may be applied by means of: (a) National laws or regulations; (b) Legally established or recognized machinery for wage determination; (c) Collective agreements between employers and workers; or (d) A combination of these various means.'

Article 3 provides, '1. Where such action will assist in giving effect to the provision of this Convention, measures shall be taken to promote objective appraisal of jobs on the basis of the work to be performed. 2. The methods to be followed in this appraisal may be decided upon by the authorities responsible for the determination of rates of remuneration, or, where such rates are determined by collective agreements, by the parties thereto. 3. Differential rates between workers, which correspond, without regard to sex, to differences as determined by such objective appraisal, in the work to be performed shall not be considered as being contrary to the principle of equal remuneration for men and women workers for work of equal value.'

'Remuneration' was defined as 'the ordinary basic or minimum wage or salary and any additional emolument payable directly or indirectly whether in cash or in kind by an employer to a worker and arising directly out of the worker's employment'. (Art. 1 (a) .)

[5] Rec. of procs., op. cit., 339.   [6] Ibid., 358; Mr Bar-Yaakov (Israel Workers).
[7] Ibid., 615. The amendments were rejected and the original proposal of the ILO adopted. An employers' amendment to add a new paragraph (c) to the effect that any difference between male and female employment based on anything other than sex was to be considered in accord with the principle was rejected as redundant and likely to weaken the text.

Unfortunately, it was the precise meaning of this fundamental principle that the Convention failed to make clear. It is the task of a definition to clarify terminology and to eliminate as far as possible the likelihood of controversy over the meaning of obligations to which parties pledge themselves.

Convention no. 100,[8] supplemented by the Recommendation, which came into force in May 1953, has been instrumental in promoting the ideal of 'equal pay',[9] and the concept has been incorporated into several later instruments.[10]

(b) *European Economic Community Legislation.* The Treaty of Rome, 1957, which set up the European Economic Community, made specific provision for equal remuneration in Article 119. The Treaty optimistically provided for a transitional period of twelve years divided into three stages of four years each during which its objectives, including the principle of equal remuneration, were to be attained.

Article 119 provides,

Each Member State shall in the course of the first stage[11] ensure and subsequently maintain the application of the principle of equal remuneration for equal work as between men and women workers.

For the purpose of this Article, remuneration shall mean the ordinary basic or minimum wage or salary and any additional emoluments whatsoever payable directly or indirectly, whether in cash or in kind, by the employer to the worker and arising out of the worker's employment.

Equal remuneration without discrimination based on sex means:

(a) that remuneration for the same work at piece-rates shall be calculated on the basis of the same unit of measurement; and

(b) that remuneration for work at time-rates shall be the same for the same job.

This is an important and useful definition and similar to that suggested in the International Labour Conference six years earlier.[12]

[8] 165 UNTS, 303 (1953).

[9] See C. W. Jenks, *Human Rights and International Labour Standards* (Stevens; Praeger, London; New York, 1960), 91–100.

[10] e.g. art. 119 of the Treaty of Rome; art 4 (3) of the European Social Charter; art. 5 (e) (i) of the Convention on the elimination of All Forms of Racial Discrimination, 1965; art. 7 (a) (i) of the International Covenant on Economic, Social, and Cultural Rights, 1966. Cf. also art. 10 (1) (b) of the Declaration on the Elimination of Discrimination against Women, 1967, and art. 11 (1) (d) of the Convention on the Elimination of All Forms of Discrimination against Women 1980.

[11] i.e. by 1 Jan. 1962.   [12] See n. 6 above.

Nevertheless, it is not without its difficulties since it unequivocally states that the principle is available for the 'same work'[13] unlike ILO Convention no. 100, which refers to 'work of equal value'. This could have been interpreted to mean that it is only when men and women are working side by side on a job or on work of identical nature that the principle is to be applied. If, for instance, men cut cloth in a particular factory and women stitch it together this is not the 'same work' if the expression is taken to mean absolutely identical, but it may be work of 'equal value' in the sense of equivalent worth. In a 1961 resolution, the member states recognized that the progressive application of the principle of equality for male and female workers has for its object the elimination of all discriminations in the fixation of salaries, in particular: (1) the application to men alone of minimum obligatory salaries or the fixing of salaries at different levels for men and women; (2) the fixing of different salary minima depending on the sex of the worker in the preparation of collective agreements, salary scales etc; (3) the fixing of different rates for work paid according to time and for piece work, for men and women; (4) the creating of distinct categories for men and women or the application of different criteria of classification when salaries are fixed by a system of professional classification; (5) generally, the maintenance in collective agreements on rates and scales, of differences of remuneration based on sex.[14] The resolution added; '*Les États membres reconnaissent aussi que sont également incompatibles avec le principe d'égalité de rémuneration les practiques qui consistent dans le déclassement systématique des travailleurs féminins, dans l'adaption de règles de qualification différents pour les hommes et pour les femmes et dans une utilisation de critères d'évaluation des fonctions pour le classement des travailleurs, qui soit sans rapport avec les conditions objectives d'exercice des dites fonctions.*' It was clearly agreed that distinctions based on differences in sex alone were to be considered irrelevant. Distinctions in remuneration based on output where piece-rates operated were perfectly valid so long as output alone was the criterion employed. Where time-rates applied no distinction based on sex could be taken into account.

In a 1968 report recent Italian decisions were examined in the

[13] See report of Mrs Schouwenaar-Franssen to the Council of Europe, Council of Europe doc. 46 (25 June 1963).

[14] See Council of Europe doc. 46 (25 June 1963); doc. 26 (8 May 1969), 11.

light of this interpretation. Two decisions recognized the absolute right of female workers to equal pay and affirmed besides that equality of remuneration ought to be deduced *de la nature des prestations concrètement fournies, et non du rendement*. On the other hand, other courts had recognized as lawful clauses in collective agreements which permit different remuneration for male and female workers according to different output, and had affirmed that equality of output is a necessary condition for equality of pay, this requirement clearly resulting from the ILO Convention no. 100 and Article 119 of the Treaty of Rome.[15]

In the Commission's view, the requirement of identical output was absolutely new and up to then had never been applied in the Community. The Commission doubted whether ILO Convention no. 100 and Article 119 could in fact serve as a basis for the application of the requirement of identical output. If it was a question of 'work of equal value' in Convention no. 100 the Commission was not convinced that this meant 'work which produces the same output'. In addition Paragraph 3 (b) of Article 119 very clearly stipulated that equality of pay meant 'that remuneration for work at time-rates shall be the same for the same job'. Therefore, although the output of work paid at time-rates may be very different, the remuneration ought, by virtue of this disposition, to be identical. It was also pointed out that output was not customarily compared when the payment of male workers was considered.[16] The Commission noted in passing that, having been ratified more recently than Convention no. 100, the provisions of Article 119 to the extent that they went further ought to prevail, and considered the view that Article 119 ought to be interpreted restrictively in the light of earlier texts difficult to defend.

However, the interpretation given to Article 119 by the Commission can be called in aid in interpreting Convention no. 100 which employs the phrase 'rates of remuneration established without discrimination based on sex', without defining it further. Article 119 defines a similar expression more fully, but in a way perfectly compatible with the ILO Convention and consistently with an interpretation suggested at the time and not controverted.[17] The application of Article 119 has caused enormous difficulty in the

[15] The Berkhouwer Report. Parlement Européen, Documents de Séance 1968–9, doc. 26 (8 May 1968), 11–12. See Council of Europe doc. SEC (67) 3204, (final) pt. 4, 3.
[16] See Parlement Européen, op. cit.   [17] See n. 6 and n. 12 above.

EEC owing to the recalcitrance of member states in giving effect to its disposition.[18]

In a 1961 resolution member states agreed to a calendar for progressive application of the principle. Discrimination in salaries greater than 15 per cent was to be eliminated by 30 June 1962; discrimination greater than 10 per cent by 30 June 1963, and all discrimination by 31 December 1964. In addition, the members agreed to refuse obligatory force to collective agreements which, in spite of the directives and recommendations of governments, did not respect this calendar.[19] Despite this resolution, little progress had been made by the specified dates.[20] In 1968 the Commission presented a draft resolution for adoption by the European Parliament[21] pointing out that the measures necessary for ensuring the complete application of the principle of equality of pay had not yet been taken, nor had procedures assuring juridical protection of the principle yet been instituted in all the member states, and one member had still not ratified ILO Convention no. 100. It requested the EEC to pledge itself urgently to take account of the situation it had imposed upon itself, and examine whether, in conformity with Article 169[22] of the Treaty of Rome, the Commission ought to formulate an opinion on the breach by one or more member states of its obligations under the treaty. The document pointed out that the question of whether Article 119 ought to be considered self-executing had not yet received a satisfactory answer and only a judgement of the Court of Justice of the European Communities seised of a concrete case would be able to establish the juridical meaning of the disposition.[23] This matter had been the subject of an

[18] On 28 July 1960, the EEC Commission called to the attention of states, ways and means which would permit them to guarantee by 1 Jan. 1962 the operation of the principle of equality of remuneration. (See Recommendation V/COM (60) 114 rev.; letter of M. Hallstein, V/4900/60.) The Social Commission approved a recommendation on 8 Nov. 1960 (see doc. 68) (11 Oct. 1961) (M Motte); and the European Parliament adopted a resolution informing member states that they were obliged to respect the date of 1 Jan. 1962 set by Article 119 (see doc. 81 (20 Oct. 1961)). On 12 June 1961 the Council created a special working group to study the application of Article 119. (See doc. 46 (25 June 1963).)

[19] Res. of 30 Dec. 1961. (See doc. 46 (25 June 1963).)

[20] See docs. V/COM (62) 321 ff.; doc. SEC (67) 3204.

[21] See Parlement Européen, Documents de Séance 1968–9, doc. 26 (8 May 1968).

[22] See A. Campbell and D. Thompson, op. cit., paras. 202, 208, and 1309, and G. Bebr, *Judicial Control of the European Communities*, (Stevens, London, 1962), 144.

[23] This did not occur until the decision in *Defrenne* v. *Sabena* [1976] ICR 547 (see below).

opinion of the Juridical Commission which, though inconclusive, inclined to the view that Article 119 produced immediate effects without the necessity for state legislation. *'L'article 119 est sans doute une disposition complexe et difficile à interpréter. Mais si elle laisse aux États un pouvoir d'appréciation, c'est tout au plus quant aux méthodes à appliquer, mais non quant aux résultats à atteindre. Si cette interprétation est correcte, les objections tombent qui sont formulées à l'endroit de l'applicabilité directe de l'article 119 sous prétexte qu'il accorderait un pouvoir d'appréciation aux États ... des arguments valables plaident en faveur de la thèse de l'applicabilité directe de l'article 119.*[24]

In the Commission's view, women ought to have a subjective right to equality of pay which they could exercise before competent state tribunals. Although the general principle of equality of men and women was found in some state constitutions,[25] only the Italian Constitution explicitly mentioned the principle of equality of remuneration,[26] but some progress was being made.[27]

In conclusion the Commission unequivocally stated its belief in the right of women to equal treatment.

[24] Doc. 26 (8 May 1968), annex ii. See also E. Vogel-Polsky, 'L'article 119 du traité de Rome peut-il être considéré comme self-executing?' *Journal des Tribunaux*, (15 Apr. 1967), no. 4570.

[25] e.g. the Preamble to the French Constitution where women are guaranteed identical rights to men in all respects. Article 3 of the Constitution of the Federal German Republic provides, *'Männer und Frauen sind gleichberechtigt.'* See doc. 26 (8 May 1968) exposé de motifs, para. 8, and pt. 4 (Conclusions).

[26] Article 37 states, '*La donna lavoratrice has gli stessi diritti, e a parità di lavoro, le stesse retribuzioni che spettano al lavoratore.'*

[27] The Commission referred to a 1963 decision of the Paris Appeal Court in a proceeding brought by an air-hostess against Air France, where in virtue of the principle of equality it declared illegal a clause in a labour contract which enabled the employer to dismiss an employee when she married. See also ILO publication, *L'égalité en matière d'emploi dans les législations et autres normes nationales.* Cf. Belgian Royal Decree of 4 August 1967 quoted in doc. 26 (8 May 1968), para. 36. Cf. also *Ministère Public* v. *Élaine Landrin* (Police Tribunal of Cannes) quoted in 7 *Journal of the International Commission of Jurists* (1966), 282; and *Bombay Labour Union* v. *Franchises (Private) Ltd.*, ibid., 137. The latter case concerned Article 15 (1) of the Indian Constitution; i.e. 'The State shall not discriminate against any citizen on grounds only of religion, race, caste, sex, place of birth or any of them.' The appellant raised a demand for the deletion of a service condition of the company which barred married women from continuing in employment. It was argued by respondent that work had to be done in a team and that there was considerable degree of absenteeism among married women thus dislocating the whole team. The Court allowed the appeal and observed that it was not impressed by the reasons given for retaining a rule of this kind. The only difference in the matter of absenteeism that

De nos jours, en effet, personne ne conteste encore aux femmes le droit de participer pleinement à toutes les activités de la vie culturelle, sociale, politique et économique. Toutes les entraves, les discriminations tant directes qu'indirectes et tous les préjugés qui font obstacle à la réalisation de cet objectif doivent être éliminés parce qu'ils constituent non seulement une limitation ou une négation du droit des femmes à l'égalité de traitement par rapport aux hommes, mais aussi une atteinte à la dignité humaine.[28]

This is a *locus classicus* of the principle of equality of the sexes. The correct view surely is that, while there are obvious physical and psychological differences between men and women, there is no evidence that women are inferior to men in respect of intelligence, judgement or capacity, and distinctions on these grounds are un-justified. The biological differences can support certain differences in function, but not discrimination with regard to rights such as educational opportunity, the franchise, or remuneration for work performed.[29] Women may legitimately receive less remuneration than men in some forms of employment, i.e. piece-work, if their output is lower, but the criterion for differentiation should be performance, not sex.

The European Commission strongly represented that in estab-lishing the principle of equal pay no consideration should be given to special measures taken for the protection of women nor to the argument that women are more frequently absent from their place of work than men.[30] This supports the view that the elimination of discrimination against women in respect of remuneration is only part of the equality principle. Special measures of protection might still be required, however, because of certain physiological differ-ences in order to achieve equality in fact.

The first important decision on the interpretation of Article 119 was *Defrenne* v. *Sabena*[31] in which the European Court of Justice held that the article was directly effective, i.e. gave rise to rights which individuals in member states could enforce in their municipal courts.[32]

could be seen was in the matter of maternity leave. But such absence could be easily provided for by having a few extra women as leave reserves.

[28] Doc. 26 (8 May 1968), 36, 12.
[29] See generally S. I. Benn and R. S. Peters, *Social Principles and the Democratic State* (Allen and Unwin; London, 1959), 117; also Frede Castberg, 'Natural Law and Human Rights' in *Les Droits de l'Homme, Revue de Droit International et Comparé*, i.15, 26.
[30] See A. Campbell and D. Thompson, *Common Market Law: Texts and Com-mentaries* (Stevens, London, 1962), para. 316.
[31] [1976] ICR 547: [1976] ECR 455.
[32] It also decided that since member states had not realized that Article 119 was

In 1975 the Council of Ministers issued Directive 75/117/EEC on equal pay and in 1976 Directive 76/207/EEC on equal access to employment, training, and working conditions.[33] This was necessary because Article 119 was confined to the issue of equal pay and its direct effects did not extend to other types of discrimination, though it has been argued, that apart from the Directive, it was open to the European Court to treat the principle of non-discrimination on the ground of sex as a general principle of law recognized in the legal system of the member states and therefore in Community law, and construe it broadly.[34]

Directive 75/117/EEC recognized that it was primarily the responsibility of member states to ensure the application of the principle of equal pay for men and women enshrined in Article 119 by appropriate legislative and administrative measures.[35] It also required states to provide the necessary judicial processes, abolish all inconsistent measures, and provide effective means for ensuring observance of the principle. Directive 76/207/EEC, after pointing out that equal treatment of male and female workers in respect of harmonization of living and working conditions constitutes one of the objectives of the Community, states that its purpose is to put into effect in member states 'the principle of equal treatment'. This means that 'there shall be no discrimination whatsoever on grounds of sex either directly or indirectly by reference in particular to marital or family status'.[36] Member states are required to take the necessary measures to ensure that (a) any laws, regulations, and administrative provisions contrary to the principle of equal treatment shall be abolished: 'any provisions contrary to the principle of equal treatment which are included in collective agreements, individual contracts of employment, internal rules of undertakings, or in rules governing independent occupations and professions shall

directly effective, and the Commission had not taken steps to implement it, claims alleging unequal treatment made before the date of the judgment should not succeed unless a worker had commenced legal proceedings before that date.

[33] *OJ* 1975, no. L, 45/19; and *OJ* 1976, no. L, 39/40 respectively.

[34] See J. M. Thomson and F. Wooldridge, 'Sex Discrimination, Equal Pay and Article 119 of the Treaty of Rome', 93 *LQR* (1971), 499, 500.

[35] This conforms with ILO convention no. 100. See also the report of the Commission to the Council of Ministers on the Application of the Principle of Equal Pay for Men and Women, COM (78) 711 (16 Jan. 1979), 140.

[36] Art. 2 (1). (Under Article 9 (1) states were required to introduce legislation necessary to comply with the directive's requirements by 12 Aug. 1978 but not all did so.)

be, or may be declared, null and void or may be amended'.[37] The necessary means of pursuing claims by judicial process must be introduced into national legal systems under Article 6. A further Directive of 19 December 1978 provides for the progressive implementation of the principle of equal treatment for men and women in matters of Social Security.[38]

Although Article 119 is directly effective, what of the directives? Under Article 189 of the Treaty of Rome, a directive is binding as to the result to be achieved upon each member state to which it is addressed but shall leave to the national authorities the choice and form of methods. Can a directive ever be directly effective in member states? It was strongly argued in the *Defrenne* case[39] that certain directives and in particular 76/207/EEC may contain provisions which do have this effect[40] and the same view is held by many commentators.[41]

The English Courts, however, have not taken the view that either of the directives can have direct 'horizontal' effects.[42] In *Hugh-Jones* v. *St John's College* Slynn J. held that although a member state cannot enforce its own national laws or administrative provisions which conflict with provisions of Community law binding on member states, 'it does not follow that an individual can rely upon a Directive in proceedings against another person in the state, not being the State itself. We do not consider that he can.'[43] The Courts in these cases have been trenchantly criticized for having summarily decided this issue themselves, rather than referring it to the European Court for a ruling, on the grounds that 'the arguments in favour and against the horizontal direct effects of Directives are very nicely

[37] Art. 3 (2). Similar measures must be taken with regard to access to all types and levels of vocational training (Art. 4).

[38] Directive 79/7/EEC, *OJ* (1979), no. L 6/24.

[39] *Defrenne* v. *Sabena* (no. 3) [1978] ECR 1365.

[40] See also the *Franz Grad* case [1976] ECR 825; *SACE* v. *Italian Ministry of Finance* [1970] ECR 1213; *Van Duyn* v. *Home Office* [1974] ECR 1337; *Verbond van Nederlandse Ondernmingen* [1977] ECR 113; *Enka BV* case [1977] ECR 2203.

[41] D. Wyatt, 'Economic and Social Policies', [1976] *European Law Review*, 414; A. J. Easson, 'Can Directives Impose Obligations on Individuals?', [1979] *European Law Review*, 67; and especially J. Thomson and F. Wooldridge, 'Equal Pay, Sex Discrimination, and European Community Law', *Legal Issues of European Integration*, 1. for a comprehensive discussion. But cf. Advocate-General Warner, 'The Relationship between European Community Law and the Natural Laws of Member States', 93 *LQR* (1977), 349, 359.

[42] *O'Brien* v. *Sim-Chem* [1980] IRLR 151 (CA); *Hugh-Jones* v. *St John's College* [1979] ICR 848. [43] [1979] ICR 848, 859.

balanced'.[44] It is probable that the European Court will adopt a teleological approach and hold that Directives 75/117/EEC and 76/207/EEC are capable of having horizontal[45] direct effects.

Article 119 has been interpreted narrowly by the European Court[46] which has held that it covers direct or overt discrimination but not indirect discrimination. The former can only be identified with the aid of the criteria based on equal pay and equal work found in Article 119 itself.[47] Indirect discrimination, on the other hand, is disguised discrimination which can only be identified by reference to more explicit implementing provisions of a Community or national character. The European Court held in *Macarthys Ltd.* v. *Smith* that Article 119 is directly applicable where men and women receive equal pay for equal work, carried out in the same establishment or service and that the work does not necessarily have to be performed contemporaneously.[48] The same case makes it clear that differentiations between men and women which are objectively justified on a ground other than sex do not infringe the treaty and are permissible.[49]

A question not yet resolved is whether an employer may pay a higher rate of pay to workers employed for forty hours a week than to workers employed for fewer hours. Equal work is not defined in the Treaty or the directives but it is arguable that full-time work is quantitatively different from part-time work and that part-time women workers do not do the same or equal work as full-time men.[50] However, it is now clear that Article 119 and Directive 75/117/EEC apply to pension schemes[51] (other than statutory

[44] Thomson and Wooldridge, op. cit., 1, 7.

[45] 'Horizontal' means that some parts of directives may be enforced against individuals and are not only directly effective *vis à vis* the member state.

[46] *Defrenne* v. *Sabena* [1976] ECR 455, *Macarthys Ltd.* v. *Smith* [1980] IRLR 211.

[47] e.g. those forms of discrimination which originate in legislative provisions or in collective labour agreements, and cases where men and women receive unequal pay for equal work carried out in the same establishment. And see *O'Brien* v. *Sim-Chem* [1979] IRLR 151 (UK Court of Appeal).   [48] [1980] IRLR 211.

[49] This justifies the view expressed by Lord Denning MR in *National Vulcan Engineering* v. *Wade* [1978] ICR 800, and other cases, that Article 119 would be interpreted by the European Court as including a similar exception to that contained in s. 1 (3) of the UK Equal Pay Act, 1970, which provides, 'An equality clause shall not operate in relation to a variation between the woman's contract and man's contract if the employer proves that the variation is genuinely due to a material difference (other than a difference of sex) between her case and his.'

[50] The view of Slynn J. in *Handley* v. *H. Mons Ltd.*[1978] ICR 147, interpreting s. 1 (3) of the Equal Pay Act, 1970, supports this view.

[51] See *Worringham and Humphreys* v. *Lloyds Bank* [1981] 2 All ER 434 (CJEC).

schemes which are not caught by Article 119).[52] The reference to 'marital or family status' in Article 2 (1) of Directive 76/207/EEC appears to cover indirect discrimination against women, whatever their marital status, on the grounds that they have dependent children.[53] A prime purpose of the directive is to make effective the principle of equal treatment of the sexes in respect of access to employment and occupation. It is doubtful whether some protective provisions in municipal legislation[54] are compatible with Article 2 (2) since sex in itself is rarely a determining factor in deciding whether persons are capable of performing certain types of work. Article 2 (2) makes clear that the principle of equal treatment requires parity but not identical treatment. Thus the directive is made without prejudice to the right of member states to exclude from its field of application those occupations and, where appropriate, the training leading thereto, for which, by reason of their nature or the context in which they are carried out, the sex of the worker constitutes a determining factor. Such occupations are likely to be rare.

Article 2 (3) specifically allows for special measures of protection 'particularly as regards pregnancy and maternity' and thus permits justifiable provisions introduced solely because of women's physiological nature. Article 2 (4) states that Directive 76/207/EEC shall 'be without prejudice' to measures to promote equal opportunity for men and women, in particular by removing existing inequalities which affect women's opportunities in the areas covered by the directive. Despite its Delphic form, this provision appears to permit at least some measures of affirmative action to bring women up to a level of real and genuine equality. An example of such a measure is Council Decision 77/804/EEC of 20 December 1977 on action by the European Social Fund for Women.[55]

[52] *Defrenne* v. *Sabena* [1976]ECR 455. This is because the character and amount of the pension was not derived from, or attributable to, the contract of employment but to the operation of legislative enactment in which the employer has no hand and the effect of which operates independently of his contractual will or intent. See *Worringham and Humphreys* v. *Lloyds Bank* [1979] IRLR 440, 444.

[53] Cf. the view of the UK Industrial Tribunal in *Thorndyke* v. *Bell Trust (North Central) Ltd.* [1979] IRLR 1.

[54] e.g. s. 21 of the Sex Discrimination Act which prohibits women from working in mines. See Wyatt [1976] ELR 417–18; *Sotgiu* v. *Deutsche Bundespost* [1974] ECR 153 and n. 126 below.

[55] OJ 1977, no. L 337/14; Council Regulation (EEC) no. 2396/71 (8 Nov. 1971) as amended by Reg. (EEC) no. L. 893/77. The Council decision provides for complementary measures of assistance to encourage the vocational training of women of or over 25 years of age without qualifications for entry or re-entry into working life.

In their review of the application of Article 119 in the United Kingdom, Thomson and Wooldridge conclude that, although British legislation does not wholly comply with the requirements of Community law, the jurisprudence of the British Courts appears to be generally careful, balanced, and correct and may be found to have a considerable influence on the European Court when it comes to consider cases referred to it under Article 119 relating to the principle of equal pay and permissible discrimination.[56]

Finally, reference should be made to *Chollet (née Bauduin)* v. *Commission of the European Communities*[57] where the European Court annulled under Article 184 of the Treaty of Rome decisions based on one of the Staff Regulations of the Officials of the European Communities which created arbitrary differences of treatment between officials. Uniform criteria must apply to officials irrespective of sex. In an Appeals Board decision the principle of non-discrimination based on sex and that of equal pay were described as fundamental principles of law as observed in the legal systems of international organizations.[58]

2. *The Political Rights of Women*

At its first session the General Assembly unanimously adopted a Resolution recalling that the principle of equal rights of men and women had been set forth in the Preamble and Article 1 of the Charter, and noting that certain member states had not yet granted to women political rights equal to those enjoyed by men. It recommended that these member states should adopt measures necessary to fulfil the purposes and aims of the Charter in that respect by granting women the same political rights as men. The matter was studied by the Commission on the Status of Women at its early sessions, and recommendations were made to the Economic and Social Council.[59] The Inter-American (Bogotá) Convention on

[56] Thomson and Wooldridge, op. cit., n. 44, at p. 14. The term 'differentiation' would have been preferable to 'discrimination'. For a survey of the measures taken to implement Directive 76/207/EEC in member states, see Commission doc. V/39/79 (1 Sept. 1979).   [57] [1972] 1 ECR 363; 18 *Recueil* (1972), 363.

[58] *Artzet* v. *Secretary-General of the Council of Europe* (no. 1) 51 Int.L.R. 438. Cf. *Zanoni* v. *European Space Research Organization* 51 Int. L.R. 430 and *Leguin* v. *Secretary-General of Council of Europe* 51 Int. L.R. 451.

[59] Res. 56 (I) (11 Dec. 1946). See ECOSOC OR, 2nd sess., annex iv, 235; 4th supp. no. 2, 6; 6th sess., supp. no. 5, 4. And see ECOSOC Res. 120A (VI) and 154 (VII); ECOSOC OR, 9th sess., supp. no. 5, 5. See also UN docs. E/CN6/131. Corr.1 and add. 1; E/CN6/143; ECOSOC OR, 11th sess., supp. no. 6, 3. See also UN doc. A/2154.

the Granting of Political Rights to Women was noted and the Secretary-General was requested to examine the possibility of a general convention.[60]

In the light of the comments and suggestions of governments, the Commission adopted a draft convention which was generally approved by the Council. It was emphasized that equal political rights for men and women were essential to a democratic regime and that the most direct and speediest means must be found to realize such equality.[61] With some further amendments the convention was adopted by the General Assembly in 1952 and entered into force on 7 July 1954.[62] Omitting the formal clause, it provided,

The Contracting Parties,

Desiring to implement the principle of equality of rights for men and women, contained in the Charter of the United Nations,

Recognizing that every person has the right to take part in the government of his country and has the right of equal access to public service in his country, and desiring to equalise the status of men and women in the enjoyment and exercise of political rights, in accordance with the provisions of the United Nations Charter and of the Universal Declaration of Human Rights,

Having Resolved to conclude a convention for this purpose,

Hereby agree as hereinafter provided:

Article I. Women shall be entitled to vote in all elections on equal terms with men without any discrimination.

Article II. Women shall be eligible for election to all publicly elected bodies, established by national law, on equal terms with men, without any discrimination.

Article III. Women shall be entitled to hold public office and to exercise all public functions, established by national law, on equal terms with men, without any discriminations.

The first two drafts had both used the word 'same' rather than 'equal' wherever it appears.[63] This was objected to, principally by

[60] ECOSOC Res. 304 B (XI). See also UN doc. E/A.C.7/S.R.132. A draft convention was submitted to the Commission's fifth session by the Secretary-General. See UN docs. A/2156/add.1, annex 1; E/CN.6/184; E/A.C.7/S.R.132; and ECOSOC OR, 13th sess., supp. no. 10, 4. The Bogotá Convention contained only one substantive article: 'The High Contracting Parties agree that the right to vote and to be elected to national office shall not be abridged by reason of sex.' (Art. 1.)

[61] ECOSOC Res. 385 B (XIII). See also UN docs. E/S.R.522; A/2156/add.1, annex 1; Also ECOSOC OR, 14th sess., supp. no. 6, 4; ECOSOC Res. 445 B (XIV) (26 May 1952); UN doc. E/S.R.575–8.

[62] GAOR, 7th sess., 3rd comm., 339–94; UN doc. A/2334; GAOR, 7th sess., plenary sess., 438–51; GA Res. 640 (VII).   [63] UN doc. A/2156/add.1, annex 1.

the United Kingdom on the grounds that it might be interpreted to mean that men might be eligible to become, for example, warders of women's prisons or heads of women's bureaux, under Article III. Distinctions between the sexes in these occupations were considered 'reasonable and non-discriminatory',[64] and at its Sixth Session, the Commission on the Status of Women therefore replaced 'same' by 'equal'.[65]

Neither of the preliminary texts had contained the words 'without any discrimination' which appear at the end of all the substantive articles but a series of Soviet amendments proposed that, at the end of each substantive article, the words, 'without any discrimination on the grounds of race, colour, nationality, property status, language or religion' should be added, on the grounds that the articles were too vague and general and did not truly reflect the fight against discrimination.[66] It was alleged that the texts could be interpreted to mean that only the equality of men and women belonging to identical groups[67] would be recognized. Other states objected that the Convention was designed to achieve for women equal rights with men, not to grant them a better status. The Soviet view appeared to have been that the Commission's task was to combat discrimination of *any* sort against women. However, 'discrimination against women' surely must be interpreted to mean discrimination against women *qua* women, and not any invidious distinction which affects men as well.

Moreover, the grounds of discrimination enumerated in the Soviet proposal were criticized as both over-inclusive in including nationality and under-inclusive in omitting political rights. The point about nationality was taken and the term 'national' altered to 'national origin';[68] otherwise, the proposal would have allowed

[64] See Comments of Governments, UN doc. E/CN.6/184, 9. The Netherlands (UN doc. E/CN.6/184/add.3) had difficulties over the meaning of 'discrimination' and purported to distinguish between 'discrimination in the sense of the draft convention' and 'discrimination' which meant reasonable or functional distinction. The definition of 'discrimination' as 'unreasonable' or 'arbitrary' distinction avoids these difficulties.

[65] UN docs. E/CN.6/L.59; E/CN.6/L.61; E/CN.6/L.62; E/CN.6/S.R.107; E/CN.6/S.R.106, 6.

[66] UN docs. E/CN.6/L.60 (Commission); A/C3/L.327/rev.1; (3rd comm.); A/L.137 (GA plenary sess.); A/C3/L.327/rev.1; UN docs. E/CN.6/S.R.105; E/CN.6/S.R.106, 8–10; A/C3/S.R.477 (GAOR, 7th sess., 3rd comm., 358) and plenary sess. (GAOR, 7th sess., plenary meetings, 443–8, 451).

[67] i.e. groups differentiated on the basis of race, ethnic origin, property, status, etc.

[68] UN docs. A/C3/S.R.475, GAOR, 7th sess., 3rd comm., 348–54; A/C3/S.R.478, GAOR, 7th sess., 3rd comm., 371–9.

political rights to alien women. In the Third Committee, all the words enumerating the grounds of discrimination were rejected, but the phrase 'without any discrimination' was retained by the narrowest possible margin in Articles I and II but was not retained in Article III.[69] This was a peculiar and confusing solution, since it was not at all clear what the phrase was intended to mean. Did it mean 'discrimination against women *qua* women', or did it mean 'invidious distinction on any ground'?

The better view is that the phrase means 'without any discrimination between men and women'. Nevertheless, it is possible to argue that the other interpretation is correct on the grounds that the deletion of the enumeration of grounds of discrimination was merely intended to avoid an under-inclusive list, and that the first interpretation was superfluous. Moreover, if the first interpretation is correct, one is left with the curious result that the words in the Soviet amendment were given a quite different meaning by the removal of its qualifying words. Articles on reservations, denunciation, reference of disputes to the International Court, and the usual machinery clauses were included but no provision was made for states to bring claims on behalf of nationals of other states before any tribunal, nor was any right of individual petition provided for.

The Convention as finally adopted is obviously primitive when compared with later instruments dealing with equality.[70] There was a lack of discussion on the meaning of 'equal rights' and the relation of this concept to non-discrimination which led to the circular form of the substantive articles. Nevertheless, recognition that 'equal' does not necessarily mean 'same' seems to have been the reason for the replacement of the latter term by the former and this was a welcome step forward.[71] Despite the infelicities of its drafting, the Convention has been immensely important as a moral and educational weapon in the campaign to improve the political rights of women.[72]

[69] Most representatives were opposed to any enumeration. (GAOR, 7th sess., plenary meetings, 440) (408th plenary meeting); UN doc. A/C3/S.R.480; GAOR, 7th sess., 3rd comm., 386–94; A/P.V.408; A/C3/S.R.481; GAOR, 7th sess., 3rd comm., 394).

[70] See generally, R. Daw, 'Political Rights of Women: A Study of the International Protection of Human Rights', 12 *Malaya L.R.* (1970), 308–36.

[71] See also the New Zealand representative in the 3rd comm., who stated: 'The special conditions . . . which several countries had found it necessary to provide for women in order to achieve a measure of equality showed that there could be *no absolute equality* between men and women in that respect.' GAOR, 3rd comm., 7th sess., 368. (UN doc. A/C3/S.R.478.)

[72] See the report of the Secretary-General on the state of the political rights of women, produced for the 23rd sess. of the GA; UN doc. A/7197 (14 Nov. 1968).

3. *The Covenants on Human Rights, 1966, and the 1967 Declaration*

Both the International Covenants on Human Rights, 1966, contain provisions stating specifically that men and women are to enjoy equal rights. Article 3 is essentially the same text in both instruments: 'The States Parties to the Covenant undertake to ensure the equal right of men and women to the enjoyment of all economic, social and cultural (civil and political) rights set forth in this Covenant.'[73] It was pointed out that the elimination of discrimination against women did not in itself guarantee equality between men and women[74] and no clear agreement existed on the content of the equality principle in this context although the concept of equality of rights for spouses had already been included in many instruments. Some representatives considered that the paragraph might be taken to decree an 'absolute' or 'precise' equality or 'identity of treatment' but others urged that what was being sought was an effective equality in fact—not the abolition of differences between the roles of men and women in marriage, but rather the equitable distribution of rights and responsibilities.[75] The inclusion of a general non-discrimination clause in the article was canvassed, but it was finally agreed that reference to discrimination was unnecessary since the matter was already covered by Article 2 (1).[76]

Meanwhile, in 1963 the Commission on the Status of Women was invited to prepare a draft declaration on the elimination of

[73] The text was adopted unanimously by the Third Committee as drafted by the Commission on Human Rights. See UN docs. E/2573, annexes 1 A and 1 B; A/5365, 23, 24, 26; A/C3/S.R.1182, 239. One representative (A/C3/S.R.1205) described Article 3 as 'superfluous' and 'sentimental'. See also UN docs. A/C3/ S.R.1182, 239–40; and A/C3/S.R.1204, 349; GA Res. 421 (V); GAOR, 5th sess., Res. 421 (V).

[74] UN doc. A/C3/L.939/rev. 1. Article 22 (4) of the Commission's draft read: 'The legislation of the States Parties to this Covenant shall be directed towards equality of rights.' See UN docs. A/5000, 24–6; E/2573 annex 1 B; A/2929, 166–71; A/C3/ S.R.1090, 1091, 1093.

[75] See ECOSOC Resolutions 504 D (XVI); 547 I (XVIII); 587 D II (XX); UN docs. A/C3/S.R.1091, 152–3 and A/C3/S.R.1093, 162–6. The Saudi Arabian representative proposed that the word 'equality' be replaced by the word 'equivalence' on the ground that the proclamation of the equal rights of men and women might injure women's interests. UN doc. A/C3/S.R.1091, 153.

[76] UN docs. A/5000, 27; A/2929, 170. In the Third Committee the Uruguayan representative said that discrimination was so repugnant that it should be referred to as little as possible even for the purpose of condemning it. To whom, he asked, would it occur to condemn leprosy or tuberculosis? See UN doc. A/C3/S.R.1091, 152; UN doc. A/C3/S.R.1095, 174.

discrimination against women[77] although to the ILO it was legally inappropriate to repeat, in an instrument not designed to establish legal obligations, measures which already constituted legal obligations for a number of states,[78] and some non-governmental organizations also doubted the practical effectiveness of such an instrument.[79] Other delegations stressed that a convention was not being drafted but a declaration designed to state principles, fix goals, and establish guide lines for the elimination of discrimination against women.[80] It would not have the compulsion of law but it would provide a yardstick to measure the progress achieved and help to educate public opinion.[81] Despite this view, it seems clear that a declaration of this nature lays down standards[82] which can be used to give content to the bare words of the Charter and if its contents are widely and uniformly accepted and applied they may become part of international customary law. While some delegates hoped that a convention would follow the Declaration others considered this unnecessary[83] in view of the texts already in existence,[84] and it was not till 1980 that a convention was finally opened for signature and ratification.

The Declaration includes articles on measures to eliminate

[77] GA Res. 1921 (XVIII) (5 Dec. 1963). A full account of the drafting history can be found in UN doc. A/6678 (GAOR, 22nd sess., annexes, agenda item 53); See ECOSOC OR 41st sess., supp. no. 7, para. 155. See also UN docs. E/CN.6/426 and add. 1 and 2; E/CN.6/L.430, annex; E/CN.6/L.437; E/CN.6/447 and add. 1; ECOSOC OR, 39th sess., supp. no. 7; ECOSOC Res. 1131 (XLI) (26 July 1966); ECOSOC OR 41st sess., supp. no. 7, UN docs. 4316, Chs. 2 and 19; A/36880, para. 112. See also M. K. Bruce, 'The Work of the United Nations relating to the Status of Women', 4 *Human Rights Jo.* (1971), 365.

[78] UN doc. E/CN.6/426, 32–4. The following ILO instruments expressly state the principle of non-discrimination on the basis of sex: the Preamble to the ILO Convention, 1919; the Declaration of Philadelphia, 1944; the Equal Remuneration Convention, 1951; the Discrimination (Employment and Occupation) Convention, 1958; the Employment Service Recommendation, 1948; the Vocational Training Recommendation, 1956 and 1962; the Plantation Convention and Recommendation, 1958; the Social Policy (Basic Aims and Standards) Convention, 1962; the Termination of Employment Recommendations, 1963; the Employment Policy Convention, 1964.

[79] e.g. the International Federation of Women Lawyers; UN doc. E/CN.6/426, 43.   [80] UN docs. E/CN.6/S.R.440–3.

[81] UN doc. A/C3/S.R.1471, 32; E/CN.6/S.R.1468, 6.

[82] What Judge Jessup in the *South West African* cases, ICJ Rep. 1966, 441, described as the 'pertinent contemporary international community standard'.

[83] UN docs. A/C3/S.R.1468, 17; A/C3/S.R.1470, 30; A/C3/S.R.1471, 34.

[84] e.g. on political rights, consent to marriage etc., nationality of married women, equal pay, discrimination in employment, discrimination in education, suppression of traffic in persons.

discriminatory laws, custom, regulations, and practices (Article 2), educating public opinion (Article 3), the right to equal suffrage (Article 4), the same rights with regard to nationality (Article 5),[85] equal rights in the field of civil law (Article 6), discrimination in penal codes (Article 7), traffic in women, and prostitution (Article 8), equal rights with regard to education (Article 9), equal rights in economic and social life (Article 10).

Article 1 simply declares that 'Discrimination, against women, denying or limiting as it does their equality of rights with men, is fundamentally unjust and constitutes an offence against human dignity'. The words 'as it does' were preferred to 'designed to' in order to avoid the inference that discrimination must always be deliberate. *Mala fides* is not essential if an act is discriminatory in effect. The absence of a definition of discrimination was regretted by certain representatives and 'equality' is not explained.[86]

The *travaux préparatoires* contain a number of exchanges of view on the meaning of the equality and discrimination principles, some of which were constructive and useful, while others revealed substantial confusion and uncertainty. An important and constructive statement by the World Union of Catholic Women's Organizations noted that it was using the word 'discrimination' in its most generally accepted, i.e. definitely pejorative sense. It should not be confused with the word 'distinction' any more than 'equality' should be taken to mean 'identity'. Although woman was equal to man in dignity and rights, she differed from him in her nature and mission and consequently in her needs. Another organization believed that any distinction based on a woman's sex or marital status constituted discrimination and that the discriminatory character of any measure was independent of the sometimes well-meaning or paternalistic intentions of those who take the measure; exceptional measures with regard to women, even when presented as privileges, were discriminatory.[87]

Several comments may be made on this statement. First, if it means that literally any distinction is discriminatory and therefore illegitimate, it is obviously unsatisfactory. Certain distinctions need to be made in the treatment of men and women because of their

---

[85] cf. the Convention on the Nationality of Married Women, 1957, (309 UNTS, 65). See Mrs Sipila (Finland) UN doc. E/CN.6/S.R.448, 10.

[86] UN docs. E/CN.6/S.R.441, 8; A/C3/S.R.1476, 61; E/CN.6/L.448/add.1., para. 24; UN docs. E/CN.6/S.R.442, 4; A/C3/S.R.1476, 61; E/CN.6/L.457.

[87] UN docs. E/CN.6/426, 45 and add. 1.

physical characteristics. Secondly, only special measures for women which are *not* privileges are legitimate under the equality principle. These distinctions seem to have been generally accepted in the drafting organs, where it was generally agreed that measures which took into account the fundamental differences between men and women could not be called discriminatory.[88]

Some representatives considered that the term 'non-discrimination' should *ex proprio vigore* imply the guarantee of the rights of women to legitimate protection on account of their special functions[89] and therefore opposed a proposal to introduce an article specifically providing for this. It was also pointed out that one draft article provided for special care and protection during pregnancy and after confinement, paid maternity leave and the right to return to former employment and other assistance.[90] Moreover, the ILO in its preliminary comments had stated its view that women should not be discriminated against because of the protective provisions in certain ILO conventions.[91]

Article 10 (2) of the Declaration consequently provided that 'In order to prevent discrimination against women on account of maternity and to ensure their effective right to work, measures shall be taken to prevent their dismissal in the event of marriage or maternity and to provide paid maternity leave, with the guarantee of returning to former employment, and to provide the necessary social services, including child-care facilities'.[92]

Since it was felt that discrimination against women should not be confused with legitimate distinctions based on physiological differences between men and women,[93] a further clause was adopted to make clear that measures taken to protect women in certain types of work, for reasons inherent in their physical nature shall not be regarded as discriminatory.[94]

[88] UN docs. A/C3/S.R.1442, 338; A/C3/S.R.1444, 401; A/C3/S.R.1468, 17; A/C3/S.R.1470, 29–30; A/C3/S.R.1471, 36; A/C3/S.R.1472, 43; A/C3/S.R.1474, 53.

[89] UN docs. E/CN.6/447, 15; E/CN.6/S.R.440, 5–7.

[90] UN doc. E/CN.6/L.445.

[91] See Conventions and Recommendations adopted by the International Labour Conference, 1919-66 (Geneva, ILO, 1966) Article 2 of Convention no. 45 provides, 'No female whatever her age shall be employed on underground work in any mine.' Article 3 of Convention no. 89 provides, 'Women without distinction of age shall not be employed during the night in any public or private industry, undertaking, or in any branch thereof other than an undertaking in which members of the same family are engaged.' See also n. 99 below.   [92] See UN docs. A/C3/L.1441/rev.1 and A/6880, 9–10.

[93] UN docs. A/C3/S.R.1472 and 1474.

[94] UN doc. A/C3/L.1441/rev.1. UN docs. A/C3/S.R.1481. One delegate voted against Paragraph 10 (3) on the grounds that the problem was one of a general

Most representatives believed that the amendment was necessary since equality of rights could not be identified with natural equality; the physical differences between men and women must be taken into account and measures which were taken to protect women by prohibiting excessively arduous work should not be described as discriminatory.[95]

Thus the framers of the Declaration clearly adopted the modern approach that the principle of non-discrimination required that there should be no 'arbitrary differentiation based on sex'. Appropriate protective measures were not arbitrary but reasonable and justified distinctions designed to achieve a real and genuine equality rather than an absolute equality or identity of treatment.[96]

4. *The 1980 Convention*

In the thirteen years that were to elapse between the Declaration and the Convention considerable changes in attitude towards equality for women and in particular towards the need for protective legislation for women were to occur. Principal reasons for these changing attitudes were the studies carried out by the International Labour Organisation, the work of the United Nations Commission on the Status of Women and of municipal equal opportunities

character affecting men and women equally. There were also young men who could not do certain kinds of work. UN docs. A/C3/S.R.1485; A/6680; GAOR, 22nd sess., annexes, agenda item 53, 10.

[95] UN doc. A/C3/S.R.1482, 90, 91. One representative referred to the Preparatory Technical Conference on the Maximum Permissible Weight to be carried by One Worker which met in 1966 in order to prepare draft conclusions for the 51st sess. of the International Labour Conference. The special provisions included for women were 'obviously not discriminatory against women'. See also UN doc. A/C3/S.R.1442, 392.

[96] UN doc. A/C3/S.R.1470, 29–30. As the Philippine representative pointed out, 'Care should be taken to give the word "equality" not a purely academic and intellectual substance, but its true and practical meaning'. (UN doc. A/C3/S.R.1444, 401.) At the twenty-first session of the Third Committee a Swedish proposal (UN doc. A/C3/L.1385) to add 'without any discrimination' to 'on equal terms' in Draft Article 4 was adopted. This was strictly unnecessary as 'on equal terms' surely implies 'without any discrimination'. (And see the comments of the Iranian representative UN doc. A/C3/S.R.1444, 404.) The purpose of the amendment was undoubtedly to bring the terminology into line with that used in the Convention on the Political Rights of Women. At the twenty-second session of the Third Committee, the Guatemalan representative opposed Article 6 (3) on the grounds that though a law permitting a child to marry at an early age would be unjust, it would not involve any discrimination as it would apply equally to both sexes. (See UN doc. A/C3/S.R.1478, 75.) This is a facile argument which ignores the factual position, since it is far more common for girls to be betrothed and married at an early age than boys.

commissions, and the growth of women's movements. The Committee of Experts on Applications of Conventions and Recommendations reporting to the International Labour Conference in 1971 pointed out that discrimination based on sex was another form of discrimination whose elimination called for constant attention and the development of a series of positive measures in various fields.[97] Experience showed in their view that many of the distinctions between the sexes which it had become customary to accept as 'normal' were really discriminatory. Law and official practice often allowed for distinctions on the basis of sex, the objective justification for which was questionable, and such distinctions should be constantly reviewed in the light of changing circumstances to see whether they were really justified from the standpoint of qualifications required by the nature of certain jobs or of the need for protection. It was becoming widely acknowledged that it was not fully legitimate to lay down that all women are physically unfitted for certain tasks when, while this might be the case for most women, it was not necessarily true for all.

A highly significant step was taken by the ILO in 1975 when it adopted a Declaration on Equality of Opportunity and Treatment for Women Workers.[98] Article 1 (1) provided that there shall be equality of opportunity and treatment for all workers and that all forms of discrimination on the grounds of sex which deny or restrict such equality are unacceptable and must be eliminated. Article 2 (2) states unequivocally that 'positive special treatment during a transitional period aimed at effective equality between the sexes shall not be regarded as discriminatory'. This formulation neatly summarizes the thesis that true equality sought by international instruments does not necessarily require identical treatment of all but that special ameliorative measures are perfectly consistent with equality and do not constitute discrimination so long as they are not continued after the need has disappeared. Later provisions also require special measures to bring out the potentialities, aptitude, and aspirations of women, including those in rural areas; to stimulate the equal access of women to top positions; to ensure equal remuneration for work of equal value, particularly in occupations in which women predominate; to ensure equality of treatment for part-time women

[97] Report III, pt. 4 B, 56th sess., of I.L. Conf., Geneva, 1971, E/CN.6/550, annex II, 1, para. 103.

[98] Adopted 25 June 1975. See UN doc. E/CN.6/603 and UN publication, sales no. E, 76 IV, 1, para. 102.

workers. Other articles declare that there shall be no discrimination against women workers on grounds of marital status, age, or family responsibilities or on the grounds of pregnancy and childbirth. Special protection in respect of maternity and work 'harmful to them from the standpoint of their social function of reproduction' should be provided but such measures 'should be reviewed and brought up to date periodically in the light of advances in scientific and technical knowledge'.

It is important to note that the Declaration does not mention protection for women other than in respect of their 'social function' of childbearing and makes no mention of night work, heavy loads, or other measures traditionally thought to be necessary. Rather, all protective measures are to be reviewed regularly to see whether they are strictly required or not. The 1979 report of the ILO to the Commission on the Status of Women continues this trend, pointing out that the ILO Plan of Action recommends that the ILO take measures to review and revise, if necessary, all protective instruments[99] in order to decide whether their provisions are still adequate in the light of experience since their adoption, and to keep them up to date in the light of scientific and technical developments.[100] Studies had found that the great majority of states have legislative limitations on night work for women, which, in so far as they take the form of outright prohibitions, are being increasingly contested. No consensus existed on the desirability of revising the existing instruments and the ILO intended to continue its research.[101]

The UK Equal Opportunities Commission concluded in 1979 that

[99] e.g. Employment (Women with Family Responsibilities) Recommendation, 1965 (no. 123); Maternity Protection Recommendation, 1952 (no. 95); Equal Remuneration Convention, 1951 (no. 100); Equal Remuneration Recommendation, 1951 (no. 90); Maternity Protection Convention, 1919 (no. 3), revised 1952 (no. 103); Night Work (Women) Convention, 1919 (no. 4) revised 1934 (no. 41) and again in 1948 (no. 89); Night Work (Agricultural) Recommendation, 1921 (no. 13); Maximum Weight Convention 1967 (no. 127); Welfare Facilities Recommendation, 1956 (no. 102). And see the report, Equal Opportunities for Men and Women Workers: Workers with Family Responsibilities, I.L. Conf., 66th sess., 1980, report VI (1) which points out that the fact that the Conference was discussing an item on 'workers' and not just 'women workers' with family responsibilities was in itself a recognition of a new trend in social policy. Convention no. 123 should be revised to cover both men and women (p. 61).
[100] UN doc. E/CN.6/631 (21 Dec. 1979), 6.
[101] See *'Night Work': Report of Tripartite Advisory Meeting*, Geneva 26 Sept.–3 Oct. 1978, doc. TAMNW/1978/VI; and working paper TAMNW/1978/I; also J. Carpenter and P. Casamian, *Night Work: Its Effects on the Health and Welfare of the Workers* (I.L. Conf. 1977).

there was no longer justification for maintaining legal provisions on hours of work which required men and women to be treated differently and it recommended that the legislation should be removed, or, where health, safety, and welfare demand it, replaced, so that it applies equally to men and women.[102] Similarly, a working party in international labour standards, as a result of an in-depth review, concluded that existing instruments on maternity protection should be revised and a research project launched to analyse new trends which might lead to the revision of Convention no. 103.[103] On the issue of affirmative action it is noteworthy that Unesco decided in 1979, in view of the handicaps facing girls and women, that until 'full equality' of education and training opportunities was assured, there was a need for special programmes for girls and women, so as to enable them to reduce and eventually eliminate the gap.[104]

It was in the light of all these developments that the Commission on the Status of Women and the General Assembly's Third Committee completed the drafting of the International Convention on the Elimination of Discrimination Against Women. The view had been expressed in the Commission on the Status of Women[105] that an international convention was needed containing measures of implementation similar to those contained in the Racial Discrimination Convention and a working group set up to examine the question invited expressions of opinion.[106] It was generally felt that, since the Declaration had no binding character, there was a need for a comprehensive convention, although the ILO had serious reservations about the viability of such an instrument. If one was desirable, however, it should be expressed in general terms and not

---

[102] See *Health and Safety Legislation: Should we distinguish between men and Women?* Report of UK Equal Opportunities Commission to the Secretary of State for Employment, March 1979, p. 96, para. 394. See also p. 389, paras. 164, 165; pp. 79–81, para. 329; p. 94, para. 379. This recommendation was attacked at the 1979 UK Trade Union Conference where Mr Bill Keys is reported to have said, 'We shall argue most strongly against the EOC's latest recommendation that virtually all the protective laws governing women in employment should be repealed . . . surely this is the most muddled, monumental thinking that has come from any commission. . . . We do not want to see equality of misery.' 'When Equality has to Stop', the *Guardian*, 5 Sept. 1979.

[103] Final Report, Official Bulletin, Special Issue, LXII (1979), ser. A.

[104] UN doc. E/CN.6/632, 21, para. 92.

[105] 'The Commission' for the purpose of this chapter refers to the Commission on the Status of Women and not the Commission on Human Rights.

[106] ECOSOC OR 48th sess., supp. no. 6, para. 16; UN doc. E/CN.6/552; E/CN.6/574; E/CN.6/573, annex. 1 and E/CN.6/A.C.1/L.2.

overlap with the conventions of the specialized agencies, particularly the ILO. The working group thereupon recommended to the Commission the preparation of a draft single comprehensive convention without prejudice to the preparation of future instruments by the United Nations or its specialized agencies. Unlike the Declaration, Article 1 of the Convention contains a definition of discrimination based upon Article 1 (1) of the Racial Discrimination Convention, 1965, i.e. 'For the purpose of the present Convention, the term "discrimination against" women shall mean any distinction, exclusion or restriction made on the basis of sex which has the effect or purpose of impairing or nullifying the recognition, enjoyment or exercise by women, irrespective of their marital status, on a basis of equality of men and women, of human rights and fundamental freedom in the political, economic, social, cultural or any other field of public life.' More controversial was Article 4, the provision analogous to Article 1 (4) of the earlier convention. This provides,

(1) Adoption by States Parties of temporary special measures aimed at accelerating *de facto* equality between men and women shall not be considered discrimination as defined in the present Convention but shall in no way entail as a consequence the maintenance of unequal or separate standards; these measures shall be discontinued when the objectives of equality of opportunity and treatment have been achieved. (2) Adoption by States Parties of special measures, including those measures contained in the present Convention, aimed at protecting maternity shall not be considered discriminatory.

At an early stage France and the United Kingdom insisted that the Convention should in no way require governments to impose 'reverse discrimination', by which they meant 'discrimination in favour of women' since, save in certain carefully defined circumstances, this would represent a permanent departure from the objective of equal status and opportunities and would not be in the long-term interest of women themselves. On the other hand, the Convention should permit (but not require) temporary affirmative action measures in special fields to equalize opportunities for women in situations where it was necessary to overcome an undesirable historical link. Other states agreed that, although such means 'may seem apparently discriminatory', they were necessary to right wrongs done against women because of their sex in the past. West Germany rightly questioned whether the physical constitution of women requires special protective measures in certain branches of work and was of the opinion that one's physical constitution is not a matter of sex but something which applies to both women and men.[107] Another delegate believed that it was fair that special measures of protection be not considered discriminatory although 'it seemingly puts women on an unequal footing'.

The language used in the debates demonstrated widespread confusion over terminology. If 'equal treatment' always means the 'same' or 'identical' treatment, then of course special measures are unequal, but if equality is used in a normative sense then the difficulty disappears. Similarly, if discrimination means unjustifiable or unreasonable differentiations then the question arises whether certain measures are objectively justifiable. This can easily be shown for measures designed to protect women's physiological function, particularly child-bearing, but as the ILO has shown, it is increasingly recognized that measures designed to protect women as such because of their physical nature might equally well be applied to some men.

Articles 10 and 11 deal specifically with questions of discrimination in Education and Employment and generally require that men and women receive the *same* treatment. Article 11 (2), however, requires states parties to take appropriate measures to protect women against dismissal on the grounds of pregnancy, maternity leave, and marital status and to introduce appropriate social services. Such protective legislation could be 'reviewed periodically in the light of scientific and technological knowledge and shall be revised, repealed or extended as necessary'. Most other provisions called for the same treatment for men and women and this occasionally gave rise to difficulties, particularly in relation to Article 16 on discrimination against women in all matters relating to marriage and family relations. Some Islamic nations objected that the rights of men and women in marriage could not be 'the same' because their roles in the family were not the same but complementary, and necessarily so for the 'physical and moral balance of children'.[108] According to this view, the article failed to take account of a fact which was a matter of common sense, namely that men and women, in order to be truly

[107] UN doc. E/CN.6/591, paras. 19, 48, 51, 56, 63. Cf. the views of France, (para. 54) that Draft Article 4 justified discrimination against women instead of fighting it, and Singapore (para. 51) which thought that the article tended to place women on a higher footing than men. Both delegates clearly misunderstood the provision. See also E/CN.6/S.R.660 and 648.

[108] UN doc. A/C3/34/S.R.70, paras. 11, 12, 31.

equal, did not need to be treated as being the same. Article 16 (1) (c)[109] which incorporated the idea 'not of equality but of identity without differentiation' between the role of the spouses was a mockery of the desired goal. This argument cut little ice with the majority of delegates who accepted that the article was dealing with an equitable distribution of rights and duties.

Other difficulties arose over the Preamble which included references to the new international economic order, neo-colonialism, and foreign occupation. The United Kingdom proposed a new preamble omitting these clauses which were 'inappropriate and unprecedented' for a legal instrument, but this was rejected on the grounds that it ignored the work done over the previous three years.[110] The United Kingdom further objected to Draft Article 16 which omitted to state that it did not apply to service in the armed forces, and to Article 9 on the grounds that the special privileges granted to women by the Convention on the Nationality of Married Women, 1957, might be jeopardized by the adoption of an article embodying the principle of full equality between the spouses.[111] Other delegates pointed out that this view was not consonant with the text which generally recognized full equality of men and women, and that the need for privileged rights, if required, was taken care of under Article 4, which allowed affirmative action as an interim measure.

More serious were the allegations that the drafting was being rushed in order that the Convention might be prepared in time for the World Conference of the United Nations Decade for Women in July 1980. It was suggested the final draft be transmitted to governments for comment and then to the General Assembly's Sixth (Legal) Committee but the view prevailed that, 'though far from being a perfect legal instrument'[112] the Convention would constitute a significant contribution to the Conference. The United Kingdom expressed serious disquiet at the way in which the Convention had been drafted and refused to sign it at the plenary session of the Conference in July 1980.[113] In the United

[109]   State parties are to 'ensure on the basis of equality of men and women . . . the *same* rights and responsibilities during marriage and at its dissolution'.
[110]   UN docs. A/C3/34/L.76, A/C3/34/14 annex i, A/C3/34/S.R.70 (GA 3rd comm.,).
[111]   UN doc. A/C3/34/14, 25.
[112]   UN docs. A/C3/34/L.75 and L.80; A/C3/34/S.R.73.
[113]   See statement by Baroness Young, plenary sess. of World Conference of the UN Decade for Women, Geneva, July 1980; and the Explanation of Vote on the Draft Convention in UN doc. A/34/830 on 18 Dec. 1979 (plenary sess., item 75.) The United Kingdom's attitude was attacked by Baroness Lockwood, Chairman of the UK Equal Opportunities Commission, in *EOC News*, Aug. 1980 and see the *Guardian*, 22 Aug. 1980.

Kingdom's view the Third Committee's working group had acted in a 'precipitate manner' and a number of matters 'could and should have been further discussed and refined'. Although objections to the formulation of the preamble Articles 9 and 29 were rehearsed, it is clear that the United Kingdom's main difficulty was with Articles 15 and 16 since 'the British system of immigration control, which the British Government consider fair and reasonable, might none the less be argued to be in contravention of these Articles as they are presently worded'. This was a reference to the British Government's new immigration rules, which clearly discriminated on the grounds of sex and have rightly been subjected to trenchant criticism.[114]

It is unfortunate that an important legal instrument was not examined in detail by the appropriate legal organs of the United Nations, and the same criticism has been levelled at the Apartheid Convention. Nevertheless, the Third Committee was assisted by expert legal advisers and relied on the precedents established by the earlier discrimination conventions and the final result should play a useful role in promoting the equality of women.[115] It is important to note that this Convention is promotional and programmatic; it does not impose immediately binding legal obligations but requires parties to take 'all appropriate measures'; it does not establish machinery to investigate complaints of non-compliance. In these respects it is a much weaker and more conservative instrument than some earlier conventions.

[114] Cmnd. 7750 (1979). See the *Guardian* and *The Times* (London), 5 Nov. 1979; T. C. Hartley, 'The New Immigration Rules', 43 *MLR* (1980), 440; Proposed new Immigration Rules and the European Convention on Human Rights (HC347 and 434 (1979–80)); 130 *NLJ* (1980), 277, 696.

[115] The text of the Convention is set out in annex iii below.

XI

EQUALITY IN THE
TREATMENT OF ALIENS

IT has long been recognized that persons who reside on the territory of countries of which they are not nationals possess a special status under international law. States have traditionally reserved the right to expel them from their territory[1] and to refuse to grant them certain rights which are enjoyed by their own nationals, e.g. the right to vote, hold public office or to engage in political activities. Aliens may be prohibited from joining the civil service or certain professions, or from owning some categories of property, and states may place them under restrictions in the interests of national security or public order. Nevertheless, once lawfully admitted to a territory, they are entitled to certain minimum rights necessary to the enjoyment of ordinary private life.[2]

The right of aliens to equality of treatment has sometimes been laid down in treaties. In the *Oscar Chinn* case[3] the Permanent Court considered the special arrangements made between the Belgian Government and the Unatra Company whereby the latter was required to reduce its transport rates but entitled to compensation for loss, with the result that other transporters were unable to compete with it. The United Kingdom claimed that Belgium was infringing the Treaty of St-Germain, 1919, which provided for commercial freedom and equality, but the Court refused to hold that the special advantages granted to Unatra were inconsistent with the treaty, since they were bound up with the position of Unatra as a company under state supervision and not with its character as a Belgian company, and would have been inapplicable to concerns not under government supervision, whether of Belgian

---

[1] See e.g. *Fong Yue Ting* v. *US*, 149 US 698 (1892), and *Italy* v. *Yugoslavia* (*Boffolo* case), 10 RIAA 528. In times of peace they should only be expelled in the interests of state security or public order. And see now, art. 13 of the Covenant on Civil and Political Rights, 1966, and art. 3 of the European Convention on Establishment, 1955. (European Treaty Series, no. 19.)

[2] See generally P. Weis, *Nationality and Statelessness in International Law* (Stevens, London, 1956); G. S. Goodwin-Gill, *International Law and the Movement of Persons between States* (Oxford University Press, 1978), ch. 5.

[3] PCIJ (1934), ser. A/B, no. 63, 65.

or foreign nationality. The Court stated: 'The form of discrimination which is forbidden is, therefore, discrimination based on nationality and involving differential treatment as between persons belonging to different national groups.'[4]

This opinion did not find favour with the minority. Judge Sir Cecil Hurst took the view that the treaties required commercial equality and that it was unnecessary to bring the case within the scope of the treaties to show that 'the discrimination was based on nationality in the sense that the differentiation was made because the persons possessed a particular nationality'.[5] Similarly Judge Altamira affirmed that a discriminatory rule violative of a treaty did not lose that character by being applied also to some nationals of the offending state.[6] The dissenting opinions are more persuasive, since it is irrelevant that the measures were not adopted from any discriminatory motive but in order to deal with the economic depression, if inequality in fact results. As Judge Anzilotti pointed out, no attempt was made to show that measures could not have been adopted to deal with the economic situation which would not have involved discrimination against aliens.[7]

In the *Rights of Nationals of the United States in Morocco* case,[8] the International Court of Justice held that certain exchange control measures introduced by Morocco, which favoured France and discriminated against the United States, violated the rights to equality of treatment enshrined in the Act of Algeciras, 1906,[9] but no attempt was made to analyse the concept of equality or discrimination.

General international law provides that aliens should not be discriminated against in their enjoyment of property rights once they have been acquired. If alien property is nationalized whereas the property of nationals remains unaffected then that act is discriminatory and prohibited under international law.[10] As Fitzmaurice points out, it has long been recognized that in certain matters, e.g. the general treatment of foreigners in a country, or compensation for property which may be expropriated or nationalized, non-discrimination as between persons of different nationality or against

---

[4] Ibid., 87.   [5] Ibid., 128.   [6] Ibid., 101–2.
[7] Ibid., 111–14. See also the comments by H. Lauterpacht in *The Development of International Law by the International Court* (Stevens, London, 1958), 262–5; and C. W. Jenks in *The Prospects of International Ajudication* (Stevens, London, 1964), 509–10.   [8] ICJ Rep. 1952, 176.   [9] Ibid., 186. See also 91–2.
[10] See in particular Gillian White, *The Nationalisation of Foreign Property* (1961), ch. 6.

foreigners as compared with persons of local nationality, amounts to a rule of international law, the breach of which gives rise to a valid claim on the part of the foreign government whose national is involved.[11]

An expropriation measure directed against the property of aliens *qua* aliens is contrary to international law either if it is intended or if it results in *de facto* discrimination.[12] It was suggested in the United Kingdom memorial in the *Anglo-Iranian Oil Company* case that an expropriation measure which affects only foreign nationals may be contrary to international law[13] and cases of 'genuine nationalization' which happen to affect a foreign national were distinguished from deliberate attempts at confiscation actuated by anti-foreign prejudice.[14] However, if 'discrimination' means 'invidious or arbitrary distinction' then there must be more than one party involved and the nationalization measures could not be illegal on the grounds of discrimination (though they might be on other grounds such as failure to provide adequate and prompt compensation) because there was no other company which was being treated more favourably.[15] Unless some basis exists for comparison of treatment, it cannot be said that there has been an invidious distinction.

When the Suez Canal Company was nationalized in 1956, the Company did not refer to the principle of non-discrimination as a legal ground for protest[16] but it was relied upon by the Netherlands

[11] G. Fitzmaurice, 'The Juridical Clauses of the Peace Treaties', 73 *Hague Recueil* (1948), ii.349. See also J. H. Herz, 'Expropriation of Foreign Property', 35 *AJIL* (1941), 243, 249; S. Friedman, *Expropriation in International Law* (Stevens, London, 1953), 189–93; Lord McNair, 'The Seizure of Property and Enterprises in Indonesia', 6 *Netherlands International Law Review* (1959), 219, 247–9; H. Rolin, ibid., 269–70; M. Sørensen, 101 *Recueil des Cours* (1960), iii.178; Shigeru Oda, 'The Individual in International Law', in M. Sørensen, ed., *Manual of Public International Law* (Macmillan, London 1968), 486.

[12] Cf. J. L. Brierly, Sir Humphrey Waldock ed., *The Law of Nations* (Clarendon Press, Oxford, 6th ed. 1963), 284. Also the advisory opinions on *German Settlers in Poland*, PCIJ, ser. B, no. 6, 24, and *Minority Schools in Albania*, ser. A/B (1935), no. 64.

[13] ICJ Pleadings, *Anglo-Iranian Oil Company* case, 93–7. See also *Württembergische Milchverwertung Südmilch AG* v. *Ugliola* [1970] CMLR 194, 202; *Re Electric Refrigerators Italy* v. *EEC Commission* [1963] CMLR 289, 311–12; S. Wex, 'A Code of Practice on Restrictive Business Practices: A Third Option', 15 *Can. YIL* (1977) 198, 222–6.

[14] Ibid., 98. Cf. also the Italian Memorial in the *Phosphates in Morocco* case PCIJ, ser. C, (1938) no. 84, 13.   [15] See 70 *Harv. L. R.* (1957), 480, 485.

[16] Though the suggestion was made by the British Foreign Secretary, Mr Lloyd, in the Security Council. (See *New York Times*, 6 Oct. 1956, 3, col. 2.) Cf. The case concerning the *Deutsche Amerikanische Petroleum Gesellschaft Oil Tankers*, 2 *UNRIAA* (1926), 777, 785.

Government in a 1959 note complaining against the nationalization of Dutch owned enterprises in Indonesia. The right of sovereign states to nationalize the property of nationals of other states was admitted provided there was no discrimination, but it was claimed that the Indonesian measures were plainly discriminatory since they were directed only against Dutch property.[17] The Organization for Economic Co-operation and Development in its Draft Convention on the Protection of Foreign Property, 1962, included as a necessary condition for a valid nationalization the principle that 'The Measures are not discriminatory . . .'[18] It is, therefore, generally accepted that nationalization measures are invalid under international law if they make distinctions between nationals and aliens to the detriment of the latter. In *Banco Nacional de Cuba* v. *Sabbatino*, the U.S. Court of Appeal, Second Circuit, held that 'When a state treats aliens of a particular country discriminatorily to their detriment, that state violates international law'.

It has frequently been claimed that the traditional rules of international law, concerning state responsibility for the acts of legislative, administrative, judicial, and other state organs, give undue preference to aliens and discriminate against a state's own nationals[20] because of the 'international standard of minimum treatment' under which an alien may expect and require from the organs of a state a certain standard of treatment regardless of what the nationals of that state may enjoy.[21] Opposed to this doctrine is the standard of 'national treatment' under which an alien may only expect to receive equality of treatment with nationals.[22]

[17] See 'Netherlands Note of December 18, 1959', 54 *AJIL* (1960), 484, 486–7.

[18] International Legal Materials, ii.241, 248. Cf. also *Anglo-Iranian Oil Company* v. *SUPOR*, 22 Int. L. R. (1955), 23, 39; *In re Helbert Wagg and Co. Ltd.* [1956] Ch. 1, 323; 22 Int. L. R. (1955), 480; *Banco Nacional de Cuba* v. *Sabbatino* (1962) 56 *AJIL*, 1104–5.

[19] 307 F. 2d 845, 866–8 (1962). The decision was reversed by the Supreme Court on the ground that, even if the expropriation was in violation of international law, as *inter alia* discriminatory, it would be unwise for the courts so to determine and thus embarrass the executive branch. 376 US 398, 433 (1964). See also M. M. Whiteman, *Digest of International Law*, (US Govt. Printing Office, Washington D.C., 1963), viii.376–82, and Gillian White, op. cit., 144.

[20] See e.g. F. V. García-Amador, 'State Responsibility in the Light of New Trends of International Laws', 49 *AJIL* (1955), 339, 344.

[21] See e.g. the *Neer* claim (1926) 4 RIAA 60; the *Hopkins* claim, ibid., 41.

[22] See the authorities quoted in J. H. Herz, 'Expropriation of Foreign Property', 35 *AJIL* (1941), 243, 259, n. 66. P. E. Corbett (*Law and Society in the Relations of States* (New York, 1951), 181) has said, 'The equality standard implies that in order to obtain compensation for injury suffered by one of its nationals abroad, a state must prove discrimination against him as a foreigner.'

In the *Hopkins* claim, the United States and Mexico General Claims Commission denied that the enjoyment by aliens of broader and more liberal treatment than that accorded by a state to its own citizens under its municipal laws amounted to a discrimination by a nation against its own citizens in favour of aliens. 'It is not a question of discrimination, but a question of difference in their respective rights and remedies. The citizens of a nation may enjoy many rights which are withheld from aliens and conversely, under international law aliens may enjoy rights and remedies which the nation does not accord to its own citizens.'[23] A number of jurists particularly from Latin America have opposed any special protection for aliens over and above that accorded by municipal law, on the grounds that this is 'unjustifiable discrimination'.[24]

At the Inter-American Conference on the International Protection of the Rights of Man, held in Mexico in 1945, it was suggested that international protection of the essential rights of man would eliminate the misuse of diplomatic protection of citizens abroad, the exercise of which has more than once led to the violation of the principles of non-intervention and of equality between nationals and aliens with respect to the essential rights of man.[25] This was taken up by the ILC's special rapporteur on the law of state responsibility, who saw both legal and political difficulties in accepting treatment giving preference to and implying privileges in favour of aliens,[26] and proposed a fusion of the principles of equality of treatment and the minimum standard of international law, in the form of a draft article:[27]

1. The State is under a duty to ensure to aliens the enjoyment of the same civil rights, and to make available to them the same individual guarantees as are enjoyed by its own nationals. These rights and guarantees shall not, however, in any case be less than the 'fundamental human rights' recognized and defined in contemporary international instruments.

2. In consequence, in case of violation of civil rights, or disregard of individual guarantees, with respect to aliens, international responsibility will be involved only if internationally recognized 'fundamental human rights' are affected.

[23] (1926) 4 RIAA 41.
[24] See e.g. García-Amador, op. cit., n. 20.
[25] See Res. XL of the Conference.
[26] First report of the special rapporteur, Mr F. V. García-Amador; *Yearbook of the International Law Commission* 1956, ii.203.
[27] *Yearbook of the ILC* 1967, ii.112. See also ibid. i.154 ff. and ii.49.

This proposal involved codifying the 'international minimum standard' and giving it content by reference to the recent developments in the law of human rights[28] and was a development of great potential significance to both the law of state responsibility and the protection of human rights. As Professor Jennings has pointed out, 'there must be some osmosis between these two principles and perhaps eventually a synthesis'.[29]

Most of the recent instruments concerning human rights tend to be cautious and vague in their treatment of the rights of aliens. There is no provision which attempts to define specifically what rights an alien may enjoy in the territory of a state and the matter is left to municipal law. The Universal Declaration of Human Rights usually refers to 'everyone' and does not specifically draw distinctions on the ground of nationality, although it is clear that the word 'everyone' in Article 21, which deals with political rights, must refer to nationals only.[30] Disqualification of aliens from exercising political rights has never been held to be discriminatory but a legitimate and reasonable restriction. A Soviet proposal that women should be granted political rights regardless of nationality in the Convention on the Political Rights of Women was withdrawn when its import was realised.[31] Nor does the Declaration of Human Rights prevent states from applying other reasonable restrictions on the rights of aliens to own property, express political opinions, or undertake certain types of work.

Although the protection of the European Convention on Human Rights applies to everyone within the jurisdiction of the states parties (Article 1), Article 16 provides that nothing in Articles 10, 11 and 14 shall be regarded as preventing the imposition of restrictions on aliens' political activity. These restrictions must also apply to Article 3 of the additional Protocol which carefully does not specify the conditions which states may attach to the exercise of the suffrage.

[28] See I. Brownlie, *Principles of Public International Law*, 3rd ed. (1979), 524–8, 596–8; S. Wex, op. cit. n. 13 above.

[29] R. Y. Jennings, 'General Course on the Principles of International Law', 121 *Recueil des Cours* (1967), ii.323, 488.

[30] Article 21 in any case refers to 'his country' which presumably must be interpreted to mean 'country of nationality'. In his report on discrimination in the matter of political rights (UN doc. E/CN.4/Sub.2/213, 41–44), Mr Santa Cruz pointed out that governments can refuse nationality to aliens or grant it accompanied by reasonable restrictions. However, any undue delay in granting nationality to those eligible may be discriminatory.

[31] See UN docs. E/C3/S.R.475, 378 and E/C3/S.R.476, 354. (Cf. also the remarks of the Brazilian delegate, UN docs. E/CN.6/S.R.106 and 107.)

The Convention on the Elimination of All Forms of Racial Discrimination specifically provides that the Convention shall not apply to distinctions, exclusions, restrictions, or preferences made by a state party to the Convention between citizens and non-citizens with the result that the rights laid down in Articles 5 and 6 which are to be assured to 'everyone' are subject to this overriding proviso and are not assured to aliens *qua* aliens,[32] though distinctions etc., made against them on the basis of race, colour, descent, or national or ethnic origin are prohibited. Nevertheless, Article 1 (3) does prohibit discrimination against any particular nationality in the legal provisions of states concerning nationality, citizenship, or naturalization,[33] while Article 5 (d) (iii) guarantees the right of everyone to equality before the law with regard to the right to nationality without distinction as to race, colour, national, or ethnic origin.[34]

Reasonable distinctions made between aliens and nationals with regard, e.g. to political and property rights and for the safeguard of national security, clearly do not conflict with the non-discrimination provisions of the Covenant on Civil and Political Rights.[35] Moreover, distinctions made between aliens and nationals in times of public emergency under Article 4 appear to be permissible as long as they are not a shield for discrimination on the grounds of race, sex, language, religion, or social origin. Article 13, included to prevent aliens from being treated arbitrarily on the grounds of foreign nationality, provides that an alien lawfully residing on the territory of a state party may be expelled from that territory only in pursuance of a decision reached in accordance with law, and except where compelling reasons of national security otherwise require, should be allowed to submit reasons against his expulsion, and to have his case reviewed by and be represented before some competent authority.[36]

[32] See E. Schwelb, 'The International Convention on the Elimination of All Forms of Racial Discrimination', 15 *ICLQ* (1966), 966, 1007–8, 1028; and E/CN.4/Sub.2/335 paras 36–9.
[33] See ibid., 1009. It has already been argued that the Scandinavian citizenship legislation does not contravene this provision.
[34] See ch. 9 above.
[35] Article 25 (political rights) refers specifically to 'citizens'. Cf. also 18 (3) and 19 (3). The protection of the Covenant extends generally to all persons within the territory or jurisdiction of the parties (art. 2).
[36] This clause appears in the Covenant in the same form as that proposed by the Commission on Human Rights. See UN doc. A/2929 113–17. Cf. art. 3 of the European Convention on Establishment, 1955, (European Treaty Series, no. 19) and the proposal to include a similar article in an additional protocol to the European Convention on Human Rights. (See Council of Europe Recommendation 234 and

More difficulty is caused by Article 2 (3) of the Covenant on Economic, Social, and Cultural Rights which permits 'developing countries, with due regard to human rights and their national economy' to determine the extent to which they would guarantee the economic rights recognized in the Covenant to non-nationals. It has already been shown that special measures for the protection of backward peoples are not necessarily discriminatory if they are designed to correct an imbalance caused by economic, social, or historical conditions or some 'natural inequality' and are not continued longer than is strictly necessary to achieve their aim.[37] Article 2 (3) contains no such proviso, the term 'developing country' is not defined, and the language used is unconscionably vague. It must therefore be regarded as an unfortunate inclusion in a covenant of this nature and likely to cause invidious and unreasonable distinctions to be made against aliens on the ground of their foreign nationality.[38]

Article 7 of the EEC Treaty provides that 'within the scope of application of this treaty and without prejudice to any special provisions contained therein, any discrimination on grounds of nationality shall be prohibited'. Although it has been argued that Article 7 prohibits any differentiation on grounds of nationality irrespective of competitive situation, disadvantage, or any justification, the better view is that 'discrimination' means *any* disadvantage on the part of the persons discriminated against.[39] 'Disadvantage' includes any kind of negative effect including the risk of such effect, and special favours granted to one may imply discrimination against another. This does not mean that differential treatment on the ground of nationality is not sometimes justified since there may be cases where special treatment of aliens is necessary in order to put

docs. 1057 (1960) and 1299 (1961).) See also A. H. Robertson, *Human Rights in Europe* (Oceana, Manchester, 1963), 151–4).

[37] In defence of the clause, it was argued that it was needed to rectify situations existing in many developing countries which left, as part of the heritage of the colonial era, the strong influence of non-nationals on the national economy. The clause was designed to restore the proper balance by enabling nationals to exercise their rights. (See GAOR, 17th sess., 3rd comm., annex 43, 6–17 (UN doc. A/5365).) The proposal was adopted narrowly 41–38, 12 abstentions.

[38] As Prof. Jennings has said, 'It is very difficult to feel any enthusiasm for this official introduction of a double standard, and of discrimination against aliens in a Covenant supposed to express universal human rights. This is a step backwards, not forwards.' See Jennings, op. cit., n. 29 above. See also E/CN.4/Sub.2/335, paras. 12–19; E/CN.4/Sub.2/392.

[39] For a full treatment see B. Sundberg-Weitman, *Discrimination on Grounds of Nationality* (North Holland, Amsterdam, 1977), 44–7 and generally.

them on the same level as nationals, but differential treatment is not justifiable if it is arbitrary[40] or unreasonable.

The best analysis of the discrimination principle by the European Court of Justice is in the *Electric Refrigerators* case[41] where it was stated that 'the differential situation of non-comparable situations does not lead automatically to the conclusion that there is no discrimination. An appearance of formal discrimination may therefore correspond in fact to an absence of material discrimination. Material discrimination would consist in treating either similar situations differently or different situations identically.' The measures taken by the European Commission in that case were held to be both justified and necessary in order to avoid discrimination. In reaching its conclusion the Court was influenced by the views of Advocate-General Lagrange who, relying on the *Minority Schools in Albania* case,[42] said that the principle of non-discrimination has a double aspect, both positive and negative. It consists 'both in treating non-comparable situations equally and in treating comparable situations unequally.' (The Court's use of words is to be preferred since the use of 'equal' in the sense of 'identical' is likely to lead to confusion.)

It is clear that Article 7 may require differential treatment in order to counter-balance the non-identical situations of nationals and aliens. Indirect discrimination is also forbidden. Thus a rule which on its face differentiates between people on the basis of criteria other than nationality none the less infringes the non-discrimination requirements of Community law[43] if its application leads in fact to the same result unless the differentiation is justified on objective grounds.[44]

More controversial is the issue of whether or not Article 7 forbids discrimination by states against their own nationals, sometimes known as 'reverse discrimination'.[45] Although the English High Court has rejected the view of the National Insurance Commissioner that he was 'unable to invoke any principle of non-discrimination

[40] Ibid., 70–85.
[41] [1963] 2 CMLR 289, 311–12. The issue here concerned Article 226 not Article 7.
[42] See p. 29 above.   [43] e.g. art. 119 as well as art. 7.
[44] See the opinion of Warner AG in *Jenkins* v. *Kingsgate Ltd.* [1981] 2 CMLR 221 and *Sotgiu* v. *Deutsche Bundespost* [1974] ECR 153; *E.E.C. Commission* v. *Ireland* (*Re Sea Fishery Restrictions*) [1978] 2 CMLR 466; *CRAM* v. *Toia* [1980] 2 CMLR 31.
[45] Although this term is well established in EEC usage it is misleading and better avoided as the use of the term in other contexts to mean 'positive measures of protection'.

against a state's own nationals' in the instant case, it left open the possibility that Community legislation only prohibits discrimination in the social services against a national of the EEC other than a national of the host nation. 'In other words, you may not discriminate against nationals of other nations of the EEC although you may be able to discriminate against your own nationals.'[46] This view not only conflicts with a literal reading of Article 7 which prohibits *any* discrimination on the grounds of nationality but is inconsistent with Council Regulation 1408/71 which refers to guaranteeing within the Community 'equality of treatment for all nationals of member-States under the various national legislations'. As Advocate-General Warner pointed out in a recent opinion, 'Article 7 of the Treaty forbids discrimination by a member-State against its own nationals as much as it forbids discrimination by a member-State against nationals of other member-States.'[48]

[46] *R* v. *National Insurance Commissioner, ex p. Warry* [1981] ICR 90.
[47] *Kenny* v. *National Insurance Commissioner* [1979] 1 CMLR 433, per Donaldson LJ.
[48] *R* v. *Saunders* [1980] QB 72. The European Court did not dissent from this view. See also Sundberg-Weitman, op. cit., ch. 9; J. Steiner 97 *LQR* (1981), 365–9; *SA des Grandes Distilleries Peureux* v. *Directeur des Services Fiscaux de la Haute-Saône* [1980] 3 CMLR 337.

XII

THE EUROPEAN CONVENTION ON HUMAN RIGHTS

1. *The Principle of Non-Discrimination*

OF all the procedures established for protecting human rights, the machinery set up by the European Convention on Human Rights and Fundamental Freedoms, 1950, is the most generally effective.[1] It nevertheless possesses some serious defects, particularly with regard to the protection of the principle of equality before the law.

In the Preamble to the Convention, the signatory governments resolved to take the first steps for the collective enforcement of certain rights set forth in the Universal Declaration of Human Rights. Several provisions of the Declaration contained provisions concerning non-discrimination and equality,[2] and these rights were naturally considered for inclusion in the European Convention. Among the rights recommended for consideration by the International Council of the European Movement, in Brussels in February 1949, and contained in Article 1 of a draft convention submitted to the Committee of Ministers in July the same year, were 'equality before the law and freedom from discrimination on account of religion, race, national origin or political or other opinion'.[3] This draft considerably influenced the First Session of the Consultative Assembly of the Council of Europe at its meeting and the rapporteur of the Legal Committee, Mr P. H. Teitgen, included the above suggestions in his list of the rights and freedoms which might be guaranteed by the Convention. During the debates many delegates affirmed the need for guarantees of equality before the law and non-discrimination. The Danish delegate pointed out that

[1] The provisions of the Convention are fully treated elsewhere: see *inter alia* A. H. Robertson, *Human Rights in Europe* (Oceana, Manchester, 1963); G. Weil, *The European Convention of Human Rights* (Sijthoff, Leyden, 1963); F. Monconduit, *La Commission européenne des droits de l'homme* (Sijthoff, Leyden, 1963); K. Vasak, *La Convention européenne des droits de l'homme* (Sijthoff, Leyden, 1965); J. E. S. Fawcett, *The Application of the European Convention of Human Rights* (Oxford University Press, 1969); F. G. Jacobs, *The European Convention on Human Rights* (Oxford University Press, 1975).   [2] Arts. 1, 2, 7, 10, 16 (1), 21 (2), and (3).
[3] Documents of the Council of Europe: docs. INF/2/E, 3, INF/5/E/R, 6–7.

the enumeration of the types of forbidden discrimination omitted any reference to sex or any provision relating to the protection of national minorities.[4] Principally due to his advocacy, references to these matters were included in the proposals presented by Mr Teitgen in August.[5] In the report of the Legal Committee to the Consultative Assembly it was explained that the resolution adopted specified that the regime of guaranteed liberties should not include any discrimination based on membership of a national minority. Since the Committee's task was to draw up a list, not of fundamental rights which must be defined in a general declaration, but only of those which appeared suitable for inclusion in an immediate international guarantee, it felt that a special provision defining rights of national minorities should not be included, without prejudice to a future examination of the matter. The clause which was approved closely approximated to the wording of Article 2 of the Universal Declaration: i.e.—'The fundamental rights and freedoms enumerated above will be guaranteed without distinction on any ground such as race, colour, sex, language, religion, political or other opinion, national or social origin, affiliation to a national minority, fortune or birth.'[6]

No other clause relating to equality or non-discrimination was included, thus modifying the original proposals of the European Movement in two important respects. First, no reference was made to a guarantee of equality before the law. Second, general protection against discrimination was no longer to be guaranteed but only protection against discrimination in respect of the rights and freedoms guaranteed in the Convention.

In his report Mr Teitgen pointed out that 'each country will maintain the right to determine the means by which the guaranteed freedoms are exercised within its territory, but its legislation in defining the measures for the achievement of these freedoms cannot make any distinction based on race, colour, sex, language, religion, political or other opinion, national or social origin, affiliation to a national minority, fortune or birth. Any national legislation which

---

[4] Reports of plenary sess. (hereafter referred to as 'rep.'), 19 Aug. 1949, 409. See e.g. Mr Lannung (Denmark), reports of the consultative Assembly (1949), 412, Mr Cingolani (Italy), 418; Mr Kraft (Denmark), 420; Mr Edberg (Sweden), 426; Mr Foster (UK) 436; Mr Everett (Ireland), 442; Mr Jaquet (France) 458; Mr MacEntee (Ireland), 462.   [5] Doc. A. 116, 2.
[6] Recommendation 38 of the Consultative Assembly, 8 Sept., 1949, See doc. Ass. 1949 no. 108, 262; doc. A 167, 4 and doc. Ass. 1949 no. 77, 205.

under the pretext of organising freedom makes any such discrimination falls within the scope of the international guarantee.'[7]

When instituting the Committee of Experts on Human Rights, in November 1949, the Committee of Ministers instructed it to pay due attention to the progress which had been made in this matter by the competent organs of the United Nations.[8] Accordingly, the preparatory report of the Council of Europe Secretariat compared the United Nations and European Draft Conventions. Article 20 of the Preliminary Draft United Nations Covenant[9] provided, '(1) All are equal before the law and shall be accorded the equal protection of the law; (2) Everyone shall be accorded all the rights and freedoms defined in this Covenant without discrimination on any ground such as race, colour, sex, language, religion, political or other opinion, national or social origin; (3) Everyone shall be accorded equal protection against any incitement to such discrimination.' Various draft texts based on the work of the Consultative Assembly were considered, some of which contained the term, 'distinction', others 'discrimination'.[10] In Article 5 of their preliminary draft, the committee of experts replaced the word 'guaranteed' by 'secured' since the aim of the Convention was not to set up an international guarantee to be undertaken by the states themselves. This was obviously intended to avoid the terminology of the minorities treaties with all its unwelcome associations.

During its second session the committee of experts considered a United Kingdom amendment to the Preliminary Draft Convention. Article 14 of the draft merely adopted the first two paragraphs of Article 20 of the United Nations Draft Covenant except for a proviso inserted after paragraph 1, i.e. 'provided that this article shall not be held to forbid the imposition of reasonable legal disabilities on minors and persons of unsound mind'. That it was thought necessary to qualify the notion of 'equality' in such a way clearly demonstrates the inchoate nature of the idea at this time. It is also noteworthy that the words 'affiliation to a national minority' were omitted from the British amendment. However, the drafting committee retained only the first six words of Paragraph 1 of the amendment, removed all references to 'equal protection of the law' and the proviso and reinstated the reference to national

[7] Rep. 1949, 1150.   [8] Doc. Ass. 1949. no. 116, para. 6, 288–9.
[9] UN doc. E/1371, 24.
[10] See docs. A809, 6 and A833, 4; CM/WP1(50)1, 10 and 12.

minorities.[11] The drafting committee was now confronted with two alternative texts.

When the Conference of Senior Officials met in Strasburg in June 1950, it adopted a simple consolidated text which provided 'The rights and freedoms defined in this Convention shall be secured without discrimination on any grounds such as . . .' and the clause relating to the principle of equality before the law was finally deleted.[12] The draft convention submitted to the fifth session of the Council of Ministers contained in Article 14 the clause, 'The enjoyment of the rights and freedoms defined in this Convention shall be secured without discrimination on any ground such as . . .'[13] This formulation emphasized that the rights and freedoms protected by the Convention were to be enjoyed and exercised to the full without discrimination on any ground. All the various ways in which the rights and freedoms recognized in the Convention may manifest themselves shall be secured (*doivent être assurés*) without discrimination. The text as it finally appears in the Convention as Article 14 reads: 'The enjoyment of the rights and freedoms set forth in this Convention shall be secured without discrimination on any ground such as sex, race, colour, language, religion, political or other opinion, national or social origin, association with a national minority, property, birth or other status.'

Its operation is restricted to some extent by Article 16: 'Nothing in Articles 10, 11 and 14 shall be regarded as preventing the High Contracting Parties from imposing restrictions on the political activity of aliens.' This article had its genesis in the report of the sub-committee which made a preliminary study of the amendments proposed by the committee of experts.[14]

The Omissions from the Convention. While the Draft Convention was being discussed at the second session of the Consultative Assembly, criticisms were made of the way in which the Committee of Ministers had altered the text. It was argued that Article 63, which allows for the optional extension of the operation of the Convention to the territories for whose international relations a

[11] UN doc. E/CN.4/355/add.2 and ECHR docs. A770, 7; CM/WP1 (50) 10, 4, and A 919.
[12] See docs. CM/WP 1 (50) 15. app. 3 and 10, and doc. CM/WP4 (50) 9, 6, 16, app. 17.   [13] Doc. CM (50) 52, 7.
[14] See doc. 796, 1. 5 Feb. 1950. As to the interpretation of art. 16, see *Gudmundsson* v. *Iceland*, Application no. 551/59.

state was responsible, ran counter to the second part of Article 2 of the Universal Declaration which was not so restrictive.[15] An amendment to delete Article 63, though carried 46–37 by the Consultative Assembly, was not accepted by the Committee of Ministers.

The original draft of the European Movement was improved by the inclusion of references to national minorities and sex in the discrimination clause but the Convention omits the more general equality and non-discrimination suggestions of the European Movement.[16] It does not provide for specific recognition of the right to equality before the law and equal protection of the laws, nor for extra guarantees for members of national minorities. There is no general prohibition of non-discrimination but only a right not to be discriminated against in respect of those rights and freedoms set forth in the Convention. Article 6 does, however, include the notion of *égalité des armes*. In *Ofner and Hopfinger* v. *Austria*[17] the Commission said, 'In the present cases, the problem is whether the notion of a fair trial embodies any right relating to the defence beyond and above the minimum rights laid down in paragraph 3. The Commission is of the opinion that what is generally called "the equality of arms", that is, the procedural equality of the accused with the public prosecutor is an inherent element of a "fair trial".' The Commission did not express an opinion as to whether the legal basis of such equality was to be found in Paragraph 3 of Article 6 since 'it is beyond doubt that, in any case, the wider and more general provision for a fair trial contained in paragraph 1 of Article 6 embodies the notion of equality of arms'. This statement was later reaffirmed in the *Pfunders* case.[18]

Nevertheless, Article 6 only provides for a procedural equality *vis-à-vis* the prosecution and the defence in criminal trials. It is not difficult to imagine situations in which a particular accused might be treated less equally than another without violence to the principle approved by the Commission under Article 6. A decision of the Austrian Constitutional Court in 1964 held that the rights of persons entitled in Austria to equality before the law had not been extended by the Convention.[19] The right to equality before the law was guaranteed by Article 7 of the Austrian Constitution and Article 2 of the state treaty to Austrian nationals alone and not to aliens.

[15] See rep. 1950, 938–40.   [16] Rep. 1950, 336.   [17] *Yearbook* 1963, 693.
[18] *Austria* v. *Italy* 30 Mar. 1963; *Yearbook* 1963, 794.
[19] See *Österreichische Juristen Zeitung* (1965), 247.

Article 14 of the Convention, which had been accepted as constitutional law since its entry into force guaranteed enjoyment of the rights and freedoms set forth therein to all people and hence to aliens as well, but the right to equality before the law was not included among those rights, and the Convention had not therefore extended the range of persons possessing this right in Austria.

In his *An International Bill of the Rights of Man*,[20] Sir Hersch Lauterpacht wrote, 'The claim to equality before the law is in a substantial sense the most fundamental of the rights of man. It occupies the first place in most written constitutions. It is the starting point of all other liberties.' Echoing this sentiment in the *South West Africa* cases, Judge Tanaka said, 'This principle— equality before the law—has been recognized as one of the fundamental principles of modern democracy and government based on the rule of law.'[21] Similarly Jenks has described the principle of respect for human rights including equality before the law as a general principle of law.[22] Nevertheless, all attempts to include a clause recognizing the principle of equality before the law were doomed to failure.

In 1958, the Legal Committee of the Consultative Assembly recommended that a further protocol to the Convention should be drafted by a committee of experts, since the Convention had (in the words of the Preamble) taken only the 'first steps', and a subcommittee was established to examine the matter.[23] Among the other political and civil rights which the Committee considered part of the 'common spiritual and legal heritage' of the member states to which the guarantee of the Convention might be extended were the rights of every individual to be recognized everywhere as a person before the law, and to equality before the law. The alternatives suggested for Article 6 were: '(a) All persons are equal before the law. The law shall afford to all persons equal and effective protection; (b) All persons are equal before the law. No one shall be subjected by the state to any discrimination based on any ground

[20] (1945), 115.   [21] ICJ Rep. 1966, 304.

[22] C. W. Jenks, *The Common Law of Mankind* (Stevens, London, 1958), 121.

[23] Res. (60) 6 of the Committee of Ministers, doc. Ass. (1960) doc. 114, para. 79. See also docs. 828, 1057, and Recommendation 234. A provision containing certain special rights for members of ethnic, religious, or linguistic minorities based on art. 25 of the Draft UN Covenant (now art. 27 of the Covenant on Civil and Political Rights) was initially considered but not proceeded with since it was unanimously agreed that such an article would not offer any sufficient new guarantee to members of national minorities.

such as sex, race, colour, language, religion, political or other opinion, national or social origin, belonging to a national minority, property, birth or other status.'

The alternative forms of Draft Article 6 revealed a basic divergence of views among the experts. An earlier draft had included a formulation almost identical to Article 24 of the United Nations draft which enshrined the principle of equality before the law and non-discrimination, but this did not find general favour. The rapporteur, however, felt that Article 6 could not be retained in this form since a general non-discrimination clause might cause insoluble problems, for instance in regard to the treatment of foreigners. It might also cover private or social relations which are not within the province of the law and put all member countries under the obligation to write into their legislation, effective guarantees against discrimination in every field of activity including such private matters as the employment of workers in private enterprises, the lease of dwellings, the limitation by private associations or trade unions of their membership to certain categories of people, and so on. He could not subscribe to a clause containing so vague, unlimited, and imprecise a commitment and, in his opinion, nor could the member states.

This view ignored the judicial guides and signposts which could be called in aid to elucidate and limit the meaning of these terms, such as the jurisprudence of the United States Supreme Court in interpreting the Fourteenth Amendment to the United States Constitution, the decisions of other municipal courts, and the work of the United Nations Sub-Commission and many other sources. The 'insoluble problem' referred to was solved in Article 1 (2) of the United Nations Convention on the Elimination of All Forms of Racial Discrimination, 1965, and was dealt with to a limited extent in Article 16 of the European Convention itself which allows states to restrict the political activities of aliens.[24] Moreover, there would not be general agreement today with the proposition that the matters described as 'private relations' are not *a priori* 'within the province of the law'.

In the rapporteur's view the first text provided for equality of protection of the rights of individuals but not necessarily for equality of rights. Thus it would not make equal pay for men and women

[24] See E. Schwelb, 'The International Convention on the Elimination of all Forms of Racial Discrimination', 15 *ICLQ* (1966), 996, 1019.

mandatory, but it would ensure that they had an equal opportunity before the law to ensure that they obtained their pay and would avoid the difficulties of interference in private and social relationships not within the province of the law.[25] Such a view cannot be permitted to pass unchallenged. The United States Supreme Court had not interpreted the 'equal protection of the laws' clause restrictively, and merely granted litigants *égalité des armes* in a court of law, but interpreted it broadly to include equality in the enjoyment of substantive rights.

The second text would not relate to the field of 'private relations', according to the rapporteur, since its purport was to require states to respect the principle of non-discrimination. Since Article 14 itself did not specifically limit the scope of the article to state action, if Article 6 were to contain such a clause, it might be concluded by an argument *a contrario* that Article 14 applied also to 'private' relations. There is little substance in this argument since the rights and freedoms guaranteed in the Convention are rights which can only be protected by the High Contracting Parties by state action. Private activities not included in section 1 or the first protocol were not subject to Article 14, and this is one reason why a convention on measures to be taken against incitement to racial, national, and religious hatred was also mooted.[26]

Both texts of Article 6 were included in the draft submitted to the Assembly and then to the Committee of Ministers but, on the advice of a committee of governmental experts, the Council of Ministers reported that 'Regarding recognition as a person in the eyes of the law, and equality before the law, the Committee did not favour their inclusion in a second protocol since it was hardly necessary, and any text likely to be accepted by all governments was open to varying interpretations. Indeed the Assembly itself had recognized the difficulty of drafting a satisfactory text on equality before the law.' It was also considered that it would produce a large number of applications which would involve the Commission in too much work investigating the facts of complaints. Even the neutered version which restricted the proposed guarantee to equal protection in the application of the law was found unacceptable and rejected.[27]

This was an unnecessarily conservative and timid attitude.

[25] See doc. 1057, 12, ff.

[26] See on this point, M.-A. Eissen, 'The European Convention on Human Rights and the Duties of the Individual', in 32 *Nordisk Tidsskrift for International Ret* (1962), 230.

[27] See docs. 1564, 55 and H (65) 16.

Moreover, it was inconsistent to assert that such an article is 'hardly necessary' and yet to complain that the Commission would be deluged with complaints requiring much investigation. If the Convention was intended to secure basic rights and freedoms, it was a pusillanimous argument that one of the most basic would involve too much work and therefore should not be included.

The American Convention on Human Rights has included the principle of equality before the law in Article 24 which provides, 'All persons are equal before the Law. Consequently, they are entitled without discrimination, to equal protection of the Law.' As has been seen, a similar formulation is found in Article 26 of the United Nations Covenant on Civil and Political Rights, and it is regrettable that the European system did not boldly allow the Commission and the Court to interpret such a clause aided by the experience of other jurisdictions with analogous provisions.

Minorities. Concern about minorities goes back to 1949 when Mr Teitgen's report on the conclusion of the European Convention raised the question of the definition of rights of national minorities.[28] One proposal was that a permanent sub-committee should be established to report annually on national minorities and groups to the Consultative Assembly, but this was not acceptable since the Legal Committee considered such a procedure similar to that applied under the League system which 'it was generally admitted . . . tended to aggravate rather than alleviate difficulties'. In 1957 the Assembly requested the Legal Committee to report on the 'Constitutions and regulations in force and the existing situations in this regard' concerning national minorities in member states of the Council of Europe, but the Council of Ministers did not consider that the information should be provided since it wished to avoid raising 'unnecessarily' a very delicate question, 'the discussion of which in public is likely to do more harm than good'.[29] In 1959, the Consultative Assembly, considering that the maximum protection should be afforded to national minorities, instructed the legal committee to study the possibility of a protocol on the rights and privileges of such minorities. In their reports, the states parties and the Secretariat took the view that minorities were already sufficiently

[28] Doc. 77 (1949) and docs. 6 (1950), 508 (1956), 522 (1956), and 551 (1956); ref. no. 272 (1959); report by M. Rolin (1957) (doc. 731).
[29] See Res. 136 (57) (1957), and docs. 1002, 923, 955.

protected from discrimination by Article 14 with regard to the rights recognized in the Convention, a safeguard rendered more effective by the right of individual application under Article 25, and the Committee reported that it was inadvisable at the time to establish a system similar to that under the League for the protection of national minorities. A more appropriate course was to settle disputes by bilateral negotiation or by the procedure established under the Council of Europe for the peaceful settlement of disputes.[30]

In 1961 the Assembly noted the existence in member states of non-dominant groups conscious of belonging to a national minority, and observed that Article 14 already afforded a certain measure of protection.[31] Nevertheless, it considered that the *collective interests* of national minorities should be satisfied to the extent compatible with safeguarding the essential interests of states to which minorities belong, and proposed a draft article: 'Persons belonging to a national minority shall not be denied the right in community with other members of their group and as far as is compatible with public order, to enjoy their own culture, to use their own schools and receive teaching in the language of their choice or to profess and practise their own religion.' The question was not deemed to be of extreme urgency because of the adequacy of the protection already afforded but, because this was not the same thing as the maximum protection, the Committee had felt justified in reconsidering the measure of protection which the Convention afforded at present. This placed persons belonging to a minority on an 'equal footing' with other individuals since persons belonging to minority groups were guaranteed the same rights and freedoms as the rest of the population and the guarantee of equality existed within a system of general protection of human rights. The advisory opinion of the Permanent Court in the *Minority Schools in Albania* case[32] was interpreted as follows: (1) Human rights and freedoms proper, i.e. the basic rights, by reason of a guarantee against discrimination in respect of them, place the minority on an equal footing with other persons within the jurisdiction of a state (present situation); (2) certain rights give the minority, as it were a kind of preferential treatment for the purpose of safeguarding its own character (proposed draft article).

[30] Recommendation 234. See docs. 999 and 1005.
[31] Recommendation 285 (following Recommendation 234). See doc. 1299 (26 Apr. 1961). The influence on terminology of the work of the UN Sub-Commission is noteworthy. (See 3rd sess., 9–27 Jan. 1950, and see Council of Europe doc. AS/Jur. XII (10) 4 (19 Jan. 1959).)   [32] PCIJ, 1935, ser. A/B, no. 64, 17.

The draft thus included the rights enumerated in Article 25 of the United Nations Draft Covenant on Civil and Political Rights but added a further right of minorities to establish their own schools and receive teaching in the language of their choice.[33] Several comments need to be made. It seems that the rapporteur and the Committee misunderstood the meaning of the term 'equality' as interpreted in the *Minority Schools in Albania* opinion. The effect of that decision was that a measure applicable both to the majority and minority groups, and thus having the appearance of *de jure* equality, had resulted in *de facto* inequality. For members of a minority to obtain a true equality of status they might have to be allowed certain special rights not required by the rest of the population. Finally, the report referred to the definition of minorities suggested by the United Nations Sub-Commission in 1950 and made two reservations concerning the use of languages and schools. It was not intended that the state should be prevented from regulating the use of languages for official purposes or that there would be a legal obligation on states to pay for teaching in minority schools though 'it was hoped this would be done where possible as a matter of policy'.

In 1963 the Committee of Ministers informed the Assembly that the experts had completed their work on the Draft Protocol, even though they had not completed their consideration of the rights of minorities. Some had felt that the inclusion of a minority clause might jeopardize the Protocol as a whole, and it was considered preferable to consider it separately.[34] In 1964 the Ministers noted the interim report of the committee of experts in which it was said to be expedient that the study be suspended until a decision had been taken on the *Belgian Linguistic* cases pending before the Commission of Human Rights, and the matter was consequently shelved.[35]

2. *The Jurisprudence of the European Commission and Court of Human Rights*

Although Article 14 of the European Convention on Human Rights appears simple and straightforward *prima facie*, no article has been more controversial in its interpretation and application. The primary

[33] Doc. 1299.
[34] See the 14th statutory report of the Committee of Ministers to the Assembly, Documents of the Assembly, Apr. 1963.
[35] *Yearbook* 1964, 74. See also H. Lannung, 'The Rights of Minorities', in *Mélanges offerts à Polys Modinos* (Editions Pedones, Paris, 1968), 181–95.

disagreement is whether or not the article can have effect *proprio motu* or whether there must also be a concurrent breach of another article of the Convention. This question has been considered by the European Court of Human Rights in the *Belgian Linguistic* case.[36]

Certain basic propositions are clearly established: (1) Discrimination *on any ground* as regards the enjoyment of the rights and freedoms in the convention is prohibited. The words 'such as' (or '*notamment*' in the French text) show that the types of discrimination are merely illustrative examples. (2) The Commission has accepted that not all differentiation is necessarily discriminatory. In some of the first applications considered,[37] it rejected the contention that the punishment of male but not female homosexuals contravened Article 14. The right to respect for private and family life in a democratic society may be subject to interference in accordance with the law of that party for the protection of health or morals under Article 8 (2), and Article 14 did not exclude the possibility of differentiating between the sexes in such measure. Presumably the tacit premiss in these cases was the assumption that male homosexuality violates the provisions of Article 8 (2) while female homosexuality does not. (3) Article 14 sanctions the principle of non-discrimination only as regards the enjoyment of the rights and freedoms set out in Section 1 of the Convention. Thus when an Italian citizen born in Germany complained that he was being discriminated against as a foreigner in that he was unable to obtain a licence to practise his profession in Germany, and demanded equality of treatment between Germans and foreigners in the work in question, the Commission pointed out that the right to exercise a profession is not among the rights guaranteed by the Convention, and since no other right guaranteed by the Commission had been violated, the application was manifestly ill-founded under Article 27 (2).[38]

However, there is a difference between the proposition that Article 14 sanctions the principles of non-discrimination only as regards the enjoyment of the rights and freedoms set out in Section 1 of the Convention, and the proposition that there can be no breach of Article 14 unless another article of the Convention has simultaneously been violated.

[36] Judgment of 23 July 1968, ser. A, no. 6. See below.
[37] Applications 104/55, 167/56, 261/57; *Yearbook* I, 228, 235, 255. But see now *X. v. United Kingdom*, Application No. 7215/75 (report of Commission).
[38] Application 86/55, *Yearbook* I, 198; also 165/56, ibid., 203.

If an applicant claims he is being discriminated against in his enjoyment of a 'right' not included in the Convention his case must be dismissed because of the inapplicability of the Convention (Article 27 (2)) but, if he makes the same claim with regard to a right recognized by the Convention, is it also necessary to show that this right has itself been breached or violated?

In *Albert Grandrath* v. *Federal Republic of Germany*[39] the applicant alleged that as a minister of the Jehovah's Witnesses he had been subjected to less favourable treatment than ministers of other religious persuasions under Article 11 of the German Act on Compulsory Military Service. He alleged that Germany had violated Articles 4 and 9 of the Convention in conjunction with Article 14. The Commission found that there had been no discrimination but by a majority was of the opinion that the application of Article 14 did not depend only on a previous finding of the Commission that a violation of another article of the Convention already existed. 'In certain cases,' it stated, 'Article 14 may be violated in a field dealt with by another article of the Convention, although there is otherwise no violation of that article. . . . Consequently if a restriction which is in itself permissible under paragraph 2 of the above Articles (Articles 4 and 9) is imposed in a discriminatory manner, there would be a violation of Article 14 in conjunction with the other article concerned.' One Commissioner was of the contrary opinion that a question of a violation of Article 14 cannot arise in an independent manner but only in connection with a violation of one of the rights guaranteed by the Convention.[40]

During the period 1962–4 six applications were lodged with the Commission by French-speaking parents of Belgian nationality on their own behalf and that of their children whom they wished to be taught in the French language.[41]

It was alleged that Belgian legislation had infringed Articles 8 and 14 of the Convention and Article 2 of the First Protocol. The Belgian Government replied that the legislation in question was entirely consonant with the Convention and Protocol and requested the Commission to reject the applications as manifestly ill-founded and inadmissible.

---

[39] Application No. 2299/64. Report of Commission adopted 12 Dec. 1966, para. 38. On the question of the autonomous operation of art. 14 see also M.-A. Eissen, ' "L'Autonomie" de l'article 14 de la convention européenne des droits de l'homme dans la jurisprudence de la commission', in *Mélanges offerts à Polys Modinos*, 122.

[40] Report of Commission, para. 47.

[41] Nos. 1474/62, 1677/62, 1691/62, 1769/63, 1994/63, 2126/64.

The Commission declared the six applications admissible with regard to alleged violations of Articles 8 and 14 of the Convention and Article 2 of the Protocol. After a friendly settlement under Article 28 (b) had been attempted unsuccessfully the Commission reported the findings of fact and its opinion as to whether these disclosed a breach of Belgium's obligations under the Convention, and transmitted its report to the Committee of Ministers, at the same time bringing the case before the European Court under Article 48 (a) of the Convention.

The majority of the Commission clearly took the view that Article 14 was not limited to cases in which there was an accompanying violation of another article since such a restricted application would 'deprive Article 14 of any practical value.' The sole effect of the discrimination in its view would be to aggravate the violation of another provision of the Convention, but such an interpretation would hardly be compatible with the wording of Article 14 which stated that the enjoyment of the rights and liberties set forth in the Convention shall be secured without any discrimination. It thus placed on states an obligation which was 'not simply negative'.

The matter was referred to the European Court of Human Rights under Article 48 of the Convention and, in its judgment on the merits, in July 1968, the Court accepted the view of the Commission that Article 2 of the Protocol and Article 8 of the Convention must be interpreted and applied by the Court not only in isolation but also having regard to the guarantee laid down in Article 14. The Court stated, 'While it is true that this guarantee has no independent existence in the sense that under the terms of Article 14 it relates solely to "rights and freedoms set forth in the Convention", a measure which in itself is in conformity with the requirements of the Article enshrining the right or freedom in question may, however, infringe this Article when read in conjunction with Article 14 for the reason that it is of a discriminatory nature.'[42]

During the hearing held in November 1966, the Commission's view of the nature of Article 14 was illustrated by reference to Article 9 which guarantees freedom of religion. The second paragraph of Article 9 authorizes certain limitations on this freedom, in

[42] European Court of Human Rights, ser. A, vol. xvi, para. 9. If there *is* a violation of a substantive article an examination as to whether there has been a violation of that article in conjunction with article 14 is not generally required unless a clear inequality of treatment in the enjoyment of the right is a fundamental aspect of the case. See *Airey* v. *Ireland*, European Court of Human Rights, ser. A, xxxii.30.

particular such as are prescribed by law and are necessary in a democratic society for the protection of public health. It would be legitimate for the authorities to forbid (for example) the ringing of church bells at certain hours of the day in the interests of public health; it would not be legitimate to permit the adherents of one religion to ring bells while compelling other denominations to remain silent. 'In such a case the Commission might find a breach not of Article 9 considered in isolation, but of Article 9 combined with Article 14, since the restrictive measure, though legitimate in itself, was applied in a discriminatory manner.'[43] It was possible for the Commission to conclude by similar reasoning that, in the present cases, there had been violations of Article 2 of the protocol combined with Article 14 of the Convention. In its memorial on the merits of the application, the Belgian government appeared to accept the argument concerning Article 9 though it did not consider that it applied also to Article 2. It stated; '*Lorsque la Convention reconnaît à l'État signataire la possibilité d'intervenir, cette ingérence est soumise au principe de non-discrimination énoncé à l'article 14.*'[44]

Both parties thus correctly recognized that where the articles of the Convention authorized certain interferences by public author-ities in the free enjoyment of those rights (i.e. interferences in the interests of national security, public safety, or the economic well-being of the country, or interference for the prevention of disorder or crime, for the protection of health or morals, or for the protection of the rights and freedoms of others) then these interferences were subject to the non-discrimination requirement of Article 14.

The scope of Article 14 is well summarized in the decision of the Court in *Marckx* v. *Belgium*[45] where it was held that although Article 14 had no independent existence it may play an important autonomous role by complementing the other normative provisions of the Convention and the Protocols. It safeguards individuals placed in similar situations from any discrimination in the enjoyment

[43] Council of Europe doc. CDH (66) 16 Prov., 20.
[44] Memorial of the Belgian Government on the merits, x, (c), *Marge d'appréciation*. It continued, '*La même analyse juridique ne s'applique pas lorsque l'on combine cet article 14 avec l'article 2, première et deuxième phrases du Protocol additionel. Cette dernière disposition, en effect, n'impose à l'État qu'un devoir d'abstention sans lui donner comme le fait l'article 9 (2) un pouvoir d'intervention.*'
[45] European Court of Human Rights, ser. A, vol. xxxi, para. 15; See also *National Union of Belgian Police* case, judgment of 27 Oct. 1975, ser. A, vol. xix, para. 44; *Belgian Linguistics* case, ser. A, vol. vi, para. 9; *Airey* v. *Ireland*, judgment of 9 Oct. 1979, series A, xxxii.30.

of the rights and freedoms set forth in those provisions. 'It is as though Article 14 formed an integral part of each of the provisions laying down rights and freedoms.'

The application of this doctrine has, however, given rise to profound disagreement in the Court. In the *Belgian Linguistics* case the Court states that although, for example, Article 6 did not compel states to institute a system of appeal courts, and a state which did so would go 'beyond its obligations under Article 6, it would nevertheless violate that Article read in conjunction with Article 14, were it to debar certain persons from these remedies without a legitimate reason while making them available to others in respect of the same type of action'.[46] Judge Fitzmaurice, in a later case, has sharply criticized this approach as 'not only wrong but manifestly wrong, and, moreover, contradictory'.[47] It was 'seriously incorrect' because the rights must *be* set forth in the Convention before the non-discrimination obligation comes into play. Yet 'in one and the same breath' the Court had said that there was no obligation under Article 6 for states to establish such a system. There was no right to be enjoyed *as* of right and hence no prohibition of discrimination if it was voluntarily provided by the state. Judge Fitzmaurice applied this criticism in his dissenting judgment in the *Belgian Police* case, and took the view that there was no obligation on the state to consult with unions and hence the question of discrimination under Article 14 did not arise. A natural and creditable distaste for discrimination in any form could not justify, in his view, a conclusion for which no legal warrant existed. The Court was not a court of ethics but a court of law.[48]

A basic difference of approach to treaty interpretation was thus revealed. The majority of the Court has firmly adopted a teleological approach while Judge Fitzmaurice has been a strict literalist. Although the teleological approach is often adopted in social, humanitarian, and law-making treaties[49] there is much to be said for

[46] *Belgian Linguistics* case, ser. A, vol. vi, para. 9.
[47] *Belgian Police* case, ser. A, vol. xix, para. 20.
[48] Ibid. para. 15. The Court had held that Article 14 did apply in these circumstances but that on the facts there had not been a breach. Judges Zekia (24–7) and Wiarda, Ganshof van der Meersch, and Bindschedler-Robert (28–9) agreed with the Court that Article 14 applied and thought that it had been breached. Judge Fitzmaurice stated that, had he thought Article 14 applied, he would have found it to be violated in conjunction with Article 11.
[49] D. J. Harris, *Cases and Materials on International Law*, (Sweet & Maxwell, London, 2nd ed. 1979), 618.

Judge Fitzmaurice's views, particularly in view of the drafting history which demonstrated adamant opposition to a general non-discrimination clause. Nevertheless, the Court in effect held that any rights granted by states even though not specifically protected by substantive articles may be breached in conjunction with Article 14 if they give effect to the aim and object of those articles. Thus access to appeal courts, though not mentioned specifically in Article 6, falls within its general rubric, and litigants may not be discriminated against in seeking to utilize them. Similarly, trade unions in order to be of any use must be able to consult with employers, negotiate with them and conclude agreements. These rights, although not specifically granted in Article 11 are necessarily implied if trade unions are to perform their functions properly, and therefore attract the protection of Article 14.

The Definition of Discrimination. Both the Commission and the Court in the *Belgian Linguistics* case carefully distinguished between discriminations and legitimate distinctions. The applicants made four points before the Commission: (1) a discrimination introduces an inequality of treatment of an arbitrary nature; (2) a distinction designed to re-establish rather than to destroy equality or based on valid reasons is legitimate; (3) a legitimate distinction can turn into a wrongful discrimination having survived the achievement of its initial aim; (4) some discriminations derive from the deliberate will of governments and are more serious while others have their origin in factors of an economic, social, or political nature or in historical circumstances.[50]

This interpretation found favour with the Commission and the Court. The Commission stressed that the motives and philosophy which have inspired a government should also be taken into account. There should be an attempt to verify the motives of the legislative body as well as the aims and effects of the legislation; the motives must be 'reasonable', the aims 'legitimate', and the effects 'justifiable'. Although the contracting states have a certain margin of discretion, the implementation organs established under the Convention have the right to review the states' appraisal of what is in the public interest. However, the Commission also believed that a state

[50] See Report of the Commission, paras. 294–6. The applicants adopted the terms used by Mr Ammoun in his draft study on discrimination in education and employed the terms 'static' and 'active' to describe discrimination.

does not discriminate if it limits itself to conferring an 'advantage', a 'privilege', or a 'favour', rather than imposing 'hardships', 'inequalities', or 'disadvantages'.[51] This terminology would have been better avoided, since advantages, privileges, or favours can amount to discrimination against those not so favoured. In order not to fall into this category they must not be 'undue preferences' but be special measures of protection taken for a limited period to remedy a particular form of backwardness, but this was not made clear by the Commission.[52]

The Court's judgment, following 'the principles which may be extracted from the legal practice of a large number of democratic states', held that the principle of equality of treatment was violated if a distinction had no objective and reasonable justification. The French text (*sans distinction aucune*) cannot be read literally, for this would lead one to judge as contrary to the Convention every one of the many legal or administrative provisions which did not secure to everyone 'complete equality' of treatment in the enjoyment of the rights and freedoms recognized. The Court's view would seem to imply that the equality aimed at by the Convention is not mathematical equality or identity but a 'real or genuine' equality.[53]

Moreover, the Court described 'discriminations' as 'unjustified distinctions' or 'arbitrary distinctions'. Both the majority judgment of the Court and the collective dissenting opinion agreed that five principles were well-founded: (1) the distinction must pursue a legitimate aim; (2) the distinction must not lack an 'objective justification'; (3) article 14 is violated when it 'is clearly established' that there is no reasonable relationship of proportionality between the means employed and the aim sought to be realized; (4) the existence of this reasonable relationship must be appreciated in the knowledge of the 'legal and factual features which characterize the life of the society in the State which is to answer for the measure in dispute'; (5) the Court cannot, in the exercise of this power of appreciation,

[51] Ibid., paras. 400–5, 425.

[52] Cf. arts. 1 (4) and 2 (2) of the Convention on the Elimination of All Forms of Racial Discrimination.

[53] European Court of Human Rights, ser. A, vi.25–50. However the Court continues: 'The competent national authorities are frequently confronted with situations and problems which, on account of differences inherent therein, call for different legal solutions; moreover certain legal inequalities tend only to correct factual inequalities.' 'Inequality' seems to be used here in the sense of 'non-identity'. However, the statement appears to recognize that special measures of protection came within the ambit of Article 14.

'assume the role of the competent national authorities, for it would thereby lose sight of the subsidiary nature of the international machinery of collective enforcement established by the Convention.' It followed from this that 'the national authorities remain free to choose the measures which they consider appropriate in those matters which are governed by the Convention' and that 'review by the Court concerns only the conformity of these measures with the requirements of the Convention'. The fact that the judges agreed on these principles yet disagreed on their application in the instant case demonstrates the problem involved in applying broad standards such as 'reasonableness' and 'justification' to particular fact situations.[54] In the *Belgian Linguistics* case, the majority of the Commission, the majority of the Court and the joint dissenting judges, though generally agreeing on the principles to be applied, nevertheless answered the questions at issue in several different ways.

A marked difference of opinion over whether there had been discrimination under Article 14 also occurred in the *Belgian Police* case. The majority of the Court held in respect of a Belgian Royal Decree of 2 August 1966 denying rights of consultation to the National Union of Belgian Police, in contrast to certain other unions which enjoyed such rights, that it had not been clearly established that the disadvantage suffered by the applicant had been excessive in relation to the legitimate aim pursued by the government, and nor had the principle of proportionality been offended.[55] Four judges[56] dissented, holding that the disadvantage in protection of occupational interests could not be justified and necessarily entailed discrimination in comparison with members of trade unions which were consulted under an earlier act. The dissenting view seems preferable since the finding that the government was not 'ill-intentioned' is hardly relevant if there is discrimination in fact. In other cases in the late 1970s, discrimination was unanimously

[54] The same difficulty has arisen in some of the American cases. See in particular *Harper* v. *Virginia State Board of Elections*, (US Supreme Court Reports) 16 L. ed. 2d. 169 and *Reynolds* v. *Sims*, 12 L. ed. 2d. 506.

[55] The Government had wished to ensure a coherent and balanced staff policy, taking due account of the occupation interests of all the staff and 'there was no reason to think that the Government had other and ill-intentioned designs'.

[56]. Judge Zekia (24–7); Judges Wiarda, Ganshof van der Meersch, and Bindschedler-Robert (28–9). Judge Fitzmaurice, had he believed Article 14 applied would have held that there had been discrimination as in the latter joint separate opinion.

established in one,[57] but in the others the differences of treatment were found not to be discriminatory as the government 'had pursued a legitimate aim by means of measures which were not disproportionate'.[58]

The important achievements of the Commission and the Court have been the use of 'discrimination' in the sense of 'arbitrary or invidious' distinction, the establishment of the tests of 'legitimate aim', 'objective justification of distinctions', and 'reasonable relationship of proportionality between the means employed and the aims sought to be realized'. They have thus made a marked contribution to the development and understanding of the principle of the equality of individuals under international law.

3. Supplementary Proposals

Because the scope of Article 14 is limited, other measures have been suggested to supplement it. The European Convention does not deal with discrimination in general nor with incitement as a separate issue. No argument could be based on Article 17 as its effect is merely negative.[59] A group which organizes incitement to racial, national, or religious hatred may be prohibited from invoking the provisions of the European Convention but the acts themselves are not prohibited or penalized. After the Council's attention had been drawn to this by a letter from the World Jewish Congress, a motion for a resolution was tabled in the Consultative Assembly in 1965 which unanimously adopted a model law on incitement to racial, national, and religious hatred.[60] Recommendation 453 recalled that the aim of the Council of Europe was to achieve greater unity between its members in observance of the rule of law and fundamental human rights, and referred to Article 14 and the United Nations Declaration on the Elimination of All Forms of Racial Discrimination. It noted that increasingly numerous elements in member states were attempting to incite the public and especially the young to racial, national, or religious hatred by means of political

[57] *Marckx* v. *Belgium*, ser. A, xxxi.15.
[58] See *The Swedish Engine Drivers'* case, no. 5614/72; *Schmidt and Dahlstromm* v. *Sweden*, no. 5589/72; *Airey* v. *Ireland*, ser. A, xxxii, *Müller* v. *Austria*, no. 5849/72; *X.* v. *United Kingdom*, no. 7215/75. See also *Sociétés X, W et Z* v. *La République Fédérale d'Allemagne*, ECHR, coll. of decs., xxxv.1.
[59] See the *Lawless* case. European Court of Human Rights, ser. A, i–iii.
[60] Mr Ivor Richards (British Labour) was appointed rapporteur for the question in the Legal Committee.

and quasi-political organizations, activities, and propaganda, in some cases under the cover of education given in schools and universities, and it appealed to all Europeans and all the organs of states to take 'appropriate measures if necessary of a legislative nature' to eliminate such abuses.[61]

In his report, Mr Richards pointed out that the model law was a novel device in the Assembly, designed to lay down certain guidelines about the type of incitement which the Legal Committee felt ought to be made a criminal offence.[62] Article 1 of the draft proposed that 'A person shall be guilty of an offence: (a) if he publicly calls for or incites to hatred, intolerance, discrimination or violence against persons or groups of persons distinguished by colour, race, ethnic or national origin or religion; (b)' if he insults persons or groups of persons, holds them up to contempt or slanders them, on account of the distinguishing particularities mentioned in Paragraph (a).'[63] It was pointed out that much controversy existed as to the efficacy of legislation of this type and the dangers of infringing other rights such as freedom of speech. In Paragraphs 14 and 15 of the report, reference was made to sociological research into questions of prejudice and discrimination, particularly by R. K. Merton,[64] who adopted four categories: the unprejudiced non-discriminator, the unprejudiced discriminator, the prejudiced non-discriminator and the prejudiced discriminator. It was concluded that apart from the prejudiced violent type of discriminator, who cannot be swayed by legislation of this sort, legislation does have an effect in discouraging discrimination and incitement to group hatred.

It was pointed out that freedom of speech does not permit licence and is not unlimited. Absolute freedom of speech has never existed, since democratic societes have always found it right and necessary

[61] Recommendation 453 (27 Jan. 1966). See report of Legal Committee, doc. 2013, and booklet containing documentary material authorized by the 4th European Council of Ministers of Justice in Berlin 25–7 May, 1966.

[62] See also the statement made at the 22nd sitting of the 17th ordinary session of the Consultative Assembly (doc. 2013).

[63] Article 2 prohibits the publication and distribution of written matter aimed at achieving the effects referred to in Article 1. Article 3, provides that a person guilty of an offence under Article 1 and/or 2 'shall be liable' without specifying the punishment, this being left to the particular state. Under Article 4, organizations whose aims or activities fall within the scope of Articles 1 & 2 shall be prosecuted and/or prohibited. The use of the insignia of such organizations is prohibited and punishable under Articles 5 (a) and 6 (a). Articles 2 (b) and 5 (b) are definition clauses.

[64] R. K. Merton, *Discrimination and the American Creed*, ed. R. M. McIver (New York, 1948). (See doc. 2013, paras. 14 and 15.)

to place limitations on it when it conflicts with overriding social interests, e.g. blasphemy, defamation, obscenity, and sedition laws. Freedom of expression carries responsibilities as well as privileges. In the same year as the historic *Brown* decision, the United States Supreme Court recognized the constitutionality of group libel laws, holding that

Free speech is not an absolute right in all circumstances. It must be accommodated to other equally basic needs of society, one of which is society's interest in the avoidance of group hostility and group conflict. A communication does not enjoy constitutional protection simply because it may express an opinion. If it is essentially designed to stir up ill will and is fraudulent, it is not in the constitutional sense an effort to communicate ideas and is therefore subject to the police power of the state. Since society gains little or nothing by group defamation, its interest in avoiding the embitterment of group relations outweighs the abstract right of freedom of expression. Racial defamation is like a slow cumulative poison, the effects of which may not be visible for years.[65]

The measures proposed in the draft recommendation and model law, would, according to the rapporteur, 'aid the creation of a free and democratic European society, in which all groups and peoples can be integrated on the basis of full equality'. In the Assembly debate, most speakers referred to the United Nations Declaration and Convention on the Elimination of all forms of Racial Discrimination, but did not envisage any overlapping of the United Nations and European initiatives. Rather, the report was thought to complement the new United Nations Convention and to accord with a policy of closer links between the world body and the Council of Europe.[66]

The model law went further than the legal provisions of most European states,[67] because Article 4 provides for the prohibition and/or prosecution of organizations whose aim or activity is incitement to racial, national, or religious hatred, and it differed from the United Nations Convention on Racial Discrimination and the Draft Convention on Religious Intolerance in several respects. First, it was intended to deal with incitement to racial, national, and religious hatred in one instrument and with the same machinery, rather than separately as in the United Nations system. Second, the model law

[65] *Beauharnais* v. *Illinois*, 343 US 250 (1952).
[66] See M Hermond Lannung, Chairman of the Committee Consultative Assembly 17th sess., 22nd sitting.
[67] See doc. 2013, app., which lists the relevant provisions of member states.

would have made a person guilty of an offence who insulted, held in contempt, or slandered persons or a group on account of distinguishing characteristics. It thus went further than the United Nations Convention on Racial Discrimination which treated as an offence the 'dissemination of ideas based on racial superiority or hatred' and generally condemned 'all propaganda . . . which attempted to justify or promote racial hatred and discrimination in any form' and contained an undertaking by the states parties 'to adopt immediate and positive measures designed to eradicate all incitement to, or acts of, such discrimination'.[68] The model law was more precise in that Articles 1 and 2 made guilty of an offence a person who published or distributed written matter (which includes any writing, sign, or visible representation) aimed at hatred, intolerance, discrimination, or violence. It also detailed more precisely the action to be taken against delinquent organizations. Under Article 4 such organizations were to be prosecuted and/or prohibited.[69] Article 4 (b) of the United Nations Convention called on states to 'declare illegal and prohibit organizations . . . which promote and incite to racial discrimination'.

One point on which the United Nations Convention goes further than the European model is in Article 4 (b) which provided that the states parties 'shall recognize participation in such organizations or activities as an offence punishable by law'. Article 5 of the model merely forbade public use of the insignia of prohibited organizations. While the latter offence can be ascertained more easily, it is difficult to understand why the outward and visible signs should be punishable but not actual behaviour.

Among instruments designed to complement the European Convention, the most important is the European Social Charter, 1961,[70] designed to protect social and economic rights. The Preamble states that social rights should be secured without discrimination on grounds of race, colour, sex, religion, political opinion, national extraction, or social origin, and the contracting parties 'accept as the aim of their policy' certain special measures of protection. Thus children and young persons have the right to a special protection against the physical and moral hazards to which they are exposed, and employed women, in case of maternity, and other employed

---

[68] Art. 4 (a) of the Convention on the Elimination of All Forms of Racial Discrimination.

[69] The French text provided: *poursuivies et, le cas échéant, interdites*.

[70] European Treaty Series. no. 38 (1965); Cmnd. 2643.

women as appropriate, have the <u>right to a special protection in their</u> work. Mothers and children, irrespective of marital status and family relations, have the right to appropriate social and economic protection. Nationals of any contracting party may engage in gainful occupation on the territory of other parties 'on a footing of equality with the nationals of the latter' but subject to restrictions based on cogent economic or social reasons.[71]

Parties undertake to recognize the right of men and women workers to equal pay for work of equal value. The rights of young persons are set out in detail in Article 7 and those of employed women in Article 8. Thus the parties undertake to provide payments for women to take leave before and after childbirth for up to 12 weeks; to consider it unlawful to dismiss women during maternity leave, and to provide nursing mothers with sufficient time off. More controversial, in view of recent developments, are the obligations to regulate the employment of women workers on night work in industrial employment and to prohibit their employment in underground mining, and, as appropriate, in 'all other work which is unsuitable for them by reason of its dangerous, unhealthy or arduous nature'. Presumably few if any occupations would now be held to fall into this category.[72]

Another European convention grants a child born out of wedlock 'the same right of succession in the estate of its father and its mother and of a member of its father's or mother's family, as if it had been born in wedlock', thus prohibiting in the territories of the states parties discrimination based on illegitimate status.[73]

[71] P. i, (7), (8), and (18). Migrant workers also have the right to 'protection and assistance' (19).
[72] See ch. 10 above. Cf. s. 21 of the UK Sex Discrimination Act, 1975, and D. Wyatt, 'Economic and Social Policies', [1976] ELR, 414, 417–18.
[73] Convention of 15 Oct. 1975 on the Legal Status of Children Born out of Wedlock, European Treaty Series, no. 85, art. 9. The Convention came into force on 11 Aug. 1978. (Similar provision is made in Article 17 (5) of the American Convention on Human Rights, 1969.)

XIII

EQUAL PROTECTION IN THE UNITED STATES AND INDIA

1. *The United States*

It is instructive to investigate the experience of the United States Supreme Court in interpreting the equality clause of the Fourteenth Amendment to the Constitution, particularly since decisions of the Court have often been used as supplementary sources of authority by counsel and judges in international tribunals. The Thirteenth, Fourteenth, and Fifteenth Amendments were passed to remedy the conditions existing after the decision in *Dred Scott* v. *Sandford*.[1] In particular, the Fourteenth Amendment[2] provided that 'No state shall make or enforce any law which shall abridge the privileges or immunities of citizens of the United States; nor shall any state deprive any person of life, liberty or property without due process of law; nor deny to any person within its jurisdiction *the equal protection of the laws*'.

The underlying purpose of the amendments was to remove all distinctions between the rights and privileges of members of different races and to guarantee complete racial equality, but they did not in effect achieve this result. In the *Slaughterhouse* cases,[3] the Fourteenth Amendment was declared to protect from the hostile legislation of the states, the privileges and immunities of the United States as opposed to the privileges and immunities of citizens of the states. The latter included those fundamental civil rights for the security and establishment of which organized society is constituted, and these remained with certain exceptions mentioned in the Federal Constitution, under the care of the state government. Similarly, the *Civil Rights* cases[4]

---

[1] 1857 US 19 How. 393, 15 L. ed. 691.

[2] The Thirteenth Amendment abolished slavery or involuntary servitude in the US except as punishment for a crime whereof the party shall have been duly convicted, while the Fifteenth Amendment provided that the right of US citizens to vote should not be denied or abridged by the US or any state on account of race, colour, or previous condition of servitude. The Thireenth Amendment was ratified on 18 Feb. 1865, the Fourteenth on 28 July 1868, and the Fifteenth on 30 Mar. 1870.

[3] 16 Wall 36, (1873) 21 L. ed. 394—and to the same effect *US* v. *Harris* 106 US 629 (1883).   [4] (1883) 109 US 3.

invalidated a Federal Civil Rights Act (which sought to forbid the denial of equal accommodations in inns, public conveyances, and places of amusement) on the grounds that the Thirteenth Amendment abolished only slavery and involuntary servitude. Denial of equal accommodation imposed no 'badge of slavery' but at most infringed rights which were protected from state aggression by the Fourteenth Amendment. Moreover, the Amendment was prohibitory upon states only. The enforcing legislation which Congress was authorized to adopt was not direct legislation on matters on which the states could not legislate, but corrective legislation to counteract and redress the effect of such laws.[5]

A decade later this doctrine was extended to its natural conclusion in *Plessy* v. *Ferguson*.[6] Brown J. said, 'A statute which implies merely a legal distinction between the white and colored races—a distinction which is founded in the color of the two races, and which must always exist so long as white men are distinguished from another race by color, has no tendency to destroy the legal equality of the two races or to reestablish a state of involuntary servitude.' This 'separate but equal' doctrine, upon which the constitutionality of segregation decisions was to depend for the next sixty years, was considered quite compatible with *Strauder* v. *West Virginia*[7] which declared that the Fourteenth Amendment required the law in the states to be the same for the Blacks as for Whites and that all persons should stand equal before the laws of the states and that no legal discrimination should be made against the Coloured race because of colour.

Not until 1952 in *Brown* v. *the Board of Education for Topeka County*[8] was the 'separate but equal' doctrine finally discarded, but it had been substantially curtailed before then. Thus in *Sweatt* v. *Painter*[9] the Supreme Court refused either to affirm or reverse *Plessy*, in holding that the separate but equal requirement was not met by the establishment of a state law school for Negroes after a

---

[5] In *Baldwin* v. *Franks* 120 US 678 (1887), a conspiracy to deprive Chinese subjects of rights secured to them by treaty, by expelling them from their homes, was held not to infringe the Second Civil Rights Statute because the word 'citizen' was used in the act in a political sense to designate one who has the rights and privileges of a citizen of a state or the US and not in the popular sense of resident, inhabitant, or person.

[6] 163 US 537, 41 (1893), but see the strong dissent by Harlan J.

[7] 100 US 303 (1880).   [8] 347 US 489–91.

[9] 339 US 629 (1950). This decision reaffirmed *Missouri (ex. rel. Gaines)* v. *Canada* 305 US 337 (1938), in which a strict equality requirement was laid down. See also *McLaurin* v. *Oklahoma State Regents* 339 US 637 (1950).

refusal to admit a Negro applicant to the state-operated 'White' school. Legal education thus became an exception to the doctrine since the Court held that separate law schools for students of different races did not provide equal education. This showed that the tests the Court would apply to determine whether true equality existed or not were becoming so exacting as to be impossible to fulfil. Other cases indicated that equality was becoming increasingly difficult to prove where segregation existed.[10] *Henderson* v. *US* concerned the denial of restaurant service to a Negro on an interstate train when, although one seat at a table reserved for Negroes was unoccupied, the others were occupied by Whites. The Court held that the fact that the railroad regulations as to separate accommodation for different races might impose on White passengers disadvantages similar to those imposed on Negro passengers was not an answer to the requirements of the Interstate Commerce Act,[11] since discriminations operating to the disadvantage of two groups were not less to be condemned because the impact was broader than if only one was affected.[12]

Discrimination *qua* discrimination is not proscribed by the Fourteenth Amendment—merely state action which results in discrimination—but what constitutes state action is not always easy to determine. In one case[13] the contention that a covenant between private individuals forbidding the sale of real estate to Negroes violated the Amendment was held to be entirely lacking in substance and colour of merit, yet it was later emphasized[14] that the judicial enforcement of private restrictions constituted state action in violation of the equal protection clause. Vinson CJ said that the enforcement by a state court of a discriminatory private covenant or agreement excluding persons from occupying or purchasing real property because of race or colour was state action notwithstanding that the restrictive covenant was valid under the applicable state law and was in accordance with the public policy of the state. The

[10] See *Mitchell* v. *US* 313 US 80 (1941); *Henderson* v. *US* 339 US 816 (1950). Cf. *McCabe* v. *Aitchison* 235 US 151 (1914).

[11] i.e. that it was unlawful for a common carrier engaged in interstate commerce to subject any person to any undue or unreasonable prejudice or disadvantage in any respect whatever.

[12] Cf. the position in the *Belgian Linguistics* case, where it was argued that the linguistic legislation applied equally to the different language groups, and was therefore not discriminatory. See ch. 12 above.

[13] *Corrigan* v. *Buckley* 271 US 323 (1926).

[14] *Shelley* v. *Kraemer*; *McGhee* v. *Sipes* 334 US 1 (1948).

Fourteenth Amendment did not protect against merely private conduct, however discriminatory it might be, and the racially restrictive agreements were not *per se* a violation of the Amendment. It was pleaded in the same case that the state courts would also enforce restrictive covenants excluding Whites, but it was held that although there was no denial of the equal protection of the laws, the rights guaranteed by the Fourteenth Amendment were in terms guaranteed to the individual and that 'equal protection of the law is not achieved by the indiscriminate imposition of inequalities'.

This marks a clear advance from the technical distinctions of the *Slaughterhouse* cases and recognizes that the equal protection of the laws provided for in the Fourteenth Amendment operates not only between groups as such but between individuals at large. Similarly, delegation to a political party of the power to fix the qualifications for primary elections was held to be the delegation of a state function, so that a party's action became the action of a state.[15] Official orders affecting the livelihoods of certain sections of the population in a discriminatory fashion have been held to violate the Fourteenth Amendment.[16] In 1952 the Court finally decided upon the vital issue whether or not the 'separate but equal' doctrine should be affirmed or overruled.[17] It concluded that in the field of public education, the separate but equal doctrine had no place, since separate educational facilities were inherently unequal. Though the Court did not expressly overrule *Plessy*, it obviously made its continued application in other fields highly improbable. *Plessy* v. *Ferguson* had its *fons et origo* in an early Massachusetts case[18] in which the State Supreme Court held that a school board had the legal power to enforce segregation. By providing a Negro child with primary education equal in all respects to that provided in other such schools, the state had not unlawfully excluded the child from public school instruction. Shaw CJ stated that the principle that 'all persons without distinction of age or sex, birth or color, origin or condition, are equal before the law' when applied to the

[15] *Allwright* v. *Smith* 321 US 649 (1941), (overruling *Grovey* v. *Townsend* 295 US 45 (1935), and relying on *US* v. *Classic* 313 US 299 (1941)).
[16] As in *Yick Wo* v. *Hopkins* 118 US 356 (1886); *Takahashi* v. *Fish and Game Conservators* 334 US 410 (1948).
[17] *Brown* v. *Board of Education of Topeka County* 347 US 489–91.
[18] *Roberts* v. *Boston* 5 Cushing (59 Mass.) 198 (1849). The doctrine there promulgated was approved *obiter* by the Supreme Court in 1877 in *Hall* v. *de Cuis* 195 US 485 and was the *ratio decidendi* of *Plessy* in 1896: See 56 *American Historical Review* (1951), 510 ff..

actual conditions of society did not lead to the conclusion that all persons 'are legally clothed with the same civil and political powers'. Laws could be enacted that were adapted to the respective relations and conditions of people or classes.[19] Since women did not at that time possess civil and political equality with men[20] it was a simple matter to conclude that the law could also distinguish between races.

In *Brown* the Court did not concern itself with a lengthy philosophical analysis of the meaning of equality as Judge Tanaka did in the *South West Africa* cases[21] but merely asked itself the question: 'Does the segregation of children in public schools solely on the basis of race, even though the physical facilities and other tangible factors may be equal, deprive the children of the minority group of equal educational opportunities?' In answering this, the Court relied largely on the evidence of psychologists and sociologists approved in the lower courts and concluded, 'to separate children from others of a similar age and qualifications solely because of their race generates a feeling of inferiority as to their status in the community that may affect their hearts and minds in a way unlikely ever to be undone'.

Subsequent cases have held that a state may no longer constitutionally require the segregation of public facilities, whether the state action is by legislative or executive action. Private conduct interfering with individual rights on the other hand does not violate equal protection unless the state itself is involved to a significant extent.[22] In several cases involving educational facilities, certain devices designed to perpetuate segregation by race were disapproved. Where a state statute closed public schools but gave aid to certain private schools it was held that: (1) the schools would still be public schools because the state would control and financially aid them; (2) the plan would discriminate geographically against communities where the schools closed, because private schools would lack the organizational, administrative, and economic advantages and probably also the accreditation of public schools.[23]

---

[19] See generally M. R. Konvitz and T. Leskes, *A Century of Civil Rights, with a Study of State Law against Discrimination* (Columbia University Press, New York, 1961).

[20] Nor did they until the Nineteenth Amendment was ratified on 26 Aug. 1920. Cf. The Equal Rights Amendment below.

[21] See ICJ Rep., 1966, 304–10, and ch. 14 below.

[22] See *Johnson* v. *Virginia* 373 US 61 (1963); *Lombard* v. *Louisiana* 373 US 267 (1963); *Peterson* v. *Greenville* 373 US 244 (1963).

[23] *St. Helena Parish School* v. *Hall* (1962) 368 US 515. Cf. in this respect the *Belgian Linguistic* cases, ch. 12 above.

Another plan allowed for a system of reasoning whereby a child could transfer back to a school in which its race was in the majority. The Court considered this a 'one way ticket leading to but one destination, i.e. the majority race of the transferee and continued segregation', and declared the plan unconstitutional since it made race an absolute criterion for granting transfers. Whatever non-racial grounds might support a state's allowing a county to abandon public schools, the object must be a constitutional one and grounds of race and opposition to integration, however disguised, do not qualify as constitutional.[24]

Other cases have extended *Brown* to cover other types of public facilities; e.g. parks,[25] inn and restaurant facilities, and interstate transportation facilities,[26] while *Cooper* v. *Aaron*[27] firmly established *Brown* as the supreme law of the land and elaborated some of its findings. The clause relates to equality between persons in a state, and not between areas, and it is unnecessary that counties *qua* counties be treated in an identical fashion.[28] Nor is evidence, showing that different persons are treated differently, enough without more to show denial of the equal protection clause, since it is the circumstances of each case which govern.[29] In *Norvell* v. *Illinois*,[30] the Court stated that 'exact equality is no prerequisite of the equal protection of the laws within the meaning of the Fourteenth Amendment'. What is meant is that equal protection does not necessarily imply identity of treatment.

It is obvious that the Supreme Court has been advancing (albeit in a haphazard and piecemeal manner) towards defining and giving a content to the equal protection clause. Modern case law interprets the central purpose of the clause as the elimination of racial discrimination emanating from official sources in the state, and this policy renders all racial classifications constitutionally suspect, and subject to the most rigid scrutiny.[31]

[24] *Goss* v. *Board of Education* 373 US 683 (1963); *McLoughlin* v. *Florida* 379 US 184.

[25] *Wright* v. *Georgia* 373 US 284 (1963); *Watson* v. *Memphis* 373 US 526 (1963).
[26] *Peterson* v. *Greenville* 373 US 244; *Taylor* v. *Louisiana* 370 US 154 (1962).
[27] 358 US 1, 7. The requirement to desegregate with all deliberate speed means 'a prompt and reasonable start towards full compliance'.
[28] *Griffin* v. *School Board of Prince Edward County* 377 US 510; cf. the question of the *jus soli* in the *Belgian Linguistics* cases, and see *Salzburg* v. *Maryland* 346 US 545.
[29] See *Kotch* v. *Board of River Port Pilot Commissioners* 330 US 522, 552; *Skinner* v. *Oklahoma* 316 US 535, 539–40.
[30] 373 US 420, and see *Douglas* v. *California* 372 US 353.
[31] *Bolling* v. *Sharpe* 347 US 497, 499; *Korematsu* v. *US* 323 US 214, 216; *Hirabayashi* v. *US* 320 US 81, 100.

For over sixty years a system of segregation on the grounds of race in the United States was found to be perfectly consonant with a constitutional clause prescribing 'equal protection' of the laws for all citizens. Such a paradoxical result deserves careful explanation, particularly since it is still widely supported.[32] One major premiss which has never been denied in any case in which the equal protection clause has been considered is that Negroes are not to be significantly disadvantaged because of their race.[33] What has caused disagreement has been whether or not segregation does significantly disadvantage Negroes. In *Plessy* the view prevailed that the laws requiring segregation of Whites and Negroes operated only in the social arena. The equal protection clause was intended to secure equality of civil and political rights but not to affect social relationships, and segregation laws providing for separate but equal facilities did not impose nor imply inequality.[34] These propositions read into the equal protection clause what is not there. The clause did not distinguish between political and civil rights on one hand and social rights on the other but proscribed all laws which differentiated between persons on an irrelevant basis.

'Equal protection' could not mean that all persons were to be treated in an identical fashion; to allow sane persons over twenty-one years of age to vote may well disadvantage infants and the insane. What is imperative is that the imposition of any disadvantages

[32] The difficulties which faced the South African Courts in attempting to reconcile the 'separate but equal' doctrine with 'equality' are illuminating. It would now appear that the attempt has been abandoned. See *George* v. *Pretoria Municipality* 1916 TPD 501; *Minister of Posts and Telegraphs* v. *Rasool* 1934 AD 167; *R.* v. *Herman*, 1937 AD 168; *R.* v. *Mozumba* 1953(1) SA 235 (J); *R.* v. *Zihlangu* 1953(3) SA 871 (C); *R.* v. *Carelse* 1943 CPD 242; *R.* v. *Abdurahman* 1950(3) SA 136 (AD); *R.* v. *Lsu* 1953(2) 484 (AD); *Reddy* v. *Durban Corporation* 1954(4) SA 304 (N); *Pietermaritzburg City Council* v. *Local Road Transportation Board* 1959(2) SA 758 (N); *Tewari* v. *Durban Corporation* 1953(1) SA 85 (N); *R.* v. *Lepile*, 1953(1) SA 225 (T); *Minister of the Interior* v. *Lockhat*, 1961(2) SA 587 (AD). See also Alfred Avins, Racial Separation and Public Accommodations: Some comparative notes between South African and American Law', 86 *SALJ* (1969), 53; Julius Lewin, 'The Struggle for Law in South Africa', 27 *Political Quarterly* (1956), 176.

[33] See generally, the illuminating article by Charles L. Black jun. 'The Lawfulness of the Segregation Decisions', 69 (1) *Yale L. J.*, 421. Also Louis H. Pollak 'Racial Discrimination and Judicial Integrity', 108 (1) *U.Pa.L.R.*, 1.

[34] Pollak points out that the separate but equal doctrine was a product of sophistication and a temporary divergence. It had earlier been apparent to the Court that separation merely by reason of race was discrimination; e.g. in *Railroad Co.* v. *Brown* 17 Wall. 445, the Court recognized that an 1866 Federal statute prohibiting a railroad from excluding persons on account of colour was not complied with by the provision of separate cars for Negroes; it read the statute as directing 'that this discrimination must cease and the colored and white races in the use of cars be placed on an equal footing'.

should be done on a rational, teleological basis which is not constitutionally prohibited. The word 'reasonable' necessarily finds its
way into 'equal protection' in the application of the latter concept to
law in general. 'Equal' comes to mean not really equal (i.e. identical)
but 'equal unless a fairly tenable reason exists for inequality'.[35]
Putting it another way, 'equality' is a relative not an absolute term
and differences in treatment are permissible if based on reasoned
considerations. Eventually, the Court accepted that segregation
even in its separate but equal guise did not provide 'true' equality.
Its result was that one group of people was confined by another to
an inferior station without the facilities to escape from it. Black
points out that the fiction of equality in such a situation is just
about on a level with the fiction of a 'finding' in an action for
trover.[36]

In *Brown* the Court in effect accepted the proposition that segregation by state law unreasonably disadvantaged Negroes. Upon
what basis did the Court reach this conclusion and how did it
measure the content of the 'equality' made mandatory by the Fourteenth Amendment? In its short opinion, the Court quoted from the
'findings' in the lower courts that segregation had a detrimental
effect upon coloured children. The effect was worse when segregation was sanctioned by the law since 'the policy of separating the
races is *usually interpreted* as denoting the inferiority of the Negro
group. This in turn produces a sense of inferiority which affects
motivation to learn and thus retards the development of Negro
children.' It added, 'Whatever may have been the extent of
psychological knowledge at the time of *Plessy* v. *Ferguson*, this
finding is amply supported by modern authority. Any language in
Plessy v. *Ferguson* contrary to this finding is rejected. We conclude
that in the field of public education the doctrine of "separate but
equal" has no place.'[37] Under 'modern authority', the Court foot-
noted a number of works by prominent social scientists written
during the previous decade, though it did not specifically base its
judgment on their findings.

In interpreting 'equal protection', the Court realized that it was
faced with a general and indeterminate requirement or 'standard' to

[35] See Black, op. cit., 422–3; and see the opinion of Judge Tanaka in the *South West Africa* cases ICJ Rep., 1966, 306.
[36] Black, 424. He also points out that some Southern courts have held that to place a White person in a Negro railroad car is actionable humiliation. Must it therefore pretend not to know that in the Negroes' position there is humiliation? (427.)
[37] 347 US 494–5.

which it had to ascribe some content. This was not achieved by recourse to its own subjective views but by reliance on certain objective criteria and extra-legal considerations, a familiar enough procedure in United States federal courts since the Brandeis brief. It is not a simple task, and in one well-known federal case, *Repouille* v. *U.S.*,[38] both Frank and Hand JJ. attempted to apply an objective standard revealed by community attitudes in their interpretation of a requirement in the nationality statutes that a person must be of 'good moral character'. They could not agree, however, on the extent to which they should rely on scientific evidence, or how community attitudes should be determined. The Nationality Act 'set as a test, not those standards which we might ourselves approve', but whether 'the moral feelings now prevalent generally in this country' would 'be outraged' by the conduct in question: that is, whether it conformed to 'the generally accepted moral conventions current at the time'.[39]

In several cases interpreting the Fourteenth Amendment 'equal protection' and 'due process' clauses, the Supreme Court considered those articles of the United Nations Charter concerning human rights and fundamental freedoms. In *Shelley* v. *Kramer*[40] the US Department of Justice cited the 1947 General Assembly resolution condemning religious and racial persecution and discrimination. In its view this helped to show that the enforcement of racial covenants was contrary to the public policy of the United States. In *Oyama* v. *California*[41] Murphy and Rutledge JJ. in their concurring opinion said, 'this nation has recently pledged itself through the United Nations Charter to promote respect for and observations of human rights and fundamental freedoms for all without distinction as to race, sex, language or religion. The alien land law stands as a barrier to that national pledge. Its inconsistency with the Charter, which has been duly ratified and adopted by the United States is but one more reason why the statute must be condemned.' Black and Douglas JJ. in their concurring opinion added, 'There are additional reasons now why that law stands as an obstacle to the free accomplishment of our policy in the international field. One of these reasons is that we have recently pledged ourselves to co-operate with the United Nations to "promote . . . universal respect for and

[38] *Repouille* v. *US* 165 F 2d. 152 (1947).
[39] Ibid., 153, per Judge Learned Hand. Judge Frank relied on 'the attitude of ethical leaders'.   [40] (1948) 334 US 1.   [41] (1948) 332 US 410.

observation of human rights and fundamental freedoms for all, without distinction as to race, sex, language or religion." How can this nation be faithful to this international pledge if state laws which bar land ownership and occupation by aliens on account of race are permitted to be enforced?'

Although in neither case did the Court rest its decision on the ground that the Charter, as a self-executing treaty, bound the United States, it was probably influenced in these cases (and in *Brown* and other cases) by the 'general sentiment of mankind' evidenced by the solemn pronouncements of the United Nations Charter.[42]

This reliance of the Supreme Court on objectively determined criteria to give content to the 'equal protection clause' of the Constitution is relevant to the interpretation of similar 'standard' clauses in international instruments. Several judges in the *South West Africa* cases accepted that there were standards of non-discrimination accepted by the world community which could be used to give flesh and viscera to the bones of the Mandate Agreement.[43]

The equal protection clause has never been thought to require the same treatment of all persons despite different circumstances.[44] Rather, it prevents states from arbitrarily treating people differently under their laws. Whether any such differing treatment is deemed to be arbitrary depends on whether or not it reflects 'an appropriate differentiating classification among those affected'.[45] Thus the Courts have evolved a doctrine of 'reasonable classification'.[46]

To be reasonable, a classification must always rest upon some real and substantial distinction bearing a reasonable and just relation to things in respect of which the classification is made,[47] which includes all who are similarly situated and none who are not. However, a classification may satisfy the 'reasonable relation' test and yet be illegitimate because the purpose or object sought to be attained is itself inherently bad. Laws which classify according to the criteria of race or colour have been held to fall into this category.

[42] See Dillard, 'Some Aspects of Law and Diplomacy' 91 *Recueil des Cours* (1957), 449.   [43] See ch. 15 below.

[44] *Tigner* v. *Texas* 310 US 141, 147 (1940).

[45] See e.g. Harlan and Stewart JJ (dissenting) in *Harper* v. *Virginia State Board of Electors* 383 US 663 (1966); 16 L. ed. 2d. 169, 181.

[46] See J. Tussman and J. tenBroek, 'The Equal Protection of the Laws', in 37 *Calif L. Rev.* (1949) 341, and S. M. Huang-Thio, 'Equal Protection and Rational Classification', [1963] *Public Law*, 412.

[47] *Southern Railway* v. *Greene* 216 US 400, 412 (1909).

In *Oyama* v. *California*[48] certain executive acts were struck down because they discriminated against a man on account of his Japanese ancestry. Similarly in *Takahashi* v. *Fish and Game Conservators*[49] the Supreme Court held that discrimination on racial grounds as an end in itself fell with the prohibition of the equal protection clause. In *Yick Wo* v. *Hopkins*[50] the Court held that unequal treatment of persons based solely on hostility to the Chinese race and nationality was unjustified.

In another case involving restrictive war-time measures against Japanese, the Court said that all legal restrictions which curtail the civil rights of a single racial group are immediately suspect. Though pressing public necessity might sometimes justify the existence of such restrictions, 'racial antagonism never can'.[51] Where a classification is made on a constitutionally suspect ground such as race, the normal presumption that legislative bodies are deemed to act constitutionally is replaced. The onus is then on a state to show that its classification is required by overriding public interest, and was not the product of purposeful discrimination.[52]

Two approaches can be discerned in the practice of the Court. The first is the traditional or passive review approach where the Court presumes the constitutionality of legislation and requires the differentiation under attack to bear a rational relation to a 'legitimate state purpose'. After establishing the latter and satisfying itself that the law has a rational basis and not an arbitrary impact, the Court investigates whether the classification is either over- or under-inclusive, i.e. whether it includes all those similarly situated with respect to the particular purpose. The application of this test has shown a consistent deference to the legislature. The second approach developed by the Warren Court and known as 'The New Equal Protection' has been the test used where the legislature's classification has affected a 'fundamental interest' or has been deemed 'suspect'.[53]

[48] 332 US 633 (1948).   [49] 334 US 410 (1948).   [50] 118 US 356 (1886).

[51] *Korematsu* v. *US* 323 US 214, 216. Cf. also *McLoughlin* v. *Florida* 379 US 184 (Stewart and Douglas JJ.) and *Aaron* v. *Cooper* 358 US 1.

[52] See *Patton* v. *Mississippi* 332 US 463 (1947); *Norris* v. *Alabama* 294 US 587 (1935); and *Arnold* v. *North Carolina* 376 US 773 (1964).

[53] See generally G. Gunther, 'The Supreme Court 1971 Term—Foreword: In Search of Evolving Doctrine on a Changing Court: A Model for a Newer Equal Protection', 86 *Harvard L. Rev.*, 1, 8; and 'Developments in the Law—Equal Protection', 82 *Harvard L. Rev.*, 1065; G. Evans, 'Benign Discrimination and the Right to Equality' 6 *Fed. L. Rev.* (1974), 26 (paper presented to the Australasian Law Schools Conference 1973); 'Forum: Equal Protection and the Burger Court', 2 *Hastings Const. L.Q.*, 645; J. Tussman and J. tenBroek, 'The Equal Protection of the Laws', 37 *Calif. L.R.* (1949), 341; P. Polyviou, *The Equal Protection of the Laws* (Duckworth, London, 1980), ch. 5.

Fundamental interests are those explicitly or implicitly guaranteed by the Constitution and include rights relating to criminal procedure, procreation, and voting, while suspect classifications include race, alienage, and poverty. Surprisingly, sex and illegitimacy have rarely been so categorized[54] and the failure of the Courts to apply the Fourteenth Amendment vigorously to sex discrimination is one reason why the ill-fated equal rights amendment was proposed.[55]

In 'suspect classification' cases[56] the Court insists that the state establish a 'compelling interest' which justifies the classification which must be drawn with a higher degree of precision than normally required. The onus of proof thus shifted to the state has proved in practice almost impossible to fulfil and the application of the 'two-tier' approach has been widely criticized. More recently a synthesis between the two tests has been attempted[57] and the Court has required a classification to have a 'fair and substantial' relation to the object of legislation, rather than merely a 'rational' relation. This was more interventionist than the traditional test but less of a hurdle than the strict scrutiny approach.[58] This development was threatened in *San Antonio Independent School District* v. *Rodriguez*[59] where the Court returned to the familiar two-tier approach, deciding, first, that education was not a fundamental interest nor wealth a suspect classification (in the particular circumstances) and, second, that a prima facie discriminatory finance system bore some rational relationship to a legitimate state purpose. However, recent cases show that classification based on gender must bear a 'close and substantial relation to important governmental objectives' so that state laws overtly or covertly designed to prefer males over females in public employment would require an exceedingly persuasive justification to

[54] But see *Frontiero* v. *Richardson* 411 US 677 (1973); and see n. 60 below.
[55] The proposed Twenty-Seventh Amendment to the US Constitution provide, 'Equality of rights under the law shall not be abridged or denied by the United States or any state on account of sex.' See B. Bayh, 'The Need for the Equal Rights Amendment' 48 *Notre Dame Lawyer* (1972), 80; P. L. Martin, 'The Equal Rights Amendment: an Overview', *St. Louis U.L.J.* (1972) 1.
[56] These include *Skinner* v. *Oklahoma* 316 US 535 (1942); *Griffin* v. *Illinois* 351 US 12 (1956); *Reynolds* v. *Sims* 377 US 533 (1964); *McLoughlin* v. *Florida* 379 US 184 (1964); *Takahashi* v. *Fish and Game Conservators* 334 US 410 (1948); *Shapiro* v. *Thompson* 394 US 618 (1969); *Katzenbach* v. *Morgan* 384 US 641 (1966).
[57] See *Reed* v. *Reed* 404 US 71 (1971); *Weber* v. *Aetna Casualty and Surety Co.* 406 US 164 (1972); *Eisenstadt* v. *Baird* 405 US 438.
[58] See Gunther, op. cit., and 'The Decline and Fall of the New Equal Protection, A Polemical Approach', 58 *Va. L.R.* (1972), 1489; 'Equal Protection in Transition: An Analysis and a Proposal', 61 *Fordham L.R.* (1973), 605.   [59] 411 US 1 (1973).

withstand constitutional challenge.[60] As Evans has pointed out, at the heart of the American equal protection doctrine, whatever its surface twists and turns, there has always been a recognition of the simple truths that numerical equality is usually impossible and often undesirable, that laws must accordingly differentiate and classify, and that the central question in evaluating them is always whether the classifications are reasonable.[61]

It was not traditionally necessary for the legislature's motive to be discriminatory if discrimination results in fact. In *Skinner* v. *Oklahoma*[62] the Court did not inquire whether there was a deliberate attempt to draw an invidious distinction between classes of persons, but merely stated that strict scrutiny of classification was required lest 'unwittingly or otherwise' invidious discriminations are made against groups or types of individuals in violation of the Constitutional guarantee of equal protection of the laws. In several cases involving the rights of indigents in criminal cases, the Court held the state responsible for a *de facto* discrimination against persons who could not afford counsel or trial transcripts even though no discriminatory motive was discovered.[63] More recent cases have held that official action will not be unconstitutional merely because it has a racially disproportionate impact; but there must be in addition a racially discriminatory intent or purpose. Nevertheless, where a clear pattern of racial under-representation emerges, the plaintiff will be held to have made out a prima facie case of discriminatory purpose, thus shifting the onus of rebuttal to the state.[64]

[60] *Personnel Administrator* v. *Feeney* 60 L. Ed. 2d. 870, 874 (1979); *Davis* v. *Passman* 60 L. Ed. 2d 846; *Reed* v. *Reed* 404 US 71; *Califano* v. *Webster* 430 US 313.

[61] Evans, op. cit. These propositions though obvious enough have caused much difficulty in the Canadian Courts. See Polyviou, op. cit., ch. 4 for a comprehensive discussion.

[62] *Skinner* v. *Oklahoma, ex rel. Williamson* 316 US 535 (1942). This case involved a sterilization statute which applied to some classes of criminals but not to others. The Court said, 'When the law lays an unequal hand on those who have committed intrinsically the same quality of offence . . . it has made as invidious a discrimination as if it had selected a particular race or nationality for oppressive treatment.' (Ibid., 541.)

[63] See *Griffin* v. *Illinois* 351 US 12 (1956); *Douglas* v. *California* 372 US 353 (1966); *Anders* v. *California* 386 US 738 (1967); and see L. G. Sager, 'Tight Little Islands: Exclusionary Zoning, Equal Protection and the Indigent', 21 *Stan. L. R.* 767, 773–8. 'While the presence of the intent to discriminate makes the imposition of responsibility more facile, there would seem to be no sound basis for making it a conclusive bar.'

[64] *Washington* v. *Davis* 426 US 229 (1976); *Village of Arlington Heights* v. *Metropolitan Housing Development Corp.* 97 S.Ct. 555 (1977); *Castaneda* v. *Partida* 97 S.Ct. 1272 (1977).

Even if a statute does not appear to draw invidious distinctions on its face, there may still be a violation of the equal protection clause if it is improperly administered. The Supreme Court has stated that 'though the law be fair on its face and impartial in appearance, yet if it is applied and administered with an evil eye and unequal hand, so as practically to make unjust and illegal discriminations between persons in similar circumstances, material to their rights, the denial of equal justice is still within the prohibition of the Constitution'.[65]

It is noteworthy that the word 'discrimination' is often used by the Supreme Court in the sense of 'distinction' and not in the sense in which it has come to be used in the practice of the United Nations, but what is clear is that the purpose of the equal protection clause is to secure every person against distinctions which are 'arbitrary', 'irrelevant', 'unreasonable', 'irrational', or 'invidious'.[66] Though there is general agreement that these are the tests which should be applied to a particular classification, there is often disagreement on the application of these standards to particular situations, as the dissenting judgments in the apportionment and poll tax cases demonstrate.[67] In *Harper* v. *Virginia State Board of Elections* it was held that to introduce wealth or payment of a fee as a measure of a voter's qualifications is to introduce a 'capricious' or 'irrelevant' factor, and constitutes an 'invidious discrimination'. Similarly, it has been held that there can be no equal justice where the kind of trial a man gets depends on the amount of money he has. In *Douglas* v. *California* the Court said that 'absolute equality' was not required. Lines can be drawn and are often sustained, and unless an indigent is provided with the benefit of counsel 'an unconstitutional line has been drawn between rich and poor'.[68]

These decisions favour the view that the equality required by the

---

[65] *Yick Wo* v. *Hopkins* 118 US 353 (1886). See also E. N. Cahn, *Commonsense about Democracy* (London, 1962), 115, 118–25.

[66] See e.g. *Williamson* v. *Lee Optical Co.* 348 US 483, 489 (1953); *Morey* v. *Doud* 354 US 457 (1957); *Skinner* v. *Oklahoma* 316 US 535 (1942); *Harper* v. *Virginia Board of Elections* 383 US 663, 674, Black J. (dissenting).

[67] *Reynolds* v. *Sims* 12 L. ed. 2d. 506. The Court reiterated its statement in *Lane* v. *Wilson* 307 US 268, 275, that the Constitution forbids 'sophisticated as well as simple-minded modes of discrimination'; *Harper* v. *Virginia State Board of Elections* 383 US 663, 668 (1966), and the dissenting judgement of Black J., at 674.

[68] *Griffin* v. *Illinois* 351 US 12 (1956); *Douglas* v. *California* 372 US 353, 357 (1966); *Anders* v. *California* 386 US 738 (1967).

equal protection clause is not mathematical exactness[69] but may include special ameliorative measures to assist the economically deprived. Until recently, the notion that the doctrine of equal protection of the laws might encompass special measures designed to assist underprivileged classes to attain a true or genuine equality had not been widely canvassed. However, it has recently been suggested that compensatory treatment to assist Negroes by means of special quotas and reservations would be fully consistent with the equal protection clause.[70] It has been argued that Harlan J.'s famous remark in his dissenting judgment in *Plessy* v. *Ferguson* that 'the law must be colorblind' should not be misunderstood as prohibiting ameliorative measures for Negroes, since there is all the difference in the world between harming someone because of an irrelevant characteristic and helping someone because of a relevant characteristic even though the characteristic be the same in both instances. Negroes, it has been said, must be assisted as Negroes, just as they have been disadvantaged as Negroes, if the Fourteenth Amendment is to serve its egalitarian purpose—just as women, children, and veterans have special laws for their protection as women, children, and veterans. Special treatment though mathematically unequal is 'more truly equal' because it gives a boost to the general level on the analogy of a handicap in a sporting contest.[71]

In *Reitman* v. *Mulkey*,[72] the Supreme Court struck down an amendment to the Californian constitution (Proposition 14) which abolished statutory measures which protected Negroes from housing discrimination. The grounds of the decision have been

[69] It has also been emphasized that the mere 'equal application' (in a mathematical sense) of a statute containing racial classifications is not enough to remove the classifications from the Fourteenth Amendment's proscription of all 'invidious racial discrimination'. See *Loving et ux.* v. *Virginia* 18 L. ed. 2d. 1010, 1016.

[70] See the important symposium, *Equality* (1965) ed. R. L. Carter, by R. L. Carter, D. Kenyon, P. Marcuse, L. Miller, quoted in R. Lichtman, 'The Ethics of Compensatory Justice', 1 *Law in Transition Quarterly* (1964), 76.

[71] Ibid. (The West German Constitutional Court has accepted that the concept of legal equality is not to be understood as an absolute or arithmetical equality without any differentiation but as a proportional and relative equality. (8 Berf CE, 51).) See Mangoldt Klein, *Das Bonner Grundgesetz*, 198–203. See also the American Model Anti-Discrimination Act prepared by the National Conference of Commissioners on Uniform State Laws which provided for certain measures of compensatory treatment for Negroes, and comments by N. Dorsen, 'The American Law on Racial Discrimination', [1968] *Public Law*, 304, and C. A. Auerbach, 'The 1967 Amendments to the Minnesota State Act Against Discrimination and the Uniform Law Commissioners' Model Anti-Discrimination Act', 52 *Minnesota L. Rev.* (1967), 231, 272–8, 321. And see the Civil Rights Act 1964, Title VI.   [72] 18 L. ed. 2d. 830.

criticized[73] but the decision can be supported on the ground that state action, i.e. Proposition 14, by abolishing special measures designed to provide a real and genuine equality for Negroes, itself denied the equal protection of the laws.

The question of the validity or otherwise of 'affirmative action' programmes arose before the Supreme Court in *De Funis* v. *Odegaard*,[74] but although the Court avoided a decision by declaring the case moot, the decision is notable for an opinion by Justice Douglas which denied that race could be taken into account in university admissions programmes at Washington University. In his view the reservation of a proportion of places for minority groups was 'fraught with dangers' mainly because of the problem of under-inclusion. The rule should be one of strict neutrality. In *Regents of University of California* v. *Bakke*,[75] a university admission programme, under which sixteen places were reserved for 'disadvantaged' minority students, was challenged by an unsuccessful White applicant. The Supreme Court in a 'Solomonic judgment'[76] ordered Bakke's admission to the Davis Medical School, but also held that race may in the right circumstances be one of the factors that universities can take into account in admitting students. It thus affirmed in part and reversed in part the decision of the California Supreme Court. The judgment is unsatisfactory and has been widely criticized.[77] Four justices[78] decided the question on the basis of Title VI of the Civil Rights Act, 1964, even though *certiorari* had been granted in order to deal with the constitutional issue. Four others[79]

[73] See 'Comments on *Reitman* v. *Mulkey:* A Recent Development in State Action Theory', 14 (1) *UCLA* Law Review (1966–7), 1.
[74] 416 US 312 (1974). See G. Dworkin, 'The *DeFunis* Case: The Right to go to Law School', *New York Review of Books*, 5 Feb. 1976, 29 ff; Dworkin, *Taking Rights Seriously* (Duckworth, London, 1977), ch. 9; 'Equal Protection and Benign Racial Classifications: A Challenge to the Law Schools', 21 *Am. L. R.* (1972), 736; R. A. Posner, 'The *DeFunis* Case and the Constitutionality of Preferential Treatment of Racial Minorities', *Sup. Ct. Rev.* (1974), 1, and symposia in 75 *Colum. R. L. Rev.*, 483; and 60 *Va. L. Rev.*, 917; P. Polyviou, *The Equal Protection of the Laws* (Duckworth, London, 1980), ch. 8. [75] 438 US 265 (1979).
[76] Lewis, 'A Solomonic Decision', *NY Times*, 29 June 1978.
[77] See e.g. G. Dworkin, 'The *Bakke* Decision: Did it Decide Anything?', 25 *New York Review of Books* (1978), 20; R. H. S. Tur, 'The Justification of Reverse Discrimination', draft paper presented at the Royal Institute of Philosophy Conference on Law, Morality, and Rights, University of Lancaster, Sept. 1979; G. Calabresi, '*Bakke* as Pseudo-Tragedy', 28 *Catholic L. Rev.* (1979), 427. But cf. D. D. Raphael, *Justice and Liberty* (Athlone Press, London, 1980), ch. 9.
[78] Burger, CJ, Stewart, Rehnquist, and Stevens JJ.
[79] Brennan, White, Marshall, and Blackmun JJ.

244 Equal Protection in the United States and India

held it constitutional for admissions programmes to take race into account so long as the stigma characteristic of traditional racial discrimination was avoided. Justice Powell agreed that, in the circumstances, Title VI had been violated but also agreed with the second four on the general issue. In his view, the medical school could not reserve a specific number of places for certain ethnic groups. On the other hand, if it had adopted the 'Harvard model' which, although taking race into account in the interests of a heterogeneous student body, did not assign a fixed number of places, this might have been permissible because it treats each applicant as an individual in the admissions process. This approach has been trenchantly criticized by Tur who claims that there is no constitutional or moral difference between the Harvard and the Washington/Davis programmes.[80] If there is a moral difference, however, it counts in favour of Washington/Davis, and if there really is a constitutional difference, it is because the Harvard model, for all its sophistication, is ultimately not an affirmative action programme at all. At Harvard, although race may have been the determining factor, an unsuccessful applicant will not know whether he has been turned down for another reason e.g. lack of musical ability. The procedure is immune from external scrutiny, whereas at Davis admissions procedures were clear and determined by public rules and at least had the virtue of honesty.[81] As was pointed out after *De Funis*, in the context of affirmative action, candour is preferable to deception and evasion.[82]

The Harvard model, which takes race into account along with other personal characteristics, is a model for a post-racist society, and the question which arises is the extent to which race can be taken into account in order to get beyond racism.[83] One view is that the Constitution must be colour-blind and never take it into account. Thus it has been argued that 'the proper constitutional principle is not, no "invidious" racial or ethnic discrimination, but no use of racial or ethnic criteria to determine the distribution of governmental benefits and burdens'.[84] Justice Douglas claimed that any state

[80] *DeFunis* v. *Odegaard* 416 US 312 (1974).
[81] Tur, 38 ff., Calabresi, 431.
[82] K. L. Harst and H. W. Horowitz, 'Symposium: Affirmative Action and Equal Protection', 60 *Va. L. Rev.* (1974), 955, 973; Dworkin, *Taking Rights Seriously*, 225; Dean Rusk, 'Preferential Treatment: Some Reflections' in Blackstone and Heslop, eds., *Social Justice and Preferential Treatment*, 154–60.
[83] See Justice Blackmun, quoted in Tur, 46.   [84] Posner, op. cit.

sponsored preference for one race over another is 'invidious' and violates the Equal Protection Clause,[85] while Justice Rehnquist more recently argued that whether described as 'benign discrimination' or 'affirmative action' the racial quota is none the less a creator of castes, a two-edged sword that must demean one in order to prefer another.[86]

The opposing view is that society cannot be completely colour-blind *in the short term* if there is to be a colour-blind society in the long term, and racial classifications are constitutionally tolerable, *at least for a limited time*, in order to achieve desirable social ends.[87] As Professor Calabresi puts it, if benign quotas are limited to Blacks and perhaps to American Indians, so long as those groups remain sufficiently disadvantaged *as groups* so that membership in them can by itself constitute disadvantage without more, there would be no major rejection of the basic universalist, meritocratic ideal. The Fourteenth Amendment must be read both to further general equality regardless of race and to permit affirmative action for certain groups regardless of individual disadvantage so long as the group remains disadvantaged.[88] To describe affirmative action as discrimination and therefore contrary to the principle of equality enshrined in the Fourteenth Amendment is to confuse terminology. As Professor Corwin rightly states, 'To be troubled about the constitutionality of the benign quota one must fail to recognize the distinction between "invidious" discrimination and "discrimination *per se*".'[89] If a 'discrimination *per se*', i.e. distinction, is reasonable and designed to further real and genuine (normative) equality then it is valid. It is this crucial point that is overlooked in Justice Rehnquist's opinions. In *Weber* he accepted the argument that Title VII of the Civil Rights Act 1964 forbade all differentiations between the races in hiring and selection for training programmes since these would offend the statute which on a literal interpretation and according

---

[85] *DeFunis* v. *Odegaard* 416 US 312 (1974).

[86] *United Steelworkers of America* v. *Weber* 61 L. ed. 2d. 480 (1980) per Rehnquist J., dissenting, p. 520.

[87] *Associated General Contractors of Massachussetts, Inc.* v. *Altschuler* 490 F. 2d. 9, 16; Karst and Horowitz; R. M. O'Neil, 'Racial Preference and Higher Education: The Larger Context', 60 *Va. L.R.* (1974), 925.

[88] Calabresi, 432, 440.

[89] E. S. Corwin, *The Constitution and What it Means Today* (Princeton University Press, 1973), 414.

to its spirit required 'equality'.[90] 'In passing Title VII, Congress outlawed all racial discrimination, recognizing that no discrimination based on race is benign, that no action disadvantaging a person because of his color is affirmative.'[91] This approach gives 'equality' the formal or mathematic meaning of 'same' or 'identity' and makes 'discrimination' a synonym of 'mere differentiation'. The majority in *Weber*[92] held that an interpretation forbidding all race conscious

[90] Article 703 (c) and (d) of the Statute made it unlawful 'to discriminate' because of race in hiring and selection of apprentices for training programmes. As Judge J. Skelly Wright has pointed out, Justice Rehnquist in 1977 urged the Court to uphold provisions of the Old Age Survivors and Disabled Benefits programme that favoured widows over widowers and characterized the difference in treatment as 'scarcely an invidious discrimination' but 'explainable as a measure to ameliorate the characteristically depressed conditions of aged widows'. This logic appears equally applicable to race-based affirmative action. (See 'Color-Blind Theories and Color-Conscious Remedies', 47 *U. Chi. L. R.* (1980), 213.) Professor A. M. Bickel's statement that discrimination on the basis of race is 'illegal, immoral, unconstitutional, inherently wrong, and destructive of democratic society' (*The Morality of Consent* (Princeton University Press, 1975), 133) has given rise to attacks on affirmative action programmes. See e.g. W. Van Alstyne 'Rites of Passage: Race, the Supreme Court and the Constitution', 46 *U. Chi. L. R.* (1979), 775; B. D. Meltzer 'The *Weber* Case: The Judicial Abrogation of the Anti-Discrimination Standard in Employment', 47 *U. Chi. L. R.* (1980), 423; P. Kurland, 'Ruminations on the Quality of Equality', *BYUL Rev.* (1979), 1, 18. But, as Justice Blackmun stated in *Bakke* (438 US 265, 407, (1978)), in order to treat persons equally we must treat them differently. 'We cannot . . . let the equal protection clause perpetuate racial supremacy.' And see G. Shatski, '*United Steel Workers of America* v. *Weber*: An Exercise in Understandable Indecision', 56 *Wash L. R.* (1980), 51. For a survey of the literature see, Simons, 77 *Mich L. R.* (1979), 513. (cf. also *Griggs* v. *Duke Power Co.* 401 US 424 (1971) and L. Lustgarten 'The New Meaning of Discrimination', [1978] Public Law, 178.)

[91] *Weber*, 520. Cf. Polyviou, 721, n. 18. A similar view has been taken in the Australian High Court. See *Cameron* v. *Deputy Federal Commissioner of Taxation* (1923) 32 CLR 68. Affirmative action is expressly permitted by Section 35 of the UK Race Relations Act, 1976, which exempts from the various forms of unlawful discrimination 'any act done in affording persons of a particular racial group access to facilities or services to meet the special needs of that group in regard to their education, training, or welfare or any ancillary benefits'. And see *The Times* leader, 26 Oct. 1977. In this context, it is useful to note the views of Lord Denning in *Cumings* v. *Birkenhead Corporation* [1972] Ch. 12, 37; 'So here if this education authority were to allocate boys to particular schools according to the colour of their hair or, for that matter, the colour of their skin, it would be so unreasonable, so capricious, so irrelevant to any proper system of education that it would be ultra vires altogether and this Court would strike it down at once. But, if there were valid educational reasons for a policy, as, for instance in an area where immigrant children were backward in the English tongue and needed special teaching, then it would be perfectly right to allocate those in need to special schools where they would be given extra facilities for learning English. In short if the policy is one which could reasonably be upheld for good educational reasons it is valid. But if it is so unreasonable that no reasonable authority could entertain it, it is invalid.'

[92] Stewart, White, Marshall, and Blackmun, JJ, and Burger, CJ agreed with Rehnquist J.'s dissent and the other judges took no part in the decision.

affirmative action would bring about an end completely at variance with the purpose of the statute which guaranteed equality for Blacks and should not be construed to foreclose private affirmative action. Thus the majority clearly, and with respect, correctly, accepts the normative and not the formal view of what equality requires. Moreover, the Court accepted that racially conscious affirmative action programmes should only continue so long as they were required and noted that because the duration of the programme in issue was finite it would perhaps terminate before the 'stage of maturity when action along this line is no longer necessary'.[93] The Court therefore accepted that affirmative action programmes are only permissible in the short term and must terminate when the disadvantaged group reaches the same level in society as the majority.[94] This is fully in line with the international instruments on equality and discrimination.

Finally, the Court held that individual employers need not have engaged in discriminatory practice in the past; their capacity for affirmative action would be measured solely in terms of a statistical disparity. Thus the Court affirmed that affirmative action should rest on distributive justice rather than compensatory criteria. The compensation argument, which has sometimes found favour in the courts,[95] is that because certain groups have suffered discrimination in the past, they should now receive special measures of assistance. The difficulty with this approach is that those advantaged by present preferential quotas are not normally the victims of past discrimination and those disadvantaged by them have rarely been guilty of past discrimination.[96] 'Compensation' is therefore being used in a 'non-standard, misleading or Pickwickian sense'[97] and the fact that some are disadvantaged by virtue of past discrimination while others are simply disadvantaged should not be relevant. Rather than seeking to compensate for past wrongs affirmative action programmes should be based on need and promote the compelling societal interest in integration and equal opportunity.[98] This concept

[93] Approving the view expressed by Blackmun J. in *Bakke* 438 US 265, 403.

[94] Calabresi, 443, states, 'And if the reparation object stems . . . from the perceived societal need to help the whole group, even when doing so entails benefitting some non-disadvantaged individuals, then that object also becomes weakened as the group ultimately finds its place as an equal in society—that is *not* as "no longer disadvantaged" but as *no more in special need* than other sometime disadvantaged groups.'

[95] *US* v. *Latlers Local 46* 471 F. 2d. 408, 413; *Anderson* v. *San Francisco Unified District School* 357 F. supp. 248–9.   [96] Harst and Horowitz, 964.   [97] Tur, 30.

[98] Calabresi, n. 77 above, and Sandalow, 'Racial Preferences in Higher Education', in B. R. Gross, ed., *Reverse Discrimination* (Prometheus Books, Buffalo, N.Y., 1967), 239–64.

of distributive justice is designed to achieve real and genuine equality.

The Court in *Weber* appears to support the 'present-day need' rather than the 'compensation' approach and to take a broader view than that of Justice Powell in *Bakke*. However, neither case deals directly with the constitutional issue which has to await the resolution of later cases.[99] But, as Tur points out, it remains an open possibility that full-blooded affirmative action, quotas included, is the least intrusive means of realizing a state of equal opportunity, and as such constitutional.[100] This will often mean that a member of a majority group disadvantaged by a minority aid programme will claim to have been discriminated against, but this attitude fails to recognize that although race was the key factor at the margin, it was his lack of ability which placed him at the margin to begin with. The choice is not to prefer an unqualified minority member over a qualified member of the majority but a selection between qualified applicants on the basis of a number of factors of which race (for example) may be one.[101]

2. *India*

Article 14 of the Indian Constitution provides that 'the state shall not deny to any person equality before the law or the equal protection of the laws within the territory of India'.[102] The first part has been said to be based on the Irish Constitution and the second on the equal protection clause of the Fourteenth Amendment to the United States Constitution.[103]

[99] *Minnick* v. *California Department of Corrections* (no. 79–1213), and *Johnson* v. *Board of Education* (no. 79–1356).

[100] Tur, 37. Tur uses the term 'reverse discrimination' which in the author's view is best avoided.

[101] Evans, op. cit.; O'Neil op. cit.; Dworkin, 24 *New York Review of Books*, 10 Nov. 1977, 15; A. R. Blackshield, ' "Fundamental Rights" and the Institutional Viability of the Indian Supreme Court', 8 *JILI* (1966), 139, 211.

[102] The Constitution came into operation on 26 Jan. 1950. Article 15 (1) further provides, 'The State shall not discriminate against any citizen on the grounds only of religion, race, caste, sex, place of birth or any of them.' See D. K. Sen, *A Comparative Study of the Indian Constitution* (Orient Longmans, Bombay, 1960–6), 227; P. K. Tripathi, *Some Insights into Fundamental Rights* (University of Bombay Press, 1972), 47–104; J. K. Mittal, 'The Right to Equality and the Indian Supreme Court; 14 *A.J. Comp. L.* 422; 'The Right to Equality in the Indian Constitution' [1970] *PL* 36 and [1971] PL 232; D. D. Basu, *Commentary on the Constitution of India* (Sarkar, Calcutta, 5th ed., 1965) i; M. V. Pylee, *Constitutional Government in India* (Asia Publishing House, London 1965); Polyviou, op. cit., ch.3.

[103] See Patanjali Sastri J. in *State of West Bengal* v. *Anwar Ali* AIR 1952 SC 75. Cf. s. 40 (6) of the Irish Constitution of 1937.

Like the United States Supreme Court, the Indian Courts have decided that the clause does not provide that all legislative differentiation is necessarily discriminatory, and have laid down a similar test of 'reasonable classification'. In the leading case, *State of West Bengal* v. *Anwar Ali*,[104] the Indian Supreme Court held that a legislative classification must be rational and not arbitrary. Not only must it be based on some qualities or characteristics which are to be found in all the persons grouped together and not in others who are left out but those qualities or characteristics must have a reasonable relation to the object of the legislation.

Das J. laid down two tests; first the classification must be founded on an intelligible differentia which distinguishes those that are grouped together from others; second, the differentia must have a rational relation to the objects sought to be achieved by the Act. In other words the differentia and the objects are distinct things and it is necessary that there be a nexus between them. This is similar to the American test laid down in *Southern Railway* v. *Greene*[105] and also the 'reasonable relationship of proportionality between the means employed and the aim sought to be realized', the test laid down by the European Court of Human Rights in the *Belgian Linguistics* case. It has been applied in a large number of Indian cases,[106] and a similar test has been applied in Pakistan.[107]

Anwar Ali also made it clear that when discrimination exists in fact, the question of motive does not arise, and any hostile or inimical intention against the particular person or class involved is no longer relevant. The test is the fact of discrimination and the intention of the legislature is thus immaterial, though a hostile or inimical intention may be useful in aiding the Court to conclude that the fact of discrimination exists.[108] This corresponds to the United States rule. The most comprehensive pronouncement on equality is to be found in *Ram Krishna Dalmia* v. *Justice Tendolkar*[109] where the court summarized the Supreme Court decisions on the subject in several propositions: (1) a law may be constitutional even though it relates to a single individual, if on account of some special

---

[104] AIR 1952 SC 75. And see *Charanjit Lal* v. *Union of India* 1950 SCR 869.

[105] 216 US 400, 412.

[106] e.g. *Kathi Raning* v. *State of Saurashtra* 1952 SCR 435; *Budhan Choudhry* v. *State of Bihar* AIR 1955 SC 190.

[107] *Jibendra Kishore Achharyya Chowdhury* v. *Province of East Pakistan* PLD 1957 SC (Pakistan) 9.

[108] Cf. P. B. Mukharji, 'Chief Justice Das and Equality before the Law', 2 *JILI* (1959–60), 161.   [109] AIR 1958 SC 538.

circumstances or reasons applicable to him and not to others, that single individual may be treated in a class by himself;[110] (2) there is always a presumption in favour of the constitutionality of an enactment and a burden on him who attacks it to show that there has been a clear transgression of a constitutional principle;[111] (3) However, though good faith and knowledge of the existing conditions on the part of the legislature are to be presumed, if there is nothing on the face of the law or the surrounding circumstances brought to the notice of a court on which a classification may reasonbly be regarded as based, the presumption of constitutionality cannot be carried to the extent of always holding that there must be some undisclosed and unknown reasons for subjecting certain individuals or corporations to discriminatory legislation;[112] (4) the legislature is free to recognize degrees of harm and may confine its restriction to those cases where need is clearest;[113] in order to sustain the presumption of constitutionality the court may take into consideration matters of common knowledge and report, and the history of the times, and may assume every state of facts which can be conceived as existing at the time of the legislation.

This would appear to be another way of saying that the court may take contemporary standards into account in evaluating the legitimacy of a particular classification.

In *Budhan Choudhry's* case,[114] the Court said that a permissible classification may be founded on many different bases, i.e. 'geographical, or according to the objects or occupations or the like'. Classifications based on geography may be reasonable[115] so long as

[110] But if no reasonable basis of classification appears on the face of the statute or is deducible from surrounding circumstances or matters of common knowledge, a court will strike down a law as an instance of 'naked discrimination'. See *Ameerunissa Begum* v. *Mahboob Begum* 1953 SCR 404; and *Ramprosad Naraim Sahi* v. *Bihar* 1953 SCR 1129.

[111] This is because it must be presumed that the legislature understands and correctly appreciates the needs of its own people, that its laws are directed to problems made manifest by experience and that its 'discriminations' (in the sense of distinctions) are made on adequate grounds. Cf. also the Privy Council decision in the Ceylonese case of *Pillai* v. *Mudanayake* [1953] AC 514 PC.

[112] Re *Kerala Education Bill* AIR 1958 SC 956; cf. *Ameerunissa Begum* v. *Mahboob Begum* 1953 SCR 404.

[113] Cf. *State of Bombay* v *Balsara* AIR 1951 SC 318; *Hans Muller* v. *Superintendent, Presidency Jail* 1955 SCR 1284.

[114] *Budhan Choudhry* v. *State of Bihar* AIR 1955 SC 190.

[115] *Purshottam* v. *Desai* AIR 1956 SC 20; *State of Uttar Pradesh* v. *Bhopal Sugar Industry* AIR 1964 SC 1179; *Bhaizalal* v. *State of Uttar Pradesh* AIR 1962 SC 981; *State of Punjab* v. *Ajaib Singh* 1953 SCR 254.

the territorial division is not selected for the purpose of effecting discrimination against a particular group of persons living in the disfavoured area, and so long as it takes account of changing circumstances. Similarly, classifications may be based on historical reasons,[116] differences in the nature of trades, callings or occupations,[117] cost effectiveness analyses,[118] the necessity of preventing only aggravated forms of mischief or harm,[119] or the need to introduce reforms gradually.[120] However, classifications based only on religion, race, caste, sex, place of birth, or any of them are clearly prohibited by Article 15 (1) of the Constitution if they draw any sort of invidious distinction between Indian citizens.[121] Recent cases have warned that the classification doctrine should not be carried to the point where, instead of being a useful servant, 'it becomes a dangerous master'.[122]

Administrative acts which are done under a statute which is not itself discriminatory on its face, may offend the equality clause if they are done with discriminatory intent,[123] and in *Anwar Ali's* case[124] Sastri J. adopted the view taken by the United States Supreme Court in *Yick Wo's* case.[125] Thus when a law is challenged as discriminatory the relevant consideration is the effect of the law and not the intention of the legislature. But when a law is itself non-discriminatory but its administration is challenged as discriminatory, the question of the intention of the administering authorities becomes material: in such a case the administrative action does not offend Article 14 unless done *mala fide* or actuated by a hostile intention. Mere errors of judgment do not suffice.

Moreover, an unimpeachable classification is not an end in itself. It has been pointed out that 'one can conceive of classifications that

[116] *Pabitra Kumar* v. *State of West Bengal* AIR 1964 SC 593.
[117] *Hathisingh Manufacturing Co.* v. *Union of India* AIR 1960 SC 931; *State of Bombay* v. *Balsara* AIR 1951 SC 318.
[118] *State of Bombay* v. *United Motors* AIR 1953 SC 252.
[119] *Sakhwant* v. *State of Orissa* 1955 1 SCR 1004 (cf. *Truax* v. *Raich* (1915) 239 US 33).
[120] *Biswambhar* v. *State of Orissa* 1954 SCR 842.
[121] Classifications may nevertheless be permissible on these grounds if they are convenient methods of putting into effect the provisions for protective measures under Article 15 (4) and 16 (4). But see below. (Cf. also S. S. Nigam, 'Equality and the Representation of the Scheduled Classes in Parliament', 2 *JILI* (1959–60), 297, 302.)
[122] e.g. *Mohd. Shujt Ali* v. *Union of India* AIR 1974 SC 1631.
[123] e.g. *Biswambhar* v. *State of Orissa* AIR 1954 SC 139, 144.
[124] 1952 SCR 284, 294–8 (see also Mukherjea J. at 331). Cf. also *Bhikusha* v. *Union of India* AIR 1963 SC 1591, 1599; and D. D. Basu, *Commentary on the Constitution of India.* op. cit., 488.   [125] See n. 65 above.

conform to all these rules and yet which are bad; classifications made in the utmost good faith; classifications that are scientific and rational, that will have direct and reasonable relation to the object sought to be achieved and yet which are bad because, despite all that, the object itself is not allowed on the ground that it offends Article 14. In such a case the object itself must be struck down and not the mere classification which after all is only a means of attaining the end desired.'[126]

The Courts have made it plain that mathematical equality is not what the Constitution requires. 'Bare equality of treatment regardless of realities is neither justice nor homage to the constitutional principle.'[127] Thus a refusal to classify may violate Article 14 where there is capricious uniformity of treatment but a 'crying dissimilarity exists in reality' and there can be 'hostile discrimination while maintaining a facade of equality.'[128] It would appear that the real and genuine equality required by Article 14 may impose affirmative duties on the Government.

Unlike the United States Constitution, the Constitution of India expressly authorizes special measures for the protection of backward groups.[129] Article 15 (4) permits 'any special provision for the advancement of any socially and educationally backward classes of citizens or for the Scheduled Castes and the Scheduled Tribes'.[130] (This provision was added by the Constitution (First Amendment) Act, 1951, Section 2, following the decision of the Supreme Court in

---

[126] See Bose J. in *Bidi Supply Co.* v. *Union of India* 1956, SCR 267 (and also in *Anwar Ali's* case. Cf. also *Lachman Das* v. *State of Punjab* AIR 1963 SC 222.

[127] *M. Match Works* v. *Assistant Collector, C.E.* AIR 1974 SC 497, 503.

[128] Ibid, 504; and see *GM, SC Railway* v *A.V.R. Siddhanti* AIR 1974 SC 1755, 1760.

[129] There is a voluminous literature. See in particular, M. Galanter, ' "Protective Discrimination" for Backward Classes in India', 3 *JILI* (1961), 39, and 'Caste Disabilities and Indian Federalism', ibid. 205; N. Radhakrishnan, 'Reservation to the Backward Classes', 13 *Indian Yearbook of International Affairs* (1964), 293, and 'Units of Social and Educational Backwardness', 7 *JILI* (1965), 262; S. S. Nigam, 'Equality and the Representation of the Backward Classes in Parliament', 2 *JILI* (1959–60), 297; M. Galanter, 'Equality and Preferential Treatment', 14 *Indian Yearbook of International Affairs* (1965), 257; A. R. Blackshield, ' "Fundamental Rights" and the Institutional Viability of the Indian Supreme Court', 8 *JILI* (1966), 139.

[130] It is a 'Directive of State Policy' that 'the state shall promote with special care the educational and economic interests of the weaker sections of the people and in particular of the Scheduled Castes and the Scheduled Tribes and shall protect them from social injustice and all forms of exploitation'. (Art. 46.) This article is 'non-justiciable' under Article 37.

State of Madras v. *Champakam Dorairajan*.)[131] Article 16 (4) also makes express provision for the reservation of appointments or posts in favour of any backward class of citizens which in the opinion of the state is not adequately represented in the state services, but neither section actually obliges governments to take action; they are merely enabling sections.

It has been emphasized that these special measures were envisaged as exceptional and temporary measures to be used only for the purpose of mitigating the *de facto* inequalities between communities and were intended to disappear with these inequalities. They were not designed to consolidate and protect a group's separate integrity.[132] Certain other constitutional provisions exist for the protection of the identity and integrity of groups. Thus religious minorities have the right to manage their own religious affairs and to maintain and administer their own institutions under Article 26; groups distinguished by language, script, or culture are guaranteed the right to conserve the same under Article 29, and linguistic and religious minorities may establish and maintain educational institutions under Article 30.

The Constitution does not provide any guidance on the basis of which groups may be scheduled as backward, nor does it place any maximum or limitation on the extent to which reservations may be made. In *Venkataramana* v. *State of Madras*[133] the Supreme Court upheld the reservation of 19.7 per cent of posts to be filled by a competitive examination for Harijans and backward Hindus but refused to allow quotas for Moslems, Christians, non-Brahmin Hindus, and Brahmins as these could not be described as backward classes. In *Kesava Iyengar* v. *State of Mysore*[134] a reservation of seven-tenths of certain posts to backward classes was upheld on the basis that a state could reserve a portion for each backward community and thus dispose of all posts, but this case has now been discredited.

---

[131] 1951 SCJ 313. This case decided that a state had no power to reserve seats for backward communities in state maintained educational institutions, and did not take account of the directive principle in Article 46. The Court also regarded as significant the fact that Article 16 (4) made special provision for reservations in the field of government employment, while Article 15 omitted any similar provision.

[132] See M. Galanter, ' "Protective Discrimination" for Backward Classes in India', 3 *JILI* (1961), 39, 42, and N. Radhakrishnan, 'Units of Social Economic and Educational Backwardness: Caste and Individual', 7 *JILI* (1965) 262, 271.

[133] 1951 SCJ 318.

[134] AIR 1956 Mysore 20 (DB) High Court of Madras.

In *Balaji* v. *State of Mysore*[135] the Supreme Court stated that special provisions for backward groups must be within reasonable limits[136] and 'speaking generally, and in a broad way, a special provision should be less than 50 per cent'. The court characterized the purpose of Articles 15 (4) and 16 (4) not merely as conferring special privileges on the backward, but as serving the interests of the whole society by promoting its weakest elements. Moreover, the Court was opposed to the adoption of caste as the sole or dominant criterion in determining social backwardness mainly because such a classification is not always logical and may contain the vice of perpetuating the castes themselves.

The notion of caste could be taken into account but it should never be the predominant test in determining social backwardness; other factors such as poverty, occupation, and habitation also come into play. As a later case put it, an authority may take caste into consideration, but if it does not the order will not be bad on that account if it can ascertain the backwardness of a group of persons on the basis of other relevant criteria.[137] The test of backwardness is 'social and educational' but it may still be permissible to classify a caste as a whole as a backward group if it possesses those characteristics.[138] Classification must be based on an 'intelligible principle' designed to further the policy and object of the constitution—the amelioration of the conditions of the really backward classes—and if the classification is 'arbitrary' or the principle of differentiation 'wholly untenable' the court would be entitled to strike it down.[139]

Although the cases show that a broad margin of discretion is left to the states, the Court must ensure that reservations work to the advantage of the backward classes[140] and do not prejudice others unduly. A rational relation must exist between the differentia used and the degree of backwardness, and the Courts must ensure that

[135] AIR 1963 SC 649. (See also *Davadasan* v. *Union of India* AIR 1964 SC 179, 186, where the majority found that the holding of *Balaji* was that any reservation greater than 50 per cent was unconstitutional. This seems an over-strict interpretation.)   [136] AIR 1963 SC 649, 663.

[137] *Chitralekha* v. *State of Mysore* AIR 1964 SC 1823; *N. K. Sharma* v. *State of Bihar* AIR 1965 Pat. 372; *State of Kerala* v. *Jacob Mathew* ILR 1964 (2) Ker. 53.

[138] *Subash Chandra* v. *State of Uttar Pradesh* AIR 1975 SC 563; *State of Andhra Pradesh* v. *U.S.V. Balaram* AIR 1972 SC 1375; *Triloki Nath* v. *State of Jammur and Kashmir* AIR 1969 SC 1.

[139] *Ramakrishna Singh* v. *State of Mysore* AIR 1960 Mys. 338; M. Galanter, 3 *JILI* (1961), 459.

[140] *See Raghuramulu* v. *State of Andhra Pradesh*, AIR (1958) AP 129 (DB) and *V. V. Giri* v. *D. Suri Dara* AIR 1959 SC 1318.

classifications do not ossify into communal quotas and thereby postpone the achievement of the real equality aimed at.[141]

The most important recent case is *State of Kerala* v. *Thomas*,[142] the Indian equivalent of the *Bakke* decision,[143] in which the Supreme Court held by a majority that a preference for scheduled castes and tribes was not discrimination based on caste or race. Racial or caste preferences in favour of a severely backward under-represented class was consistent with the right of equality which meant 'actual equality' and not merely 'formal equality'.[144] The *Kerala* preference thus did not violate the constitutional right of equality of opportunity of a state employee denied promotion because he was not a member of the preferred backward class. As Ray CJ stated, 'The rule of parity is the equal treatment of equals in equal circumstances. The rule of differentiation is enacting laws differing between different persons or things in different circumstances . . . the rule of differentiation is inherent in the concept of equality.'[145] Equality thus means parity of treatment under parity of conditions and does not connote absolute equality.[146]

Article 15 (3) of the Constitution provides that states may make 'any special provision for women'. It has been generally agreed that special protection for women which helps them to attain a more genuine equality with men is in the interests of society, and that they are justifiable even if men are thereby put at a temporary disadvantage.[147]

The 1963 Constitution of the Federation of Malaysia includes special measures of protection for the aboriginal peoples and the Malays, by providing for the reservation of positions in the public services, the grant of special scholarships and educational facilities and certain preferences in the granting of business licences. However, these special rights are entrenched in the constitution and

[141] It has been argued that reservations based on caste have led to the perpetuation of caste-consciousness and the promotion of inter-caste tension (see S. S. Harrison, *India: The Most Dangerous Decade* (1960), 103, 104), and that there is a fierce struggle among castes to be classified as backward to be entitled to reservations. (See M. N. Srinivas, 'Caste in Modern India' in 16 *Journal of Asian Studies* (1957), 529.)

[142] AIR 1976 SC 490: [1979] 1 SCR 906.

[143] A. M. Katz, 'Benign Preferences: An Indian Decision and the *Bakke* case', 25 *AJCL* (1977), 611.

[144] [1979] 1 SCR 929, per Ray CJ, 951, per Mathew J., 981, per Krishna Iyer J.

[145] [1979] 1 SCR 929.   [146] Ibid.

[147] See *Dattatraya* v. *State of Bombay* AIR 1953 Bom. 311; and *Ramchasdra Mahton* v. *State of Bihar* XIV Bihar LJ Reps. (1966), 112.

cannot be abolished without the consent of the Conference of Rulers.[148] It has been properly pointed out that if the true purpose of these measures was to enable competition with the more progressive races then they should cease once parity is reached.[149]

Conclusions. Several principles can be deduced from the United States and Indian cases. (1) Distinctions drawn between groups of persons by legislation are not necessarily discriminatory. (2) In order for the distinctions to be legitimate, the classification of persons into groups which are to be treated differently must have a real and substantial basis, and a reasonable and just relation to the purpose of the legislation. (3) There is presumption that legislative bodies act constitutionally, but this presumption may be reversed if a classification is made solely on the basis of a natural inequality such as race. (4) A discriminatory motive is not an essential element if legislation is discriminatory in effect. (5) However, if an administrative act performed under a statute impartial on its face is challenged as discriminatory, the intention of the administering authorities is material. (6) Distinctions will be illegitimate if they are arbitrary, unreasonable, irrational, invidious, capricious, or irrelevant. (7) The point at which distinctions become discriminatory should be determined in the light of the current social situation[150] and current community standards.[151]

The Indian Constitution specifically provides for special measures of protection for the amelioration of the condition of depressed groups; nevertheless the equality principle may be effective *proprio motu* to achieve the same result, if it is interpreted to require a real and genuine rather than a mathematical or exact equality, and the

---

[148] See s. 153 and 159 of the Constitution of Malaysia, 1963.

[149] See S. M. Huang-Thio, 'Constitutional Discrimination under the Malaysian Constitution', 6 *Malaya L.R.* (1964), 1, 15. This article shows the difficulties which arise if the term 'discrimination' is equated with the term 'distinction'. Thus it is stated (p. 4) that 'a blanket prohibition against discrimination has the adverse effect of precluding the state from taking ameliorative measures to remove the various disabilities of the depressed classes'. If discrimination is taken to mean 'invidious distinction' and not to preclude special temporary measures of protection (cf. art. 1 of the 1965 Racial Discrimination Convention) then this difficulty disappears.

[150] Cf. *Pillai* v. *Mudanayake* [1953] AC 514 (PC) where the Privy Council applied the maxim, *omnia praesumuntur rite esse acta.*

[151] Cf. *Reynolds* v. *Sims* 12 L. ed. 2d. 506; and *Harper* v. *Virginia State Board of Electors* 16 L. ed. 2d. 169, 174, where it was said that notions of what constitutes equal protection for the purposes of the equal protection clause do change, and that the Courts have never been confined to historic notions of equality.

principle of non-discrimination is interpreted to forbid only dis-
advantageous distinctions and not special measures of protection.[152]
It is suggested that such a result would be perfectly consonant with
the interpretation of discrimination adopted in recent international
conventions.

[152] Measures for the preservation of linguistic and religious rights of minorities
should be continued as long as required; but ameliorative measures should be
temporary.

XIV

THE SOUTH WEST AFRICA CASES AND THE PRINCIPLE OF EQUALITY

In the *South West Africa* cases,[1] Liberia and Ethiopia requested the International Court of Justice to determine whether or not the Republic of South Africa was still bound by the Mandate agreement it had made with regard to the territory of South West Africa and, if so, whether it was in breach of its obligations under that agreement. Although the Court did not examine the actual merits of the claim on the basis that 'the applicants cannot be considered to have established any legal right or interest appertaining to them in the subject matter of the present claims',[2] the judgments (in particular, the dissenting opinion of Judge Tanaka) and the pleadings contain important observations on the principles of equality and non-discrimination.

In their final submissions the applicants claimed *inter alia* that:

Respondent, by laws and regulations, and official methods and measures, which are set out in the pleadings herein, has practised apartheid, i.e. has distinguished as to race, colour, national or tribal origin in establishing the rights and duties of the inhabitants of the Territory; that such practice is in violation of its obligations as stated in Article 2 of the Mandate and Article 22 of the Covenant of the League of Nations; and that Respondent has the duty forthwith to cease the practice of apartheid in the Territory;[3]

Respondent, by virtue of economic, political, social and educational policies applied within the Territory, by means of laws and regulations, and official methods and measures, which are set out in the pleadings herein, has, in the light of applicable international standards or international legal norms, or both, failed to promote to the utmost the material and moral well being and social progress of the inhabitants of the Territory; that its failure to do so is in violation of its obligations as stated in Article 2 of the Mandate and Article 22 of the Covenant; and that the Respondent has the duty forthwith to cease its violations as aforesaid and to take all practicable action to fulfil its duties under such Articles.[4]

[1] ICJ Rep. 1962, 318 (1st phase) and ICJ Rep. 1966, 4 (2nd phase).
[2] ICJ Rep. 1966, 51.
[3] Applicants' final submissions, CR 65/35, 69 (submission no. 3).
[4] Ibid., 69–70 (submission no. 4).

The applicants alleged the existence of international standards and/or an international norm of non-discrimination or non-separation, which, though differing in quality, possessed the same content. On occasions the applicants complained that the respondent had misinterpreted the applicants' theory of the case by repeatedly referring to the 'norm' and 'standards' of non-differentiation.[5] This, the applicants correctly pointed out, was more than a semantic distinction but struck at the heart of the true significance of the applicants' arguments.[6] In their opinion many types of differentiation were permissible, such as that provided for in the minorities treaties; what was not permissible was 'discrimination', i.e. (in this context) distinctions made on the irrelevant grounds of race, colour, or national or tribal origin.

To justify its policy of apartheid in South West Africa, however, the respondent quoted many examples of *different* treatment, such as the minorities treaties, special protection for women, separate conveniences for men and women, separate public holidays for different religious communities and different public schools for various language groups and the two sexes, and alleged that on the applicants' argument, these could not be provided by United Nations members.[7] Judge Tanaka properly rejected this contention, pointing out that it was impossible to assert that such cases of different treatment violated the norm of non-discrimination.[8]

Using the minorities treaties as an example, the Judge made two points. First, the norm of non-discrimination, as 'the reverse side of the notion of equality before the law' prohibited a state from excluding members of minority groups from rights, interests, and opportunities enjoyed by the majority population group. Second, the members of a minority group were guaranteed the protection of their own religious and educational activities. What was essential was that the guarantee was conferred in order to protect interests which the minority group wishes to maintain. There had to be an opportunity to reject the guarantee, since if it was imposed upon them its whole rationale fell to the ground. Although Judge Tanaka did not discuss the *Minority Schools in Albania* case, he nevertheless implied that the possibility of cultivating religious, educational, or linguistic values is a necessary condition of enjoying citizenship on

[5] See e.g. CR 65/31, 13. [6] CR 65/31, 16. [7] Rejoinder, i.145.
[8] Dissenting opinion of Judge Tanaka, *South West Africa* cases (2nd phase), ICJ Rep. 1966. The text may be found in I. Brownlie, *Basic Documents on Human Rights* (Oxford University Press, 1971), 456 ff.

equal terms.[9] The spirit of the minorities treaties was 'positive and permissive', not 'negative and prohibitive'.

In the case of apartheid it was probably reasonable that ethnic groups should be treated in some matters differently from one another. Different treatment required reasonableness to justify it. Acceptable reasons for differential treatment included the protection of certain fundamental rights and freedoms as in the case of minorities, the protection of infants (e.g. their incapacity to make contracts for non-necessaries), and, for that matter, the physical differences between men and women. Although individuals may be classified together for the purpose of differential treatment they do not constitute respectively a group strictly speaking. A racial group could not be categorized in a similar fashion because the scientific and clear-cut definition of race was not established, and, in any case, the physical characteristics used as criteria to distinguish one race from another do not constitute in themselves relevant factors as the basis for different political or legal treatment. If any necessity did exist for treating one race differently from another, this was not derived from physical characteristics or racial qualifications but from *other* factors—religious, linguistic, educational, or social, which in themselves are not related to race or colour.

The principle of equality means that all human beings are equal before the law and have equal opportunities without regard to such things as religion, language, eduction, sex, or social group. On the other hand, human beings, being endowed with individuality and living in different surroundings and circumstances need in some aspects, politically, legally, and socially, different treatment. Although equal treatment is a principle, its 'mechanical application', ignoring all concrete factors, engenders injustice. Accordingly it requires different treatment taking into consideration the concrete circumstances of individual cases. Differential treatment is permissible and *required* by the considerations of justice; it does not mean a disregard of justice. 'Equality being a principle, and different treatment an exception, those who refer to the different treatment must prove its *raison d'être* and its reasonableness.'[10] Different treatment is legally justifiable to the extent that it is just and reasonable, and the onus is on him who alleges the necessity for different treatment to demonstrate it. In the educational field, is it reasonable that children of diverse population groups should be

---

[9] ICJ Rep. 1966, 307.   [10] Ibid., 309

educated separately? Because of the value of the maternal tongue as the medium of instruction an affirmative answer can be given, with the important proviso that such separate instruction is in accordance with the wishes of the particular parents concerned.[11]

Judge Tanaka took the view that any distinction on a racial basis is contrary to the principle of equality.[12] Certainly, this would seem to be true where racial groups are treated separately as racial groups with regard to the use of public facilities and accommodations, but there may, nevertheless, be circumstances in which the making of distinctions on the basis of racial classification are occasionally justified. This situation could arise where individuals have previously been significantly disadvantaged on racial grounds.[13] Where this is so, certain special measures of assistance would not seem to conflict with the principle of equality, so long as they are optional and not imposed and are intended as ameliorative measures not to be continued longer than is strictly necessary. However, such classifications should be treated with great caution since it is not often that the use of other criteria such as economic and cultural levels will not suffice.

An argument that the establishment of job ceilings could be justified by the principle of reciprocity or balance was demolished by Judge Tanaka. He pointed out that it was not enough to say that the rights and freedoms of natives are restricted in one area while the corresponding rights and freedoms of the white inhabitants were restricted in another. The principle of equality was not observed because 'each unequal treatment constitutes an independent illegal conduct; the one cannot be counterbalanced by the other, a set-off is not permitted between two obligations resulting from illegal acts.'[14] A similar argument may be found in the jurisprudence of the United States Supreme Court[15] and the same considerations apply to respondent's arguments in the *Belgian Linguistics* cases that equality is preserved by treating each linguistic area in the same way.

---

[11] Cf. *Meyer* v. *Nebraska* 262 US 390.   [12] ICJ Rep. 1966, 314.
[13] This would mean that race was in these circumstances a relevant factor, just as sex is a relevant factor in providing special measures of protection for women.
[14] ICJ Rep. 1966, 313.
[15] e.g. *Henderson* v. *US* 339 US 816, (1950) 94 L. ed. 1302. The Court said 'The fact that the railroad's regulations as to separate accommodation for different races might impose on white passengers in proportion to their numbers, disadvantages similar to those imposed on negro passengers was not an answer to the requirements of [the Act] since discriminations that operate to the disadvantage of two groups are not less to be condemned because the impact is broader than if only one is affected.'

The latter case reveals another side of the equality principle since, although it might seem prima facie to be a case in which a group was requesting special treatment and privileges on the basis of language rather than claiming victimization because of discrimination, in fact, it is an example of a situation in which discrimination occurs because unidentical groups are being treated in the *same* way instead of being treated *differently* in proportion to their differences. In order to attain true equality, each population group should have had the same opportunity to have their children taught in their maternal tongue. The differential treatment consists in providing instruction only in the language of one particular section of the population and the onus is on those who seek to impose different treatment to justify it.[16] This they may be able to do if they can show that the measures adopted were consonant with the test of reasonableness and this in turn depends on all the attendant circumstances. For example, there may be too few pupils or insufficient teachers or the cost may be prohibitive. It would probably not be reasonable to provide teaching for a small group of alien origin in their own language, but for a major language group it may well be different. The deciding factors should be other considerations such as ease of administration and cost.

In Judge Tanaka's opinion the principle of equality before the law required that what are equal are to be treated equally and what are unequal to be treated differently[17] but this did not answer the question, 'What is equal and what is different?' Since all human beings, notwithstanding minor differences, are equal in their dignity as persons, from the point of view of human rights and fundamental freedoms they must be treated equally.

The core of his argument is to be found in his third proposition. 'The principle of equality does not mean absolute equality, but recognizes relative equality, namely different treatment proportionate to concrete individual circumstances. Different treatment must not be given arbitrarily; it requires reasonableness, or must be in conformity with justice, as in the treatment of minorities, different treatment of the sexes regarding public conveniences, etc. In these cases, the differentiation is aimed at the protection of those con-

---

[16] Cf. M. P. Golding, 'Principled Decision-Making and the Supreme Court', in R. S. Summers, ed., *Essays in Legal Philosophy* (Basil Blackwell, Oxford, 1968), 208, 233, 236.

[17] This, he pointed out, is what Aristotle termed *justitia commutativa* and *justitia distributiva*. (ICJ Rep. 1966, 305.)

cerned, and is not detrimental and therefore not against their will.'[18]

This statement is a clear rejection of the mathematical or numerical interpretation of equality, and support for the normative view that equality in law permits and requires special treatment in accordance with different needs. As the Judge pointed out earlier, 'To treat different matters equally in a mechanical way would be as unjust as to treat equal matters differently.'[19] The criterion for a justifiable differentiation is reasonableness which is the converse of arbitrariness.

However, in order to show that a differentiation is unreasonable or unjust, it is not necessary to demonstrate *mala fides* if the differentiation is discriminatory in effect. This will be so if the difference in treatment is imposed upon the individuals affected who do not have the choice whether to accept it or not. Apartheid was fundamentally unreasonable and unjust because it involved making distinctions on the basis of race rather than on grounds which might be justifiable such as linguistic or cultural differences. Distinction on a racial basis was itself contrary to the principle of equality which was of the character of natural law, and accordingly illegal.[20]

Although Judge Tanaka's views on the nature of equality were merely *obiter dicta* in the *South West Africa* cases, his exposition is undoubtedly the *locus classicus* on the subject, and has had a profound influence on later thinking.

---

[18] ICJ Rep. 1966, 313. [19] Ibid., 305
[20] Ibid., 314. The author does not wholly accept Judge Tanaka's exposition. For example, it has already been suggested that there may be rare occasions when distinctions on racial grounds may be permissible, and his use of terminology is occasionally confusing. Although he generally used the term 'discrimination' in the sense of 'unreasonable, arbitrary distinction' on other occasions he sometimes appeared to use it in the sense of 'distinction' *simpliciter*. Thus he once referred to a 'permissible discrimination', ICJ Rep. 1966, 307.

XV

NON-DISCRIMINATION AS A LEGAL PRINCIPLE

1. *Standards*

IN their pleadings in the *South West Africa* cases the applicants claimed *inter alia* that there existed applicable international standards or an international legal norm or both, in the light of which the respondent by its policies of apartheid had violated its obligations under Article 2 of the Mandate and Article 22 of the League Covenant to promote to the utmost the material and moral well being of the inhabitants of the territory.[1] These alleged standards or norms were said to prohibit discrimination and constitute a legal limitation of the respondent's discretionary power. Apartheid was defined by the applicants as a situation where 'the status, rights, duties, opportunities and burdens of the population are determined and allotted arbitrarily on the basis of race, colour and tribe in a pattern which ignores the needs and capacities of the groups and individuals affected and subordinates the interests and rights of the great majority of the people to the preferences of a minority'.[2]

There were two alternative aspects to the applicants' arguments:[3] first that there existed a norm or rule of international law prohibiting the practice of apartheid; or second, that there existed certain 'standards' which could be used to interpret the Mandate agreement but to which the governing effect of a legal rule was not attributed. The nature of these 'standards' and the criteria by which they are recognized and incorporated as part of the legal obligations of parties to an agreement require consideration. It is a truism that only in a few paradigm situations can a legal rule cover exhaustively every situation that may arise. Usually a rule has a core of settled

[1] See applicants' final submissions, 19 May 1965, CR 65/35, 69–70 (and CR 65/2–34).   [2] *South West Africa* cases, pleadings: memorials, 108.

[3] This alternative aspect led to a good deal of misunderstanding between the parties. The applicants complained that their position was being misinterpreted by the respondent. See CR 65/96, when counsel for the applicants cited the occasions on which objection was raised to respondent's misrepresentation of the applicants' position.

meaning and a large penumbra where its application is in doubt. It is in this latter area that 'extra-legal standards' are often used to evaluate a factual situation. A 'standard' as opposed to a legal rule is a typical category of indeterminate reference.[4] Rarely can a court apply a formula mechanically to a given situation and where judgments cannot be decided by logical exercises but require a decision as to what justice requires in the circumstances, then standards such as reasonableness, fairness, just cause, and due care are appealed to. Legal rules or norms which allow for reference to such standards, although they are legal propositions, provide for variations of their content and application in different situations. They direct the court 'to derive the rule to be applied from daily experience'.[5]

In a vast area of legal relations legal rules refer to indeterminate guides which are given content by the received ideals of judges and by incorporating the widely shared convictions of society.[6] As Pound points out, standards are general limits of permissible conduct to be applied according to the circumstances of each case and are the chief reliance of modern law for individualization of application. They provide a method for incorporating the *mores* of a society and 'the felt necessities of time and place' into the law.[7] Cardozo writes of standards of behaviour which are types or patterns to which statutes or decisions may be expected to conform. These have their roots in the *mores* of the day and though they may lack an official imprimatur this will not always hinder us from resting securely on the assumption that the omission will be supplied when occasion so demands.[8]

Examples abound of the role of standards in municipal law. In the House of Lords, Lord Reid, speaking of natural justice, described as a 'perennial fallacy' the idea that because something cannot be cut and dried or nicely weighed or measured, therefore it does not exist. 'The idea of negligence is equally insusceptible of exact definition, but what a reasonable man would regard as a fair procedure in particular circumstances and what he would regard as negligent in particular circumstances are equally capable of serving as tests in law.'[9]

[4] See J. Stone, *Legal Systems and Lawyers' Reasonings*, (Stevens, London, 1964) 263. [5] O. W. Holmes, *The Common Law* (Macmillan, London, 1881), 123.

[6] For a discussion of the role of 'extra-legal standards', see Prof. R. M. Dworkin, 'Is Law a System of Rules?' 35 *U. Chicago L. Rev.* (1967), 14, reprinted in Summers, ed., *Essays in Legal Philosophy* op. cit., 25.

[7] Roscoe Pound, 'Hierarchy of Sources and Forms in Different Systems of Law' 7 *Tulane L. Rev.* (1933), 475.

[8] Benjamin Cardozo, *The Growth of the Law* (Princeton University Press, 1924), 52. [9] *Ridge* v. *Baldwin* [1963] AC 40, 64, 65.

This is how a court relies on objectively ascertained criteria in coming to a decision. In the same way, American cases interpreting the Fourteenth Amendment have used the objective criteria derived from scientific studies and evidence of international agreements such as the United Nations Charter and the Universal Declaration of Human Rights to give content to the standard of 'equal protection'.[10]

Similarly, international law contains many references to vague standards and abstract concepts. Many norms refer to standards; e.g. in the field of state responsibility towards aliens, there is a duty incumbent upon states to respect a minimum international standard of civilization in their treatment of aliens[11] which is very close to a doctrine of the reasonable state.[12] In *Techt* v. *Hughes*[13] Cardozo J. preferred to lay down a fluid standard to regulate the impact of war on treaties, than to apply the rigid set of rules which then existed. In this way flexibility of the law was attained at the expense of exact precision. There are many instances in which international courts have relied on standards. For example in the *Chorzow Factory* case,[14] the principle of estoppel was clearly invoked by implication. In the *Morocco* case[15] the court invoked the standards of reasonableness and good faith when considering the power of customs officials to make valuations, while in the *Fisheries* case[16] the judgment was based to a large extent on the reasonableness of Norway's claim in the light of all the circumstances. Similarly, in the *Waters of the Meuse*,[17] Judge Manley Hudson held that equity was a general principle of law and that 'equality was equity'. Interpreting Article 15 of the European Convention, the European Court of Human Rights held in the *Lawless* case[18] that the existence at the relevant time of a public emergency threatening the life of the nation was *reasonably* deduced by the Irish government from a combination of several factors.

[10] See, in addition, the cases and articles referred to by Judge Jessup in his opinion in the *South West Africa* cases, ICJ Rep. 1966, 434 ff.

[11] But see the discussion (p. 198 above) of García-Amador's reports as special rapporteur on the law of state responsibility. Judge Jessup criticized the way this subject was dealt with by counsel in the *South West Africa* cases. (ICJ Rep. 1966, 435.)

[12] See also M. S. McDougal and N. A. Schlei; The Hydrogen Bomb Test in Perspective, 64 *Yale L.J.* (1955), 648, 659, 660.

[13] 229 NY 222 (1920).   [14] PCIJ, ser. A, no. 17.

[15] Case concerning, *Rights of Nationals of the United States of America in Morocco*, ICJ Rep. 1952, 176, 212.

[16] ICJ Rep. 1951, 116.   [17] PCIJ ser. A/B, fasc. no. 70, 76 ff.

[18] *Lawless* v. *Republic of Ireland*, European Court of Human Rights, ser. A, vol. iii.

Standards by their nature can be expanded to cover any lacuna in the law, and Lauterpacht is surely correct in denying the existence of a *non liquet* in international law.[19] Dillard has suggested three points which are relevant to a consideration of the role of law in settling disputes in the national or international domain.[20] First, the concept of a judicial process whereby the court in a somewhat mechanistic way merely applies the law to the facts, fails to take standards adequately into account. Secondly, the power of the court increases in direct proportion as the norms increase in generality. Even if the court pays lip service to 'objective' standards, the difficulty of ascertaining these standards leaves such wide room for discretion as to make the court's power to affect future conditions a significantly felt institutional problem. Thirdly, in the framing of codes and drafting of treaties as well as in the determination of the kinds of controversies suitable for judicial decision, the significant differences between rules (in the narrow sense), principles, and standards can become critically important.[21]

Under the League mandate system, the mandatories were clearly expected to comply with certain standards in the fulfilment of the 'sacred trust'. Quincy Wright pointed out that Article 22 of the League Covenant laid down broad principles to be developed in more detail by other provisions.[22] Standards for guiding policy and action in mandated areas were established by three distinct procedures, i.e. quasi-judicial, technical, and legislative. There was (a) the growth of a jurisprudence from decisions on particular questions, (b) the agreement on principles for its own use by the Mandate Commission, and (c) the passage of formal resolutions by the Council or Assembly. Wright saw the evolution of general standards as 'perhaps the most important development of the mandate system'.[23]

It was with these considerations in mind that members of the Court wrote their opinions in the *South West Africa* cases. Though Judge Jessup avoided the applicant's contention that there existed a

---

[19] H. Lauterpacht, *The function of law in the International Community* (Clarendon Press, Oxford, 1933) 61 ff.

[20] See H. C. Dillard, 'Some Aspects of Law and Diplomacy', 91 *Recueil des Cours* (1957), 449, 486. Dillard also shares Lauterpacht's doubts concerning the validity of the distinction between 'legal' and 'political' disputes. See p. 486. See also J. Stone, '*Non-Liquet* and the Function of Law in the International Community', 35 *BYIL* (1959), 126.

[21] Dillard, 485.

[22] Quincy Wright, 'The Establishment of Standards' in *Mandates under the League of Nations* (Chicago, 1930), ch. 7, 219.

[23] Wright, 225.

peremptory norm of international law of non-discrimination, he nevertheless accepted that the judicial task of the Court in interpreting Article 2 of the Mandate agreement was to be performed by applying appropriate objective standards. After reviewing the role of standards in the judicial process, he decided that it would not be a legally justifiable conclusion to hold that the mandatory had an unreviewable discretion.[24]

The difficulties in reaching the objectives of the sacred trust were formidable and the routes to the objectives multiple, but this did not mean that the choice of policies made by the mandatory was not subject to review. Nor did it follow that each member of the Court had to decide subjectively whether he believed the mandatory had chosen wisely or correctly since the law abounded in examples of standards or criteria which are applied by the courts as tests of human conduct.[25] In his view, there were objective criteria which could be used to test the mandatory's conduct of the Mandate. Article 2 of the Mandate should be interpreted by reference to the *pertinent, contemporary, international, community standard*.[26] This could be found in the accumulation of expressions of condemnation of apartheid, especially as recorded in the resolutions of the United Nations General Assembly. Counsel for the respondent had agreed that 'the effect of obtaining the agreement of an organization like the United Nations would, for all practical purposes, be the same as obtaining the consent of all the members individually', and that would probably be of 'decisive practical value' as the United Nations 'represented most of the civilized states of the world'.[27]

Judge Jessup pointed out that it is equally true that obtaining the disagreement and condemnation of the United Nations is of decisive practical—and juridical—value in determining the applicable standard. The Court was bound to take account of such a consensus as providing the standard to be used in the interpretation of Article 2 of the Mandate.[28] Judge Tanaka, though he preferred to argue the

[24] ICJ Rep. 1966, 438, 441
[25] He pointed out that Judge Kaeckenbeeck as President of the Arbitral Tribunal in Upper Silesia wrestled successfully with many problems, such as the way to test discrimination through the use of discretionary powers. (ICJ Rep. 1966, 434.)
[26] ICJ Rep. 1966, 441 (emphasis added). (Cf. also M. Sørensen, 'The Quest for Equality', in *International Conciliation* (1956), no. 507, 291.)
[27] *South West Africa* case pleadings, CR 65/15, 28.
[28] This conclusion did not rest on the thesis that General Assembly resolutions have a general legislative character or create new rules of law. (See also C. J. R. Dugard, 'The *South West Africa* Cases, Second Phase, 1966', 83 *SALJ* (1966), 429, 455, 456.)

existence of a legal norm of non-discrimination, also averred that the equality principle (as an integral part of the United Nations Charter) could be applied to the Mandate agreement as a principle of interpretation.[29]

Formidable and persuasive as these arguments are, they are not without difficulties. There is a clear acceptance of the proposition that in interpreting an international agreement which refers to vague standards which are to be achieved, the discretion of a state in choosing its method of obtaining an objective is limited by certain criteria objectively ascertained, i.e. the consensus of the contemporary international community. It is thus that the *content* of the standards which are to be achieved is measured.

Article 2 of the Mandate required the mandatory 'to promote to the utmost the material and moral well being and social progress of the inhabitants of the territory'. In the consensus of the 'pertinent world community' as discovered by the declarations and resolutions of the United Nations, 'material and moral well-being and social progress of the inhabitants' is incompatible with a system of apartheid or racial discrimination.

This theory raises the whole question of the legal status of resolutions and declarations of the General Assembly. It is obvious that if the consensus of contemporary world community concerning equality can be used to interpret the vague wording of the Mandate, *a fortiori*, it can be used to interpret a document such as the United Nations Charter itself in which there are specific references to discrimination. Judge Jessup carefully refused to hold that the principle of apartheid violated a general rule (norm) of international law, since this might seem to be passing judgment on the legality of acts performed within the Republic of South Africa.[30] Yet, by allowing United Nations resolutions and declarations to be used as authoritative aids to interpretations of the Mandate, he must also admit them to assist in the interpretation of the Charter itself to which South Africa is a party.

It has often been suggested that although the Universal Declaration of Human Rights in itself may not be a legal doctrine involving legal obligations, it is of legal value inasmuch as it contains an authoritative interpretation of the human rights and fundamental freedoms which do constitute an obligation binding on United

[29] ICJ Rep. 1966, 290. (But cf. opinion of *ad hoc* Judge Van Wyk, 159–68.)
[30] ICJ Rep. 1966, 433.

Nations members under the Charter.[31] Lauterpacht has strongly criticized such a view. In his opinion, to maintain that a document contains an authoritative interpretation of a legally binding instrument was to assert that the former document itself is as legally binding and as important as the instrument which it is supposed to interpret.[32]

The main difficulty here is caused by the words 'authoritative interpretation'. If this language is rejected in favour of a terminology incorporating standards, the situation does not involve contradictions. Professor Waldock describes the declaration as having 'high authority as the accepted formulation of the common standards of human rights'.[33] Professor Brownlie speaks of it as an *authoritative guide* to the interpretation of the provisions of the Charter, and as having 'indirect legal effect'.[34] The distinction is important. An 'authoritative interpretation' cannot be rebutted or gainsaid, whereas a 'guide to interpretation', however authoritative, cannot have this effect. It merely provides evidence of opinions of governments as to interpretation but without having binding effect *per se*. It is *evidence* which can be used to give content to a standard. Moreover, the Universal Declaration claims in its preamble to be 'a statement of the common standards of achievement for all people and all nations'.

Accordingly, when a dispute as to the meaning of a human rights provision in an instrument (e.g. the Charter) arises, the Declaration can be used as a guide to the meaning of the formal general proposition sought to be interpreted, and will be given a great deal of weight as a statement of pertinent contemporary international standards. In the same way, other resolutions and declarations of the United Nations provide evidence of such standards and should be accorded suitable importance not only by international tribunals seeking to interpret an international instrument containing references to standards, but also by states seeking to regulate their internal affairs in accordance with international law.

[31] See e.g. L. B. Sohn, 'The Universal Declaration of Human Rights: A Common Standard of Achievement?' 8 *Journal of the International Commission of Jurists* (1967), no. 2, 17, 25, 26.

[32] H. Lauterpacht, op. cit., 409.

[33] C. H. M. Waldock, 'Human Rights in Contemporary International Law and the Significance of the European Convention', in *The European Convention on Human Rights, ICLQ Supp.* (1965), no. 11, 15.

[34] I. Brownlie, *Principles of Public International Law* (Oxford University Press, 3rd ed. 1979), 571.

2. Norms

The alternative argument of the applicants in the *South West Africa* cases was that there had evolved over the years and now existed a generally accepted international human rights norm of non-discrimination. It was defined by international undertakings in the form of principles, conventions, and declarations, by judicial decisions, by the practice of states, and by constitutional and statutory provisions which incorporated such a norm into the body of laws of states.[35] To support this claim the applicants relied to a large extent on the many resolutions concerning discrimination and apartheid which had been passed by organs of the United Nations, particularly the General Assembly.

This contention was rejected by Judge Jessup on the ground that since international bodies lack a true legislative character, their resolutions alone cannot create law.[36] Nevertheless, as Sloan points out, the non-obligatory status of Assembly resolutions is far from being as definitely established as has been assumed by most writers. 'The most that can be said is that there is a presumption against these recommendations possessing binding legal force.'[37] It seems clear that some General Assembly resolutions such as those concerned with the internal working of the United Nations do have a full legal effect in that they are binding upon both the members and the organs of the United Nations, thus creating obligations and legal situations which did not exist before.[38]

In the *Voting Procedure* case,[39] Judge Lauterpacht said, 'Although decisions of the General Assembly are endowed with full legal effect in some spheres of the activity of the United Nations and with limited legal effects in other spheres, it may be said, by way of a broad generalization, that they are not legally binding upon the Members of the United Nations.'[40] A similar view was taken by Judge Fitzmaurice in the *Expenses* case.[41]

[35] *South West Africa* cases, pleadings: reply, 274.
[36] ICJ Rep. 1966, 432, 441.
[37] F. B. Sloan, 'The Binding Force of a "Recommendation" of the General Assembly in the United Nations', 25 *BYIL* (1948), 1, 16.
[38] See D. H. N. Johnson, 'The Effect of Resolutions of the General Assembly', 32 *BYIL* (1955–6), 97–122.
[39] ICJ Rep. 1955, 67.
[40] Ibid., 115 and cf. Judge Klaestad, 88.
[41] ICJ Rep. 1962, 210, (and also Judge Winiarski, 233). But cf. the views of Judge Alvarez in the *Fisheries* case, ICJ Rep. 1951, 116, 152, and his dissenting opinion in the *Reservations* case, ICJ Rep. 1951, 15, 52.

However, even if it may be said that recommendations of the General Assembly and the Security Council are generally not binding and cannot in themselves create new rules of law, this is quite another thing from saying that they have no legal effect. On the contrary, they may be strong evidence of the existence of general principles of law recognized by civilized nations or be evidence of the *opinio juris* necessary for the formation of customary law.

Considerable discussion has taken place over the legal status of General Assembly resolutions which purport to be declarations of legal principles, particularly with regard to the Declaration of Legal Principles Governing the Activities of States in the Exploration and Use of Outer Space.[42] The United States took the view that this resolution created law, but this opinion was not universally accepted by other states, and no general *opinio juris* can be deduced from the debates. Professor Cheng has suggested that certain law-finding resolutions, if adopted unanimously may dispense with the need for state practice, by themselves providing evidence of the *opinio juris*. In his view there was no reason why a new *opinio juris* should not develop overnight so that a new rule of international customary law might come into existence instantly.[43] He found support for this contention in General Assembly Resolution 96 (I) of 11 December 1946 which affirmed that genocide was a crime under international law, but here it seems that the General Assembly was merely declaring that it recognized certain pre-existing legal principles and was not endeavouring to create new principles 'instantly'. In spite of the attractions of this approach it should be rejected since 'instant customary law' is inconsistent with the usual meaning of customary law which requires a repeated practice.[44] Thus Article 38 (1) (b) of the Statute of the International Court of Justice calls for 'evidence

---

[42] GA Res. 1962(XVIII). See also GA Res. 1721 A (XVI).

[43] See Bin Cheng, 'The United Nations Resolutions on Outer Space: "Instant" International Customary Law?' in 5 *Indian Journal of International Law* (1965), 23, 46.

[44] This is not to say that new law-creating processes may not be developing. Thus J. E. S. Fawcett has tentatively suggested that an international declaration would establish rules of law if at least four conditions are satisfied: i.e. that the sponsoring states have authority to make the declaration; that the declaration serves a common interest; that the principles declared are capable of functioning as rules of law without further elaboration; and that the sponsoring states intend to observe them as such. See J. E. S. Fawcett, *International Law and the Uses of Outer Space* (Oceana, Manchester, 1968), 7. D. H. N. Johnson, op. cit., 121, has also suggested that there is nothing to prevent members incurring binding legal obligations by the act of voting for resolutions in the General Assembly provided there is a clear intention to be so bound.

of a general practice'. Judge Tanaka has refused to admit that individual resolutions, declarations, judgments, decisions, etc., are binding on the members of the United Nations. 'What is required for customary international law is the repetition of the same practice; accordingly in this case, resolutions, declarations, etc., on the same matter in the same or diverse organs must take place repeatedly.'[45] He also pointed out that the appearance of international organizations had influenced the mode of generation of customary law. 'In the contemporary age of highly developed techniques of communication and information, the formation of a custom through the medium of international organizations is greatly facilitated and accelerated; the establishment of a custom would require no more than one generation or even far less than that.'[46] The better answer, therefore, is that, although customary law may develop very rapidly, it cannot come into existence instantly.[47]

It is clear that the participation of states in General Assembly resolutions provides evidence of state practice.[48] Certainly, there is no reason why they should not provide such evidence, particularly in view of the fact that diplomatic dispatches are admissible for this purpose. Nevertheless, resolutions of international organs are not *sui generis*. As Professor Jennings points out, 'A resolution of an international body may represent the collective view of states: it may also represent little or nothing of the sort. Often only time and the interaction of decisions indicating, when taken together, an unmistakable trend will enable one to sort out the important from the insignificant.'[49] The continual recitation by the General Assembly of certain principles that are described as binding obligations because of their roots in established sources of international law serves to reinforce the claim that the particular resolution containing them enunciates legally binding principles. The repetition of references to previous resolutions demonstrates that those resolutions contain principles of an important nature which are 'temporally stable' and thus distinguishes them from matters which are of temporary concern.[50]

[45] ICJ Rep. 1966, 292.   [46] Ibid., 291.
[47] As Prof. Jennings says, 'custom seems to belie its nature by developing if not quite instantly at any rate with surprising celerity'. See R. Y. Jennings, 'General Course on Principles of International Law', 121 *Recueil des Cours* (1967) ii.323–5, 334.
[48] But cf. *ad hoc* Judge Van Wyk, ICJ Rep. 1966, 169.
[49] R. Y. Jennings, 'Recent Developments in the International Law Commission', 13 *ICLQ* (1964), 385, 393.
[50] See S. A. Bleicher, 'The Legal Significance of Re-Citation of General Assembly Resolutions', 63 *AJIL* (1969), 444–77.

One of the most constantly recited resolutions has been General Assembly Resolution 217 (III), the Universal Declaration of Human Rights. It has been estimated that the Declaration was referred to in later resolutions seventy-five times in the first nineteen years since its adoption.[51] In some recommendations, the Universal Declaration has been referred to as if it were on the same level as the Charter itself. Thus the 1960 Declaration on the Granting of Independence to Colonial Countries and Peoples provided that 'all states shall observe faithfully and strictly the provisions of the Charter of the United Nations, the Universal Declaration of Human Rights, and the present Declaration'.[52] In the General Assembly, the Cyprus representative pointed out that this declaration was 'second only to the Charter of the United Nations and the Universal Declaration of Human Rights on both of which it is based and both of which it revitalizes'.[53] Similar language was used in the 1963 Declaration on the Elimination of All Forms of Racial Discrimination and the 1965 Convention on the same subject.

There is, therefore, considerable authority now for the view that the principles of the Universal Declaration by widespread and constant recognition have been clothed with the character of customary law.[54] S. A. Bleicher has stated the General Assembly Resolutions 217 (III) and 1514 (XV) 'appear to have attained, or at least progressed well down the road to attaining, the status of accepted principles of international law'.[55] A more forthright statement has been made by L. B. Sohn: 'In a relatively short time the Universal Declaration of Human Rights has thus become a part of

[51] Ibid., 444.

[52] GA Res. 1514 (XV). Schwelb has commented: 'This is a far cry from a mere standard of achievement: it says they "shall observe". One could object to this that apparently the General Assembly exceeded its powers by addressing such a peremptory demand to member states. The fact is, however, that this Declaration was adopted against no opposing vote by 96 votes with seven abstentions, and it was re-enacted in 1961 with 102 votes for and 4 abstentions and in 1962 by 107 votes and 4 abstentions.' E. Schwelb, 'The United Nations and Human Rights' in 11 *Howard L.J.* (1966), 356, 367.

[53] GAOR 15th sess., plenary meetings, P.1281; and see ibid., 1002–3 (Ceylonese representative), 1136, (Nepal representative), and 1256 (Cyprus representative). But cf. 1266 (Swedish representative).

[54] See Sir Humphrey Waldock, 'Human Rights in Contemporary International Law and the Significance of the European Convention', *ICLQ, supp.* no. 11 (1965), 1, 15; and *Recueil des Cours* (1962) ii.32, 199. See also E. Schwelb, *Human Rights and the World Community*.

[55] Bleicher, op. cit., 477. Prof. Jennings also takes the view that the Universal Declaration is 'Certainly not without some legal efficacy'. See Jennings, op. cit., 504.

the constitutional law of the world community; and together with the Charter of the United Nations, it has achieved the character of a world law superior to all other international instruments and to domestic laws.'[56] Another problem which arises is whether or not the consent of all states is required for the creation of a customary rule. This is particularly relevant in the case of South Africa which has consistently opposed General Assembly resolutions dealing with questions of non-discrimination and apartheid.

The applicants in the *South West Africa* cases pointed out that Article 38 (1) (b) of the Court Statute does not require unanimous consent as a prerequisite to the existence of a customary norm. What was required was rather a consensus of an overwhelming majority, a convergence of international opinion, a predominance of view.[57] This interpretation found favour with Judge Tanaka who said that Article 38 (1) (b) does not exclude the possibility of a few dissidents for the purpose of the creation of a customary international law.[58] Nor does it seem that a protesting state can exclude itself from the generality of such a customary law for the same reason.[59] The International Court has sometimes appeared to suggest that a customary rule must have been acquiesced in by a particular state that is alleged to be bound by it.[60] However, in the cases concerned, the Court was dealing not with a general customary rule but with an alleged local or special custom.[61] Fitzmaurice has shown that there are important differences between the formation of a general custom and a special custom. Only in the latter situation is it necessary to show consent or at least acquiescence on the part of the particular state or states to be bound.[62] Were customary law not formed by a process more akin to consensus than to consent, there would be no need for a new state to be bound by existing general customary law irrespective of its consent. Thus it would not seem

[56] L. B. Sohn, 'The Universal Declaration of Human Rights: A Common Standard of Achievement', 8 *Journal of the International Commission of Jurists* (1967), no. 2, 17, 26.
[57] *South West Africa* cases, CR 65/35, 14–15.
[58] ICJ Rep. 1966,291. Cf. also Lord McNair, *The Law of Treaties* (Oxford University Press, 1961), 214, n. 5.
[59] See Jennings, op. cit., 336.
[60] e.g. *The Asylum* case ICJ Rep. 1950, 266, 276; the *Morocco* case, ICJ Rep. 1952, 176, 200; *Right of Passage over Indian Territory* case, ICJ Rep. 1960, 6.
[61] See A. A. D'Amato, 'The Concept of Special Custom in International Law,' 63 *AJIL* (1969), 211.
[62] Sir Gerald Fitzmaurice, 92 *Recueil des Cours* (1957), ii.1, 100; and *BYIL* (1953), 68–9.

possible for states to exclude themselves from the operation of any customary rule that may exist concerning human rights.[63]

It might be argued that the completion of the International Covenants on Human Rights indicated that member states did not consider that the Universal Declaration expressed binding obligations, but there are sufficient differences both in regard to substance and implementation to make the existence of overlapping obligations perfectly plausible; existing customary law exists alongside the provisions of the Covenants[64] although the fuller substantive provisions of the Covenants may in time better reflect the obligations of customary law than those of the Declaration. In the light of all these considerations, it is difficult to deny that the Universal Declaration of Human Rights, and, in particular the principles of equality of individuals and non-discrimination which it contains, constitute part of customary international law.

Specific mention was made in Article 62 (2) of the Charter of the power of the General Assembly to make recommendations concerning human rights, distinct from its general power to make recommendations under Article 10, and the Universal Declaration might accordingly be regarded as an authoritative interpretation of the Charter provisions on human rights.[65] Mr Cassin was confident that if the International Court of Justice was seised of a case of violation of human rights it would regard it as a question of positive international law and considered it to be quite clear that 'recommendations regarding human rights were rather different from other recommendations, since Articles 55 and 56 of the Charter created a general obligation for states to co-operate with the United Nations in promoting respect for human rights and a general obligation obviously carried more weight when given practical form by a recommendation'.[66] Similarly, in Sloan's opinion, it might be argued that the protection of human rights falls or will be brought into a sphere of action where binding resolutions may be made.[67]

Finally, arguments can be adduced to support the view that the basic principles of human rights, as, in particular, the principles of equality, may form part of the general principles of law recognized by civilized nations. Article 38 (1) (c) of the Court Statute does not

[63] This is quite apart from the question of *jus cogens* which will be considered below.   [64] Cf. S. A. Bleicher, op. cit., 465, and R. Y. Jennings, op. cit., 337.
[65] Commission of Human Rights, debate on periodic reports, 1953. See UN doc. E/CN.4/S.R.404/rev.1, 11–16, especially Mr. Ingles (Philippines).
[66] See UN doc. E/CN.4/S.R.405, 4–16.   [67] F. B. Sloan, op. cit., 24.

mean that a majority of civilized nations, by legislating on a particular domestic matter, could compel a minority to introduce similar legislation.[68] What it does permit is the borrowing from comparative law sources of certain fundamental legal concepts and underlying or guiding principles.[69] As Bin Cheng has said, general principles of law can be considered as 'juridical truth'.[70]

Certainly, the constitutions and laws of the great majority of 'civilized' nations embody to some extent the principles of equality before the law. Sen has demonstrated that a considerable number of constitutions embody the principle of equality,[71] and according to Peaslee, approximately 73 per cent of national constitutions contain clauses respecting equality.[72] Moreover, it has been suggested that resolutions of the General Assembly can also serve to determine that certain rules are 'general principles of law recognized by civilized nations'.[73] Respect for human rights including equality has also been recognized as a general principle of law by C. W. Jenks.[74]

The claim that the principle of equality is a general principle of law has been supported by Judge Tanaka[75] but not widely canvassed elsewhere in the Court. In any case it is not necessary to rely upon this argument as more support exists for the contention that the principle can be based on customary sources.[76]

3. *The Equality of Individuals as a Jus Cogens principle*

Jus Cogens has been described as the body of those general rules of law whose non-observance may affect the very essence of the legal system to which they belong to such an extent that the subjects of the law may not, under pain of absolute nullity, depart from them in virtue of particular agreements. The rules of *jus dispositivum* are valid only in so far as there are no inconsistent rules freely chosen by

[68] See *ad hoc* Judge Van Wyk, *South West Africa* cases, ICJ Rep. 1966, 170.
[69] Judge Tanaka, ibid., 295, (and see generally 294–300).
[70] Bin Cheng, *General Principles of Law as Applied by International Courts and Tribunals* (Stevens, London, 1953), 24.
[71] D. K. Sen, *A Comparative Study of the Indian Constitution* (Orient Longmans, Bombay, 1966), 200–3.
[72] Amos J. Peaslee, *Constitutions of Nations* (Nijhoff, The Hague, 2nd ed., 1956), i.7. Later editions give no figure.   [73] See S. A. Bleicher, op. cit., 477.
[74] C. W. Jenks, *The Common Law of Mankind* (Stevens, London, 1958), 121.
[75] ICJ Rep. 1966, 294–300.
[76] The importance of the discrimination conventions should not be forgotten. It is submitted that as well as laying down rules of law applicable between the parties, they are also evidence of the growth of customary rules which they codify.

the parties. Thus *jus cogens* restricts the freedom of the parties; its rules are absolutely binding.[77]

Although the concept is not new, it is only recently that it has begun to assume any importance in international practice and the thinking of statesmen.[78] Lord McNair has pointed out that it is difficult to imagine any society, whether of individuals or of states, whose law sets no limit whatever to freedom of contract. In every civilized community there are some rules of law and some principles of morality which individuals are not permitted by law to ignore or to modify.[79]

Before World War II Verdross argued for the existence of *jus cogens*, which he described as a general principle prohibiting states from concluding treaties *contra bonos mores*,[80] quoting in support the views of Judge Schücking in the *Oscar Chinn* case. '*Jamais . . . la Cour n'appliquerait une convention dont le contenu serait contraire aux bonnes mœurs.*'[81] Subsequently, when the International Law Commission formulated its proposals for the codification of the law of treaties, a draft article concerning the concept of *jus cogens* was included,[82] and the Vienna Convention on the Law of Treaties includes Article 53 entitled 'Treaties conflicting with a peremptory norm of general international law (*jus cogens*)' and provides, 'A treaty is void if, at the time of its conclusion, it conflicts with a peremptory norm of general international law. For the purposes of the present Convention, a peremptory norm of general international law is a norm accepted and recognized by the International community of states as a whole as a norm from which no derogation is permitted and which can be modified only by a subsequent norm of

[77] See E. Suy, *The Concept of Jus Cogens in International Law*, in *Papers and Proceedings*, ii, of the Conference on International Law held at Lagonissi, Greece, in Apr. 1966 by the Carnegie Endowment for International Peace.

[78] Sir Humphrey Waldock, special rapporteur on the law of treaties for the International Law Commission, has said that the concept was not perhaps familiar to statesmen and would not be readily assimilated by them. *Yearbook of the ILC 1963*, i.77–8.

[79] Lord McNair, *The Law of Treaties*, (Oxford University Press, 1961), 213–14.

[80] A. Verdross, 'Forbidden Treaties in International Law', 31 *AJIL* (1937), 571–7. And see also his later article, '*Jus Dispositivum* and *Jus Cogens* in International Law,' 60 *AJIL* (1966), 55.   [81] PCIJ ser. A/B, no. 63, 150.

[82] See GAOR 21st sess., supp. no. 9., UN doc. A/6309/rev.1. See also GA Res. 2166 (XXI), and 61 *AJIL* (1967), 248; *Yearbook of the ILC 1963*, ii.52; GAOR 18th sess., supp., no. 9, UN doc. A/5509; 58 *AJIL*, 245, 264; UN docs. A/CN.4/175, A/CN.4/183/add.1, and A/C6/376. See also the references compiled by E. Schwelb, in Some Aspects of International *Jus Cogens* as Formulated by the International Law Commission', 61 *AJIL* (1967), 946.

general international law having the same character.' Article 64
further provides that 'If a new peremptory norm of general international law emerges, any existing treaty which is in conflict with
that norm becomes void and terminates'.[83] The International Law
Commission did not, however, provide any examples of *jus
cogens*—for two reasons. It was felt, first, that such an inclusion
might lead to misunderstanding as to the position of other possible
cases and, second, that a complete list of such cases was impossible
without a prolonged study of the matter.[84]

Most members of the Commission felt that no definition was
necessary because the idea of *jus cogens* was clear in itself and *jus
cogens* rules were those which existed in the interest of the international community as a whole.[85] In his 1963 report, the special
rapporteur[86] pointed out that the formulation of a *jus cogens* rule
was not free from difficulty since there was as yet no generally
accepted criterion by which to identify a general rule of international
law as having such a character. It was undeniable that the majority
of general rules of international law were not *jus cogens* principles
and that states could contract out of them by treaty.[87] Nevertheless,
the special rapporteur considered that it might be advantageous to
indicate by way of example some of the 'more conspicuous' instances
of treaties that were void by reason of their inconsistency with a *jus
cogens* rule. Among the examples he included any act or omission
characterized by international law as an international crime, any act
or omission in the suppression of which every state is required by
international law to co-operate.

Thus where international law, as in the cases of the slave trade,
piracy, and genocide, places a general obligation upon every state
to co-operate in the suppression of certain acts, a treaty contem-
plating or conniving at their commission must be tainted with
illegality. The principle of non-discrimination would be a strong
candidate for inclusion under this heading, if it is correct that the
widely repeated condemnations of discrimination have ripened into
a rule of customary international law.

At the conference on the Concept of *Jus Cogens* in International
Law held in Greece in 1966, Professor Suy produced a compre-

---

[83] See UN doc. A/Conf. 39/27, 25, 31 (23 May 1969).

[84] See ILC report on work of 15th sess., GAOR, 18th sess., supp. no. 9, UN doc.
A/5509, 11–12; 58 *AJIL*, 245, 264.

[85] See *Yearbook of the ILC* 1963, i.66–77.

[86] Sir Humphrey Waldock.   [87] See *Yearbook of the ILC* 1963, ii.53.

hensive analysis of the views concerning *jus cogens* of the leading writers on international law. From this survey one can deduce that writers on international law almost unanimously agree that an international *jus cogens* exists.[88] Although the great difficulty of defining the notion was stressed it was generally agreed that the following were contrary to the *jus cogens*: (1) agreements to undertake the use of force as an instrument of national policy; (2) agreements contrary to fundamental humanitarian principles such as the prohibition of slavery, of traffic in women and children, and of genocide.

Moreover, several writers emphasized that *jus cogens* should include respect for human rights as such. The establishment of minimum standards of humanitarian treatment, and the protection of human rights were also emphasized by the conference participants in their discussion of its content.[89] Moreover, it was generally agreed that the most important provisions of the Charter and particularly those contained in Articles 1 and 2 were peremptory norms of general international law binding on members and non-members alike.[90] Lord McNair has suggested that those provisions of the Charter which purport to create legal rights and duties possess a constitutive or semi-legislative character, with the result that states cannot contract out of them or derogate from them by treaties made between them, and that any treaty whereby they attempted to produce this effect would be void.[91] Also, Article 103 of the Charter provides that the obligations of members under the Charter shall prevail over their obligations under any other international agreement.[92]

Clearly the protection of human rights is one of the main purposes of the Charter under Article 1 (3), and Articles 55, 56, and 76 (c)

[88] Conference on International Law, Lagonissi, Greece, 3–4 Apr. 1966, under the auspices of the Carnegie Endowment for International Peace. *Papers and Proceedings*, ii.24–48. See also the Bibliography, ibid., 77.

[89] e.g. G. Dahm, *Völkerrecht* (Kohlhammer, Stuttgart, 1958–61); H. A. Rolin, 'Les principes du droit international public', 77 *Recueil des Cours* (1950), 434; Van der Meersch, *Vienna Colloqium*, doc. H/Coll (65) 14, 16; see 1966 Conference, *Papers and Proceedings* ii.29, 43–4, 92–9, 104, 107.

[90] Ibid., 99, 111. Cf. also the views of E. Schwelb, 'Some Aspects of International *Jus Cogens* as Formulated by the International Law Commission,' 61 *AJIL* (1967), 946, 960.   [91] Lord McNair, *The Law of Treaties*, 217.

[92] Sir Humphrey Waldock has commented: 'Nevertheless, it remains true that Article 103, which is entirely general in its terms and therefore appears to cover both prior and future agreements, lays down the principle of the priority of the Charter and not that of the invalidity of inconsistent treaties.' (*Yearbook of the ILC* 1963, ii.56.)

certainly purport to create legal rights and duties. It would appear, therefore, that the protection of human rights can be considered to possess a *jus cogens* character, and this view was accepted by Judge Tanaka who argued, 'If we can introduce in the international field a category of law, namely *jus cogens*, recently examined by the International Law Commission, a kind of imperative law which constitutes the contrast to the *jus dispositivum*, capable of being changed by way of agreement between states, surely the law concerning the protection of human rights may be considered to belong to the *jus cogens*.'[93]

This is an eminently sensible view, but some writers tread more cautiously; for example, Virally has said '*Il est difficile par exemple, de poser en règle qu'un principe abstrait, comme l'obligation de respecter les droits de l'homme, fait partie du* ius cogens. *Cela n'est probablement vrai que de certaines des règles qui découlent de ce principe.*'[94]

Genocide and slavery are favourite examples of practices which are generally accepted to be contrary to the *jus cogens*. In the advisory opinion on the *Reservations to the Genocide Convention*,[95] the International Court of Justice quoted from General Assembly Resolution 96 (I) where the Assembly stated that genocide was a crime under international law which shocked the conscience of mankind, resulted in great losses to humanity, and which was contrary to the moral law and to the spirit and aims of the United Nations. The first consequence of this conception was that 'the principles underlying the Convention are principles which are recognized by civilized nations as binding on States, even without any conventional obligations.'[96]

This language is perfectly compatible with the interpretation that the provisions of the Convention not only bind states without any conventional obligation, but also partake of the character of *jus cogens*, and this view has been accepted by Rosenne. Speaking in the International Law Commission, he said, 'In its advisory opinion on the Reservation to the Genocide Convention, the International Court of Justice had established the *jus cogens* duty of all states to

[93] *South West Africa* cases, dissenting opinion of Judge Tanaka, ICJ Rep. 1966, 298. And see notes 101 and 102 below.
[94] M. Virally, 'Réflexions sur le "*Jus Cogens*"', *Annuaire Français de Droit International* (1966), 5, 28. He was prepared to accept that 'la ségrégation raciale' was contrary to the *jus cogens*.
[95] ICJ Rep. 1951, 15.
[96] Ibid., 23.

co-operate in the suppression of genocide, holding that the duty was quite independent of the Genocide Convention itself and derived from the General Assembly resolutions on the subject.'[97]

It is clear that genocide and slavery are extreme examples of the denial of the principle of equality of individuals, and if these practices can be considered to be contrary to the *jus cogens*, then it is not unreasonable to suppose that other examples of the denial of the principle may also be contrary to the doctrine. This view is supported by the interpretation adopted in the Sixth Committee of the meaning of genocide in General Assembly Resolutions 96 (I) and 180 (II). It was considered that although the Genocide Convention should deal with genocide *stricto sensu*, the content of what was termed 'cultural genocide' also constituted criminal acts which should be earnestly condemned.[98] It was merely felt that this particular convention was not the correct instrument to provide for its prevention and punishment. It would not be unsafe, therefore, to take the view that the remarks which have been made with regard to genocide in the sense of the physical destruction of groups may be applied *mutatis mutandis* to 'cultural genocide'.

Even if one adopts the narrow view preferred by Virally, it seems that the principles of equality and non-discrimination as fundamental human rights are prime candidates for inclusion in the list of *jus cogens* principles. Thus as Schwelb points out, 'it there is a subject matter in present-day international law which appears to be a successful candidate for regulation by peremptory norms, it is certainly the prohibition of racial discrimination.'[99] Similarly, Professor Brownlie has stated that the 'least controversial' examples of *jus cogens* include genocide, racial and religious non-discrimination and non-discrimination as to sex.[100] There would not seem to be any reason why other aspects of the principle of equality apart from racial discrimination should not also form part of its content.[101]

---

[97] *Yearbook of the ILC* 1963, i.74.

[98] See GAOR 3rd sess., 6th comm., 193–205. See also ch. 6 above. ('Cultural genocide' refers to any deliberate act committed with intent to destroy the language, religion, or culture of a national, racial, or religious group on the grounds of the national or racial origin or religious belief of its members. See UN doc. E/447, art. 3.)

[99] Schwelb, op. cit., n. 90 above, 956.

[100] I. Brownlie, *Principles of Public International Law* (Oxford University Press, 3rd ed. 1979), 513 (and n. 4). He thus goes further than his more tentative remarks in the first edition (1966), 417.

[101] The Discrimination (Employment and Occupation) Convention 1958 and the Convention against Discrimination in Education 1960 have also been claimed to form part of the *jus cogens*: Schwelb, 953.

One objection which could be raised is that some of the Conventions which prohibit types of discrimination contain denunciation clauses, many of which were adopted without debate.[102] This fact is prima facie incompatible with the proposition that the law which such conventions lay down is part of the *jus cogens*, since *jus cogens* permits no derogation from it. Nevertheless, it is clear that treaty law may exist contemporaneously with customary law,[103] and states do not cease to be bound by the latter even if they denounce a treaty in which a particular part of customary law is codified. As Sir Humphrey Waldock has pointed out, the Genocide Convention contained, in addition to the substantive clauses relating to the prevention and suppression of genocide, certain procedural clauses in respect of which a right of denunciation was appropriate. If a particular rule is part of the *jus cogens* it would be 'manifestly absurd' to suggest that by denouncing a treaty containing it a state was no longer bound by that rule, though it may no longer be subject to the particular procedural provisions contained in the treaty.[104]

There are thus sound reasons for accepting that the principles of equality and non-discrimination, in view of their nature as fundamental constituents of the international law of human rights, are part of the *jus cogens*. The International Court of Justice gives support to this view in both the *Barcelona Traction* case and the *Namibia* opinion. In the former the Court held that obligations of states to the international community as a whole were, in view of their importance, obligations *erga omnes*. Such obligations derive in contemporary international law from the 'outlawing of acts of aggression, and of genocide, as also from the principles and rules concerning the basic rights of the human person, including protection from slavery and racial discrimination'.[105] Thus basic human rights and racial discrimination in particular are placed in the same category as matters generally acknowledged to form part of *jus cogens*, i.e. the outlawing of aggression and genocide, and are said to be owed to

[102] See e.g. art. 21 of the Convention on the Elimination of All Forms of Racial Discrimination, and UN docs. A/C3/S.R.1368, and A/6181, paras. 195–6.

[103] Cf. Bleicher, 'The Legal Significance of the Re-Citation of General Assembly Resolutions', 63 *AJIL* (1969), 444, 465.

[104] *Yearbook of the ILC* 1963, i.131. For a full discussion of this point, see Schwelb, op. cit., n. 86 above, 953–5.

[105] *Barcelona Traction, Light and Power Co.* case, ICJ Rep. 1970, paras. 33–4. See also I. Brownlie, *Principles of Public International Law* (Oxford University Press, 3rd ed. 1979), 596–8.

all. Similarly, in 1971 the Court pointed out[106] that under the Charter of the United Nations, the former mandatory (South Africa) had pledged itself to observe and respect, in a territory having an international status, human rights and fundamental freedoms for all without distinction as to race. 'To establish instead and to enforce distinction, exclusions, restrictions, and limitations exclusively based on grounds of race, colour discrimination or national or ethnic origin which constitute a denial of fundamental human rights is a flagrant violation of the purposes and principles of the Charter.' Since under Article 1 (3) of the Charter discrimination on the grounds of sex, language, or religion is prohibited, it follows from the advisory opinion that to establish and enforce distinctions based on any of these grounds would also be a flagrant violation of the Charter.[107]

[106]   *Namibia* opinion ICJ Rep. 1971, para. 131.
[107]   UN doc. E/CN.6/552.

XVI

CONCLUSIONS

BELIEF in equality—the view that unless there is a reason for it, recognized as sufficient by some identifiable criterion, one man should not be preferred to another, is a deep-rooted principle in human thought.[1] The principle has been recognized as one of the fundamental principles of modern democracy and government based on the rule of law, and has been assimilated into many legal systems. As Lauterpacht has said, 'The claim to equality before the law is in a substantial sense the most fundamental of the rights of man. It occupies the first place in most written constitutions. It is the starting point of all other liberties.'[2] In international law the principle has usually been stated in the negative form, as one of non-discrimination.

Traditional international law did not concern itself with discrimination except as an element to be considered in determining the legality of a state's treatment of foreigners. A number of peace treaties sought to provide guarantees of religious freedom and thereby protect particular religious minorities from discriminatory treatment and there were occasional cases of humanitarian intervention, but, in general, international law did not regulate a state's treatment of its own nationals. Consequently, it was indifferent to discrimination by a state against particular ethnic, religious, or other groups in its territories. After World War I there was a more systematic attempt to provide international guarantees for the protection of minorities, and there were moves to make inequality of the sexes a matter of international concern, particularly in the International Labour Organization. Dissatisfaction with the minorities regime, and particularly the important debates in the League Assembly, led to a new emphasis after World War II. The United Nations Charter stressed the principle of protection of human rights for all without discrimination, and subsequently the anti-colonial campaign and racial problems in many parts of the world

[1] See Sir Isaiah Berlin, 'Equality as an Ideal', 56 *Proceedings of the Aristotelian Society* (1955–6), 301.
[2] Sir Hersch Lauterpacht, *An International Bill of the Rights of Man* (Columbia University Press, New York, 1945), 115.

have combined to make discrimination one of the great issues of the time. Consequently, the legal content of the principles of equality and discrimination are a matter of prime importance to international as well as municipal lawyers. There is now much evidence to demonstrate that the principles of equality of individuals and non-discrimination are rules of international law and provide standards[3] which can assist in the interpretation of international instruments.

In his 1949 report on the *Main Causes and Types of Discrimination* the Secretary-General of the United Nations confined the term 'discrimination' to 'any conduct based on a distinction made on grounds of natural or social categories which have no relation either to individual capacities or merits or to the concrete behaviour of the individual person'. A proposal in the Commission on Human Rights to qualify the word 'discrimination' by 'arbitrary' in the Universal Declaration was rejected principally on the grounds that discrimination already meant 'invidious distinction' and had the derogatory meaning of 'unfair, unequal' treatment.[4] This interpretation was adopted by the United Nations Sub-Commission on the Prevention of Discrimination and Protection of Minorities. The various studies carried out by the Sub-Commission[5] and the work of other bodies such as the United Nations Committee on Information from Non-Self-Governing Territories[6] have been instrumental in giving content to the principle, as has the jurisprudence of the European Court of Human Rights, which has described 'discrimination' as unjustified or arbitrary distinction.[7] Modern international instruments, such as the Conventions on the Elimination of Racial Discrimination and Discrimination against Women, also use 'discriminate' in its pejorative sense. Under international law, states may make certain distinctions with regard to the enjoyment of human rights and fundamental freedoms without violating the equality principle. The principle does not require absolute equality or identity of treatment but recognizes relative equality, i.e. different treatment proportionate to concrete individual circumstances. In order to be legitimate, different treatment must be reasonable and not arbitrary, and the

---

[3] See G. Goodwin-Gill, *International Law and the Movement of Persons between States* (Oxford University Press, 1978), 78.

[4] See UN docs. E/CN.4/Sub.2/40/rev.1, 26; E/CN.4/S.R.52, 6–17; E/CN.4/S.R.53, 2, 5–10; E/CN.4/S.R.54, 2–3.

[5] See in particular the study of discrimination against persons born out of wedlock, UN doc. E/CN.4/Sub.2/265, 25.

[6] e.g. UN doc. A/2219, pt. iii, 53.

[7] ch. 12 above.

onus of showing that particular distinctions are justifiable is on those who make them.[8]

Distinctions are reasonable if they pursue a legitimate aim and have an objective justification, and a reasonable relationship of proportionality exists between the aim sought to be realized and the means employed. These criteria will usually be satisfied if the particular measures can reasonably be interpreted as being in the public interest as a whole and do not arbitrarily single out individuals or groups for invidious treatment. For example, it is reasonable to withhold the exercise of political rights from aliens, infants, and the insane.

A discriminatory motive is not a necessary ingredient of a violation of the principles of equality, though it will make the finding of such a violation easier. As the recent anti-discrimination conventions put it, distinctions are discriminatory if they have 'the purpose or effect of nullifying or impairing equality of treatment'. That 'non-discrimination' is a negative way of stating the principle of equality is illustrated by the jurisprudence of the West German Federal Constitutional Court, which has repeatedly affirmed that the principle of equality is violated when a reasonable and objectively evident reason for different treatment cannot be found. It has also recognized that an essential difference may even require different treatment.[9]

Thus the principle of equality has two aspects, one negative and one positive. The minorities treaties after World War I included both aspects in that they made provision both for the prevention of discrimination and for the protection of minorities. As the Secretary-General's study *The Main Types and Causes of Discrimination* points out, both prevention of discrimination and protection of minorities 'represent different aspects of the same principle of equality of treatment for all'.[10] Although the Sub-Commission set up under the United Nations was intended to deal with both these matters, only the first attained prominence in the practice of the organization, at least until recently. This was because the protection of minorities under the League of Nations system was felt to have

---

[8] See Judge Tanaka, *South West Africa* cases, ICJ Rep., 1966, 309, 314. (Cf. also M. P. Golding, in R. S. Summers, ed., *Essays in Legal Philosophy* (Basil Blackwell, Oxford, 1968), 236.

[9] See K. Doehring, 'Non-Discrimination and Equal Treatment under the European Human Rights Convention and the West German Constitution with Particular Reference to Discrimination against Aliens', 18 *AJCL* (1970), 305, 307, 316.

[10] UN doc. E/CN.4/Sub.2/40/rev.1, para. 9.

exacerbated a difficult political problem. Nevertheless, it would appear that the positive side of the principle of equality has re-appeared in another guise, i.e. the provision of special measures of protection for economically, socially, and culturally deprived groups.

It is now generally accepted that the provision of special measures of protection for socially, economically, or culturally deprived groups is not discrimination, so long as these special measures are not continued after the need for them has disappeared. Such measures must be strictly compensatory and not permanent or else they will become discriminatory. It is important that these measures should be optional and not against the will of the particular groups affected, and they must be frequently reconsidered to ensure that they do not degenerate into discrimination.[11] The other type of protective measure which is permissible is the provision of special rights for minority groups to maintain their own languages, culture, and religious practices, and to establish schools, libraries, churches, and similar institutions. These measures are not discriminatory because they merely allow minorities to enjoy rights which are exercised by the rest of the population. Such measures produce 'an equilibrium between different situations' and should be maintained as long as the groups concerned wish.

Non-discrimination and equality of treatment are equivalent concepts.[12] As the Permanent Court said in the *Minority Schools in Albania* case, 'Equality in law precludes discrimination of any kind.'[13] 'Discrimination' is defined under international law to mean only unreasonable, arbitrary, or invidious distinctions, and does not include special measures of protection of the two types described above. Putting it positively, the equality principle forbids discriminatory distinctions but permits and sometimes requires[14] the provision of affirmative action. The principle of the equality of individuals under international law does not require a mere formal or mathematical equality but a substantial and genuine equality in fact.

[11] A similar approach was being developed in the jurisprudence of the United States Supreme Court in the late 1970s. See ch. 13 above.

[12] Cf. J. E. S. Fawcett, *The Application of the European Convention of Human Rights* (Oxford University Press, 1969), 239.

[13] PCIJ ser. A/B, no. 64, 19.

[14] Article 4 of the Racial Discrimination Convention of 1965 requires affirmative action by states, but the 1980 Convention on Discrimination against Women merely permits it.

ANNEX I

International Convention on the Elimination of all Forms of Racial Discrimination

The States Parties to this Convention,

Considering that the Charter of the United Nations is based on the principles of the dignity and equality inherent in all human beings, and that all Members States have pledged themselves to take joint and separate action, in co-operation with the Organization, for the achievement of one of the purposes of the United Nations which is to promote and encourage universal respect for and observance of human rights and fundamental freedoms for all, without distinction as to race, sex, language or religion,

Considering that the Universal Declaration of Human Rights proclaims that all human beings are born free and equal in dignity and rights and that everyone is entitled to all the rights and freedoms set out therein, without distinction of any kind, in particular as to race, colour or national origin,

Considering that all human beings are equal before the law and are entitled to equal protection of the law against any discrimination and against any incitement to discrimination,

Considering that the United Nations has condemned colonialism and all practices of segregation and discrimination associated therewith, in whatever form and wherever they exist, and that the Declaration on the Granting of Independence to Colonial Countries and Peoples of 14 December 1960 (General Assembly resolution 1514 (XV)) has affirmed and solemnly proclaimed the necessity of bringing them to a speedy and unconditional end,

Considering that the United Nations Declaration on the Elimination of All Forms of Racial Discrimination of 20 November 1963 (General Assembly resolution 1904 (XVIII)) solemnly affirms the necessity of speedily eliminating racial discrimination throughout the world in all its forms and manifestations and of securing understanding of and respect for the dignity of the human person,

Considering that any doctrine of superiority based on racial differentiation is scientifically false, morally condemnable, socially unjust and dangerous, and that there is no justification for racial discrimination, in theory or in practice, anywhere,

Reaffirming that discrimination between human beings on the grounds of race, colour or ethnic origin is an obstacle to friendly and peaceful relations among nations and is capable of disturbing peace and security among peoples and the harmony of persons living side by side even within one and the same State,

Convinced that the existence of racial barriers is repugnant to the ideals of any human society,

Alarmed by manifestations of racial discrimination still in evidence in some areas of the world and by governmental policies based on racial superiority or hatred, such as policies of apartheid, segregation or separation,

Resolved to adopt all necessary measures for speedily eliminating racial discrimination in all its forms and manifestations, and to prevent and combat racist doctrines and practices in order to promote understanding between races and to build an international community free from all forms of racial segregation and racial discrimination,

Bearing in mind the Convention concerning Discrimination in respect of Employment and Occupation adopted by the International Labour Organization in 1958, and the Convention against Discrimination in Education adopted by the United Nations Educational, Scientific, and Cultural Organization in 1960,

Desiring to implement the principles embodied in the United Nations Declaration on the Elimination of All Forms of Racial Discrimination and to secure the earliest adoption of practical measures to that end,

Have agreed as follows:

Part I

Article 1

1. In this Convention, the term 'racial discrimination' shall mean any distinction, exclusion, restriction or preference based on race, colour, descent, or national or ethnic origin which has the purpose or effect of nullifying or impairing the recognition, enjoyment or exercise, on an equal footing, of human rights and fundamental freedoms in the political, economic, social, cultural or any other field of public life.

2. This Convention shall not apply to distinctions, exclusions, restrictions or preferences made by a State Party to this Convention between citizens and non-citizens.

3. Nothing in this Convention may be interpreted as affecting in any way the legal provisions of States Parties concerning nationality, citizenship or naturalization, provided that such provisions do not discriminate against any particular nationality.

4. Special measures taken for the sole purpose of securing adequate advancement of certain racial or ethnic groups or individuals requiring such protection as may be necessary in order to ensure such groups or individuals equal enjoyment or exercise of human rights and fundamental freedoms shall not be deemed racial discrimination, provided, however, that such measures do not, as a consequence, lead to the maintenance of separate rights for different racial groups and that they shall not be continued after the objectives for which they were taken have been achieved.

Article 2

1. States Parties condemn racial discrimination and undertake to pursue by all appropriate means and without delay a policy of eliminating racial discrimination in all its forms and promoting understanding among all races, and, to this end:

   (*a*) Each State Party undertakes to engage in no act or practice of racial discrimination against persons, groups of persons or institutions and to ensure that all public authorities and public institutions, national and local, shall act in conformity with this obligation;

   (*b*) Each State Party undertakes not to sponsor, defend or support racial discrimination by any persons or organizations;

   (*c*) Each State Party shall take effective measures to review governmental, national and local policies, and to amend, rescind or nullify any laws and regulations which have the effect of creating or perpetuating racial discrimination wherever it exists;

   (*d*) Each State Party shall prohibit and bring to an end, by all appropriate means, including legislation as required by circumstances, racial discrimination by any persons, group or organization;

   (*e*) Each State Party undertakes to encourage, where appropriate, integrationist multi-racial organizations and movements and other means of eliminating barriers between races, and to discourage anything which tends to strengthen racial division.

2. States Parties shall, when the circumstances so warrant, take, in the social, economic, cultural and other fields, special and concrete measures to ensure the adequate development and protection of certain racial groups or individuals belonging to them, for the purpose of guaranteeing them the full and equal enjoyment of human rights and fundamental freedoms. These measures shall in no case entail as a consequence the maintenance of unequal or separate rights for different racial groups after the objectives for which they were taken have been achieved.

Article 3

States Parties particularly condemn racial segregation and *apartheid* and undertake to prevent, prohibit and eradicate all practices of this nature in territories under their jurisdiction.

Article 4

States Parties condemn all propaganda and all organizations which are based on ideas or theories of superiority of one race or group of persons of one colour or ethnic origin, or which attempt to justify or promote racial hatred and discrimination in any form, and undertake to adopt immediate and positive measures designed to eradicate all incitement to, or acts of, such discrimination and, to this end, with due regard to the principles embodied in the Universal Declaration of Human Rights and the rights expressly set forth in Article 5 of this Convention, *inter alia*:

(*a*) Shall declare an offence punishable by law all dissemination of ideas based on racial superiority or hatred, incitement to racial discrimination, as well as all acts of violence or incitement to such acts against any race or group of persons of another colour or ethnic origin, and also the provision of any assistance to racist activities, including the financing thereof;

(*b*) Shall declare illegal and prohibit organizations, and also organized and all other propaganda activities, which promote and incite racial discrimination, and shall recognize participation in such organizations or activities as an offence punishable by law;

(*c*) Shall not permit public authorities or public institutions, national or local, to promote or incite racial discrimination.

Article 5

In compliance with the fundamental obligations laid down in Article 2 of this Convention, States Parties undertake to prohibit and to eliminate racial discrimination in all its forms and to guarantee the right of everyone, without distinction as to race, colour, or national or ethnic origin, to equality before the law, notably in the enjoyment of the following rights:

(*a*) The right to equal treatment before the tribunals and all other organs administering justice;

(*b*) The right to security of person and protection by the State against violence or bodily harm, whether inflicted by government officials or by any individual, group or institution;

(*c*) Political rights, in particular the rights to participate in elections—to vote and to stand for election—on the basis of universal and equal suffrage, to take part in the Government as well as in the conduct of public affairs at any level and to have equal access to public service;

(*d*) Other civil rights, in particular:

   (i) The right to freedom of movement and residence within the border of the State;

   (ii) The right to leave any country, including one's own, and to return to one's country;

   (iii) The right to nationality;

   (iv) The right to marriage and choice of spouse;

   (v) The right to own property alone as well as in association with others;

    (vi) The right to inherit;
    (vii) The right to freedom of thought, conscience and religion;
    (viii) The right to freedom of opinion and expression;
    (ix) The right to freedom of peaceful assembly and association;

(*e*) Economic, social and cultural rights, in particular:
    (i) The rights to work, to free choice of employment, to just and favourable conditions of work, to protection against unemployment, to equal pay for equal work, to just and favourable remuneration;
    (ii) The right to form and join trade unions;
    (iii) The right to housing;
    (iv) The right to public health, medical care, social security and social services;
    (v) The right to education and training;
    (vi) The right to equal participation in cultural activities;

(*f*) The right of access to any place or service intended for use by the general public, such as transport, hotels, restaurants, cafés, theatres and parks.

Article 6

States Parties shall assure to everyone within their jurisdiction effective protection and remedies, through the competent national tribunals and other State institutions, against any acts of racial discrimination which violate his human rights and fundamental freedoms contrary to this Convention, as well as the right to seek from such tribunals just and adequate reparation or satisfaction for any damage suffered as a result of such discrimination.

Article 7

State Parties undertake to adopt immediate and effective measures, particularly in the fields of teaching, education, culture and information, with a view to combating prejudices which lead to racial discrimination and to promoting understanding, tolerance and friendship among nations and racial or ethnical groups, as well as to propagating the purposes and principles of the Charter of the United Nations, the Universal Declaration of Human Rights, the United Nations Declaration on the Elimination of All Forms of Racial Discrimination, and this Convention.

PART II

Article 8

1. There shall be established a Committee on the Elimination of Racial Discrimination (hereinafter referred to as the Committee) consisting of eighteen experts of high moral standing and acknowledged impartiality elected by States Parties from among their nations, who shall serve in their personal capacity, consideration being given to equitable geographical distribution and to the representation of the different forms of civilization as well as of the principal legal systems.

2. The members of the Committee shall be elected by secret ballot from a list of persons nominated by the States Parties. Each State Party may nominate one person from among its own nationals.

3. The initial election shall be held six months after the date of the entry into force of this Convention. At least three months before the date of each election the Secretary-General of the United Nations shall address a letter to the States Parties inviting them to submit their nominations within two months. The Secretary-General shall prepare a list in alphabetical order of all persons thus nominated, indicating the States Parties which have nominated them, and shall submit it to the States Parties.

4. Elections of the members of the Committee shall be held at a meeting of States Parties convened by the Secretary-General at United Nations Headquarters. At that meeting, for which two-thirds of the States Parties shall constitute a quorum, the persons elected to the Committee shall be those nominees who obtain the largest number of votes and an absolute majority of the votes of the representatives of States Parties present and voting.

5. (*a*) The members of the Committee shall be elected for a term of four years. However, the terms of nine of the members elected at the first election shall expire at the end of two years; immediately after the first election the names of these nine members shall be chosen by lot by the Chairman of the Committee.

(*b*) For the filling of casual vacancies, the State Party whose expert has ceased to function as a member of the Committee shall appoint another expert from among its nationals, subject to the approval of the Committee.

6. States Parties shall be responsible for the expenses of the members of the Committee while they are in performance of Committee duties.

Article 9

1. States Parties undertake to submit to the Secretary-General of the United Nations, for consideration by the Committee, a report on the legislative, judicial, administrative or other measures which they have adopted and which give effect to the provisions of this Convention:

(*a*) within one year after the entry into force of the Convention for the State concerned; and (*b*) thereafter every two years and whenever the Committee so requests. The Committee may request further information from the States Parties.

2. The Committee shall report annually, through the Secretary-General, to the General Assembly of the United Nations on its activities and may make suggestions and general recommendations based on the examination of the reports and information received from the States Parties. Such suggestions and general recommendations shall be reported to the General Assembly together with comments, if any, from States Parties.

Article 10

1. The Committee shall adopt its own rules of procedure.
2. The Committee shall elect its officers for a term of two years.
3. The secretariat of the Committee shall be provided by the Secretary-General of the United Nations.
4. The meetings of the Committee shall normally be held at United Nations Headquarters.

Article 11

1. If a State Party considers that another State Party is not giving effect to the provisions of this Convention, it may bring the matter to the attention of the Committee. The Committee shall then transmit the communication to the State Party concerned. Within three months, the receiving State shall submit to the Committee written explanations or statements clarifying the matter and the remedy, if any, that may have been taken by that State.

2. If the matter is not adjusted to the satisfaction of both parties, either by bilateral negotiations or by any other procedure open to them, within six months after the receipt by the receving State of the initial communication, either State shall have the right to refer the matter again to the Committee by notifying the Committee and also the other State.

3. The Committee shall deal with a matter referred to it in accordance with paragraph 2 of this Article after it has ascertained that all available domestic remedies have been invoked and exhausted in the case, in conformity with the generally recognized principles of international law. This shall not be the rule where the application of the remedies is unreasonably prolonged.

4. In any matter referred to it, the Committee may call upon the States Parties concerned to supply any other relevant information.

5. When any matter arising out of this article is being considered by the Committee, the States Parties concerned shall be entitled to send a representative to take part in the proceedings of the Committee, without voting rights, while the matter is under consideration.

Article 12

1. (*a*) After the Committee has obtained and collated all the information it deems necessary, the Chairman shall appoint an *ad hoc* Conciliation Commission (hereinafter referred to as the Commission) comprising five persons who may or may not be members of the Committee. The members of the Commission shall be appointed with the unanimous consent of the parties to the dispute, and its good offices shall be made available to the States concerned with a view to an amicable solution of the matter on the basis of respect for this Convention.

(*b*) If the States parties to the dispute fail to reach agreement within three months on all or part of the composition of the Commission, the members of the Commission not agreed upon by the States parties to the dispute shall be elected by secret ballot by a two-thirds majority vote of the Committee from among its own members.

2. The members of the Commission shall serve in their personal capacity. They shall not be nationals of the States parties to the dispute or of a State not Party to this Convention.

3. The Commission shall elect its own Chairman and adopt its own rules of procedure.

4. The meetings of the Commission shall normally be held at United Nations Headquarters or at any other convenient place as determined by the Commission.

5. The secretariat provided in accordance with Article 10, paragraph 3, of this Convention shall also service the Commission whenever a dispute among States Parties brings the Commission into being.

6. The States parties to the dispute shall share equally all the expenses of the members of the Commission in accordance with estimates to be provided by the Secretary-General of the United Nations.

7. The Secretary-General shall be empowered to pay the expenses of the members of the Commission, if necessary, before reimbursement by the States parties to the dispute in accordance with paragraph 6 of this Article.

8. The information obtained and collated by the Committee shall be made available to the Commission, and the Commission may call upon the States concerned to supply any other relevant information.

Article 13

1. When the Commission has fully considered the matter, it shall prepare and submit to the Chairman of the Committee a report embodying its findings on all questions of fact relevant to the issue between the parties and containing such recommendations as it may think proper for the amicable solution of the dispute.

2. The Chairman of the Committee shall communicate the report of the

Commission to each of the States parties to the dispute. These States shall, within three months, inform the Chairman of the Committee whether or not they accept the recommendations contained in the report of the Commission.

3. After the period provided for in paragraph 2 of this Article, the Chairman of the Committee shall communicate the report of the Commission and the declarations of the States Parties concerned to the other States Parties to this Convention.

Article 14

1. A State Party may at any time declare that it recognizes the competence of the Committee to receive and consider communications from individuals or groups of individuals within its jurisdiction claiming to be victims of a violation by that State Party of any of the rights set forth in this Convention. No communication shall be received by the Committee if it concerns a State Party which has not made such a declaration.

2. Any State Party which makes a declaration as provided for in paragraph 1 of this Article may establish or indicate a body within its national legal order which shall be competent to receive and consider petitions from individuals and groups of individuals within its jurisdiction who claim to be victims of a violation of any of the rights set forth in this Convention and who have exhausted other available local remedies.

3. A declaration made in accordance with paragraph I of this Article and the name of any body established or indicated in accordance with paragraph 2 of this Article shall be deposited by the State Party concerned with the Secretary-General of the United Nations, who shall transmit copies thereof to the other States Parties. A declaration may be withdrawn at any time by notification to the Secretary-General, but such a withdrawal shall not affect communications pending before the Committee.

4. A register of petitions shall be kept by the body established or indicated in accordance with paragraph 2 of this Article, and certified copies of the register shall be filed annually through appropriate channels with the Secretary-General on the understanding that the contents shall not be publicly disclosed.

5. In the event of failure to obtain satisfaction from the body established or indicated accordance with paragraph 2 of this Article, the petitioner shall have the right to communicate the matter to the Committee within six months.

6. (*a*) The Committee shall confidentially bring any communication referred to it to the attention of the State Party alleged to be violating any provision of this Convention, but the identity of the individuals or groups of individuals concerned shall not be revealed without his or their express consent. The Committee shall not receive anonymous communications.

(*b*) Within three months, the receiving State shall submit to the Committee written explanations or statements clarifying the matter and the remedy, if any, that may have been taken by that State.

7. (*a*) The Committee shall consider communications in the light of all information made available to it by the State Party concerned and by the petitioner. The Committee shall not consider any communication from a petitioner unless it has ascertained that the petitioner has exhausted all available domestic remedies. However, this shall not be the rule where the application of the remedies is unreasonably prolonged.

(*b*) The Committee shall forward its suggestions and recommendations, if any, to the State Party concerned and to the petitioner.

8. The Committee shall include in its annual report a summary of such communications and, where appropriate, a summary of the explanations and statements of the States Parties concerned and of its own suggestions and recommendations.

9. The Committee shall be competent to exercise the functions provided for in this Article only when at least ten States Parties to this Convention are bound by declarations in accordance with paragraph 1 of this Article.

Article 15

1. Pending the achievement of the objectives of the Declaration on the Granting of Independence to Colonial Countries and Peoples, contained in General Assembly resolution 1514 (XV) of 14 December 1960, the provisions of this Convention shall in no way limit the right of petition granted to these peoples by other international instruments or by the United Nations and its specialized agencies.

2. (*a*) The Committee established under Article 8, paragraph 1, of this Convention shall receive copies of the petitions from, and submit expressions of opinion and recommendations on these petitions to, the bodies of the United Nations which deal with matters directly related to the principles and objectives of this Convention in their consideration of petitions from the inhabitants of Trust and Non-Self-Governing Territories and all other territories to which General Assembly resolution 1514 (XV) applies, relating to matters covered by this Convention which are before these bodies.

(*b*) The Committee shall receive from the competent bodies of the United Nations copies of the reports concerning the legislative, judicial, administrative or other measures directly related to the principles and objective of this Convention applied by the administering Powers within the Territories mentioned in sub-paragraph (*a*) of this paragraph, and shall express opinions and make recommendations to these bodies.

3. The Committee shall include in its report to the General Assembly a summary of the petitions and reports it has received from United Nations

bodies, and the expressions of opinion and recommendations of the Committee relating to the said petitions and reports.

4. The Committee shall request from the Secretary-General of the United Nations all information relevant to the objectives of this Convention and available to him regarding the Territories mentioned in paragraph 2 (*a*) of this Article.

Article 16

The provisions of this Convention concerning the settlement of disputes or complaints shall be applied without prejudice to other procedures for settling disputes or complaints in the field of discrimination laid down in the constituent instruments of, or in conventions adopted by, the United Nations and its specialized agencies, and shall not prevent the States Parties from having recourse to other procedures for settling a dispute in accordance with general and special international agreements in force between them.

Part III

Article 17

1. This Convention is open for signature by any State Member of the United Nations or member of any of its specialized agencies, by any State Party to the Statute of the International Court of Justice, and by any other State which has been invited by the General Assembly of the United Nations to become a Party to this Convention.

2. This Convention is subject to ratification. Instruments of ratification shall be deposited with the Secretary-General of the United Nations.

Article 18

1. This Convention shall be open to accession by any State referred to in Article 17, paragraph I, of the Convention.

2. Accession shall be effected by the deposit of an instrument of accession with the Secretary-General of the United Nations.

Article 19

1. This Convention shall enter into force on the thirtieth day after the date of the deposit with the Secretary-General of the United Nations of the twenty-seventh instrument of ratification or instrument of accession.

2. For each State ratifying this Convention or acceding to it after the deposit of the twenty-seventh instrument of ratification or instrument of accession, the Convention shall enter into force on the thirtieth day after the date of deposit of its own instrument of ratification or instrument of accession.

Article 20

1. The Secretary-General of the United Nations shall receive and circulate to all States which are or may become Parties to this Convention reservations made by States at the time of ratification or accession. Any State which objects to the reservation shall, within a period of ninety days from the date of the said communication, notify the Secretary-General that it does not accept it.

2. A reservation incompatible with the object and purpose of this Convention shall not be permitted, nor shall a reservation the effect of which would inhibit the operation of any of the bodies established by this Convention be allowed. A reservation shall be considered incompatible or inhibitive if at least two-thirds of the States Parties to this Convention object to it.

3. Reservations may be withdrawn at any time by notification to this effect addressed to the Secretary-General. Such notification shall take effect on the date on which it is received.

Article 21

A State Party may denounce this Convention by written notification to the Secretary-General of the United Nations. Denunciation shall take effect one year after the date of receipt of the notification by the Secretary-General.

Article 22

Any dispute between two or more States Parties with respect to the interpretation or application of this Convention, which is not settled by negotiation or by the procedures expressly provided for in this Convention, shall, at the request of any of the parties to the dispute, be referred to the International Court of Justice for decision, unless the disputants agree to another mode of settlement.

Article 23

1. A request for the revision of this Convention may be made at any time by any State Party by means of a notification in writing addressed to the Secretary-General of the United Nations.

2. The General Assembly of the United Nations shall decide upon the steps, if any, to be taken in respect of such a request.

Article 24

The Secretary-General of the United Nations shall inform all States referred to in Article 17, paragraph 1, of this Convention of the following particulars:

(*a*) Signatures, ratifications and accessions under Articles 17 and 18;

(*b*) The date of entry into force of this Convention under Article 19;

(*c*) Communications and declarations received under Articles 14, 20 and 23;

(*d*) Denunciations under Article 21.

Article 25

1. This Convention, of which the Chinese, English, French, Russian and Spanish texts are equally authentic, shall be deposited in the archives of the United Nations.

2. The Secretary-General of the United Nations shall transmit certified copies of this Convention to all States belonging to any of the categories mentioned in Article 17, paragraph 1, of the Convention.

In faith whereof the undersigned, being duly authorized thereto by their respective Governments, have signed the present Convention, opened for signature at New York, on the seventh day of March, one thousand nine hundred and sixty-six.

B

The General Assembly

Recalling the Declaration on the Granting of Independence to Colonial Countries and Peoples contained in its resolution 1514 (XV) of 14 December 1960,

Bearing in mind its resolution 1654 (XVI) of 27 November 1961, which established the Special Committee on the Situation with regard to the Implementation of the Declaration on the Granting of Independence to Colonial Countries and Peoples to examine the application of the Declaration and to carry out its provisions by all means at its disposal,

Bearing in mind also the provisions of Article 15 of the International Convention on the Elimination of All Forms of Racial Discrimination contained in the annex to resolution 2106 A (XX) above,

Recalling that the General Assembly has established other bodies to receive and examine petitions from the peoples of colonial countries,

Convinced that close co-operation between the Committee on the Elimination of Racial Discrimination, established by the International Convention on the Elimination of All Forms of Racial Discrimination, and the bodies of the United Nations charged with receiving and examining petitions from the peoples of colonial countries will facilitate the achievement of the objectives of both the Convention and the Declaration on the Granting of Independence to Colonial Countries and Peoples,

Recognizing that the elimination of racial discrimination in all its forms is vital to the achievement of fundamental human rights and to the assurance of the dignity and worth of the human person, and thus constitutes a pre-emptory obligation under the Charter of the United Nations,

1. *Calls upon* the Secretary-General to make available to the Committee on the Elimination of Racial Discrimination, periodically or at its request, all information in his possession relevant to Article 15 of the International Convention on the Elimination of All Forms of Racial Discrimination;

2. *Requests* the Special Committee on the Situation with regard to the Implementation of the Granting of Independence to Colonial Countries and Peoples, and all other bodies of the United Nations authorized to receive and examine petitions from the peoples of the colonial countries, to transmit to the Committee on the Elimination of Racial Discrimination, periodically or at its request, copies of petitions from those peoples relevant to the Convention, for the comments and recommendations of the said Committee;

3. *Requests* bodies referred to in paragraph 2 above to include in their annual reports to the General Assembly a summary of the action taken by them under the terms of the present resolution.

ANNEX II

(a) Articles Concerned with Equality and Non-Discrimination in the International Covenant on Civil and Political Rights, 1966

Article 2

1. Each State Party to the present Covenant undertakes to respect and to ensure to all individuals within its territory and subject to its jurisdiction the rights recognized in the present Covenant, without distinction of any kind, such as race, colour, sex, language, religion, political or other opinion, national or social origin, property, birth or other status.

2. Where not already provided for by existing legislative or other measures, each State Party to the present Covenant undertakes to take the necessary steps, in accordance with its constitutional processes and with the provisions of the present Covenant, to adopt such legislative or other measures as may be necessary to give effect to the rights recognized in the present Covenant.

3. Each State Party to the present Covenant undertakes:

   (*a*) To ensure that any person whose rights or freedoms as herein recognized are violated shall have an effective remedy, notwithstanding
   that the violation has been committed by persons acting in an official
   capacity;

   (*b*) To ensure that any person claiming such a remedy shall have his right
   thereto determined by competent judicial, administrative or legislative
   authorities, or by any other competent authority provided for by the
   legal system of the State, and to develop the possibilities of judicial
   remedy;

   (*c*) To ensure that the competent authorities shall enforce such remedies
   when granted.

Article 3

The States Parties to the present Covenant undertake to ensure the equal right of men and women to enjoyment of all civil and political rights set forth in the present Covenant.

Article 4

1. In time of public emergency which threatens the life of the nation and the existence of which is officially proclaimed, the States Parties to the present Covenant may take measures derogating from their obligations under the present Covenant to the extent strictly required by the exigencies of the situation, provided that such measures are not inconsistent

with their other obligations under international law and do not involve discrimination solely on the ground of race, colour, sex, language, religion or social origin.

2. No derogation from Articles 6, 7, 8 (paragraphs 1 and 2), 11, 15, 16 and 18 may be made under this provision.

3. Any State Party to the present Covenant availing itself of the right of derogation shall immediately inform the other States Parties to the present Covenant, through the intermediary of the Secretary-General of the United Nations of the provisions from which it has derogated and of the reasons by which it was actuated. A further communication shall be made, through the same intermediary on the date on which it terminates such derogation.

Article 6

1. Every human being has the inherent right to life. This right shall be protected by law. No one shall be arbitrarily deprived of his life.

2. In countries which have not abolished the death penalty, sentence of death may be imposed only for the most serious crimes in accordance with the law in force at the time of the commission of the crime and not contrary to the provisions of the present Covenant and to the Convention on the Prevention and Punishment of the Crime of Genocide. This penalty can only be carried out pursuant to a final judgment rendered by a competent court.

3. When deprivation of life constitutes the crime of genocide, it is understood that nothing in this article shall authorize any State Party to the present Covenant to derogate in any way from any obligation assumed under the provisions of the Convention on the Prevention and Punishment of the Crime of Genocide.

4. Anyone sentenced to death shall have the right to seek pardon or commutation of the sentence. Amnesty, pardon or commutation of the sentence of death may be granted in all cases.

5. Sentence of death shall not be imposed for crimes committed by persons below eighteen years of age and shall not be carried out on pregnant women.

6. Nothing in this article shall be invoked to delay or to prevent the abolition of capital punishment by any State Party to the present Covenant.

Article 14

1. All persons shall be equal before the courts and tribunals. In the determination of any criminal charge against him, or of his rights and obligations in a suit at law, everyone shall be entitled to a fair and public hearing by a competent, independent and impartial tribunal established by law. The Press and the public may be excluded from all or part of a trial for reasons of

morals, public order (*ordre public*) or national security in a democratic society, or when the interest of the private lives of the parties so requires, or to the extent strictly necessary in the opinion of the court in special circumstances where publicity would prejudice the interests of justice; but any judgment rendered in a criminal case or in a suit at law shall be made public except where the interest of juvenile persons otherwise requires or the proceedings concern matrimonial disputes or the guardianship of children.

2. Everyone charged with a criminal offence shall have the right to be presumed innocent until proved guilty according to law.

3. In the determination of any criminal charge against him, everyone shall be entitled to the following minimum guarantees, in full equality:

- (*a*) To be informed promptly and in detail in a language which he understands of the nature and cause of the charge against him;
- (*b*) To have adequate time and facilities for the preparation of his defence and to communicate with counsel of his own choosing;
- (*c*) To be tried without undue delay;
- (*d*) To be tried in his presence, and to defend himself in person or through legal assistance of his own choosing; to be informed, if he does not have legal assistance, of this right; and to have legal assistance assigned to him, in any case where the interests of justice so require, and without payment by him in any such case if he does not have sufficient means to pay for it;
- (*e*) To examine, or have examined, the witnesses against him and to obtain the attendance and examination of witnesses on his behalf under the same conditions as witnesses against him;
- (*f*) To have the free assistance of an interpreter if he cannot understand or speak the language used in court;
- (*g*) Not to be compelled to testify against himself or to confess guilt.

4. In the case of juvenile persons, the procedure shall be such as will take account of their age and the desirability of promoting their rehabilitation.

5. Everyone convicted of a crime shall have the right to his conviction and sentence being reviewed by a higher tribunal according to law.

6. When a person has by a final decision been convicted of a criminal offence and when subsequently his conviction has been reversed or he has been pardoned on the ground that a new or newly discovered fact shows conclusively that there has been a miscarriage of justice, the person who has suffered punishment as a result of such conviction shall be compensated according to law, unless it is proved that the nondisclosure of the unknown fact in time is wholly or partly attributable to him.

7. No one shall be liable to be tried or punished again for an offence for which he has already been finally convicted or acquitted in accordance with the law and penal procedure of each country.

Article 16

Everyone shall have the right to recognition everywhere as a person before the law.

Article 23

1. The family is the natural and fundamental group unit of society and is entitled to protection by society and the State.
2. The right of men and women of marriageable age to marry and to found a family shall be recognized.
3. No marriage shall be entered into without the free and full consent of the intending spouses.
4. States Parties to the present Covenant shall take appropriate steps to ensure equality of rights and responsibilities of spouses as to marriage, during marriage and at its dissolution. In the case of dissolution, provision shall be made for the necessary protection of any children.

Article 24

1. Every child shall have, without any discrimination as to race, colour, sex, language, religion, national or social origin, property or birth, the right to such measures of protection as are required by his status as a minor, on the part of his family, society and the State.
2. Every child shall be registered immediately after birth and shall have a name.
3. Every child has the right to acquire a nationality.

Article 25

Every citizen shall have the right and the opportunity, without any of the distinctions mentioned in Article 2 and without unreasonable restrictions:
  (*a*) To take part in the conduct of public affairs, directly or through freely chosen representatives;
  (*b*) To vote and to be elected at genuine periodic elections which shall be by universal and equal suffrage and shall be held by secret ballot, guaranteeing the free expression of the will of the electors;
  (*c*) To have access, on general terms of equality, to public service in his country.

Article 26

All persons are equal before the law and are entitled without any discrimination to the equal protection of the law. In this respect, the law shall prohibit any discrimination and guarantee to all persons equal and effective protection against discrimination on any ground such as race, colour, sex, language, religion, political or other opinion, national or social origin, property, birth or other status.

Article 27

In those States in which ethnic, religious or linguistic minorities exist, persons belonging to such minorities shall not be denied the right, in community with the other members of their group, to enjoy their own culture, to profess and practise their own religion, or to use their own language.

(b) Articles concerned with Equality and Non-Discrimination in the International Covenant on Economic, Social, and Cultural Rights, 1966

Article 2

2. The States Parties to the present Covenant undertake to guarantee that the rights enunciated in the present Covenant will be exercised without discrimination of any kind as to race, colour, sex, language, religion, political or other opinion, national or social origin, property, birth or other status.
3. Developing countries, with due regard to human rights and their national economy, may determine to what extent they would guarantee the economic rights recognized in the present Covenant to non-nationals.

Article 3

The States Parties to the present Covenant undertake to ensure the equal right of men and women to the enjoyment of all economic, social and cultural rights set forth in the present Covenant.

Article 4

The States Parties to the present Covenant recognize that, in the enjoyment of those rights provided by the State in conformity with the present Covenant, the State may subject such rights only to such limitations as are determined by law only in so far as this may be compatible with the nature of these rights and solely for the purpose of promoting the general welfare of a democratic society.

Article 5

1. Nothing in the present Covenant may be interpreted as implying for any State, group or person any right to engage in any activity or to perform any act aimed at the destruction of any of the rights or freedoms recognized herein, or at their limitation to a greater extent than is provided for in the present Covenant.

2. No restriction upon or derogation from any of the fundamental human rights recognized or existing in any country in virtue of law, conventions, regulations or custom shall be admitted on the pretext that the present Covenant does not recognize such rights or that it recognizes them to a lesser extent.

Article 7

The States Parties to the present Covenant recognize the right of everyone to the enjoyment of just and favourable conditions of work, which ensure, in particular:

(a) Remuneration which provides all workers, as a minimum, with:

(i) Fair wages and equal remuneration for work of equal value without distinction of any kind, in particular women being guaranteed conditions of work not inferior to those enjoyed by men, with equal pay for equal work;

Article 10

The States Parties to the present Covenant recognize that:

1. The widest possible protection and assistance should be accorded to the family, which is the natural and fundamental group unit of society, particularly for its establishment and while it is responsible for the care and education of dependent children. Marriage must be entered into with the free consent of the intending spouses.

ANNEX III

The Convention on the Elimination of All Forms of Discrimination against Women, 1980

The States Parties to the present Convention,

Noting that the Charter of the United Nations reaffirms faith in fundamental human rights, in the dignity and worth of the human person and in the equal rights of men and women,

Noting that the Universal Declaration of Human Rights affirms the principle of the inadmissibility of discrimination and proclaims that all human beings are born free and equal in dignity and rights and that everyone is entitled to all the rights and freedoms set forth therein, without distinction of any kind, including distinction based on sex,

Noting that the States Parties to the International Covenants on Human Rights have the obligation to ensure the equal right of men and women to enjoy all economic, social, cultural, civil and political rights,

Considering the international conventions concluded under the auspices of the United Nations and the specialized agencies promoting equality of rights of men and women,

Noting also the resolutions, declarations and recommendations adopted by the United Nations and the specialized agencies promoting equality of rights of men and women,

Concerned, however, that despite these various instruments extensive discrimination against women continues to exist,

Recalling that discrimination against women violates the principles of equality of rights and respect for human dignity, is an obstacle to the participation of women, on equal terms with men, in the political, social, economic and cultural life of their countries, hampers the growth of the prosperity of society and the family and makes more difficult the full development of the potentialities of women in the service of their countries and of humanity,

Concerned that in situations of poverty women have the least access to food, health, education, training and opportunities for employment and other needs,

Convinced that the establishment of the new international economic order based on equity and justice will contribute significantly towards the promotion of equality between men and women,

Emphasizing that the eradication of *apartheid*, of all forms of racism, racial discrimination, colonialism, neo-colonialism, aggression, foreign occupation and domination and interference in the internal affairs of States is essential to the full enjoyment of the rights of men and women,

Affirming that the strengthening of international peace and security, relaxation of international tension, mutual co-operation among all States irrespective of their social and economic systems, general and complete disarmament, and in particular nuclear disarmament under strict and effective international control, the affirmation of the principles of justice, equality and mutual benefit in relations among countries and the realization of the right of peoples under alien and colonial domination and foreign occupation to self-determination and independence, as well as respect for national sovereignty and territorial integrity, will promote social progress and development and as a consequence will contribute to the attainment of full equality between men and women,

Convinced that the full and complete development of a country, the welfare of the world and the cause of peace require the maximum participation of women on equal terms with men in all fields,

Bearing in mind the great contribution of women to the welfare of the family and to the development of society, so far not fully recognized, the social significance of maternity and the role of both parents in the family and in the upbringing of children, and aware that the role of women in procreation should not be a basis for discrimination but that the upbringing of children requires a sharing of responsibility between men and women and society as a whole,

Aware that a change in the traditional role of men as well as the role of women in society and in the family is needed to achieve full equality between men and women,

Determined to implement the principles set forth in the Declaration on the Elimination of Discrimination against Women and, for that purpose, to adopt the measures required for the elimination of such discrimination in all its forms and manifestations,

Have agreed on the following:

Part I

Article 1

For the purposes of the present Convention, the term 'discrimination against women' shall mean any distinction, exclusion or restriction made on the basis of sex which has the effect or purpose of impairing or nullifying the recognition, enjoyment or exercise by women, irrespective of their marital status, on a basis of equality of men and women, of human rights and fundamental freedoms in the political, economic, social, cultural, civil or any other field.

Article 2

States Parties condemn discrimination against women in all its forms, agree to pursue by all appropriate means and without delay a policy of eliminating discrimination against women and, to this end, undertake:

(*a*) To embody the principle of the equality of men and women in their national constitutions or other appropriate legislation if not yet incorporated therein and to ensure, through law and other appropriate means, the practical realization of this principle;

(*b*) To adopt appropriate legislative and other measures, including sanctions where appropriate, prohibiting all discrimination against women;

(*c*) To establish legal protection of the rights of women on an equal basis with men and to ensure through competent national tribunals and other public institutions the effective protection of women against any act of discrimination;

(*d*) To refrain from engaging in any act or practice of discrimination against women and to ensure that public authorities and institutions shall act in conformity with this obligation;

(*e*) To take all appropriate measures to eliminate discrimination against women by any person, organization or enterprise;

(*f*) To take all appropriate measures, including legislation, to modify or abolish existing laws, regulations, customs and practices which constitute discrimination against women;

(*g*) To repeal all national penal provisions which constitute discrimination against women.

Article 3

States Parties shall take in all fields, in particular in the political, social, economic, and cultural fields, all appropriate measures, including legislation, to ensure the full development and advancement of women, for the purpose of guaranteeing them the exercise and enjoyment of human rights and fundamental freedoms on a basis of equality with men.

Article 4

1. Adoption by States Parties of temporary special measures aimed at accelerating *de facto* equality between men and women shall not be considered discrimination as defined in the present Convention, but shall in no way entail as a consequence the maintenance of unequal or separate standards; these measures shall be discontinued when the objectives of equality of opportunity and treatment have been achieved.

2. Adoption by States Parties of special measures, including those measures contained in the present Convention, aimed at protecting maternity shall not be considered discriminatory.

Article 5

States Parties shall take all appropriate measures:
  - (*a*) To modify the social and cultural patterns of conduct of men and women, with a view to achieving the elimination of prejudices and customary and all other practices which are based on the idea of the inferiority or the superiority of either of the sexes or on stereotyped roles for men and women;
  - (*b*) To ensure that family education includes a proper understanding of maternity as a social function and the recognition of the common responsibility of men and women in the upbringing and development of their children, it being understood that the interest of the children is the primordial consideration in all cases.

Article 6

States Parties shall take all appropriate measures, including legislation, to suppress all forms of traffic in women and exploitation of prostitution of women.

Part II

Article 7

States Parties shall take all appropriate measures to eliminate discrimination against women in the political and public life of the country and, in particular, shall ensure to women, on equal terms with men, the right:
  - (*a*) To vote in all elections and public referenda and to be eligible for election to all publicly elected bodies;
  - (*b*) To participate in the formulation of government policy and the implementation thereof and to hold public office and perform all public functions at all levels of government;
  - (*c*) To participate in non-governmental organizations and associations concerned with the public and political life of the country.

Article 8

States Parties shall take all appropriate measures to ensure to women, on equal terms with men and without any discrimination, the opportunity to represent their Governments at the international level and to participate in the work of international organizations.

Article 9

1. States Parties shall grant women equal rights with men to acquire,

change or retain their nationality. They shall ensure in particular that neither marriage to an alien nor change of nationality by the husband during marriage shall automatically change the nationality of the wife, render her stateless or force upon her the nationality of the husband.

2. States Parties shall grant women equal rights with men with respect to the nationality of their children.

PART III

Article 10

States Parties shall take all appropriate measures to eliminate discrimination against women in order to ensure to them equal rights with men in the field of education and in particular to ensure, on a basis of equality of men and women:

- (*a*) The same conditions for career and vocational guidance, for access to studies and for the achievement of diplomas in educational establishments of all categories in rural as well as in urban areas; this equality shall be ensured in pre-school, general, technical, professional and higher technical education, as well as in all types of vocational training;
- (*b*) Access to the same curricula, the same examinations, teaching staff with qualifications of the same standard and school premises and equipment of the same quality;
- (*c*) The elimination of any stereotyped concept of the roles of men and women at all levels and in all forms of education by encouraging coeducation and other types of education which will help to achieve this aim and, in particular, by the revision of textbooks and school programmes and the adaptation of teaching methods;
- (*d*) The same opportunities to benefit from scholarships and other study grants;
- (*e*) The same opportunities for access to programmes of continuing education, including adult and functional literacy programmes, particularly those aimed at reducing, at the earliest possible time, any gap in education existing between men and women;
- (*f*) The reduction of female student drop-out rates and the organization of programmes for girls and women who have left school prematurely;
- (*g*) The same opportunities to participate actively in sports and physical education;
- (*h*) Access to specific educational information to help to ensure the health and well-being of families, including information and advice on family planning.

Article 11

1. State Parties shall take all appropriate measures to eliminate

discrimination against women in the field of employment in order to ensure, on a basis of equality of men and women, the same rights, in particular:

(*a*) The right to work as an inalienable right of all human beings;

(*b*) The right to the same employment opportunities, including the application of the same criteria for selection in matters of employment;

(*c*) The right to free choice of profession and employment, the right to promotion, job security and all benefits and conditions of service and the right to receive vocational training and retraining, including apprenticeships, advanced vocational training and recurrent training;

(*d*) The right to equal remuneration, including benefits, and to equal treatment in respect of work of equal value, as well as equality of treatment in the evaluation of the quality of work;

(*e*) The right to social security, particularly in cases of retirement, unemployment, sickness, invalidity and old age and other incapacity to work, as well as the right to paid leave;

(*f*) The right to protection of health and to safety in working conditions, including the safeguarding of the function of reproduction;

2. In order to prevent discrimination against women on the grounds of marriage or maternity and to ensure their effective right to work, States Parties shall take appropriate measures:

(*a*) To prohibit, subject to the imposition of sanctions, dismissal on the grounds of pregnancy or of maternity leave and discrimination in dismissals on the basis of marital status:

(*b*) To introduce maternity leave with pay or with comparable social benefits without loss of former employment, seniority or social allowances;

(*c*) To encourage the provision of the necessary supporting social services to enable parents to combine family obligations with work responsibilities and participation in public life, in particular through promoting the establishment and development of a network of child-care facilities;

(*d*) To provide special protection to women during pregnancy in types of work proved to be harmful to them.

3. Protective legislation relating to matters covered in this article shall be reviewed periodically in the light of scientific and technological knowledge and shall be revised, repealed or extended as necessary.

Article 12

1. States Parties shall take all appropriate measures to eliminate discrimination against women in the field of health care in order to ensure, on a basis of equality of men and women, access to health care services, including those related to family planning.

2. Notwithstanding the provisions of paragraph 1 of this article, States Parties shall ensure to women appropriate services in connexion with pregnancy, confinement and the post-natal period, granting free services where necessary, as well as adequate nutrition during pregnancy and lactation.

Article 13

States Parties shall take all appropriate measures to eliminate discrimination against women in other areas of economic and social life in order to ensure, on a basis of equality of men and women, the same rights, in particular:

(*a*) The right to family benefits;

(*b*) The right to bank loans, mortgages and other forms of financial credit;

(*c*) The right to participate in recreational activities, sports and all aspects of cultural life.

Article 14

1. States Parties shall take into account the particular problems faced by rural women and the significant roles which rural women play in the economic survival of their families, including their work in the non-monetized sectors of the economy, and shall take all appropriate measures to ensure the application of the provisions of this Convention to women in rural areas.

2. States Parties shall take all appropriate measures to eliminate discrimination against women in rural areas in order to ensure, on a basis of equality of men and women, that they participate in and benefit from rural development and, in particular, shall ensure to such women the right:

(*a*) To participate in the elaboration and implementation of development planning at all levels;

(*b*) To have access to adequate health care facilities, including information, counselling and services in family planning;

(*c*) To benefit directly from social security programmes;

(*d*) To obtain all types of training and education, formal and non-formal, including that relating to functional literacy, as well as, *inter alia*, the benefit of all community and extension services, in order to increase their technical proficiency;

(*e*) To organize self-help groups and co-operatives in order to obtain equal access to economic opportunities through employment or self-employment;

(*f*) To participate in all community activities;

(*g*) To have access to agricultural credit and loans, marketing facilities, appropriate technology and equal treatment in land and agrarian reform as well as in land resettlement schemes;

(*h*) To enjoy adequate living conditions, particularly in relation to housing, sanitation, electricity and water supply, transport and communications.

PART IV

Article 15

1. States Parties shall accord to women equality with men before the law.

2. States Parties shall accord to women, in civil matters, a legal capacity identical to that of men and the same opportunities to exercise that capacity. In particular, they shall give women equal rights to conclude contracts and to administer property and shall treat them equally in all stages of procedure in courts and tribunals.

3. States Parties agree that all contracts and all other private instruments of any kind with a legal effect which is directed at restricting the legal capacity of women shall be deemed null and void.

4. States Parties shall accord to men and women the same rights with regard to the law relating to the movement of persons and the freedom to choose their residence and domicile.

Article 16

1. States Parties shall take all appropriate measures to eliminate discrimination against women in all matters relating to marriage and family relations and in particular shall ensure, on a basis of equality of men and women:

    (*a*) The same right to enter into marriage;

    (*b*) The same right freely to choose a spouse and to enter into marriage only with their free and full consent;

    (*c*) The same rights and responsibilities during marriage and at its dissolution;

    (*d*) The same rights and responsibilities as parents, irrespective of their marital status, in matters relating to their children; in all cases the interests of the children shall be paramount;

    (*e*) The same rights to decide freely and responsibly on the number and spacing of their children and to have access to the information, education and means to enable them to exercise these rights;

    (*f*) The same rights and responsibilities with regard to guardianship, wardship, trusteeship and adoption of children, or similar institutions where these concepts exist in national legislation; in all cases the interests of the children shall be paramount;

    (*g*) The same personal rights as husband and wife, including the right to choose a family name, a profession and an occupation;

    (*h*) The same rights for both spouses in respect of the ownership, acquisition, management, administration, enjoyment and disposition of property, whether free of charge or for a valuable consideration.

2. The betrothal and the marriage of a child shall have no legal effect, and all necessary action, including legislation, shall be taken to specify a minimum age for marriage and to make the registration of marriages in an official registry compulsory.

PART V

Article 17

1. For the purpose of considering the progress made in the implementation of the present Convention, there shall be established a Committee on the Elimination of Discrimination against Women (hereinafter referred to as the Committee) consisting, at the time of entry into force of the Convention, of eighteen and, after ratification of or accession to the Convention by the thirty-fifth State Party, of twenty-three experts of high moral standing and competence in the field covered by the Convention. The experts shall be elected by States Parties from among their nationals and shall serve in their personal capacity, consideration being given to equitable geographical distribution and to the representation of the different forms of civilization as well as the principal legal systems.

2. The members of the Committee shall be elected by secret ballot from a list of persons nominated by States Parties. Each State Party may nominate one person from among its own nationals.

3. The initial election shall be held six months after the date of the entry into force of the present Convention. At least three months before the date of each election the Secretary-General of the United Nations shall address a letter to the States Parties inviting them to submit their nominations within two months. The Secretary-General shall prepare a list in alphabetical order of all persons thus nominated, indicating the States Parties which have nominated them, and shall submit it to the States Parties.

4. Elections of the members of the Committee shall be held at a meeting of States Parties convened by the Secretary-General at United Nations Headquarters. At that meeting, for which two thirds of the States Parties shall constitute a quorum, the persons elected to the Committee shall be those nominees who obtain the largest number of votes and an absolute majority of the votes of the representatives of States Parties present and voting.

5. The members of the Committee shall be elected for a term of four years. However, the terms of nine of the members elected at the first election shall expire at the end of two years; immediately after the first election the names of these nine members shall be chosen by lot by the Chairman of the Committee.

6. The election of the five additional members of the Committee shall be held in accordance with the provisions of paragraphs 2, 3 and 4 of this article, following the thirty-fifth ratification or accession. The terms of two of the additional members elected on this occasion shall expire at the end of two years, the names of these two members having been chosen by lot by the Chairman of the Committee.

7. For the filling of casual vacancies, the State Party whose expert has ceased to function as a member of the Committee shall appoint another expert from among its nationals, subject to the approval of the Committee.

8. The members of the Committee shall, with the approval of the General Assembly, receive emoluments from United Nations resources on such terms and conditions as the Assembly may decide, having regard to the importance of the Committee's responsibilities.

9. The Secretary-General of the United Nations shall provide the necessary staff and facilities for the effective performance of the functions of the Committee under the present Convention.

Article 18

1. States Parties undertake to submit to the Secretary-General of the United Nations, for consideration by the Committee, a report on the legislative, judicial, administrative or other measures which they have adopted to give effect to the provisions of the present Convention and on the progress made in this respect:

   (*a*) Within one year after the entry into the force for the State concerned; and

   (*b*) Thereafter at least every four years and further whenever the Committee so requests.

2. Reports may indicate factors and difficulties affecting the degree of fulfilment of obligations under the present Convention.

Article 19

1. The Committee shall adopt its own rules of procedure.

2. The Committee shall elect its officers for a term of two years.

Article 20

1. The Committee shall normally meet for a period of not more than two weeks annually in order to consider the reports submitted in accordance with article 18 of the present Convention.

2. The meetings of the Committee shall normally be held at United Nations Headquarters or at any other convenient place as determined by the Committee.

Article 21

1. The Committee shall, through the Economic and Social Council, report annually to the General Assembly of the United Nations on its activities and may make suggestions and general recommendations based on the examination of reports and information received from the States Parties. Such suggestions and general recommendations shall be included in the report of the Committee together with comments, if any, from States Parties.

2. The Secretary-General shall transmit the reports of the Committee to the Commission on the Status of Women for its information.

Article 22

The specialized agencies shall be entitled to be represented at the consideration of the implementation of such provisions of the present Convention as fall within the scope of their activities. The Committee may invite the specialized agencies to submit reports on the implementation of the Convention in areas falling within the scope of their activities.

PART VI

Article 23

Nothing in this Convention shall affect any provisions that are more conducive to the achievement of equality between men and women which may be contained:

   (*a*) In the legislation of a State Party; or
   (*b*) In any other international convention, treaty or agreement in force for that State.

Article 24

States Parties undertake to adopt all necessary measures at the national level aimed at achieving the full realization of the rights recognized in the present Convention.

Article 25

1. The present Convention shall be open for signature by all States.
2. The Secretary-General of the United Nations is designated as the depositary of the present Convention.
3. The present Convention is subject to ratification. Instruments of ratification shall be deposited with the Secretary-General of the United Nations.
4. The present Convention shall be open to accession by all States. Accession shall be effected by the deposit of an instrument of accession with the Secretary-General of the United Nations.

Article 26

1. A request for the revision of the present Convention may be made at any time by any State Party by means of a notification in writing addressed to the Secretary-General of the United Nations.

2. The General Assembly of the United Nations shall decide upon the steps, if any, to be taken in respect of such a request.

Article 27

1. The present Convention shall enter into force on the thirtieth day after the date of deposit with the Secretary-General of the United Nations of the twentieth instrument of ratification or accession.
2. For each State ratifying the present Convention or acceding to it after the deposit of the twentieth instrument of ratification or accession, the Convention shall enter into force on the thirtieth day after the date of the deposit of its own instrument of ratification or accession.

Article 28

1. The Secretary-General of the United Nations shall receive and circulate to all States the text of reservations made by States at the time of ratification or accession.
2. A reservation incompatible with the object and purpose of the present Convention shall not be permitted.
3. Reservations may be withdrawn at any time by notification to this effect addressed to the Secretary-General of the United Nations, who shall then inform all States thereof. Such notification shall take effect on the date on which it is received.

Article 29

1. Any dispute between two or more States Parties concerning the interpretation or application of the present Convention which is not settled by negotiation shall, at the request of one of them, be submitted to arbitration. If within six months from the date of the request for arbitration the parties are unable to agree on the organization of the arbitration, any one of those parties may refer the dispute to the International Court of Justice by request in conformity with the Statute of the Court.
2. Each State Party may at the time of signature or ratification of this Convention or accession thereto declare that it does not consider itself bound by paragraph 1 of this article. The other States Parties shall not be bound by that paragraph with respect to any State Party which has made such a reservation.
3. Any State Party which has made a reservation in accordance with paragraph 2 of this article may at any time withdraw that reservation by notification to the Secretary-General of the United Nations.

Article 30

The present Convention, the Arabic, Chinese, English, French, Russian and Spanish texts of which are equally authentic, shall be deposited with the Secretary-General of the United Nations.

IN WITNESS WHEREOF the undersigned, duly authorized, have signed the present Convention.

INDEX OF CASES

INDIAN AND PAKISTAN CASES

N.K. Sharma v. *State of Bihar* AIR 1965 Pat. 372. **p. 254**
Pabitra Kumar v. *State of West Bengal* AIR 1964 593. **p. 251**
Pillai v. *Mudanayake* [1953] AC 514 (P.C.) **pp. 250, 256**
Purshottam v. *Desai* AIR 1956 SC 20. **p. 250**
Raghuramulu v. *State of Andhra Pradesh* AIR 1958 AP 129. **p. 254**
Ram Krishna Dalmia v. *Justice Tendolkar* AIR 1958 SC 538. **p. 249**
Ramakrishna Singh v. *State of Mysore* AIR 1960 Mys 338. **p. 254**
Ramchasdra Mahton v. *State of Bihar* xiv Bihar L.J. Reps. (1966) 122. **p. 255**
Ramprosad Naraim Sahi v. *State of Mysore* 1953 SCR 1129. **p. 250**
Sakhwant v. *State of Orissa* 1955 I SCR 1004. **p. 251**
State of Andhra Pradesh v. *U.S.V. Balaram* AIR 1975 SC 563. **p. 254**
State of Bombay v. *Balsara* AIR 1951 SC 318. **pp. 250, 251**
State of Bombay v. *United Motors* AIR 1953 SC 252. **p. 251**
State of Kerala v. *Jacob Mathew* ILR 1964 (2) Ker. 53. **p. 254**
State of Kerala v. *Thomas* AIR 1976 SC 490; [1979] 1 SCR 906. **p. 255**
State of Madras v. *Dorairajan* AIR 1951 SC 226. **p. 10**
State of Punjab v. *Ajaib Singh* 1953 SCR 254. **p. 250**
State of West Bengal v. *Anwar Ali* AIR 1952 SC 75. **pp. 248, 249, 252**
State of Uttar Pradesh v. *Bhopal Sugar Industry* AIR 1964 SC 1179. **p. 250**
Subash Chandra v. *State of Uttar Pradesh* AIR 1975 SC 563. **p. 254**
Triloki Nath v. *State of Jammu and Kashmir* AIR 1969 SC 1. **p. 254**
V. V. Giri v. *D. Suri Dara* AIR 1959 SC 1318. **p. 254**
Venkataramana v. *State of Madras* 1951 SCJ 318. **p. 253**

DECISIONS OF NATIONAL COURTS

Cameron v. *Deputy Federal Commission of Taxation* (1923), 32 CLR 68. **p. 246**
Cumings v. *Birkenhead Corporation* [1972] Ch. 12. **p. 246**
George v. *Pretoria Municipality* 1916 TPD 501. **p. 234**
In re *Helbert Wagg & Co. Ltd.* [1956] Ch. 1; (1955), 22 Int. L.R. 480. **p. 197**
Israel v. *Eichmann* (1961) 36. Int. L.R. 5. **p. 114**
King-Ansell v. *Police* [1979] 2 NZLR. 531. **p. 108**
Mills v. *Cooper* [1967] 2 QB 459. **p. 108**
Minister of the Interior v. *Lockhat* 1961 (2) SA 587 (AD) **p. 234**
Minister of Posts and Telegraphs v. *Rasool* 1934 AD 167. **p. 234**
Pietermaritzburg City Council v. *Local Road Transportation Board* 1959 (2), SA 758 (N). **p. 234**
Reddy v. *Durban Corporation* 1954 (4), SA 136 (AD). **p. 234**
R. v. *Addurohman* 1950 (3) SA 136 (AD). **p. 234**
R. v. *Carelse* 1943 CPD 242. **p. 234**
R. v. *Herman* 1937 AD 168. **p. 234**
R. v. *Lepile* 1953 (1) SA 225 (T). **p. 234**
R. v. *Lsu* 1953 (2) SA 484 (AD). **p. 234**
R. v. *Mozumba* 1953 (b) SA 235 (J). **p. 234**
R. v. *Zihlangu* 1953 (3) SA 871 (C). **p. 234**
Tewari v. *Durban Corporation* 1954 (4) SA 304 (N). **p. 234**

GENERAL INDEX

Aboriginals, 15, 143, 255
affirmative action, 98, 131, 145, 243 ff., 288
  see also special measures of protection
aliens
  political activities, 211
  Racial Discrimination Convention, 158
  rights of, 17, 48, 152, 180–1, 194–203, 236
apartheid, 1, 13, 81, 92–4, 111–16, 119, 260, 269
  in sport, 116
  Racial Discrimination Convention, 155
  Special Committee on, 93
  see also segregation
arbitrariness, 2, 4, 186, 201, 221, 241
Aristotle, 2, 5

backwardness, 221, 252 ff.
Berlin, Sir Isaiah, 3, 285
Brandeis brief, 236
Brownlie, I., 59, 81, 199, 259, 270, 282–3

Calabresi, G., 243 ff.
Capotorti, F., 94, 142, 147, 150
Cardozo, B., 265
Cassin, R., 57–8, 63–4, 66, 112, 153, 276
caste, 1, 255 ff.
Cecil, Lord Robert, 16, 35
Chamberlain, Sir Austen, 25
Cheng, B., 272, 277
classification, reasonable, 3, 4, 9, 95 ff., 237 ff.
clausula rebus sic stantibus, 47
colonialism, 81, 119, 154, 274
  granting of independence to colonial countries and peoples, 92, 119, 154
Commission on Human Rights, 65 ff., 72 ff., 122, 131–2
Commission on the Status of Women, 61, 65, 72, 104, 118, 128, 132, 182, 186, 188–9

compensatory treatment, 7, 8
  see also affirmative action and special measures of protection
Conventions:
  Apartheid, 111–16
  Consent to Marriage, Minimum Age for Marriage and Registration of Marriage, 104
  Discrimination (Employment and Occupation), 104, 124–8, 156, 164
  Discrimination in Education, 104, 128–35, 156
  Elimination of All Forms of Racial Discrimination, 79, 104, 152–65, 200, 210, 225, 286
  Elimination of All Forms of Discrimination Against Women, 104, 168, 189, 286
  Equal Remuneration, 103
  European Convention of Human Rights, 13, 33, 50, 164, 199, 204–7
  European Social Charter, 226
  Genocide, 102, 104–13
  ILO Conventions, 98, 147, 166–8
  Law of Treaties (Vienna), 278
  Legal Status of Children Born out of Wedlock, 227
  Non-applicability of Statutory Limitations to War Crimes and Crimes Against Humanity, 113
  Nationality of Married Women, 192
  Political Rights of Women, 13, 104, 161, 171–99; Inter-American Convention, 104, 178
  Promotional, 103, 192–3
  Slavery, 104, 116–21
  Treaty of Berlin, 21
  Treaty of Paris, 20
  Treaty of Rome (EEC), 168–78, 201
  Treaty of Siena, 20
Covenants on Human Rights, 75–7, 86, 97, 104, 112, 131, 136–52, 165, 182, 200, 214

national standard of treatment, 195 ff.
natural justice, 265
Nazis, 12
Nietzsche, 3
non-governmental organisations, 62, 97 ff.
non-self-governing territories
    racial discrimination in, 88 ff.
norms
    humanitarian, 23
    of non-discrimination, 258 ff., 264, 271–7
numerus clausus, 131

Outer Space
    Declaration of Legal Principles, 272

Paine, T., 2
peremptory norms of international law,
    see jus cogens
Permanent Court of International Justice, 12, 24–33
piracy, 279
political rights, 162–3
Polyviou, P., 240
positive action, 98, 145
    see also affirmative action, special measures of protection, protective measures
preferential treatment, 213, 221
privileges, 10–15
promotional conventions, 103, 192–3
proportionality, 221–3
protective measures, 8, 146, 186, 213, 288

quotas, 100, 242, 255

racial hatred, incitement to, 226
Raphael, D. D., 7
Rawls, J., 3, 6
reasonable classification, 4, 9, 237 ff., 249–63, 287
religious intolerance, 62 ff., 111, 121–3, 225
    genocide, 121
    minorities, 22–6
    proposed clauses in League Covenant, 15–20
    reservations, 100, 242
    reverse discrimination, *see* discrimination
Richards, I., 224

sameness, 3, 7, 98, 180–1, 191
Schwelb, E., 105, 141, 155, 157, 161, 163, 200, 210, 274, 278, 280, 282
Segregation, 110, 228 ff.
    see also apartheid
seminars on discrimination, 99–101
'separate but equal' doctrine, 160, 229 ff.
slavery, 1, 11, 70, 81, 104, 112, 116–21, 229, 279–82
    see also apartheid and colonialism
social justice, 6
    see also justice, equality (normative)
Sørensen, M., 10, 59
special measures of protection, 7, 11, 12, 13, 25, 51, 59, 90, 95–101, 124–7, 131, 135, 143, 153, 158–9, 185, 187–8, 226, 242–3, 247, 252–7, 288
    ILO, 125–7
    Unesco, 135, 143 ff.
    women, 187–8, 226
standards of non-discrimination, 237, 258 ff., 264–70
states
    equality of, 16, 19, 38
    rights and duties of, 71
    sovereignity of, 18
status, 1, 8, 11, 68, 117, 194
Sub-Commission on the Prevention of Discrimination and Protection of Minorities, 12, 47, 60 ff., 72–87, 112, 119, 126, 129–30, 132, 214, 286 ff.
    studies by, 76–7, 88 ff.

Tanaka, Judge, 209, 232, 258–77, 281
Teitgen, P. H., 204–5
trade unions
    right to join, 164, 220
traffic in women, *see* slavery
Tur, R. H. S., 243, 247–8

United Nations
    Charter, 20, 41, 52 ff., 88 ff., 154, 266, 270
    Dumbarton Oaks proposals, 53–4, 59
    Economic and Social Council, 72 ff., 97, 104, 106, 116–17
    Fourth Committee, 89
    General Assembly, 91, 116, 121
    International Law Commission, 106, 115–16, 198, 279, 281
    High Commissioner, 101